Applied Welfare Economics

Applied Welfare Economics: Cost-Benefit Analysis of Projects and Policies presents a consistent framework for applied welfare economics and is grounded in a comprehensive theory of cost-benefit analysis, specifically focused on offering a practical approach to policy and project evaluation. After opening with a theoretical discussion of the concept of social welfare, a critical analysis of the traditional doctrine of welfare economics embodied in the Two Fundamental Theorems, and a presentation of social cost-benefit analysis, the book introduces readers to an applied framework. This includes the empirical estimation of shadow prices of goods, the social cost of labour and capital, and the assessment of risk. This book also discusses the state of the art of international experience with CBA, including *ex-post* evaluation of major projects, and the use of cost-benefit analysis in regulatory policy. The empirical chapters draw from first-hand research, gained by the authors and their collaborators over many years of advisory work for the European Commission and other international and national institutions. This second edition presents updated data, more international examples, and more coverage of topics such as the social discount rate for projects or policies with very long run impacts and the application of CBA in new contexts. It also includes end-of-chapter questions to aid student's learning. Applied Welfare Economics is a valuable textbook for upper-level courses on welfare economics, cost-benefit analysis, public policy analysis, and related areas.

Massimo Florio is Professor of Public Economics and Jean Monnet Chair "ad personam" of EU Industrial Policy at the University of Milan, Italy.

Chiara Pancotti is Senior Researcher at the Centre for Industrial Studies, Italy and former adjunct Professor of Cost-Benefit Analysis at University of Milan, Italy.

Routledge Advanced Texts in Economics and Finance

For more information about this series, please visit: www.routledge.com/Routledge-Advanced-Texts-in-Economics-and-Finance/book-series/SE0757

Applied Welfare Economics

Cost-Benefit Analysis of Projects and Policies

Second Edition

Massimo Florio and Chiara Pancotti

Routledge
Taylor & Francis Group

LONDON AND NEW YORK

Cover image: © den-belitsky / Getty Images

Second edition published 2023
by Routledge
4 Park Square, Milton Park, Abingdon, Oxon, OX14 4RN

and by Routledge
605 Third Avenue, New York, NY 10158

Routledge is an imprint of the Taylor & Francis Group, an informa business

© 2023 Massimo Florio and Chiara Pancotti

First edition published by Routledge 2014

British Library Cataloguing-in-Publication Data
A catalogue record for this book is available from the British Library

Library of Congress Cataloging-in-Publication Data
Names: Florio, Massimo, author. | Pancotti, Chiara, author.
Title: Applied welfare economics : cost-benefit analysis of projects and policies / Massimo Florio and Chiara Pancotti.
Description: Second Edition. | New York, NY : Routledge, 2023. | Series: Routledge advanced texts in economics and finance | Revised edition of Applied welfare economics, 2014. | Includes bibliographical references and index. |
Identifiers: LCCN 2022008469 (print) | LCCN 2022008470 (ebook) | ISBN 9781032043005 (hardback) | ISBN 9781032022185 (paperback) | ISBN 9781003191377 (ebook)
Subjects: LCSH: Welfare economics, | Cost effectiveness.
Classification: LCC HB846 .F579 2023 (print) | LCC HB846 (ebook) | DDC 330.12/6—dc23/eng/20220330
LC record available at https://lccn.loc.gov/2022008469
LC ebook record available at https://lccn.loc.gov/2022008470

ISBN: 978-1-032-04300-5 (hbk)
ISBN: 978-1-032-02218-5 (pbk)
ISBN: 978-1-003-19137-7 (ebk)

DOI: 10.4324/9781003191377

Typeset in Bembo
by codeMantra

Contents

PART THREE
Experience   233

Figures

Tables

Boxes

Preface

What can we say about the unit value of a good to society? To many people, the answer is simple. Market prices give us the right information. Hence, social welfare is no more than the value of the output of a country, i.e. prices times quantities in a given year. Some economists would then add a proviso: 'if markets are undistorted', or 'if there are no market failures'. The view that market prices, with some 'local' adjustments, are all we need to know to answer the opening question of this book is, however, inadequate, and – in a deep sense – could be misleading. Even under competitive markets, prices can be far from being socially optimal, except perhaps when one adopts an extremely narrow and controversial view of social welfare. This narrow view goes back to Vilfredo Pareto, the 'pure' economist, but was wisely rejected by Vilfredo Pareto himself, the social scientist.

Interdependencies in an economy are so wide, and the possible criteria for social welfare so different, that virtually nothing can be said on the social benefits and costs of the provision of energy, transport, education, water, environmental protection, urban regeneration, health, and several other goods just using the prices we observe. In a deep sense, there are no 'right' prices, only observable prices and a constellation of possible socially optimal prices that cannot be directly observed. Trying to discover the social opportunity cost of goods, the 'shadow prices', is, however, possible and useful. This book tries to convey the message that such work of exploration and discovery of social values is feasible and necessary to evaluate public projects and policies.

Several chapters draw on lecture notes from graduate teaching of Welfare Economics over around twenty years. One of us (Florio) started teaching this subject in 1990 to students of PhD programmes in both Public Finance and Economics at the University of Pavia, and then he went on to teach the same topic at the PhD programme and Master course in Economics and Political Sciences at the University of Milan. Pancotti also taught cost-benefit analysis to graduate students at the University of Milan (degree in Economics and Political Science) for several years. We both (Florio and Pancotti) think that for scientific research in any field, a deep understanding of some crucial questions and concepts is often more important, or at least should come earlier, than learning cookbook recipes about solving problems. Moreover, some chapters of this book draw from the authors' extensive experience of evaluation work for international institutions, particularly the European Commission, and teaching to civil servants and professionals in different countries and at the Milan Summer School in CBA, co-organized over ten years by the University of Milan and the Centre for Industrial Studies.

We propose a mixture of theory and practice of social cost-benefit analysis. Although this is a feature of several other books, the balance here is in favour of a consistent frame that goes from a review of first principles to the critical discussion of experience. The book is written for students with a background in Economics at an intermediate level, but the main text is readable by a wider audience interested in Applied Welfare Economics. Professionals, who are often provided with recipes for welfare analysis without much intellectual justification, could also appreciate the book.

The book is organized around three parts (Theory, Empirics, Experience) and eleven chapters. The structure of the book is as follows.

Part One – 'Theory' – lays down some concepts. This part includes three chapters:

- Chapter 1, 'On social welfare', considers the role of government or social planner in Welfare Economics and reviews both some standard and less standard social welfare functions. It also discusses the foundations of Gross Domestic Product accounting, stating that this concept, albeit important in practice, is implicitly based on a narrow utilitarian social welfare function, criticized by Amartya Sen and others.
- Chapter 2, 'The two fundamental theorems re-examined', presents the traditional two fundamental welfare theorems, introducing the concepts of goods, individual endowments, ownership claims on net products of firms, producers' prices, rations and lump-sum taxes, and the government objective function. The critiques to the theorems by Stiglitz are briefly discussed to show why the received interpretation of the welfare theorems is not helpful for evaluating policies and projects.
- Chapter 3, 'Shadow prices and the social planner', deals with the definition of the key concepts of public production plans, policies, and shadow prices. This chapter draws from a simplified version and elaboration of the Drèze and Stern (DS) model, which provides a general definition of shadow prices in a second-best planning framework. On the basis of this frame, the chapter explains some DS formulas of the marginal social values in a closed economy.

Part Two – 'Empirics' – is about translating the theory into the empirics of welfare analysis. It comprises the following chapters:

- Chapter 4, 'The social cost of goods', moves from the DS framework to a more applied setting for shadow price calculation. It shows how to translate inputs and outputs at observed prices into a welfare analysis that uses shadow prices, and how financial performance criteria, such as the Net Present Value and the Internal Rate of Return, can be turned into economic criteria. In this context, empirical estimation of conversion factors and the relationship between short-cut formulas and general equilibrium theory are discussed.
- Chapter 5, 'The social cost of labour', addresses the opportunity cost of labour, i.e. the shadow wage rate. After discussing, at a theoretical level, the relationship between macroeconomic disequilibria and market wages, the chapter describes a unified model for estimating shadow wages. Using aggregate regional data, it shows how to derive specific shadow wage rates, and relative conversion factors, under different labour market conditions.
- Chapter 6 'The social cost of capital', focuses on the estimation of the social discount rate and reviews alternative approaches to valuing future benefits and costs against the present ones. The discussion includes the relationship between private

and social return to capital, the role of the welfare of future generations in the inter-temporal planner's problem, and the declining discount rates.

- Chapter 7, 'Welfare weights and distributional impacts', reviews the topic of distribution issues in project and policy evaluation. The logic behind welfare weights, to what extent weighting is different from the standard interpretation of the Pareto criterion, and how it depends upon the type of social welfare function, is discussed.
- Chapter 8, 'Risk assessment', introduces the uncertainty affecting the future trend of most variables or parameters used in the calculation of the economic return, and shows how risk assessment is important for project selection. After presenting the theory of risk analysis, the chapter discusses to what extent the theoretical perspective is applied in practical evaluation and reflected in the existing methods to simulate Monte Carlo experiments.

Part Three – 'Experience' – presents different perspectives of real-world features that relate to evaluation practices:

- Chapter 9, 'International evaluation practices', is about the experience of international organizations and public sector bodies in project appraisals. The official evaluation guidelines adopted by the European Commission (EC) (DG Regional Policy), the European International Bank, World Bank, and selected national authorities are reviewed. The chapter discusses to what extent practice on the ground complies with the official guidelines.
- Chapter 10, '*Ex-post* project evaluation', explores the practice of *ex-post* CBA, first, by discussing how an *ex-post* CBA should be carried out from a methodological point of view, then, describing how its results can be used in the decision-making process, and, finally, by illustrating the actual use and limitations in the international practice.
- Chapter 11, 'The use of cost-benefit analysis in regulatory policy', offers an overview of the use of CBA in regulatory policy, by presenting its principal historical developments and methodological tenets, and sheds light on the practices that have taken shape over time in different institutional contexts.

Acknowledgements

Emanuela Sirtori, economist at CSIL (Centre for Industrial Studies, Milan), beyond her contribution as co-author of some of the chapters, has coordinated the preparation of the first edition of this book. Without the intelligent, skilful, and dedicated efforts by Emanuela, this book simply could not exist. Elisa Borghi and Chiara Del Bo, formerly PhD students in the University of Milan and now lecturers respectively in LIUC and Milan, have collected the initial lecture notes for some chapters. Without their help in assembling a preliminary text, this book would not have kicked off. Several other researchers have worked with the authors on CBA topics over the years, particularly at CSIL, forming possibly one of the most experienced teams in Europe in terms of project and policy evaluation. Part of this book draws from lectures held during the nine editions (from 2011 to 2019) of the Milan Summer School on Cost Benefit Analysis of Investment Projects, organized by CSIL in collaboration with the University of Milan. Co-authors of some chapters include Gelsomina Catalano, Chiara Del Bo, Stefano Lombardi, Matteo Pedralli, Davide Sartori, Emanuela Sirtori, and Silvia Vignetti. Their specific contributions are acknowledged in the appropriate places. Other chapters draw from previous papers with Chiara Del Bo, Carlo Fiorio (both at University of Milan), and Riccardo Puglisi (University of Pavia).

Moreover, three anonymous reviewers at Routledge, and other experts, have provided helpful advice. We are particularly grateful for their important comments to Francesco Angelini (European Investment Bank), Rinaldo Brau (University of Cagliari), Gianni Carbonaro (European Investment Bank), Sara Colautti (CSIL), Silvia Fedeli (University of Rome), Ugo Finzi (formerly at the World Bank, senior advisor at CSIL), Mario Genco (CSIL), Per-Olov Johansson (Stockholm School of Economics), and Gareth Myles (University of Exeter). Per-Olov and Gareth have extensively commented on Part One of the book, and we are particularly grateful for their constructive criticism on the first edition.

The permission by the publishers and co-authors to utilize previously published material is acknowledged for the following article:

- Del Bo, C., Fiorio, C. and Florio, M. (2011) 'Shadow wages for the EU regions', *Fiscal Studies*, 32 (1): 109–143.

In spite of all this helpful advice and collaboration, the authors are the residual claimant of any remaining errors.

In Memoriam of Eduardo Ley

In May 2013 Florio asked Eduardo Ley to offer his advice on some chapters of this book, as he kindly did on other projects many times over several years. He replied to Emanuela Sirtori: this time it was impossible for him because of some health problems. After some weeks he sent a review of "The gift of doubt" (a biography of Albert Hirschman by M. Gladwell). Some days after this, Eduardo passed away on July 1, 2013. We were not aware of his illness. He was an outstanding applied economist, before at University Carlos III in Madrid, then at Resources for the Future in Washington D.C., from where he moved to the IMF and later to the World Bank. Eduardo was passionate about the importance of cost-benefit analysis and about strategies to deal with poverty and optimist about the contribution that we as economists can make to social welfare by offering realistic advice. Eduardo was also energetic, generous, and always ready to joke about something. An accomplished economist, a fine person, a friend that we shall miss. In this book, that he will not read, we hope there is, however, here and there, something coming from our conversation and mutual understanding over a too short friendship.

Milan, December 2013

Abbreviations

A	Axiom
AD	Arrow–Debreu
BAU	Business-as-usual
B/C	Benefit–Cost ratio
CBA	Cost-benefit Analysis
CBO	Congressional Budget Office
CDF	Cumulative Distribution Function
CES	Constant Elasticity of Substitution
CF	Conversion factor
CGE	Computable General Equilibrium
CGP	Commissariat général du Plan
CIF	Cost, Freight and Insurance
CS	Consumer's surplus
CSIL	Centre for Industrial Studies
CV	Compensating Variation
DG	Directorate General
DGREGIO	Directorate-General for Regional and Urban Policy
DS	Drèze-Stern
EBRD	European Bank for Reconstruction and Development
EC	European Commission
EIB	European Investment Bank
EIRR	Economic Internal Rate of Return
ENPV	Economic Net Present Value
EU	European Union
EU-15	European Union 'Old' Member States
EUR	Euro
EV	Equivalent Variation
FIRR	Financial Internal Rate of Return
FIRR(K)	Financial Rate of Return on Capital
FNPV	Financial Net Present Value
FOB	Free on Board
FOC	First-order Condition
FSE	Fairly Socially Efficient
GAO	Government Accountability Office
GBP	British Pound

GDP	Gross Domestic Product
GNI	Gross National Income
GVA	Gross Value Added
HDI	Human Development Index
ICT	Information and Communication Technologies
IEG	Independent Evaluation Group
IID	Independent and Identically Distributed
IMF	International Monetary Fund
IRR	Internal Rate of Return
ISPA	Structural Instrument for Pre-Accession
JASPERS	Joint Assistance to Support Projects in European Regions
LM	Little and Mirrlees
LRMC	Long Run Marginal Cost
MCPF	Marginal Cost of Public Funds
METB	Marginal Excess Tax Burden
MSV	Marginal Social Value
NNP	Net National Product
NPC	Nominal Protection Coefficient
NPV	Net Present Value
NUTS	Nomenclature of Territorial Units for Statistics
OECD	Organization for Economic Cooperation and Development
OIRA	Office of Information and Regulatory Affairs
OMB	Office of Management and Budget
PDF	Probability Distribution Function
POPE	Post Operations Project evaluation
PPP	Purchasing Power Parity
QKU	Quasi-Keynesian unemployment
R&D	Research and Development
RAILPAG	Railway Project Appraisal Guidelines
REIRR	*Ex-post* or re-estimated economic Internal Rates of Return
RIA	Regulatory Impact Assessments
RLD	Rural Labour Dualism
RPI	Retail Price Index
s.t.	Subject to
SCF	Standard Conversion Factor
SDR	Social Discount Rate
SER	Shadow Exchange Rate
SPC	Shadow Price of Capital
SRRI	Social Rate of Return on Investment
SRTP	Social Rate of Time Preference
SWB	Subjective Well-Being
SWF	Social Welfare Function
SWR	Shadow Wage Rate
UK	United Kingdom
ULD	Urban Labour Dualism
UN	United Nations
UNDP	United Nations Development Programme

US	United States
USD	United States dollars
VAT	Value Added Tax
WB	World Bank
WBM	World Bank Model
WTA	Willingness-to-accept
WTP	Willingness-to-pay

Main notation

h	Index for households or individuals, ranging from 1 to H. When distinguishing between two individuals, h and k are used, $k \neq h$.
i	Index for goods, ranging from 1 to I
j	Index for firms or production units, ranging from 1 to J
x	Consumption
X	Set of all the feasible vectors of consumption plans for every h
y	Aggregate production plan: $y = \sum_{j} y^j$
Y	Set of all the feasible vectors of production plans for every j
z	Net supply of goods by the public sector
p	Producer prices
q	Consumer prices
U	Utility function
W	Government's objective function
$W(U^h)$	Direct social welfare utility function
$V(v^h)$	Indirect social welfare utility function
G	Government or social planner
E	State of the economy
e^h	Consumption initial endowment
Π^j	Total profit of firm j
d_j^h	Profit share (i.e. ownership share) of individual h in firm j
ζ_j	Government's profit share in firm j
$E(s)$	Aggregate net demand (depending on a generic signal)
z_i	Net private demand (depending on p and q)
s	Signals (i.e. variables influencing private agents' behaviour)
$\bar{s}$	Exogenous signal
t	Indirect taxes (or subsidies) on goods, such that $t_i = (q_i - p_i)$
ℓ	Lump-sum taxes (or subsidies)
$\bar{x}$	Quantity constraint on consumption
$\bar{y}$	Quantity constraint on production
$\bar{x}_+$ or $\bar{y}_-$	Upper or lower bound of consumption ration
$\bar{y}_+$ or $\bar{y}_-$	Upper or lower bound of the ration on output
ϕ	Public policy function
l	Labour
f	Exchange rate

L	Lagrangian function
λ	Lagrangian multiplier
dx	Marginal change of consumption
dz	Marginal change of public supply (i.e. small project)
m	Lump-sum income
r	Government's transfer
v	Net impact on the Social Welfare Function of a marginal change of an input or output (i.e. the shadow price)
b	Marginal social utility of lump-sum transfers to households
β	Marginal social utility of households' lump-sum income (i.e. the welfare weights)
ε	Elasticity
∂	Partial derivative
K	Capital
*	Apex indicating that its element assumes an equilibrium value
$\sim$ or $^\wedge$ or $'$	Apexes indicating that their elements assume a value generally different from the equilibrium one
$>$	Symbol used for ordering preferences. It is equivalently used for $>h$. Weak preference is indicated by $>$

Vector notation

In general, variables in R^I are restated simply by $z = (z_1, \ldots, z_i)$ or similar conventions.

$x = y$ for vectors means $x_1 = y_2$, $x_2 = y_2$, etc.; the same applies for $x \geq y$. Superscripts usually stand for identification of an agent, such as x^h, y^j, etc. Subscripts usually stand for the identification of goods, such as x_i. Row and column vectors are not distinguished by specific symbols.

Part One
Theory

1   On social welfare

DOI: 10.4324/9781003191377-2

Overview[1]

Does building a hospital in a district increase the well-being of its residents? Does privatization of a utility company improve a country's economic conditions? What is the social impact of a new regulation that extends compulsory education by one year? To answer these questions, the concept of social welfare and its evolution needs to be defined. This is not easy.

Adam Smith's interest in the *Wealth of Nations* is a prominent example of a long intellectual effort in explaining an elusive concept: what is collective wealth? Are wealth and welfare synonyms? These deep philosophical questions have been answered over centuries in different ways and across social disciplines, particularly Ethics, Political Science, Sociology, and eventually Economics.

The main contribution of Economics to this old debate is twofold: first, the idea that the wealth of a nation can be measured; and second, that this measurement can be consistent with a rigorous theory that associates the well-being of individuals with that of a society. The former idea is embodied in some of the adopted accounting conventions to define Gross Domestic Product (GDP) or related macroeconomic indicators. The latter idea is, to a certain extent, associated with the broader concept of a Social Welfare Function (SWF). Historically, GDP accounting is an imperfect application of often confused or abstract theories of economic welfare. Both GDP and SWF concepts are, however, still controversial.

In this chapter, these two ideas are discussed in the context of the 'Economics of welfare', as the subject was defined one century ago by Arthur Cecil Pigou (Pigou 1912), even though a broader and more flexible definition of Welfare Economics is adopted here. This book aims at presenting empirical methods to estimate whether a change in the world (determined by a policy or a project) is beneficial or not to society, according to certain accounting conventions. Before doing this, the concept of social welfare needs to be introduced and discussed.

The literature on the topic is wide and any attempt to cover it implies personal choices about what to consider more relevant. Several strands of research reject the welfaristic perspective of analysis mostly discussed in this chapter and seek alternatives. Some of these, such as the non-welfaristic approach by Sen, or Happiness Economics, are briefly presented in the chapter. Other approaches are only briefly mentioned in the Further Reading section.

An introductive chapter such as the present one cannot be too ambitious and it simply intends to suggest two ideas: first, that the use of observed prices to measure individual and collective well-being has intrinsic limitations; second, that social welfare is an elusive concept, and any attempt to capture it in a simple formula should be regarded as only one among many alternatives. A theorist needs, in a sense, to be dogmatic, make some assumptions, and move on from them. An applied welfare economist should be open-minded and flexible and admit that social welfare is an artificial concept that can be analyzed in different ways. In a heuristic perspective, different concepts are tailored to answer different questions. This should be acknowledged from the beginning of a journey in the evaluation of projects and policies in the real world, with all its ever-changing complexity and diversity. This journey starts with the discussion of GDP as it has been widely adopted by governments as the economic policy yardstick. The discussion shows not only why Applied Welfare Economics cannot rely on GDP as a welfare measure, but also why there is no one-fits-all alternative. Dealing with ambiguity and multi-dimensionality is a fascinating feature of this topic.

The structure of this chapter is as follows: Section 1.1 introduces the concept of social welfare; Section 1.2 is about GDP as a welfare indicator and its extension as Net National Product (NNP); Section 1.3 deals with individuals and social welfare, Section 1.4 is about goods, and Section 1.5 is about utility; Section 1.6 mentions Sen's critique to welfarism; Section 1.7 defines paternalism; Section 1.8 introduces the perspective of Happiness Economics; and finally Section 1.9 briefly compares the normative with the positive approach. Further readings are suggested in Section 1.10.

1.1 The concept of social welfare

1.1.1 Gross Domestic Product as welfare measurement

Nowadays, GDP seems a familiar concept to many. Until the end of World War II, however, there was no international convention about how to measure the product of a country.[2] Keynes (1936) in the *General Theory* struggled to find a way to build a macroeconomic theory without a clear concept of domestic product. The first step towards a workable and comparable definition of GDP was undertaken by the commission established at the United Nations (UN) in the post-war years, under the chairmanship of Sir Richard Stone. While the guidelines provided by the Stone Commission were simple and contained in a slim book (Stone 1947), the growing complexity of the task over the years is reflected in SNA 2008, the most recent convention among the UN, International Monetary Fund (IMF), World Bank, Organisation for Economic Co-operation and Development (OECD) and Eurostat: the System of National Accounts (European Communities *et al.* 2009).

All these efforts can be regarded as accounting rules, with a practical purpose. In fact, people are accustomed to reading seemingly precise figures. For example, in 2012, GDP in the United States was USD (United States dollars) 15,609 billion in Purchasing Power Parity (PPP) terms, while that of China was USD 12,387 billion in PPP. In the same year, GDP (in PPP) per capita was USD 49,601 in the United States and USD 9,142 in China and the 2011–2012 yearly change of the former was 3 per cent and of the latter 10 per cent (IMF data). But what exactly do these figures mean in terms of well-being of the average American or Chinese citizen, and for the countries as a whole?

A possible answer to this question is simply to consider GDP (or related concepts, such as Gross National Income – GNI[3]) as an attempt to measure the product of a nation, hence its consumption and investment (public and private). In doing so, one of the problems faced by economists back in the eighteenth century was how to avoid any possible confusion between stocks and flows of goods and how to sum them. This problem is far from being solved today. For example, the consumption of an existing stock should be properly accounted; however, in the System of National Account, there is no clear way to measure the depletion of non-reproducible stocks of goods, such as petroleum, natural forests, landscape, or clean air. If those goods are 'natural capital goods', their depletion is a negative investment. For instance, Dasgupta (2021) explains that if one destroys biodiversity so as to build a shopping mall, the national accounts record the increase in produced capital (the shopping mall is an investment), but not the disinvestment in natural capital unless it commanded a market price.

Therefore, the core question is: what is the value of a good to society?

To show how values arise from ratios of quantities, we can consider a very simple economy, where there is just one consumer (or where all consumers are identical and earn the same income). This economy produces just one agriculture good a, one manufactured good m,[4] and one service s, for example, the transport of these goods. It is a closed economy. If the agriculture good is the only one that goes to final consumption, and manufacturing and transportation are only instrumental to the production of food, the yearly added value of the agriculture industry Y_a is:

$$Y_a = X_a - X_m P_m - X_s P_s \tag{1.1}$$

where X are quantities in physical units of goods and P are prices in units of *numéraire* (i.e. unit of account). Prices are constant. The key question in this story is this: what are prices? Other interesting questions are put aside now, such as what are quantities of goods? Or what are goods? How can they be measured? The two latter issues will be considered later on, particularly in Chapter 2. Here the focus is on prices, as these are the main concern for evaluation.

People are accustomed to think of prices as being expressed in money terms, but this convenient fact obscures the welfare content of the abstract entity that it is defined as price. Suppose there is no money at all. Given that the only consumption good is a, some type of food, the *numéraire* can be the a-good itself, as it is natural to measure well-being here in terms of food. Thus, GDP is nothing more than the welfare level of the economy expressed in food units or perhaps in its caloric content. Taking $P_a = 1$, the social value of food produced is now just X_a. Price is here nothing more than a conversion factor that changes (linearly) the social value of one unit of m in some units of a. Thus, if x is the measurement unit (1 ton of food, or 1 billion calories), then $P_m = \dfrac{x_a}{x_m} = z$. Similarly, for the price of transport and food: $P_s = \dfrac{x_a}{x_s} = w$ and $P_a = \dfrac{x_a}{x_a} = 1$.

After using these conversion factors, the GDP contribution of the agriculture expressed in terms of units of food under (1.1) is:

$$Y_a = X_a - X_m \left(\frac{x_a}{x_m} \right) - X_s \left(\frac{x_a}{x_s} \right). \tag{1.2}$$

Hence, in this economy, GDP is the added value of each sector measured in units of food, given certain weights or parameters 1, z and w that can be interpreted as 'prices' but are actually only conversion factors of quantities:

$$\text{GDP} = Y_a = \left(X_a - z X_m - w X_s \right) + z X_m + w X_s = X_a. \tag{1.3}$$

In other words, GDP is the total amount of the consumption good produced, valued as the *numéraire*. Thus, given a technology (or a social rule) converting manufactured goods and transport in food, and being optimally used (i.e. no more can be produced with the resources available), the added value of the economy is a certain amount of food available for consumption. This seems a sensible way to describe welfare, at least for a rudimentary economy, ignoring distributive issues. One unit more of food increases social welfare by the same amount.

In a simple economy like this one, the association between the concept of welfare and GDP is obvious: the more food people have, the less they starve, thus presumably the happier they are. To interpret GDP as a welfare measure, it is necessary to say that welfare increases one-for-one with increased food consumption. Clearly, the crucial trick here is the assumption that, for a given technology, a set of conversion factors exists that can exactly change kilocalories into kilometres of transport and trucks into units of equivalent food and welfare.

It is important to observe that these conversion factors are not 'market prices'. They are ratios arising from bartering among agents, given their preferences and hence their willingness to pay for a good. Prices can be conversion factors computed by a social planner, or given by social norms,[5] or selected by a random process under certain constraints (e.g. negative prices are not admitted, etc.). As discussed later on, avoiding the confusion between market prices (including prices in 'competitive' markets) and social accounting prices is the core idea of Applied Welfare Economics. The theory of value was the key concern of classical economists, from Ricardo to Marx. One market interpretation was given by Walras and re-elaborated in the neoclassical theory of value by Arrow and Debreu. That general equilibrium view of what the social value of a good is, was criticized by Piero Sraffa and others. Implicitly, the neoclassical view on prices and social values was criticized by Keynes and Stiglitz, among several others. There is nothing intrinsically neoclassical in Welfare Economics, at least in the broad sense of the term adopted in this book.

1.1.2 Income and final consumption

It is well known that GDP as a welfare concept can be expressed equivalently in two other ways: either as the sum of the wages paid to workers in terms of food in each of the three sectors or as the sum of workers' final consumption (there is no saving). This is the well-known idea that in a closed economy, the sum of the value of net outputs (the added value of each industry) equals the compensation of production factors and final households' consumption. And this is also the amount of food available to households, again an indicator of their well-being. This triple dimension of measuring the well-being of an economy where food or calories are the *numéraire* is briefly discussed below.

If there are N workers in the economy (or the unique consumer distributes his working time across the three activities) such that the employment is $N_s = n_a + n_m + n_s$, then the average compensation (per capita income) per worker must be $\frac{x_a}{N}$. If skills are assumed to be homogeneous, and labour is assigned to each industry optimally (e.g. productivity per worker in terms of food is the same across industries),[6] there will be a unique wage rate that is exactly $\frac{x_a}{N}$. Thus, the employment (and the wage share) of each industry is determined accordingly. Note that:

$$\frac{X_a - zX_m - wX_s}{n_a} = \frac{X_a}{N} \tag{1.4}$$

obviously implies:

$$n_a = \frac{N(X_a - zX_m - wX_s)}{X_a}. \tag{1.5}$$

Similar relations apply to n_m and n_s.

Thus, one might have a labour *numéraire*, and at that point, an alternative to food as a *numéraire* could be the equivalent labour content of each good as a welfare measure.

The 'food' equivalent of a good can be seen as its 'benefit' or demand side, while the 'labour' content is its supply or cost side. This would be a very crude but interesting example of cost-benefit analysis for a simple economy. There is nothing really important in measuring GDP in terms of calories of food or in terms of hours of equivalent work. The social value of working time can always be computed in terms of calories of food, and conversely, the social value of one calorie of food in terms of working time necessary to get it, and prices expressed in one way or another. Moreover, in this example, no special importance is attached to the 'rule' for the determination of wages in a non-capital economy. In contrast, the story is much more complex (and controversial) in an inter-temporal context, when savings and capital, and social norms for allocating capital endowments, may determine wages, quasi-rents or human capital, interests, and profits.

1.1.3 A digression on money in welfare economics

In this simple economy, money is not needed. It is enough to attach a labour (or food) price to each good. When euros or dollars are used in the context of welfare analysis in the rest of this book, in general, the use of a 'monetary' value has nothing to do with 'money' in the usual meaning.

A serious misunderstanding of a typical application of Welfare Economics, such as social cost-benefit analysis, is to think that this attaches a 'money' value to everything, including life saved. The marginal utility of money or income is briefly discussed later. Here, we simply state that while it is convenient that existing currencies are used as a *numéraire*, one euro of welfare is not the same thing as one actual observed euro. It is true, however, that there may be some relation between actual and welfare money, but most of the welfare analysis is carried out in a non-monetary context (e.g. monetary policy and inflation are not considered) even when a currency is used as *numéraire*.[7]

As a small digression, actual money can be private or public, even if the unit of account has been public (i.e. established by a government) for several centuries. The reason for both private and public money is traditionally associated with the measurement of values (*numéraire*), means of payment (transaction money), reserves of value, and means of speculation. All these functions are associated with complex issues, including knowledge, uncertainty, and time, that cannot be discussed here. Thus, for most of the discussion below, accounting prices expressed in euros or in whatever currency for welfare purposes, should not be confused with the actual currency. For example, the welfare content in terms of food of the actual money can be very different from the food content of accounting euros in a cost-benefit analysis (or can be coincidental in special circumstances only).

1.2 The welfare assumptions behind GDP and NNP

From the previous discussion, it is apparent that the correspondence between GDP and social welfare is not straightforward. While the notion of using the sum of consumption or incomes or output values is appealing and simple, on closer inspection, it is full of dubious assumptions. Three questions must be considered:

I   Why is a good included in the calculation?
II   What is the appropriate price (conversion factor) in terms of a *numéraire* for the welfare analysis of such good?
III   Can consumption of goods across individuals simply be summed to get a sensible notion of social welfare?

It is now recalled how the conventional GDP concept answers these questions. First, GDP includes all goods produced by the private and public sectors for which either a price or a cost can be observed in money terms. Thus, a large number of things that indeed can make people happier or furious, such as a beautiful landscape or a traffic jam, are not included. Housewife production is omitted too. In fact, probably some of the most important goods in our life are not included in GDP; see further discussion below. This is not just a matter of lack of markets, but a much more important and subtle issue that has to do with incomplete information, such that, in a sense, what is a good is never a closed set. Any attempt by economists to build a synthetic indicator of social welfare is flawed because of the uncertainty about what is (objectively or subjectively) considered as good to human beings of the present and future generations.

Second, GDP uses only two types of prices: market prices (net or gross of indirect taxes, i.e. production or consumption prices) and production cost (typically for public sector services). The problem for welfare analysis is that many, or perhaps all of these observed prices, are poorly related to the (optimal) marginal social value of goods. This book presents several examples of this fact. At this stage, it seems enough to say that markets and governments often misprice key production factors (capital, labour, knowledge, natural resources and institutions, including freedom and democracy) in welfare terms (with zero price a frequent occurrence for socially valuable goods). Hence any output produced with those inputs is also mispriced.

As for the third question, the way the GDP concept is designed in national accounts does not consider inequality of the welfare effects of consumption. As shown in the previous example, what is done is simply to sum up the consumption of each agent in the economy. Under homogeneity of skills, and no capital, wages and consumption are identical across individuals in a pure labour economy. Heterogeneity in skills, can be regarded as a lottery that assigns some characteristics to individuals: some of them may have physical or mental impairment and others are able to do everything. This fact leads to different productivity, different wages, and different consumption. By construction, GDP is totally indifferent to the fact that in one state of the world, there is a certain social distribution of abilities (or of any asset) and in another one a completely different pattern, even though the average consumption may be identical. Thus, a country where there is just one extremely well-paid individual and 99 people get almost nothing would be welfare equivalent to another country where there are 100 individuals who get the same average salary. Most people would not feel comfortable with this indifference. Looking at the latter situation, one would see perhaps that nobody is homeless, starving, or affected by avoidable illness. In the former society, 99 per cent of the time, one will see deprivation and misery all around. How can it be reasonably said that the collective welfare of each society is the same?

This question also arises when an inter-temporal perspective is adopted and the society to be considered is the future one. The extensive literature on 'Green National Accounting' can be seen as an attempt to extend equity across generations. However, some of this literature refers to a representative consumer and ignores that today, and presumably tomorrow, opportunities and well-being are very different across individuals.

The relevant concept of this stream of literature is the Net National Product (NNP). There are several possible definitions of this measure, but basically, they revolve around the idea that sustainable consumption is not the same as current consumption, as the former implies that the capital stock of the country (or of the planet) is preserved, while the latter can be supported by depletion of capital.

While idea of NPP is appealing and related to inter-generational equity, it involves a number of conceptual and computational difficulties. First of all, what actually is capital (including natural resources, human capital and any other capital good) implies that production opportunities that will arise tomorrow, based on new knowledge, can be identified now. Second, sustainable consumption in an inter-generational perspective means that you need to solve an inter-temporal growth programme.

Thus, accounting NNP conventions based on prices observed today would not work. A variant of this reasoning is that utility, not consumption, should be held constant (*ceteris paribus*) across generations. Both versions of 'green accounting' (sustainable consumption and sustainable utility) need shadow prices and possibly social discounting; the two concepts are discussed in the following chapters of this book.

The next section discusses how a specific social welfare function (Bentham) is to a certain extent associated with the GDP concept and why this SWF is unappealing. As far as NNP is based on similar welfare foundations, there is no difference between the two concepts in this perspective.

1.3 Individual and social welfare

The oldest view on how to convert individual welfare into social welfare is associated with Jeremy Bentham (1789). The 'utilitarian' SWF is simply:

$$\text{SWF} = \sum_i U_i (.). \tag{1.6}$$

This is the sum of individual utilities. If utilities are proportional to income (or to present and future consumption) so and the marginal utility of income is constant, GDP is a Bentham-type SWF as it sums incomes of a country (up to a linear transformation).[8]

However, summing utilities (in whatever way they are measured) and incomes is a different affair. In the previous example of one-consumer equivalent economy, GDP was the sum of food produced or consumed and was suggested a natural indicator of social well-being. The correspondence would be obvious if all individuals had the same marginal utility of income. This condition is equivalent to saying that income distribution is optimal. Otherwise, it would be possible to increase social welfare by moving one unit of money away from those with lower marginal use for it to those more deserving. This is not the case in the real world.

Before discussing this seemingly simple SWF function, and its alternatives, some words must be spent on individual utilities. This theme has been discussed by microeconomists over more than one century.

One crucial point here that there is a set of observable variables, for example, quantities of goods X_1, X_2, ..., X_I consumed by an individual h and an individual k, and that a certain algebraic transformation of these observables generates a non–observable, but still measurable, new variable: a utility. Then these utilities are aggregated, as in Bentham-type SWF, as cardinal and interpersonally comparable numbers (it is assumed here familiarity with cardinality versus ordinality of utility; see the Further Reading section 1.10 below). Thus one can say, in a precise sense, that social welfare in one country is greater than in another country or that states of the world can be compared. This is what GDP does and why it was conceived.

Is it sensible to proceed in this way? This issue was very controversial in the first half of the last century. The rejection of cardinality and interpersonal comparability in utility has been the tenet of a number of microeconomists. While some interpersonal comparability can be achieved when looking at ordinal levels, as in Rawlsian SWF (see below), the main alternative to the old welfare economics in the tradition of Bentham was simply to avoid any form of interpersonal comparisons of utility by assuming that utility is an ordinal concept: one can say that he prefers a state of the world compared to another one, but he cannot say that his preference is associated with a cardinal number. It is not possible to directly measure distances in such a space because the fact that social welfare as seen by individual 1, i.e. SW_1, is preferred to social welfare as seen by individual 2, i.e. SW_2, tells nothing about how intensively SW_1, welfare dominates over SW_2. Then, the fact that for another consumer SW_2, is preferred to SW_1 cannot be compared to conclude which one would lose 'more' if SW_2 or alternatively SW_1 is extracted.

As further discussed in Chapter 2, the rejection of cardinal utility and interpersonal comparability is instrumental to a very special definition of social welfare, associated with Vilfredo Pareto, and its subsequent versions.

Clearly, if the observables, such as consumption, or income and prices, cannot be associated to build respectively direct or indirect utility functions, it would be impossible to construct a concept of social utility that allows for comparisons. Thus, this crucial step needs to be discussed briefly. Is there anything wrong or illogical in building an unobservable variable (function of utility) based on observable variables? Is the new variable ('utility') anything real? This is an epistemological issue that has no absolute answer. Other sciences use artificial variables, for example, Physics uses imaginary numbers as ingredients of quantum mechanics. Imaginary numbers have no natural real-world counterparts, but using them in equations of quantum mechanics allows for precise predictions. A possible answer to the question of unobservable variables is to assume a heuristic perspective. Building an artificial, unobservable variable, as a manipulation of some observables, can be seen as legitimate if it generates predictions that can be verified or disproved.

Suppose, just to discuss an example among many others, that individual utility is assumed by an applied economist to be a constant elasticity of substitution (CES) function of consumption of $I = (1,\dots,i,\dots,I)$ goods:

$$U^h\left(X_1,\dots,X_I\right) = \left[\sum_{i=1}^{I}\alpha_i X_i^{\rho}\right]^{1/\epsilon}. \tag{1.7}$$

where the weights are such that $\sum_{i=1}^{I} \alpha_i = 1$ and $\rho > 0$ is a parameter. For the properties of CES utility (and its macroeconomic counterpart), see the references in the Further Reading section (1.10).

When the CES assumption (or any other) is made, it is important to understand that no independent measurement of the functional form of utility, so defined, is possible. Thus, it is not possible to *directly* test the assumption simply because utility cannot be observed and consumption data cannot be fitted to an unobservable. The only thing one can do is to use consumption data X and see if the observed pattern works well in terms of prediction when CES is assumed and the parameters α and ρ are estimated. In fact, CES utility is associated with a well-defined demand function, which lends itself to econometric testing when prices and incomes are included as controls. As it happens, the indirect version of the CES utility (see Box 1.1) is also a nice way to cardinalize utility, as per cent changes of utility are equal to Hicksian equivalent variations of income. But nothing ensures that the CES utility applies to any specific individual. In fact, several alternative assumptions could have been made, as Box 1.1 shows. Only empirical testing under different assumptions would tell which model works better in a given context.

Box 1.1 Some utility functions

Direct utility functions

CES utility: $U^h(X_1,\ldots,X_I) = \left[\sum_{i=1}^{I} \alpha_i X_i^\rho\right]^{1/\rho}$, where $\sum_{i=1}^{I} \alpha_i = 1$.

Cobb–Douglas: $U^h(X_1,\ldots,X_I) = \prod_{(i=1)}^{I} X_i^{(\alpha_i)}$, where $\alpha_i \geq 0$. This is special case of

Stone–Geary utility function $U^h(X_1,\ldots,X_I) = \prod_{i=1}^{I} (X_i - \gamma_i)^{\alpha_i}$ when $\gamma_i = 0$.

Linear utility: $U^h(X_1,\ldots,X_I) = \sum_{i=1}^{I} X_i$.

Quasi-linear utility: $U^h(X_0,X_1,\ldots,X_I) = X_0 + U^h(X)$.

Indirect utility function

The indirect utility function is the function $V(p,m)$ that gives the maximum utility achievable at given prices (p) and income (m):

$$\begin{cases} V(p,m) = \max U(x) \\ \text{s.t.} \\ px = m. \end{cases}$$

Some examples are the following:

Isoelastic (CES) indirect utility function: $V(p,m) = \left[\sum_{i=1}^{I} a_i^{1-\sigma} p_i^{\sigma}\right]^{-1/\sigma} m$, where

$$\sigma = \frac{\rho}{\rho-1}.$$

Cobb–Douglas indirect utility function: $V(p,m) = \prod_{i=1}^{I}\left(\frac{\alpha_i}{\alpha p_i} m\right)^{\alpha_i}$, $\alpha_i \geq 0$, $\alpha = \sum_{i=1}^{I} \alpha_i$

Source: Author, based on references in Section 1.10.

Are individual utility functions (in this book, individual welfare and utility are used synonymously) just being 'invented'? While a theorist will insist on respecting certain axioms that sound 'logical' or 'desirable' (the role of axioms in Welfare Economics is mentioned in Chapter 2), an applied economist will insist that some predictions can be made and tested.

Thus, any individual welfare function that assumes continuity and differentiability, and such that the first partial derivative is positive and the second derivative is negative to consumption of one good, will imply some testable predictions. For example, it will assume that a consumer's can be observed, even if individual satisfaction cannot be directly observed. This is the 'revealed preference' approach that has been widely used in the empirical estimation of consumer functions: given a certain income and price level, a marginal propensity to consume a specific good is expected. It is an empirical parameter that can be estimated for samples of individual consumers, or countries and so on, across years. If income doubles while prices remain constant, a still positive but decreasing marginal propensity to consume can be observed or not, indirectly testing our assumption on the form of the individual welfare function.

A different approach is to directly ask consumers what they would prefer to do if income doubles. Or to ask them to assign a score to their degree of happiness on a certain scale. This is the 'stated preference' approach that is largely used in cost-benefit analysis (contingent valuation and choice experiments, sometimes called conjoint analysis) and in Happiness Economics (see, e.g., Layard 2005); see below.[9]

The two approaches and their applications are discussed later and in Chapter 4, but here we simply state that adopting a certain individual welfare function in principle should not be an arbitrary choice, as this can be tested empirically. The empirical test may be difficult for a number of reasons, including lack of data and irrational consumer behaviour. However, in principle, indirect testing of the assumptions made on individual welfare functions is often possible, and should be done whenever data are available.

After all, building a SWF means that (a) some individual welfare functions are assumed and (b) they are then combined into an aggregate formula. In principle, this is a legitimate procedure, as far as the two steps are understood and tested. We do not dwell here anymore on the first step, which is discussed in several Microeconomics textbooks.

An important remark, in this context, is that consumers react to signals they observe, typically prices, in the usual meaning, and in most cases take them as parameters. Thus, actual-observed-prices or other observed signals determine the behaviour of agents, while it may be the case – and in fact it is often the case – that those signals are distorted from a social welfare perspective. In fact, a key motivation of Welfare Economics is the existence of a wedge between observed prices and 'shadow prices' reflecting the marginal social value of goods.

1.4 Determinants of individual welfare: goods

In most of this book, individual welfare is defined as a real function of real variables, and a cardinal perspective in utility is adopted. This is a sensible way to deal with building social welfare functions, as is discussed below.

A direct utility function of individual h then takes the general form:

$$U^h = U^h(X),\tag{1.8}$$

where $X = X_1, X_2, [\ldots]$ is a vector of quantities of goods.

Alternatively, an indirect utility function takes the form:

$$V^h = V^h(m^h, p),\tag{1.9}$$

where m^h is income of the h-th individual and p is a vector of prices. It is assumed that in general $dU/dx > 0$, $dV/dm > 0$, $dV/dp < 0$, while $U''(x) < 0$.

One has, however, to be careful with the definition of 'goods'. The dimension of goods and price vectors is the same (where zero is a possible price for some goods). But we have previously asked the question: what are goods? We said above that, GDP accounting conventions includes only goods for which a price or a cost can be observed. Here we need to be more general.

In fact, goods are defined as any objects that potentially increase individual welfare. This definition means that U or V must be comprehensive. For example, all objects priced zero by markets or governments that increase individual welfare must be included. There are many goods that are not explicitly included in GDP but that can increase or decrease welfare. Examples are health condition, waiting time, environment, and years of life.

It is noteworthy that 'bads' are the complements of goods and are better defined taking their 'good' counterparts. Thus, the health condition of a person can be described on a scale from 0 to 100, with '100 illness' equal to death, but it is more convenient to reverse the scale and use 100 as 'perfect health' and 0 as death.

In this context, the 'law' of diminishing marginal utility of goods has been justified on logical grounds by early microeconomists. While, in general, this 'law' seems sensible, it is not entirely compelling. Certainly, one should agree the one-millionth cup of coffee consumed is not enjoyed as much as the first of the morning. However, it is not immediately understandable why the same 'law' of diminishing welfare return should apply to other goods, such as health.

However, when health components are disentangled one by one, it seems that the ability to enjoy abilities has its own limitations. For instance, the happiness of healing from total blindness or deafness is certainly very great and it seems sensible to say that moving from a good condition to an excellent one is less rewarding than from a very poor condition to a good one. In principle, as mentioned, this can be tested by revealed or stated preferences for health conditions, even if the problem of placing a metric on the level of health is not a trivial one. One idea that is often encountered in this context is the 'marginal willingness-to-pay' (WTP) for a good or 'marginal willingness-to-accept' (WTA) for a bad (see Chapter 4). In the form previously stated, some of the capabilities in the meaning of Sen can be treated as goods: a point that is discussed later in this chapter.

1.5 Determinants of social welfare: individual utilities

1.5.1 Aggregating individual utilities

Similarly to individual welfare, there are again two steps for building any SWF. First, one needs to decide its arguments and second, to decide the functional form.

Given that the SWF should be a way to represent the well-being of a community, the best avenue is to think that somebody cares for this concept. This can be the welfare economist himself, or a government, or politician with a certain vision of what is good for the society. It should be insisted that an 'objective' SWF cannot be built, but it is always necessary to assume a perspective, i.e. a set of value judgements that convey the evaluation criteria of one specific subject.

The most straightforward perspective is that of a social planner who is only interested in maximizing the welfare of individuals. This viewpoint was originally due to Pareto (1916) in the *Trattato di Sociologia Generale*, where he says that in order to sum up the utilities of different individuals you need to assign weights to them. To do this, one cannot consider as equally important, for example, the welfare of honest people and of criminals, where the latter find their welfare in harassing the former.

Interestingly, this is a completely different view from that advocated by Pareto (1909) in the *Manuel d'Economie Politique*, and in fact the one that is now reported as the Pareto criterion in standard microeconomics textbooks (see Box 1.2). According to the economist Pareto, the only acceptable social criterion is one where any improvement in the welfare of an individual does not come at the expense of any other individual in the society (see more on this in Chapter 2). This is what may be expected if there is no way to compare individual utilities. If there are two states of the world, when SW_1 is preferred to SW_2 by at least one agent, and all the other agents are indifferent to them, SW_1 is socially preferred to SW_2 (the difference between the weak and strong Pareto criteria is mentioned in the next chapter). However, it is obvious that this criterion is very restrictive, as in a community it is enough that one member says that he suffers from a change to stop that change even if it is supported by a majority of $H - 1$ individuals (with H whatever large a number).

Thus, the more promising approach adopted in Applied Welfare Economics is similar to the Pareto-sociologist criterion: a weighted sum of individual utilities.[10] The main

Box 1.2 Pareto economist versus Pareto sociologist

Pareto the economist – Pareto (1909)

For a generic consumer h the change in total ophelimity (subjective utility) is the following: $dU_h = \varphi_{ha}dx_{ha} + \varphi_{hb}dx_{hb} + \cdots - \varphi_{hs}dx_{hs}$, where dx are small changes in consumption of goods a, b, ... or in supply of effort and other goods s; φ_a are (positive and negative) marginal utility for each good and service. If there are H consumers, the following system is obtained:

$$\begin{cases} d\lambda_1 = p_a dx_{1a} + p_b dx_{1b} + \cdots - p_s dx_{1s} \\ \qquad\qquad \cdots \\ d\lambda_H = p_a dx_{Ha} + p_b dx_{Hb} + \cdots - p_s dx_{Hs} \end{cases} \quad \text{(A)}$$

from which is derived:

$$\begin{cases} dU_1 = \mu_1 d\lambda_1 \\ \qquad \cdots \\ dU_H = \mu_H d\lambda_h \end{cases} \quad \text{(B)}$$

where: $\mu_1 = \varphi_{1a}/p_a \quad \mu_2 = \varphi_{2a}/p_a$, etc $\quad$ (C)

$d\lambda$ are changes in total consumption, which are determined as the weighted sum of variations in consumption of goods and services, where weights are given by their prices p_a, p_b, ..., p_s. To obtain the system (B), a further weighting is needed, introducing the coefficients defined in (C), which represent the ratio between elementary ophelimity and price of a *numéraire* good a. Pareto notes that, contrary to system (A), the sum of system (B) or its single components is not possible. Thus, he says, to maximize collective ophelimity an indirect criterion based on system (A) is needed. To have a maximum, a necessary condition is a null differential: $d\Lambda = 0$, where $d\Lambda = d\lambda_1 + d\lambda_2 + \cdots d\lambda_h$. At the maximum, a further increase of aggregate consumption without a negative change for at least one individual is not possible. The same holds for production. This is the well-known Pareto-optimum (for one version of it, see Chapter 2).

Pareto the sociologist – Pareto (1916)

Pareto explains extensively the distinction between the concept of maximum collective utility in Economics and in Sociology in the *Trattato di Sociologia Generale* (1916). His argument is the following. Given that individuals' ophelimities are not comparable, he assumes the possibility of introducing positive quantities a_1, a_2,... etc. such that: $a_1 d\varphi_1 + a_1 d\varphi_2 + \cdots + a_1 d\varphi_h = 0$. To find the weights a_1, a_2,... etc. he assumes relaxing an implicit assumption in the individual ophelimity function, that each individual has not only a system of preferences defined according to his states of ophelimity, but also a system of subjective evaluations relative to the ophelimity levels of the other $H - 1$ individuals. In this way, he defines the following system:

$$\begin{cases} a_{11}d\varphi_1 + a_{12}d\varphi_2 + \cdots + a_{1H}d\varphi_H = 0 \\ a_{21}d\varphi_1 + a_{22}d\varphi_2 + \cdots + a_{2H}d\varphi_H = 0 \\ \qquad\qquad\qquad \vdots \\ a_{H1}d\varphi_1 + a_{H2}d\varphi_2 + \cdots + a_{HH}d\varphi_H = 0. \end{cases}$$

Each individual states his/her own weighting of his/her own ophelimity $d\varphi_i$ and that of the other $H - 1$ agents. For each individual, the maximum is obtained when the weighted sum of changes in ophelimity is equal to zero. Then, the H subjective evaluations must be weighted: this is the essential function of the government, which assigns its own evaluation system β_i to each individual assessment a_i.

Thus, maximum utility for the sociological collectivity will be:

$$M_1 d\varphi_1 + M_2 d\varphi_2 + \cdots + M_H d\varphi_H, \text{ where } M_i = a_i \beta_i$$

According to Pareto, the economic optimum as in Pareto (1909) has to be seen as the extreme limit beyond which the pure economic reasoning cannot go without contradictions. He maintains that the determination of the coefficients a and β cannot be derived with the instruments introduced by Pareto (1909), but have to be determined with those developed by Pareto (1916).

Source: Florio (1988).

difference with the Bentham criterion lies in the fact that individual utilities, instead of being just summed, are first weighted, then summed. This idea was formalized by Bergson (alias Burk 1938) and developed by Paul Samuelson (1947), hence the current name of Bergson–Samuelson for an SWF of the generic form $W = W(U)$, where U is a vector of dimension H; see below, equation (1.12). One possible linear specification is this:

$$W = \sum_h w^h U^h. \tag{1.10}$$

The Bentham SWF is hence a special case of Bergson–Samuelson SWF, when $w^h = 1$ for each h (any set of equal weights can be normalized to unity), where w are 'welfare weights', coefficients that in the Bergson–Samuelson (BS) frame take the form $dW/dU > 0$.

Another form, taking an integral instead of a sum and used when there is a population continuum, is simply:

$$W = \int_{h=1}^{H} f\left(U^h\right) dU^h. \tag{1.11}$$

Before dwelling on any specific functional form, it is worthwhile to make two remarks. In Sen (1986) terms, the Bergson–Samuelson SWF is welfaristic, as it is based only on the welfare of agents, and is individualistic, as only individual welfare matters. It is shown below that (a) there may be other ways to model individualistic functions and (b) there may be SWFs that are not (only) individualistic.

According to many welfare economists, for example, Boadway and Bruce (1984), the most general form for any SWF is simply:

$$W = W\left(U^h\left(.\right)\right). \tag{1.12}$$

In fact, this is the most general form of an *individualistic* SWF. One way to interpret this SWF as Paretian is to say that there should be three specific restrictions on it: (a) the function must be well defined in the utility space; (b) it must be strictly increasing in each individual's utility; and (c) indifference curves should have some formal properties.

However, this would be the Pareto sociologist, not the economist, despite any implied 'ordinalism' retained by Samuelson (1947). Atkinson and Stiglitz (1980) say:

> The standard procedure for arriving at a complete ordering is to postulate a Paretian Social Welfare Function. This function, which may be written as $\Gamma\left(U^1,U^2,U^3,...U^h\right)$ where U^h denotes the utility of individual h, is Paretian in the sense of respecting individual valuations. It is therefore consistent with the Pareto criterion, but goes beyond it in assuming that gains and losses can be compared.
> (Atkinson and Stiglitz 1980: 339)

Clearly, the fact that losses and gains can be added is not in the spirit of Pareto the economist. Having said this, let us briefly discuss why the Bergson–Samuelson-SWF is often regarded as appealing.

An indirect utility function of the form $V^h = V^h\left(m^h, p\right)$ is considered, where m^h is the lump-sum income, i.e. income that is independent of the agent's behaviour. Assuming that the agent has to take prices as parameters, a natural way to express the welfare weights in this context is:

$$\beta^h = \left(\frac{\partial W}{\partial V^h}\right)\left(\frac{\partial V^h}{\partial m^h}\right). \tag{1.13}$$

Thus, the profile of all the welfare weights can depend simply upon a function that expresses a social valuation of the income of any individual. In Chapter 7, the application of welfare weights to social cost-benefit analysis is discussed in detail. Here their interpretation is stressed.

1.5.2 Interpretation of welfare weights

One way to interpret the β^h generating function is that it simply reflects individual welfare profiles, i.e. the fact that individuals may have a decreasing marginal utility of income. While this view has been advocated, it is probably too strong and unnecessary. In fact, even if each individual may have a negative second derivative to income, similarly to the utility of each individual good, there are two possible objections. First, it is not obvious that for an individual to have decreasing welfare returns to each good implies also decreasing return to income. A change in income, in fact, has the potential to increase the consumption of any good, including those that were out of reach before the increase. Thus it is not clear why the satisfaction deriving from an additional unit of income for somebody who is already very rich should be less than if he was poorer. This fact would be very difficult to test, because obviously the marginal willingness-to-pay for an increase of income is the increase of income itself; hence the same kind of revealed or stated preference approach that was briefly discussed above cannot be used.[11]

A well-known example of a function that has decreasing returns on each of its arguments but constant returns to scale is the Cobb–Douglas, which can be interpreted here in welfare terms in the trivial case of two goods: $U = x_1^{\alpha} x_2^{1-\alpha}$.

This individual utility function says that individual utility in a two-goods space is such that (ignoring some issues about ordinality versus cardinality of the involved functions):

$$\log U = \alpha \log x_1 + (1-\alpha)\log x_2.$$

It can be easily generalized to I goods, provided that the exponents of the partial utility derived from each good sum to one.

Box 1.3 Cobb–Douglas utility function generalized to several goods

The Cobb–Douglas utility function generalized to I goods is $U(x) = \prod_{i=1}^{I} x_i^{\alpha_i}$.

Marginal utility is positive $\dfrac{\partial U}{\partial x_i} = \alpha_i \dfrac{U}{x_i} > 0$ but decreasing in the consumption of the good, $\dfrac{\partial^2 U}{\partial x_i^2} = \alpha_i(\alpha_i - 1)\dfrac{U}{x_i^2} < 0$ provided that $0 < \alpha_i < 1$.

However, the function has constant returns to scale if the sum of the exponents is one. In fact, consider a symmetric increase in the consumption of all goods equal to $\lambda = 1$, then:

$$\prod_{i=1}^{I}(\lambda x_i)^{\alpha_i} = \prod_{i=1}^{I}(\lambda)^{\alpha_i}\prod_{i=1}^{I}(x_i)^{\alpha_i} = \lambda^{\sum_{i=1}^{I}\alpha_i}\sum_{i=1}^{I}(x_i)^{\alpha_i} = \lambda\prod_{i=1}^{I}(x_i)^{\alpha_i} \text{ iff } \sum_{i=1}^{I}\alpha_i = 1$$

Source: Author, based on references in Section 1.10.

A second and even more crucial objection to the interpretation of the welfare weights as an 'objective' reflection of individual welfare functions is that we cannot assume that the welfare profiles of each individual are identical.

The safest interpretation of the vector in the spirit of Pareto-sociologist, Bergson and several other welfare economists is that these coefficients express a social norm, a convention. In this case they express a convention on income distribution, or – in other words – aversion to inequality of a given society.

Chapter 7 comes back on this, dealing with welfare weights and distributive consideration in policy or project evaluation. The remark stressed here is that this value judgement on equity needs not to be imposed by a benevolent dictator or by the applied economist. It can result from a political process that delegates to the government the translation, for example, in tax codes or in public spending budgets, of the view of a democratic majority of voters. It is, however, difficult to think of this as the outcome of a unanimity rule as implied by the Pareto-economist criterion, because there will be losers in the process.

In addition to the Bentham and Bergson–Samuelson SWF (respectively equations 1.6 and 1.10), the third classic example is Rawls (1971), based on his *Theory of Justice*. The idea here was that if all individuals are under a veil of ignorance about where they are going to be placed by a random assignment of welfare, it would be rational for anybody to subscribe to a social norm that compares states of the world focusing only on the bottom of the scale (see Box 1.4).

Box 1.4 Some variants of individualistic SWF

As an exercise, some conventional and less conventional but still individualistic SWFs can be hypothesized drawing from the microeconomic theory of production and other fields. In fact, any SWF can be regarded as an algorithm that transforms inputs, i.e. individual welfare indexes, into an output, social welfare. Here below some examples are reported, but several others can be found in the literature.

- The Rawls SWF takes the form: $W = \min\left(U^1, \ldots U^h \ldots, U^H\right)$. Bentham, Bergson–Samuelson and Rawls SWFs are all special forms of an isoelastic function of a parameter (isoelastic frame): $W = \left(\dfrac{1}{1-a}\right)\sum\limits_{i=1}^{I}\left(U_i^{1-a}\right)$ where a is a constant and is greater than or equal to zero. This expression can be manipulated according to the transformation: $W' = (1-a)W^{\frac{1}{1-a}}$ to obtain the CES form: $\left[\sum\limits_{i=1}^{I}\left(U_i^{1-a}\right)\right]^{\frac{1}{1-a}}$. For the Bentham SWF $a = 0$, for Bergson–Samuelson $a < 1$, and for $a \to \infty$ the SWF becomes Rawlsian, ignoring the corner values.

- Additive separable functions whose arguments are functions of scalars U_i, which in turn are functions of indexes or scalars $W = \sum\limits_{i=1}^{I} a_i f\left(U_i\left(x_i\right)\right)$.

- Average functions of the form: $W = \dfrac{1}{I}\sum\limits_{i=1}^{I} Y_i$ such as GDP per capita.

- Egalitarian functions: $W\left(u^1, \ldots, u^H\right) = \sum\limits_{h} u^h - \lambda \sum\limits_{h}\left[u^h - \min_h\left(u^h\right)\right]^h$. A simple one in this class is $W_{Gini} = \bar{m}\left(1-G\right)$, where G is the Gini index and $\bar{m}$ is the average per capita income.

- Linear welfare functions characterized by an interaction term highlighting possible social evaluation of the mutual relations between pairs of types u_i and u_j: $W = \sum_i^I a_i U_i + \sum_i^I b_{ij} U_i U_j$. When $b = 0$, it is obtained the standard specification of a linear Bergson–Samuelson SWF.

- A non-additive but conjunctive SWF, also called Bernoulli–Nash: $W = \prod_i U_i^{ai}$. This is again equivalent to the Bergson–Samuelson but when it is expressed in logarithmic form. It can take the following geometric average form: $W = \sqrt[I]{\prod_{i=1}^{I} U_i}$.

- A disjunctive SFW where aggregate welfare is the product of the inverse of the deviation from the maximum level of feasible utility (there is satiation) from i and the actual level, weighted for the exponent a_i: $W = \prod_i \dfrac{1}{\left(U_i^{\max} - U_i\right)^{a_i}}$,

- Generalized CES: $W = \left[\left(a_i U_i\right)^c + \left(a_j U_j\right)^{-c}\right]^{1/c}$.

Boadway and Bruce (1984) discuss the relationship between different families of SWF and issues of measurability and comparability of utility.

Source: Author, based on references in Section 1.10.

1.6 Sen's critique of individualistic Social Welfare Function

Sen (1986) offers a critical review of the ethical principles underlying the individualistic view of Welfare Economics. He firmly rejects the position of Robbins (1938) about the meaninglessness of interpersonal comparability of utility. He also attacks the Pareto criterion. More recently, he has extended his criticism to Rawls as he sees that the ethical foundation of the traditional efficiency criterion is extremely poor. There are two crucial arguments in Sen's work:

- one is related to the importance that individuals usually attach to objectives differently from their own well-being;
- the second argument suggests that an individual's success is related to the broader concept of capabilities. This leads to a non-individualistic and non-welfaristic view of what collective welfare is.

The discussion in Sen (1986) points to a re-assessment of the meaning of freedom for an individual. An individual is free if he or she has a fair chance to achieve welfare for himself/herself, and this implies having some fundamental capabilities. An individual is also free if he/she has the opportunity to pursue ideals or states of the world that may be oriented to altruism or to other desired changes that are difficult to be seen as 'egoistic'. Personal felicity, in this perspective, is not necessarily what a human being wants to achieve (or at least not in the conventional meaning). Moreover, freedom might be considered to have an intrinsic value.

While this discussion may be seen as purely abstract, it has important empirical and predictive implications. If human behaviour is influenced by capabilities, freedom and non-individualistic choices, any model based on the standard economic framework will miss a large part of actual states of affairs in societies. For a broad discussion of the question 'Equality of What?' see Sen (1992), while for his reading of the broader subject of Social Choice Theory, see Sen (1986).

In the perspective of Applied Welfare Economics, two additional issues can be raised: first, how to distinguish 'functionings' from 'capabilities', and second, how to use these ideas for empirical analysis. According to Sen, the definition of 'functionings' is indeed very large, as in principle, any individual condition that has an impact on individual welfare is a functioning. The difference between this framework and the traditional one in welfare analysis can be seen by taking the example of health. High consumption of drugs may increase utility by curing illness. But a very low consumption of drugs, because the health condition is good, cannot be said to decrease welfare. Thus, the health condition of an individual is a functioning *per se*. From a neoclassical perspective, which is considered in Chapter 2, the drug is not the proper definition of the good, but it should relate to a state of world where people are affected by illness. While this line of defence can make, to a certain extent, the notions of goods and of functionings mutually compatible, the notion of capabilities seems more challenging to accommodate.

According to Sen, each individual has a given set of opportunities to achieve some functionings, and this capability set cannot be described in terms of what the individual 'has' but in terms of what he 'can have'. This enlarges very much the scope of social welfare because clearly income (the typical resource available to individuals) is only one element at one's disposal to achieve some functionings. Moreover, while functionings are in principle observable, and studies of social conditions have been doing this for many decades (by sociologists, anthropologists, social psychologists), it is less clear how to measure capabilities. Some dimensions, such as freedoms, are covered by international databases, and it seems that basically what Sen has in mind is an integration of a liberal view of society in welfare analysis.

This subject has been growing enormously in the last 20 years and has influenced the views about development policies (e.g. the Millennium Goals of the United Nations or the Human Development Index by the United Nations Development Programme – UNDP). However, it seems difficult to operationalize Sen's ethical position, except for some 'goods' that are at the intersection between functionings, capabilities and well-being, such as education, the value of life expectancy or equality of consumption. As a matter of fact, the concepts behind the Human Development Index (HDI), for example, are firmly within the approach to Applied Welfare Economics adopted in this book, while the construction of the index itself is difficult to match with a precise theory of welfare. The same would apply to any multi-dimensional aggregate social indicators, where the implicit or explicit weights are not microfounded. In fact, as Fleurbaey (2009) suggests, there is a paradox in any attempt to build a social welfare index based on functionings since a contradiction arises when a certain pattern of preferences for capabilities is assumed for a given society:

> If a single index is defined in order to weight the various dimensions of life for all individuals, uniformly, there is no chance that the weights will respect the

individuals' own values about life and the procedure would appear paternalistic or perfectionist. If, on the contrary, one seeks to respect each and every individual's view about the relative importance of the various dimensions of life, one is taking the welfarist route, it is said, and ends up dealing with utility functions.

(Fleurbaey 2009: 1065)

1.7 Paternalism and not (only) individualistic Social Welfare Functions

Until now, individuals are assumed to be the best judges of what gives them pleasure. This sounds logical and widely acceptable. But is this assumption tenable without further inquiry?

Since Musgrave (1969), who proposed the notion of merit wants, it has been observed that one can conceive a SWF where the social planner has its own preferences over consumption profiles.

The general form of these SWFs is:

$$W = W\left[U^h\left(.\right), X_i\right].$$
(1.14)

Thus, the government may want to push the consumption of certain goods that have collective value beyond the individual appreciation. Examples are education or protection of the environment. It is also possible to notice that governments often oppose the consumption of certain goods, for example, drugs.[12]

The motivation for these not entirely individualistic SWFs is that the social planner acts here not just as the neutral expression of individual interests but as an active organizer of society, having in mind specific goals. The justification for this 'paternal' role of government may be that agents are myopic, or have incomplete preferences, or in general, ignore externalities and impacts on future generations. For a review of government paternalism see Le Grand and New (2015).

Again, this is quite far from the Pareto-economist approach, which is purist about individualism as the foundation of economics. However, any SWF except the narrowest definition of Pareto optimality is a form of paternalism, because nothing ensures that, for example, altruism is embodied in the individual preferences of all citizens in the same way. In this perspective, even the most standard Bergson–Samuelson SWF is paternalistic. Moreover, any SWF has to include or exclude some agents as legitimate carriers of preferences: children, and other people who are considered unable to have 'voice' or 'standing' in their preferences. This is also a fundamental form of paternalism, as it defines the boundaries of the society for the calculation of welfare.

Applied Welfare Economics needs to be intrusive to be able to draw policy advice. It is known that some citizens like too much alcohol or tobacco or do not care about climate change and its impact on unborn generations. These people are forced by governments to pay taxes or suffer rationing of consumption and emissions to protect health and the environment beyond their desires.

These arguments fall outside individualism as the methodological foundation of economics. The founding fathers of the profession, including Adam Smith and Vilfredo Pareto, who were well aware that governments have certain responsibilities, never took such a foundation seriously. While according to Smith governments should act considering a set of ethical values, Pareto concluded that governments are unavoidably influenced by elites representing certain interests and that any ethic of those elites serves specific interests. In the following section, the divide between the tradition of Welfare Economics and public choice, and between 'normative' and 'positive' analysis in Public Economics, is briefly mentioned, but this is not the place to discuss this fundamental divide of perspective of analysis.

Having said this, the formal structure of a SWF with specific merit goods is such that, to specify it, a certain weight needs to be assigned to individual-based preferences versus community-based preferences.

One trivial example is an augmented Bergson–Samuelson SWF of the form:

$$W = \sum w^h U^h (x) + \sum b_i x_i \,, \tag{1.15}$$

where w are the ordinary welfare weights (as in equation 1.10) and b are the welfare weights that express the collective preference for some goods i beyond individual preferences.

A practical and well-known example of an implicit SWF of this type, which combines standard of living and some macro merit goods, is again the Human Development Index formulated by the UNDP, even if it has been justified by Sen (1987) and others on different grounds.

Altruism and paternalism can be combined in a SWF that takes the following form:

$$\mathrm{SWF} = W\left(..., U^h\left(x^h; U^k; x^k_M, ...\right)\right) \tag{1.16}$$

where the social welfare depends upon individual utilities U^h, and these, in turn, depend, for each individual h, upon own consumption x^h, others' utilities U^k, and others' consumption of a subset of goods x^k_M, i.e. merit goods. An example is a society where individuals care about their own subjective welfare, others' subjective welfare, but also about others' level of access to health services or protection from unhealthy food, independently from the subjective utility. Any cost-benefit analysis in this society would take into account these concerns. Chapters 2 and 7 further discuss altruism.

Again, there is no need to think of a benevolent dictator imposing the paternalistic SWF. A democratic society where there are 99 citizens who care about climate change in the next century and one who does not care will elect a government that reflects the preferences of the majority, and will assign a certain weight to environmental objectives. This, in turn, will be reflected in social cost-benefit analysis of any decision, through a system of shadow prices that will include those preferences. This is not fundamentally different from a more traditional shadow pricing of goods that includes social preferences for welfare distribution, in ways that are presented in the following chapters.

Box 1.5 The Human Development Index (HDI)

The Human Development Index (HDI) was introduced in 1990 in the first Human Development Report (UNDP 1990). The breakthrough for the HDI was the creation of a single statistic as a frame of reference for both social and economic development. The HDI sets a minimum and a maximum for each dimension, called goalposts, and then shows where each country stands in relation to these goalposts, expressed as a value between 0 and 1. The HDI facilitates instructive comparisons of the experiences within and between different countries.

The HDI is a summary measure of human development. It measures the average achievements in a country in three basic dimensions of human development:

- a long and healthy life, as measured by life expectancy at birth;
- knowledge, measured by mean of years of schooling for adults aged 25 years and more and expected years of schooling for children of school entering age; and
- a decent standard of living, as measured by Gross National Income (GNI) per capita in purchasing power parity (PPP) terms in US dollars.

Before the HDI itself is calculated, an index needs to be calculated for each of the three dimensions. To calculate these indices (life expectancy, education, GNI per capita), minimum and maximum values (goalposts) are chosen for each underlying indicator.

Performance in each dimension is expressed as a value between 0 and 1 by applying the following general formula:

$$\text{Dimension index} = \frac{\text{actual value} - \text{minimum value}}{\text{maximum value} - \text{minimum value}}.$$

The HDI is then calculated as a simple average of the dimension indices. Fleurbaey (2009) critically discusses this and similar social indicators as representing social welfare in a theoretically defensible way.

The table below reports the goalposts considered for calculating the HDI.

Dimension	Indicator	Minimum	Maximum
Health	Life expectancy	20	85
Education	Expected years of schooling (years)	0	15
	Mean years of schooling (years)	0	18
Standard of living	Gross national income per capita (2011 PPP USD)	100	75,000

Source: UNDP (2019).

1.8 Happiness Economics

The traditional tenet of neoclassical Welfare Economics was that individuals are, after all, the best evaluators of what is good to them. Suppose this assumption, in the tradition of Bentham and Edgeworth, is taken at face value. Why not to simply ask people to report their assessment about how happy they are about their own condition in a given country and time, and from this infer the aggregate social welfare of the country?

In the last two decades, several researchers have stressed the legitimacy and relevance of introducing 'happiness', i.e. self-assessed well-being or satisfaction, for the evaluation of economic welfare. Layard (2005) and Frey and Stutzer (2018), *inter alia*, offer comprehensive surveys in this area. This subjective well-being assessment can, in principle, be done by surveys where citizens are asked simple questions of the form 'On a scale from "very satisfied" to "very unsatisfied" how happy are you with your present life?'. The survey approach can be carefully designed to pick up appropriate sampling patterns, for example, in terms of timing of the interview, ways the question is asked (by telephone, in person, etc.) and the individual information analysed and aggregated by appropriate statistical methods. Testing different scales has revealed that respondents are influenced by something well known to experimental psychologists. A cardinalization of the answers is possible if the questions are asked in percentage of time the respondent says he/she is in a bad or good emotional state. More elusive is, however, the issue of the intensity of such feelings. How to combine intensity and duration of self-assessed well-being remains a difficult issue.

The core of this empirical research programme is the study of the determinants of social happiness. In a sense, this has led people to appreciate how narrow was the perspective of the old utilitarian view of Welfare Economics, which focused on consumption of goods as the unique argument of utility. While utility is a subjective unobservable (it has been described as a mental state by early writers), it seems sensible to consider what determines such mental states. The discovery that respondents' happiness is influenced by health status and unemployment (per se, not just because of its impact on income), social relations, civil rights, and freedom adds new dimensions to what should be considered in social welfare. The interpretation is not easy, however. For example, there may be an econometric issue of endogeneity: are poor social relations a consequence or determinants of low happiness levels? Issues of omitted variables would also be a potential factor that biases estimated coefficients in empirical models.

With all the possible cautions, the most important result of this recent literature is that GDP is not strongly correlated with social happiness. One possible reason is the so-called treadmill effect, which in turn can be attributed to shifting hedonic benchmarks or aspiration levels. The former is due to the declining effect of pleasant stimuli, and is not a surprise for neoclassical Welfare Economics, which has long assumed that the marginal utility of consumption of one specific good decreases. However, empirical research tends to go beyond this and suggests a decreasing happiness effect of income, a very controversial issue in terms of the tenets of 'New Welfare Economics' in the style of Lionel Robbins and others. The aspiration treadmill is a more subtle effect, and one that possibly goes in the opposite direction: if an individual is rich, his/her benchmark may be somebody who is richer than him/her, and this shifts satisfaction for his/her current position in the social scale. This is compatible with social welfare functions with an element of envy in utility. As the reference points will shift over time and across countries, a time and cross-country effect should be introduced in subjective well-being (SWB).

An interesting aspect of the debate about Happiness Economics is related to cognitive dissonance. Do people actually understand what increases their utility? In some cases, people are not informed about the effects, even in the short run, not to mention a longer time horizon, of their consumption choices. Thus, it may be the case that there is a divergence between utility and SWB. However, this criticism is self-defeating because a third party should assess what is 'objectively' good for an individual, and this discards the definition of utility as a subjective, albeit unobservable, variable.

Whatever the deep philosophical implications of the observed lack of strong positive correlation between SWB and GDP, it is not easy to dismiss this fact, confirmed by many studies (see Layard 2005 for some of the evidence). In principle, one could go so far as to say that governments should maximize their country's SWB, not its GDP. Interestingly, if one takes this view, it would be necessary to reconsider how to accommodate inequality in an aggregate SWB indicator. Thus, much of the previous discussion about value judgement of equity, altruism, envy, and paternalism, is not at all discarded by considering aggregate SWB instead of GDP (or in this perspective even NNP, which is, after all, a variant of an 'objective' social welfare indicator).

Eventually, empirical happiness research can be seen as a complement to other perspectives in Applied Welfare Economics, possibly drawing from specific evidence on certain aspects of SWB. For example, Florio (2013) uses happiness data about prices and quality of services of network industries (telecommunications and energy) in the EU 'Old' Member States (EU-15), over several years, to evaluate the welfare effects of policy reforms, in combination with more traditional, 'objective' information about prices and service level indicators. The combination of subjective and objective empirical data seems an interesting way to look at different aspects of welfare effects of policy reforms. An applied welfare economist should see this as an advantage. In cost-benefit analysis, there is a well-established tradition of using subjective evidence to estimate the willingness-to-pay or willingness-to-accept, as discussed in Chapter 4; thus the Happiness Economics perspective, with all the necessary caveats, is certainly not alien to Applied Welfare Economics.

1.9 'Positive' analysis

Until now, a social planner has been implicitly assumed to maximize the welfare of the society. In fact, the planner or government here is just an algorithm that reflects the views of the agents (or of a part of the agents, perhaps a majority) in some way and to a certain extent.

This view of government, as mentioned, was rejected by Pareto and others, who considered it too abstract. The view of the state as a Leviathan was first advanced by Hobbes, and in various forms, it survives in both conservative and radical political thinking. For example, Barzel (2002) proposed an elaborated economic theory of the state as a protector of society from violence, and in turn as an exploiter of citizens. Marx looked at the state as the expression of the dictatorship of the bourgeoisie on other classes, particularly the working class.[13]

A tradition of Economics has tried to formalize these views in the form of 'positive' or empirical objective functions of the government. This tradition is particularly associated with the work of Buchanan, Tullock, and others, and one may look at Mueller (2003) for a wide review of this tradition. Forte (2010) offers an original discussion of a public choice perspective in Public Economics. He starts from a reconsideration of Pareto, Sidgwick,[14] Edgeworth, and Pigou, and suggests that the ethical foundations of the neoclassical tradition should be enlarged to accommodate the individual perceptions of what social welfare should be. These 'individual Social Welfare Functions' are similar to what has been previously discussed in this chapter in terms of altruism and envy, but the interesting point here is how to aggregate such preferences. The public choice perspective relies on aggregation not on a third party, i.e. the evaluator or the social planner, but on a cooperative game among individuals. This goes back to old ideas by Wicksell (1901, 1958a, 1958b), but is framed in modern game theory (as in Shapley 1969): it is not a majority rule, but the agreement by participants in a game of its rules, and then (possibly) an equilibrium follows. The equilibrium is not necessarily optimal in some external 'social welfare' perspective but is feasible in a public choice one.

The core of the public choice way to look at the government's action is to say that governments are never welfare maximizers. They are the expression of a political process in which policymakers, bureaucrats and voters play complex games to ensure control of the state and its powers. Some of the public choice authors are more pessimistic than others about the outcome of the game when a powerful government is captured by a part of the society. An elected policymaker needs to secure for himself/herself the favour of his/her constituency, but at the same time has a private agenda in terms of perks, side payments, honours, and reputation. An example, among many, of a SWF of this type, i.e. influenced by vested interests, is given in Laffont (2005); see Box 1.6. This function is a linear combination of the usual welfare maximization and the private utility of policy-makers who want to extract rents from a policy (privatization in that context).

Clearly, there is a very precise distinction between this kind of analysis and the search for what is socially efficient. An useful reference to understand the difference in perspective between 'normative' Welfare Economics and the 'positive' perspective of public choice is the debate between Buchanan and Musgrave (1999), two authors who gave a great personal contribution to either view.

Box 1.6 An example of government's Social Welfare Function with corruption

Suppose there are a government and a firm and that:

S = social value of a unit of a public service

$C = \beta - e$ = production cost; β = technological parameter; e = effort to reduce costs.

The Social Welfare Function is given by the sum of welfare levels of the different individuals. The agent (the supplier of the public service) receives from the principal (the government) a transfer equal to the cost C plus an incentive t. The transfer to the agent costs $(C+t)(1+\lambda)$ to taxpayers, where $\lambda > 0$ is the social cost of public funds. Thus, consumers-taxpayers' welfare is $V = S - (C+t)(1+\lambda)$. The corresponding agent's welfare is:

$$U = t - \Psi(e).$$

Social welfare is equal to $W = V + U = S - (1+\lambda)(\beta - e + t) + t + \Psi(e)$ or, analogously, $W = V + U = S - (1+\lambda)(\beta - e + \psi(e)) - \lambda U$.

A benevolent government with complete information would choose an incentive such that $\Psi' = (e^*) = 1$.

However, the government is controlled by politicians with a private agenda trying to extract rents (b).

Assume that the cost for the public firm is $(b + a)$ and that corruption is represented by $\delta \geq 1$. Then, the government maximizes the following Social Welfare Function:

$$W = \delta b + S - (1+\lambda)(\beta - e + b + a + \Psi(e)) - \lambda U.$$

The SWF is a pure utilitaristic function when $\delta = 1$. Maximizing W, under the constraint of a non-negative U, the government will have non-negative rents b, and the optimal b will be strictly positive if $\delta > 1 + \lambda$.

Source: Author, based on Laffont (2005).

In the rest of the book, the normative view is firmly adopted, and the public choice perspective is no more considered. This is not because it would be sensible to consider governments in the real world as welfare maximizers. It would be extremely naïve to think that politicians do not often have their own interests, and certainly, there is a lot to say in favour of the intuitions of Pareto, Marx, Schumpeter and several other realistic social scientists. While the 'positive' perspective should be regarded as a legitimate and interesting field of empirical analysis of government in Social Sciences, for an economist, it would be helpful to say something about welfare maximization as a benchmark and, in other words, to adopt the viewpoint of 'What if government is benevolent?'.

After all, to evaluate the outcomes of different real-world governments and their decisions, a benchmark is needed. How could one say whether a government's action, perhaps captured by social élites or ruling classes, is good or bad for society, if the evaluator does not have the tools to measure social welfare changes across time and countries? Going back to the opening questions of this chapter, in the real world, where a new bridge or a hospital will be located is certainly the result of political influence and not just of welfare calculation. But the 'What if?' perspective needs to be adopted when impartial, independent, transparent advice has to be offered. This should and can be done.

Admittedly, any measurement of such welfare changes is not entirely value-free. It will reflect some assumptions accepted by the evaluator about desirable income distribution, interactions between individual achievements, and possibly some merit goods. However, in the spirit of Myrdal (1969), these values, embodied in specification of functions, in parameters, and eventually in national accounts as GDP or other macroeconomic indicators, can be made transparent and tested for their consequences in the evaluation. Thus, picking up one among the possible specifications on normative SWF is not an arbitrary choice by the analyst. It is the consequence of a set of values embodied in the proposed social criterion and must not be confused with the empirical estimation of observable government objective functions.

The rest of this book offers some tools for a normative analysis of a government's policies and projects. Before presenting these tools, however, a second preliminary step is still needed: a critical reconsideration of the fundamental welfare theorems as the starting point of Applied Welfare Economics. This is done in the following chapter.

1.10 Further reading

Some material in Part One of the book assumes familiarity with intermediate Microeconomics texts, such as Varian (1992, 2014) or Mas Colell *et al.* (1995). The debate between old and new Welfare Economics (the first one grounded in the two ideas of social utility maximization and eventually in diminishing marginal utility, the second one based on the criticism of Pareto and the assumption of the impossibility of interpersonal comparability of utility) has been discussed several times, for example, by Sen (1986, 1987). Johansson (1991) is a very clear introduction to modern Welfare Economics.

For an account of the ethical and interdisciplinary considerations behind this debate, and for an update on new approaches, see Adler and Posner (2006). In their view, the whole history of the debate revolves around three views of welfare:

a. *Mental-state view*: utility is a mental state that in principle can be measured and summed across individuals. The idea goes back to Bentham, John Stuart Mill and

Sidgwick, and is revived by such recent approaches as hedonism (Feldman 2004), happiness economics (Frey and Stutzer 2018) and experimental psychology (Kahneman and Tversky 2000). Supporters of the simple sum of individual welfare changes in cost-benefit analysis are Harberger (1971b) and Mishan (1976).

b. *Objective-good view*: this is based on identifying a list of things that everybody should agree are beneficial in a fundamental sense. For Nussbaum (2000) these are: life itself, bodily health and integrity, use of senses, imagination and thought, emotions, practical reason, affiliation, interaction with other species, play, and control of the environment. Sen's view about resources and capabilities (and ideals) as priors to welfare can be seen as a variant of this approach (resourcism).

c. *Preference-based view*: this is the one that has been discussed most in the chapter, as it goes back to Pareto, and non-Paretian (the economist) but still preferentialist ('prioritarism') views such as Bergson–Samuelson and Pareto (the sociologist) or lexmin social orderings as in Rawls.

Adler and Posner (2006) (building in part on Harsanyi 1955) propose a compromise solution as they suggest a 'restricted, preference-based' welfare definition. They argue that an outcome A is better than another outcome B if and only if a rational, well informed, deliberative individual prefers at a certain time outcome A to outcome B and his preference is self-interested. This approach is labelled as 'weak welfarism' and takes the structure: (W, F), where W is the maximization of welfare (regarded as a moral concept) and F is a vector of other factors.

For a recent review of the debate on social welfare see Backhouse *et al.* (2021).

Finally, it has to be remarked that the current debate on welfare is highly interdisciplinary: for example, Adler and Posner are legal scholars, Martha Nussbaum is a philosopher and several of the authors that have been mentioned above are not economists (even if they, like Harsanyi or Kahneman, have been awarded a Nobel prize in Economics).

1.11 Summary of Chapter 1

- People are accustomed to evaluating government policies for their impact on GDP per capita and growth. However, this accounting is justified only on very restrictive assumptions on the underlying SWF and the welfare information conveyed by prices.
- The concept of GDP has been designed to allow the aggregation of consumption of each agent in the economy. It allows for no consideration of inequality of the welfare effects of consumption. Moreover, a large number of goods (and bads) that influence individual welfare are outside the scope of GDP calculation. Hence, GDP can be a misleading welfare indicator.
- Green accounting and NNP need inter-temporal shadow prices and do not solve the welfare issue of GDP, because both NNP and GDP disregard welfare aggregation issues.
- The SWF is a way to represent the well-being of a community. Building a SWF means, first, to assume some individual welfare functions, and then to combine them into an aggregated formula. Different utility functions can be assumed.
- Welfare weights can be applied to individual utilities. These could be interpreted as weights that reflect different individual welfare profiles, i.e. the fact that individuals may have a decreasing marginal utility of income. They can also reflect a value

judgment, imposed by the government or by the economist, on equity needs in income or consumption distribution.

- Sen criticized the ethical principles underlying the individualistic view of Welfare Economics and stressed that individuals can also attach importance to objectives different from their own well-being. Moreover, he suggested that welfare can be achieved only if some fundamental capabilities are in place.
- It is also possible to determine SWFs in which the social planner has its own preferences over consumption profiles. Thus the social planner can be considered as an actor who is not the expression of individual interest but acts as an active organizer of society, following his own goals.
- The Human Development Index developed by the UNDP is an example of a welfare indicator that attempts to combine capabilities and well-being, such as education and the value of life expectancy, to evaluate development.
- Happiness Economics offers an interesting new perspective for empirical analysis, but a definition of a SWF in terms of subjective well-being poses complex problems.
- The applied welfare economist will offer his calculations to policy-makers, to opposition parties, to anybody who is interested at in looking at the consequences of decisions. Applied Welfare Economics tries to introduce some precision in these calculations, without assuming that governments will necessarily conform to them (whereas 'positive' Public Economics deals with real-world behaviours of policy-makers, voters, lobbies, social classes, etc.).

End chapter questions

- Gross Domestic Product is the most well-known indicator of aggregate economic activity. Briefly discuss the major problems and issues of using GDP as a yardstick of economic performance and proxy of social welfare.
- Explain the difference between ordinal and cardinal utility.
- The Social Welfare Function is a way to represent the well-being of a community. What assumptions have to be made to define and build a Social Welfare Function?
- What are the properties of the following utility function $U = x_1^{\frac{1}{3}} x_2^{\frac{2}{3}}$? Why in welfare economics does the assumption that individuals have a decreasing marginal utility of income is often too strong and unnecessary?
- Design a Social Welfare Function with specific merit goods where weights are assigned to individual-based preferences versus community-based preferences. Is there any practical example of a function that combines individualism and paternalism?
- In which sense Sen's approach is similar to the Pareto sociologist one?

Notes

1 Thanks are due to Elisa Borghi and Chiara Del Bo, who helped to draft the lecture notes for the Master in Economics and Political Science at the University of Milan, upon which the first three chapters elaborate.
2 A preliminary idea of GDP was first presented by Simon Kuznets in 1937 in his report to the US Congress 'National income, 1929–32'.
3 While GDP can be defined as the total market value of all final goods and services produced in a country in a year, GNI includes, also, the income a country receives from other countries, minus similar payments made to other countries. In the perspective of economic globalization, some economists regret the shift of focus from GNI to GDP in government

statistics, as this tends to ignore the impact on wealth production abroad. Florio (2001) discusses inconsistencies in national accounts.

4   In the remainder of the book, *m* is generally used to indicate income.

5   Maurice Godelier (1971) tells an interesting story on values in an ancient barter economy, where salt is the *numéraire*.

6   If productivity is different across sectors in terms of food–equivalent per capita, it would be socially better to move workers to where productivity is higher, and away from where it is lower.

7   See, however, Roberts (1980), who investigates when price-independent prescriptions about welfare are theoretically justified.

8   If individual marginal utility is decreasing with income levels, a Bentham-type SWF can differ from the sum of incomes.

9   Chapter 4 deals with revealed and stated preference approaches.

10 Bergson (1983) discusses the formula proposed by Pareto (1916) as a variant of the conventional Benthamian SWF, which anticipates the treatment of income distribution contained in Bergson (1938).

11 Myles (1988, 1990) discusses an interesting case where the marginal utility of income can be increasing because of vertical product differentiation.

12 In this case, the partial derivative of W relative to the 'bad' will be negative, even if the partial derivative of U is positive for some individuals.

13 Coco and Fedeli (2014) discuss the possible foundations of Marxian Public Economics, with a comment by Florio (2014).

14 Among his most influential books, see Sidgwick (1874, 1883, 1891).

2 The two fundamental theorems re-examined

Overview

After the introductory discussion of Social Welfare Functions in the previous chapter, this one turns to their maximization mechanisms: markets and plans. A recurrent theme of the previous discussion on GDP and other accounting conventions for aggregating individual welfare is the limited meaning of observed prices as the relevant information for social welfare accounting. As prices are, after all, ratios of quantities, or conversion factors, from where do these numbers arise? And can the mechanisms that generate the right information for welfare analysis be identified? The role of this chapter is to argue that the traditional interpretation of the fundamental welfare theorems, for which market mechanisms provide the correct prices in a welfare perspective, is not very helpful for an applied economist. Differently from observed prices, the concept of shadow prices is a central notion of cost-benefit analysis. Thus, before explicitly introducing this subject in Chapter 3, it can be useful to discuss some misunderstandings about the roles of markets and governments as generators of information.

This discussion is mainly abstract, and readers who are directly looking for an applied perspective may consider entirely skipping this chapter or read only some parts of it. Other readers, however, may be interested in examining the reasons for frequent misinterpretations of the roles of markets and governments in achieving efficient outcomes. Starred sections are recommended for those readers who possibly already have some grasp of general equilibrium theory and the two theorems. The concept of shadow prices, which is the core concept in Chapter 3 and most of this book, is better understood when looking at its general (dis)equilibrium foundations (even when, for practical reasons, partial equilibrium estimation or other shortcuts are needed).

This chapter, after some introductory remarks and some preliminary intuitions about the interpretation of the two welfare theorems (Section 2.1), considers a standard Arrow–Debreu economy augmented by the government (Sections 2.2* and 2.3*). In this frame, the concepts of goods, individual endowments, ownership claims on net products of firms, producers' prices, rations and lump-sum taxes and the government objective function are introduced. Section 2.4* discusses the objectives and constraints of consumers, producers, and government, while Section 2.5 is about the Walrasian equilibrium. The chapter then presents the meaning of the two welfare theorems free from any ideology (Section 2.6). Sections 2.7 and 2.8 present the Stiglitz's critique (1994) on the theorems' informative structure and a critical analysis of the Second Theorem. Finally, Section 2.9 briefly discusses the role of the government in Welfare Economics to show that governments do not necessarily need to be Paretian and markets do

DOI: 10.4324/9781003191377-3

not need to clear, as rationing equilibria are widespread. The discussion is completed by the Further Reading section, which presents a limited selection of the vast theoretical literature on these topics, and by an appendix on lump-sum taxes.

2.1 Theorems versus intuitions

The standard exposition of the normative theory of Public Economics usually starts with a recall of the two fundamental theorems of Welfare Economics, followed by an analysis of possible deviations of the real world from the conditions assumed by these theorems. Then, the study of the first-best (non-distortive) and second-best (with distortions, typically on prices) public intervention is introduced.

The two theorems are often presented as follows[1]:

First Theorem: If (1) families and firms act under perfect competition, taking prices parametrically, (2) there is a complete system of markets and (3) there is perfect information, then a competitive equilibrium, if it exists, is Pareto-efficient.

(Atkinson and Stiglitz 1980: 343)

Second Theorem: If (1) consumers' indifference curves and firms' production sets are convex, (2) there is a complete set of markets, (3) there is perfect information, and (4) transfers and lump-sum taxes can be introduced at no cost, then each Pareto-efficient allocation can be obtained as a competitive equilibrium through appropriate taxes and lump-sum transfers.

(Atkinson and Stiglitz 1980: 343)

After these statements, the reader of Public Economics textbooks is usually redirected to microeconomic theory that deals with some issues related to preferences and the other 'if' involved in the theorems. The formal statement of the theorems is presented later and found to be more concise: prices can support a demand–supply equilibrium, and this equilibrium is Pareto optimal. Hence, equilibrium prices are the right signal for welfare evaluation.

The orthodox interpretation of the two theorems suggests that market mechanisms, and the associated prices, generate the most efficient social outcome[2]:

The First Fundamental Theorem of Welfare Economics, is a mathematical statement of Adam Smith's notion of the invisible hand leading to an efficient allocation. Prices provide the incentives so that firms and households guided by prices and self-interest can, acting independently, find an efficient allocation. [...] There it is in modern mathematical form – just what Adam Smith (1976) would have said.

(Starr 1997: 146, 238)

Taken together, the two welfare theorems are the theoretical basis of liberal thinking.

(Laffont 1988: 5)

[...] the Fundamental Theorems go beyond Adam Smith's aphorism on the 'invisible hand', defining precisely in which sense a market allocation is desirable, the conditions which need to be satisfied and circumstances under which these conditions will be satisfied by the market.

(Boadway and Bruce 1984: 82)

The role of the state in this model is reduced to its simplest expression and it is identified with the one assigned by the liberal ideology of the XIX century: apart from the production of fundamental collective goods, defence, security – not included in our model – the state has to monitor the good functioning of markets.

(Guesnerie 1980: 80)[3]

Adam Smith, however, never proposed a theorem. Claiming a logical link between Smith's 'Invisible Hand' and Pareto optimality of competitive markets hides an ancient illusion: the desire of giving a scientific foundation, and thus objectivity, to the grand debate on the reciprocal roles of the market and government. In turn, efficiency and equity concepts are often neatly separable in the frame of the two theorems. This was, with variable degrees of critical discussion of the theorems, the standard presentation of the reference manual of the new Public Economics by Atkinson and Stiglitz (1980); see also Myles (1995), Jha (1998), Hindriks and Myles (2006),[4] and several others. Hence, in this frame, the desirable role of public intervention is often confined to offering remedies to traditional 'market failures' (Bator 1958) and it is even more restricted when possible 'policy failures' are also considered. However, one can claim that this 'free-market' interpretation of the two theorems can generate a misunderstanding about the proper foundations of the economic theory of government. This chapter aims at stressing this aspect, as Applied Welfare Economics needs to be firmly rooted in a view of what governments should do and how their actions can be evaluated.

The rest of the chapter takes stock of the traditional interpretations of the two theorems, distinguishing the analytical contribution from their implications for Welfare Economics. These implications, as shown later, are ambiguous. In summary, the two theorems use, first, a paradigm of positive economics, i.e. the Walrasian equilibrium, and, second, an a priori criterion of normative economics, i.e. Paretian efficiency. Both aspects need a critical examination as the appropriate foundations of Welfare Economics from an applied perspective. The examination of the axiomatic structure of the equilibrium paradigm justifies the alternative view, proposed by trends in the literature (see, e.g., Backhouse and Boianovsky 2013; Murakami 2016). According to this alternative view, Walrasian equilibria are special cases of non-Walrasian equilibria, characterized by demand and supply functions with quantity constraints. At the same time, a well-developed literature on the social welfare shows that Paretian efficiency is a special criterion, without a particular a priori privileged position in the wide range of rules for social choice (see Chapter 1).

If, however, one wants to accept the Walras–Pareto paradigm as the reference case or as the starting point of the analysis, the establishment of the exact interpretation of equilibrium prices in the model is still crucial. Those prices are shadow prices, the solution to a system of equations, given the objective functions and the constraints. They may or may not be related to observable market prices as well as to planned prices. The potential divergence is crucial for the applied welfare economist.

Shadow prices can also be found for non-Walrasian equilibria, and alternative states of the world can be evaluated, through these shadow prices, both with Paretian and non-Paretian social welfare criteria.

The two theorems, reduced to their essential analytical core, say nothing more than the following proposition: under certain formal conditions, a Walrasian equilibrium is Pareto-efficient, and to each Pareto-efficient, allocation corresponds to a Walrasian equilibrium. According to this formulation, the two theorems are abstract propositions, with a limited interpretative and normative value in an applied perspective. In fact, research in Applied Welfare Economics should begin with the evaluation of these limitations. According to Hindriks and Myles (2006), Public Economics often starts with a consideration of the 'practical shortcomings' of the two theorems and looks for more applicable approaches.

As mentioned, from the beginning of the general economic equilibrium theory with Walras (1874), economic analysis and pre-analytic intuitions of the role of the market (and of public intervention) intertwined. Thus, Pareto (1909) could interpret the theory from a free-market perspective, while Barone (1935), Lerner (1946), and Lange and Taylor (1948) could reuse the same analytical basis to formulate a theory of socialist planning (Heal 1973). Not surprisingly, Stiglitz (1994) criticized the two theorems, as they would have fed symmetric errors into the roles of the market and the state. Stiglitz's view is discussed later (Section 2.7).

The now standard theoretical setting was formulated by Kenneth Arrow and Gerad Debreu, working independently at the beginning of the 1950s, and successively jointly by Arrow and Debreu (1954) and Debreu (1959). The increasingly sophisticated instruments found in the subsequent literature, e.g. Arrow and Hahn (1971), Hildebrand and Kirman (1988), and Starr (1997), among many others, have not entirely eliminated the initial tension between mathematical modelling on the one hand and intuitions, value judgement, ideologies, on the other.

2.2 The Arrow–Debreu (AD) economy (*)

This section re-examines the implications for Welfare Economics of the axiomatic structure of the general equilibrium analysis in its standard version: the Arrow–Debreu (AD) model, augmented with a public sector.[5] The problems of existence, uniqueness, and stability of the equilibrium and many details are skipped. The axiomatic structure of the AD frame is quite complex, and the following is a simplification of a formal analysis of the explicit and implicit axioms found in the various formulations proposed in the literature.[6]

An AD economy can be defined as a collection of analytical objects, stylized analogues of observable items in real economies, grouped according to well-defined axiomatic properties. For example, the following collection of 15 sets is considered:

$$E \equiv \{I, H, X, J, Y, U, d, e, p, G, W, t, \ell, \bar{x}, \bar{y}\},$$ (2.1)

where:

- I is the set of the AD goods, each labelled as $i = 1, \ldots, I$.
- H is the set of consumers, where each consumer is identified by a name $h = 1, \ldots, H$.
- X is the set of all the feasible vectors of consumption plans for every h, composed of the sets X^h, each one including all the vectors $x^h = \left(x_1^h, x_2^h, \ldots, x_I^h\right)$.
- J is the set of production units, each one identified by a code $j = 1, \ldots, J$.

- Y is the set of all the feasible vectors of production plans, composed of the sets Y^{ij}, which include all the vectors $y^j = \left(y_1^j, y_2^j, \ldots, y_I^j\right)$.

- U is a set of utility functions, $U^h = U^h(\cdot)$, each corresponding by assumption to a consumer's preference system $\succeq_h$.

- d is a vector of ownership shares assigning to each consumer h the net product of every $j : d_j^h = \left(d_1^h, d_2^h, \ldots, d_J^h\right)$.

- e is the set of initial endowments of consumer goods for every consumer: $e^h = \left(e_1^h, e_2^h, \ldots, e_I^h\right)$.

- p is the vector of the relative production prices $p = (p_1, p_2, \ldots, p_I)$. An arbitrary good is the *numéraire*, provided it has an equilibrium price greater than zero.

- G is the government, an agent.

- W is the objective function of the government: $W = W\left(U^h, \ldots\right)$

- t is a vector of government's taxes/subsidies on goods, such that $t_i \equiv q_i - p_i$ where q_i is the consumer price.

- ℓ is a vector of government's personalized lump-sum taxes $\ell = \left(\ell^1, \ell^2, \ldots, \ell^H\right)$.

- $\bar{x}$ is a vector of government's quantity constraints on consumption: $\bar{x} = (\bar{x}_1, \bar{x}_2, \ldots \bar{x}_I)$.

- $\bar{y}$ is a vector of government's quantity constraints on production plans: $\bar{y} = (\bar{y}_1, \bar{y}_2, \ldots \bar{y}_I)$.

In summary, E includes:

- a set of I goods;
- three groups of agents: H consumers, J producers, and G, the government;
- the production sets;
- the consumption sets;
- two sets of objective functions: I individual utility functions and the Social Welfare Function;
- six sets of signals: prices for I goods; 2 quantity constraints (upper and lower bound) for I goods; personalized lump-sum taxes for consumers H; indirect taxes on I; $I \cdot H$ initial endowments; and $H \cdot J$ property shares.

The simplified AD frame connects these objects in the following way. The government wants to maximize social welfare, which is a function (at least in part) of individual welfare. The government can use four instruments: ℓ, t, $\bar{x}$, $\bar{y}$. Consumers want to maximize their individual welfare, which is (at least in part) a function of their individual consumption levels; production units want to distribute the highest net product py to their owners; production prices are endogenous, while d and e are exogenous. As shown in a subsequent section, however, you can also imagine a government that directly manipulates d and e.

A state of E is a configuration $\hat{E}$ such that all the variables correspond to the determined numerical values. In particular, an allocation is defined as a determined configuration of consumed and produced quantities $(\hat{x}, \hat{y})$.

There is no analytical reason for a model of E to be built in this particular way. For example, often in the general equilibrium literature G, W, t, ℓ, t, $\bar{x}$, $\bar{y}$ are not explicitly included in E. However, in this case, the interpretation of the Second Welfare Theorem with statements such as 'The government, through lump-sum taxes, can reach any Pareto optimum by a competitive equilibrium' becomes ambiguous. Given that the government, its objectives and constraints are not well defined nor included in the model, their elaboration is beyond the proper scope of the formal analysis. This ambiguity does not arise when the theorems are formally stated; see below.

An example of this slip from theory to an interpretation well outside the theory is the following:

> The Second Fundamental Theorem of Welfare Economics represents a significant defense of the market economy's resource allocation mechanism [...]. This is the basis of the common prescription in public finance that any attainable distribution of welfare can be achieved using a market mechanism and lump sum taxes [...]. On this basis, public authority intervention in the market through direct provision of services (housing, education, medical care, child care etc.) is an unnecessary escape from market allocation mechanisms with their efficiency properties.
>
> (Starr 1997: 151)

What to include or not to include in the model is important, given that this choice can affect the model's ability to represent the economy by an analogy that justifies it.[7]

The endogenous or exogenous status of the variables included in the model is an analytical convention to be evaluated case by case. Suppose the following partition is used:

- Exogenous: $I, H, J, X, Y, U, W, d, e, G$;
- Endogenous: $x, y, \bar{x}, \bar{y}, p, t, \ell$.

With this framework in mind, the model can be interpreted as follows. Given goods, consumers, firms, production and consumption technologies, ownership rights and initial endowments, and given the individual welfare functions and a government characterized by a Social Welfare Function, the social planner determines the consumption and production plans and the vector of government's instruments (personalized lump-sum taxes, indirect taxes, quantity constraints) satisfying the objectives and constraints.

However, moving even only one item from a list to the other is enough to change the interpretation, as the formal features of the model change accordingly. For example, predetermined non-personalized lump-sum taxes or exogenous rations may change the story dramatically. Readers are invited to try to move one variable from one to the other set and discuss the consequences in terms of interpreting the setting.

Informally, if the exogenous variables in a system of equations are 'too many', the model is overdetermined, whereas if they are 'not enough' the model is underdetermined.[8] A possibility to make some variables exogenous is simply to give them a zero value; then, if $\bar{x} = \bar{y} = 0$, the government can use only some types of lump-sum and indirect taxes. If p is exogenous (fixed production prices) but t is endogenous, then q is also endogenous. If ℓ is a fixed amount, equal among all the consumers, then the vector of lump-sum taxes is exogenous,[9] and so on.

2.3 The axiomatic structure (*)

The standard AD frame is characterized by a quite complex axiomatic structure. A list of the most cited axioms (A) is the following (for a formal exposition, see the specific literature, starting with, e.g., Arrow and Debreu 1954; Debreu 1959; Geanakoplos 1987):

A.1 Enumerability, finiteness, and measurability of goods.

A.2 Every h can form the consumption plans $x^h \in X^h \subset R^I$ where R is the set of real numbers.

A.3 $U^h(x,...)$ is reflexive, complete, transitive, and continuous.

A.4 Non-satiation $\forall h, \forall x_i^h$.

A.5 Convexity of X^h and quasi-concavity of U^h.

A.6 $e^h \subset R_+^I \forall h$ (consumers have no debts in kind).

A.7 $d_j^h \geq 0 \forall h$ (consumers have no negative property rights) $\sum_h d_j^h = 1$.

A.8 No exit or entry in the market (J is given). If 0 is in the production set, firms can stop production at no cost.

A.9 $\forall j \; \exists$ the technological space Y^{ij}; feasible plans $y^j \in Y^J$; a partition of the net product $\Pi^j \equiv py^j$ through shares d_j^h; and inactivity $y^i = 0$ is possible at zero cost.

A.10 Y^i is strictly convex.

A.11 Y is closed and superiorly bounded even if all the e^h are used in production.

A.12 e^h is transferable at no cost.

A.13 Anonymity (the identification code for goods cannot include h and j).

The list can be shortened or extended according to analytical purposes; for example, the axioms about convexity are not necessary for proof of the First Theorem but are needed for the proof of the Second Theorem. Moreover, some axioms group different hypotheses (e.g. A.3 on consumers' rationality) and there are some hidden axioms. The following discussion provides some examples.

Each axiom can, in turn, be discussed according to two complementary perspectives:

i   realism or observable economies;
ii the degree of consistency or inconsistency with respect to other axioms.

To briefly illustrate these issues and for its particular relevance for applied economists, axiom A.1 can be considered. Given 'completeness of markets', it is assumed that goods' 'labels' identify unambiguously quality, space, time, and state of the world for each of the goods.[10] Let $\alpha, \beta, \gamma, \delta$ be the vectors associated with each of these four characteristics. Let $\alpha = 1, 2, ..., A; \beta = 1, 2, ..., B$, etc. be the relative indexes. Then, as an example, $x_{228,71,12,41}^h$ could be the quantity of the good for the hth consumer with subscript indexes about these four characteristics. Let $z \in R^4$ be the particular combination; then p_z, y_z, ℓ_z etc. have to be interpreted accordingly.

In fact, those 'public' goods à la Samuelson, and even the ordinary private goods, can exist as analytical objects only if other, and more fundamental, public goods are produced, i.e. conventions, standards, etc. However, who is producing these fundamental goods? Who is demanding them? Who is paying for their cost of production? These goods are external to the AD frame, which, in a precise sense, assumes that goods such as knowledge are given and hence have no social value. This is, however, obviously absurd in a dynamic setting, where growth is determined by new knowledge and not just by exogenous capital, goods, and labour.

This is just an example of a whole class of problems related to the axiomatization of an economic environment. So much for the issue of realism. Consistency is a different issue.

It is also worthwhile stressing that an axiom often has to be interpreted jointly with others. For example, A.1 with A.13 implies that i and j indexes are not admissible characteristics of a good. Why not? Obviously, not on the formal ground. For example, a price for good w (a bundle of characteristics) $p_{\alpha,\beta,\gamma,\delta,h,j} \equiv p_w$ is, analytically, not too different from $p_{\alpha,\beta,\gamma,\delta} \equiv p_z$ i.e. the price for a less specified good z, from which it is distinguished 'only' because $w \in R^6$, $z \in R^4$.

However, if the model's 'prices' are *ad personam* and if a price for each h and for each j exists, it can no longer be said that 'every agent considers the price parametrically' in the usual meaning. The pre-analytical intuition of the 'market' as an impersonal mechanism ceases, as prices would be intrinsically related to personalized goods. If for each transaction, a different price is formed for different agents, then price discrimination, Lindahl prices (Lindahl 1919) and numerous cases of imperfect competition are includable in the model; however, the meaning of the equilibrium would change. This is not an issue of realism but an intrinsic formal characteristic of the theory's axiomatic structure itself.

In a more applied perspective, it is interesting to list and discuss cases of goods in observable economies in which the price (demand and supply) is intrinsically (virtually or actually) *ad personam* or related to 'small groups'.

2.4 Consumers, producers, and government: objectives and constraints (*)

An example of standard modelling of households' planning is this: the h-th consumer determines the optimal consumption plan x^h solving the following constrained program:

$$
\begin{cases}
\max_{x^h} U^h\left(x_1^h,\ldots,x_I^h\right) \\
\text{subject to (s.t.)} \\
\sum_{i=1}^{H} p_i x_i^h \leq \sum_{i=1}^{H} p_i e_i^h + \sum_{j=1}^{J} d_j^h \Pi^j \\
\bar{x}_- < x^h < \bar{x}_+
\end{cases}
\tag{2.2}
$$

Where Π^j are companies' profits. By convention, $x_i^h < 0$ is a good sold by the consumer, whereas $x_i^h > 0$ is a purchased good. If $U^h\left(x^h\right)$ depends only on x^h and if it is quasi-concave by A.5, then an appropriate demand function is derived, as for example $x_i^h = x_i^h\left(p, d^h, e^h, \Pi\right)$, where the vectors in the argument are exogenous from the point of view of the hth consumer. A.1, A.2 and A.3 define the neoclassical consumer's rationality. Π is distributed according to A.9, while the vector e^h is non–negative by A.6 $\left(e^h \in R_+^I\right)$. A.4 guarantees that x^h is always less preferred to x'^h, with at least one element $x_i'^h > x_i^h$.

In the previous section, an explicit axiom of complete or perfect information is missing. The fact that the consumer is perfectly informed is often seen as a logical consequence of A.1, A.2 and A.3, but the model would work even if the future state of the world were imperfectly known, provided that the information is symmetric.

Axiomatic properties of the standard model are violated if there is asymmetric information as explained later in this chapter.

If $U^h(\cdot)$ depends only on x^h, then the following is implied: each item that can potentially increase individual welfare through consumption has to be an AD good, therefore for A.5 (convexity of X^h) it has to be always substitutable at the margin with another AD good. Everything has a price, but, again, non-AD 'goods' are not just priced zero by assumption, they must disappear from E, and are not 'listed'.

The individual welfare (and the social welfare) in the standard model is an exhaustive concept, with no exceptions allowed. A single exception would be enough to destroy the concept of equilibrium.

Moreover, following the discussion in Chapter 1, it is also possible to imagine more complex $U^h(\cdot)$, i.e. $U^h \equiv U^h\left(x^h, U^k\right)$, where $k \neq h$ (envy, altruism). In these economies, utilities are interdependent, as discussed in the previous chapter. The consequences for the standard model are problematic. It is just an example of the previous theme: if U^k affects h's welfare, then it is in some way an AD good as well, and it must have a 'price'.

Other themes for discussion are the following. For convex X^h sets, U^h are quasi-concave. If these functions are not strictly quasi-concave,[11] two goods can be perfect substitutes for more than one consumer, and the relative indifference curve in an Edgeworth box can have straight portions (see Figure 2.1). Thus the standard theory needs additional axioms to avoid multiple equilibria (see Starr 1997).

Another discussion topic is related to the budget constraint. With strict equality in the budget constraint, consumers spend the entire profit income and consume their initial endowments fully. This is consistent with A.4 and with the absence of the temporal dimension in a proper sense. For a correct interpretation of the budget constraints, let e_l^h be the initial labour endowment expressed in hours of work; $-y_l^j$ be the purchase of working hours by the jth production unit; then $-x_l^h$ is the selling of working hours by the hth consumer.

With strict equality in the budget constraint, potential working hours in the initial endowments not sold become leisure time enjoyed by the consumer, valued at their opportunity cost, equal to p_l, i.e. the hourly wage.

It is often convenient to choose working time as the *numéraire* and let $p_l = 1$. This convention is often used in models of optimal taxation of goods. It is a good way to critically analyze the standard theory by rethinking every value in terms of its labour content because it will make apparent the lack of realism involved in transferring labour skills/endowments from one consumer to another through lump–sum taxation.[12]

Eventually, if $t \neq 0$, then $p \neq q$. Demand functions become $x^h = x^h\left(q, \Pi, e^h, d^h\right)$.

Initial endowments will have a different value in terms of labour/leisure time for sellers and for buyers. Therefore, a tax on labour income generates a wedge between the gross and the net wage. Suppose that t is the only available instrument for the government and that this agent is constrained to a balanced budget.

Therefore, $t_i > 0$ for some goods, while $t_i > 0$ for other ones. It follows that, given the vectors e^h and the products pe^h for the seller and qe^h for the buyer, consumers will result in being discriminated according to the exogenous share of taxed or subsidized goods in the initial endowment of each consumer. Every h will try to maximize the sales of subsidized goods ($t_i < 0$) and to minimize purchases of taxed goods ($t_i > 0$).[13]

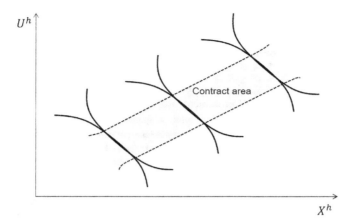

Figure 2.1 Indifference curves with (non-strict) quasi-concave utility.
Source: Author.

The discussion now moves to firms. There are only private firms in this economy. Production units adopt the following program:

$$\begin{cases} \max_{y^j} py^j \\ \text{s.t.} \\ \overline{y}_- < y^j < \overline{y}_+ \end{cases} \qquad (2.3)$$

The production function $y^j = y^j(p)$ is subject to axioms A.8, A.9, A.10 and A.11 and to the convention of considering $y^j > 0$ as an output and $y^j < 0$ as an input.

Among the inputs of some firms, there can be the outputs of other firms. The sign convention eliminates any duplication, therefore $\Pi > py$ is the net product even in an economy with intermediate goods.

By A.10, strict convexity implies decreasing returns to scale. With the weak convexity assumption, constant returns are considered as well, while increasing returns are retained as inconsistent with the standard model. An interesting empirical problem is the frequency of increasing returns in the observable world: see *infra*, for example, the discussion on the acquisition of information as a fixed cost. If increasing returns are frequent in the observed economies, this is another source of criticism of the realism of the model (see below about the role of information).

Many other issues related to the production dimension of the standard theory are skipped, as the chapter cannot be exhaustive in this discussion and only aims at giving some hints on the reading of the two theorems.

Now the government is explicitly considered. The government adopts the following program:

$$\max_{x^h} W = W\left[U^h\left(x^h\right)\right] \qquad (2.4)$$

Subject to (s.t.) the Pareto criterion: $\left\{\hat{x}^h\right\}$ is P-efficient if and only if $\nexists \left\{\tilde{x}^h\right\}$ such that $U^h\left(\tilde{x}^h\right) \geq U^h\left(\hat{x}^h\right)$, $\forall h$ and, at least for some $h, U^h\left(\tilde{x}^h\right) > U^h\left(\hat{x}^h\right)$.

As government's instruments are, $\bar{x}, \bar{y}, t, \ell$, therefore $x^h = x^h\left(q, \bar{x}, \bar{y}, \ell, d, \Pi, e\right)$.

A feasible allocation is $\hat{x}$ is P-efficient in a weak sense if there is not another feasible allocation $\tilde{x}$ preferred to $\hat{x}$ by all consumers. An allocation $\hat{x}$ is P-efficient in a strong sense if there does not exist another allocation $\tilde{x}$ weakly preferred to $\hat{x}$ and with $\tilde{x} \succ \hat{x}$ at least for one consumer.

It is possible to prove that for continuous and monotonic utility functions, an allocation $\hat{x}$ is P-efficient in a weak sense if and only if it is P-efficient in a strong sense. Therefore, given the standard neoclassic assumptions, these two concepts are equivalent (Varian 1992: 323).

Note that the fact that G constrains its own Social Welfare Function to arguments $U^h(x^h)$ according to the Pareto criterion is *de facto* an additional axiom, not included in the standard axiomatic structure A.1–A.13.

Let us define the non-Paretian individualistic social welfare criterion, a function $W(U^h)$ that does not satisfy the Pareto criterion even if it is still based on U^h only. Moreover, a non-individualistic Social Welfare Function is defined as a function $W(U^h, \ldots)$ in which there are other arguments as well as the individual utilities. This is clearly difficult to accommodate in the standard intuition of the theorems, as the resulting 'equilibrium' prices, if an equilibrium in some sense exists (see below), would have a different meaning as compared with the intuition of prices resulting from market equilibria. This is particularly important if one considers the quantity constraints in production and consumption.

Going back to Pareto optimality, a trivial solution for the government problem is to fix $\bar{x} = \hat{x}$, or to constrain agents' consumption exactly to the P-optimum. In this case, all other instruments are null, and firms simply match the demand by consumers. Prices would not play any specific role.

Which variables are exogenous is relevant for P-optimality. For example, if lump-sum taxes are endogenous and W is consistent with the strict Pareto criterion, this mental experiment can be performed. Let the government casually extract ℓ^h, for example, stochastically taxing the income produced by profit participation: $\ell^h = \varphi\left(\sum d_j^h \Pi\right)$ with $\ell > \sum_j d_j^h \Pi$ in some cases (subsidies) and $\ell < \sum_j d_j^h \Pi$ in some other cases (taxes).

In this case, it is not possible for $\sum_h \ell^h = 0$ to find a P-superior x^h by simply reducing taxes, because subsidies would also be reduced for some h. A non-Paretian W is needed to compare the U^h and to determine ℓ endogenously.

2.5 The Walrasian equilibrium

A Walrasian equilibrium is a state $\hat{E}$ of an AD economy such that it is possible to find vectors of prices, consumption and production plans, and government instruments such as taxes and subsidies, rations, etc.:

$$\hat{E} \equiv \left[\hat{p}, \{\hat{x}^h\}, \{\hat{y}^j\}, \{\hat{s}\}\right] \tag{2.5}$$

(where all government's instruments are denoted by $\hat{s}$) such that:

i $\hat{x}^h \in X^h$

ii $y^j \in Y^j$

iii $\hat{p}x^h \leq \hat{p}e^e + \displaystyle\sum_{j=1} d_j^h \hat{p}\hat{y}^j, \; \forall h$

iv $U^h\left(\hat{x}^h\right) \geq U^h\left(\tilde{x}^h\right), \; \forall x^h \in X^h$ s.t. budget constraint

v $\hat{p}\hat{y}^j \geq \hat{p}\tilde{y}^j, \forall \tilde{y}^j, \in Y^j$

vi $\hat{x} \leq \hat{y} + e.$

The equilibrium condition (vi) is the aggregate equilibrium of demand and supply as:

$$x = \sum_h \sum_i x_i^h (\cdot) \tag{2.6}$$

$$y = \sum_j \sum_i y_i^j (\cdot). \tag{2.7}$$

The Walrasian equilibrium is often called the 'competitive' equilibrium. However, this terminology is more suggestive or evocative than rigorous. In what sense can one say that $\hat{E}$ is conceptually connected to 'competitive' markets? Would this require a different definition and characterization of these markets? In some texts,[14] 'non-parametric' is taken to be the same as 'competitive', but we can assume that in a command economy prices are centrally fixed, and one would not use 'competition' to describe such a situation. One way to see this is to consider rationing.

In the observed world, the government often uses rationing (imposing maximum and minimum constraints over consumption and production). What are the possible justifications for this behaviour?

Let us define a non-Walrasian equilibrium as a state of E such that for some goods and agents $\bar{x}$ and $\bar{y}$ are binding, agents maximize their objective function under the appropriate constraints on X^h and Y^j, and a non-zero vector $\hat{p}$ consistent with and optimal under the constraints can be found (see, e.g. Benassy 1990).[15] This concept is recalled again below. Now the concept of net demand is presented.

Net demand $Z_i(p)$ is defined as:

$$Z_i (p,t) \equiv x_i (q) - y_i (p) - \sum_{h=1}^{H} e_i^h. \tag{2.8}$$

Given this definition, vectors $\hat{p}$ and $\hat{t}$ must be such that $Z_i\left(\hat{p}, \hat{t}\right) \leq 0, \; \forall i$ and, if $Z_i\left(\hat{p}, \hat{t}\right) < 0$, then $\hat{p} = \hat{q} = 0$ (i.e. goods available in E but redundant have a null value). For the proof, see Varian (1992: 318), as adapted in Box 2.1.

Box 2.1 Walras law and government

If $(H - 1)$ agents are satisfying the budget constraint with strict equality, then the hth agent also is satisfying it. The Walrasian equilibrium in an AD economy including the government implies automatically the balancing of the government budget.

Proof

Summing up all the individual budget constraints and calling $x_i \equiv \sum_{h=1}^{H} x_i^h$, it is obtained that:

$$\sum_{i=1}^{I} p_i x_i = \sum_{j=1}^{J} \sum_{h=1}^{H} d_j^h \Pi^j + \sum_{h=1}^{H} \sum_{h=1}^{I} p_i e_i^h$$

Or, remembering that $\sum d_j^h = 1$, and the definition of profits

$$\sum_{i=1}^{I} p_i x_i = \sum_{j=1}^{J} p_i \gamma_i^j + \sum_{h=1}^{H} \sum_{i=1}^{I} p_i e_i^h$$

Hence: $\sum_{i=1}^{I} p_i Z_i(p) = 0$

The aggregate value of net demand is zero for every vector p. A vector of indirect taxes is introduced and it is found that $R \equiv \sum t_i x_i = 0$ is verified, where R represents fiscal revenues. In fact, it must be that:

$$\sum_{i=1}^{I} p_i x_i + \sum_{i=1}^{I} t_i x_i = \sum_{i=1}^{I} p_i \gamma_i + \sum_{i=1}^{I} \sum_{h=1}^{H} p_i e_i^h$$

Therefore:

$$\sum_{i=1}^{I} p_i Z_i(p,t) = -\sum_{i=1}^{I} t_i x_i.$$

The term on the left-hand side is null when there is no excess of demand (Walrasian equilibrium). Therefore, the right-hand side is also null and this implies zero fiscal revenues (taxes collected equal subsidies paid) or $t_i = 0$. The government as an economic agent in this context must balance its budget or simply would not have any revenue (including from income taxes).

Source: Adapted from Varian (1992).

This shows that in this context, the government should not distort prices. Equivalently, it should not distort quantities. Hence, the government has nothing to do (except possibly to implement lump-sum taxes and transfers, as is discussed below).

2.6 The two theorems without ideology

The two fundamental theorems can be concisely expressed as follows (skipping the necessary and sufficient conditions).

First Theorem

Let $\hat{E} \equiv \left[\hat{p}, \{ \hat{x}^h \}, \{ \hat{y}^j \} \right]$ be a Walrasian equilibrium, then $\{ \hat{x}^h \}$ and $\{ \hat{y}^j \}$ are Pareto-efficient allocations. For an example of proof, see Myles (1995) or Starr (1997).

Second Theorem

Let $\{ \hat{x}^h \}$, $\{ \hat{y}^j \}$ be a Pareto efficient allocation. Then, a vector $\hat{p} \neq 0$ exists such that $\left[\hat{p} \{ \hat{x}^h \}, \{ \hat{y}^j \} \right]$ is a Walrasian equilibrium. Again see Myles (1995) or Starr (1997) for a proof.

There are several other ways to state the theorems. The Second Theorem, for example, is often expressed in terms of an economy with transfers (or lump-sum taxes and subsidies); see Hindriks and Myles (2006) for an informal presentation. It is helpful, however, to focus here on the most concise version of the theorems. Indeed they do not necessarily imply a role of the government, which, as mentioned, would imply stating a Social Welfare Function and the admissible set of instruments that a (more or less) informed and benevolent government wants to implement.

The crucial issue is to think of (relative) prices, given a *numéraire*, as 'conversion factors' of the quantity of one good into the quantity of another good (see Chapter 1). Suppose again labour time is the *numéraire*. The First Theorem says that – given certain axioms – when there is no excess demand for any good at certain conversion factors of labour into each of the other goods, it is impossible to improve the welfare of an individual without decreasing the welfare of another one. In other words, only by forcing an individual to accept something he dislikes, such as working more or less than he/she would like to do, could improve the welfare of any other individual, given the fact that conversion factors are exactly those arising from the maximization of the welfare of individuals and the profit of firms. It is important to observe that, as discussed later on, there is no need to assume that these equilibrium prices, i.e. conversion factors of quantities, arise from values traded in money terms or through barter.

In this context, there is no compelling analytical reason to interpret the Second Theorem in the context of an economy with transfers. The formal content of the theorem simply states that a set of conversion factors can support any Pareto allocation, for example, labour time in terms of other goods, such that by using those ratios of quantities the net excess demand is zero for any good. This is trivially true if there is just one feasible Pareto allocation, as the First Theorem establishes exactly this, and the reciprocal proposition must be right as well in this particular case.

Suppose, instead, there are two feasible Pareto allocations. What the Second Theorem then says is that each of the two can be supported by a set of conversion factors in terms of labour time that leaves everybody exactly with the quantity of goods they want to consume and firms with the quantity of goods they want to produce. In particular, in both the Pareto points, workers would enjoy exactly the leisure time they want, and firms get the employees they need.

Again, this has *per se* nothing to do with either taxation or trades. If the two Pareto allocations exist in two random states of the world, for example, because God distributes labour abilities in uneven ways across individuals, then what the Second Theorem says is just that each of the two P-points can be compatible with a set of 'relative prices' in terms of labour time such that there is no excess of demand. How this set of conversion factors is used or computed (by a planner, an auctioneer, or a software) is not explained by the theorem itself. Moreover, the theorem has nothing to say about why a government or anybody should prefer one of the two allocations.

It has been already observed that a Walrasian equilibrium[16] is only by a vague analogy called a competitive equilibrium, notwithstanding the interchangeable use of these two terms in the literature. But what is competition in an AD frame?

As stated above, a hidden axiom in the standard definition of the Walrasian equilibrium is the prohibition for agents to conclude contracts at prices different from the equilibrium ones.[17] This implies a mechanism for selecting the 'right' prices among all the possible ones and blocking information and/or contracts at non-equilibrium prices.

This mechanism, implied but not explicitly included in the standard formulation of the First Theorem, was understood in the Walras tradition as a peculiar auction, very different from those observed in the real world. An auctioneer calls prices, agents declare demand and supply at those prices, but contracts are not closed until the declared prices are precisely those equating demand and supply. It can be assumed that the auctioneer, examining every time the excess of demand and supply, could adjust the prices until convergence occurs at the equilibrium. Ingenious proposals have been formulated in dynamic models (Arrow and Hahn 1971).

This is not the place for a discussion of the formal problem of stability of the model. Suppose for a moment that this problem has been solved, i.e. the mechanism spontaneously converges conveniently toward the equilibrium price vector. In any case, in the Walrasian 'auction', the market is not represented more than any other mechanism of adjustment and convergence.

In the classic model of optimal taxation by Diamond and Mirrlees (1971), the Walrasian equilibrium and the corresponding second-best Pareto optimum are preserved, taking advantage of the ambivalence of the standard model. Therefore, a vector of optimal taxes t can be calculated and sent as a message to firms, which, however, are assuming p parametrically to preserve production efficiency, while consumers are parametrically assuming q. This environment is explicitly designed by the authors as fully under the informative control of the government; therefore here, decentralization through prices has little to share with the Walrasian auctioneer. There is nothing to auction.

It can, for example, be supposed that the auctioneer is the government itself, to which all the ownership rights can be assigned (or they can be equally distributed to all consumers) to obtain a process of decentralized planning, or 'market socialism'; see below.

However, this interpretation also seems to be artificial and outside the formal model. By substituting the auctioneer with a software a set of random numbers are generated and notional agents' demands recorded: after a sufficiently significant number of draws (with respect to the algorithm and the problem's characteristics), the software will find out the equilibrium price vector, if it exists, and will communicate it to agents, along with the permit to conclude contracts.

The substitution of equilibrium price signals with corresponding quantity signals would be absolutely equivalent (the algorithm can take advantage of the relative duality) and, in this case, there would be a centralized planning based on command. This will preserve the properties of the First Theorem: the Walrasian equilibrium would still be Pareto-efficient, but there would be no decentralization of the decisions, nor, in the weak sense of the 'market socialism', through prices.[18]

It is possible to discuss the information costs in both the mechanisms (centralized versus decentralized, private versus public ownership). However, the crucial point is that very different mechanisms are virtually consistent with the formal aspects of the First Theorem. The fact is that the convergence mechanism itself (its informative properties, its costs and its rules) is not included in the standard AD economy, nor can it be included with just vague interpretations, like those cited in Section 2.2.

2.7 The critiques by Stiglitz to the theorems

Joseph Stiglitz has strongly criticized the First Theorem:

> I argue that the first fundamental theorem in Welfare Economics [...] is fundamentally flawed. Quite contrary to that theorem, competitive economies are almost never efficient (in a precise sense [...]).
>
> (Stiglitz 1994: 27)

Stiglitz's attack is complementary to our discussion above: the issue for him is the gap between the informative structure of the AD economy and the structure that can be inferred by interpreting the world with an alternative modelling. This new perspective is the one adopted in the Economics of Information. Its core feature is that available information is not fixed, but can be acquired only by paying some costs, and sometimes these costs are so high that they result in market incompleteness. Under this perspective, the hidden axiom on the existence of forces that drive the economy to the equilibrium seems to be contradicted by a wide range of results, reviewed by Stiglitz (1994), showing that if informative imperfection is considered, as it is for the interpretation of the real world, then disequilibria emerge systematically.

This line of attack deserves attention, as it allows one to reinterpret the debate on the two theorems under the light of the new paradigm of the Economics of Information, which is an alternative to the neoclassic orthodoxy (and that in perspective implies a different perception of the role of the public sector).

If the hidden axiom about symmetric or 'fixed' information (meaning that the model's informative structure is not affected by any agents' action) is no longer applicable, the general relevance of the First Theorem also disappears. The equilibria towards which agents tend are not necessarily Pareto-efficient. Therefore, this offers the government a potential role, as using some of its exclusive tools could increase the social welfare unambiguously.

These are, in summary, some of the themes proposed by Stiglitz (1994):

1 Externalities of the first type: incompleteness of the market for risks. If, under uncertainty, the return of each project is influenced by the behaviour of other investors (e.g. by the number of producers investing in similar projects), there is a widespread externality. The probability distribution of the return for the individual is a function of the probability distribution of other agents' returns (therefore, the risks are not independent, and the risk premium cannot be decided by an insurance mechanism).

2 Externalities of the second type: adverse selection. If, for example, the quality of the workforce is variable, even if the average quality is known, the behaviour of certain

groups of agents (e.g. those with lower levels of ability) could influence the average and generate an externality on the producers.

3 Externalities of the third type: incentive problems. Suppose that each individual considers as given the insurance contract's price; then, the incentive to deliver effort to avoid the risky event is lower, and this increases the social cost of insurance with respect to the private cost (the price could increase indefinitely).

4 Incompleteness of the goods market: markets are intrinsically complete when the existence of transaction costs is allowed for. With a great number of goods and states of nature, for an infinite number of future dates, the social costs of organizing all these markets could be so high that the main part of the resources would be used for that. Hence, there would be a trade-off between markets' organization and production.

5 Moreover, according to Stiglitz, a logical contradiction seems to appear between the hypothesis of market completeness, which implies extremely refined specifications of the feasible transaction in terms of quality, date, place, state of the world, and the assumption of competitiveness. This usually implies that the number of competitors is sufficiently high to make prices 'parametric'. In the case of the labour market, detailed contracts possibly imply different contracts for different agents, i.e. *ad personam* contracts (but they would violate axiom A.13). In order to have a contract relative to the same good (of the same quality, place, time, etc.), agents must share the same information. However, in the real world, informative symmetry cannot always be present. In turn, the informative asymmetry generates problems of adverse selection and moral hazard, identified as a cause of non-insurability of certain contracts, and therefore this fact reinforces the case for market incompleteness.

6 There can be an inconsistency between the assumptions of complete markets and perfect information. If prices relative to future events do not allow inferences on all relevant information (e.g. if the forward price of wheat does not allow for the effect of weather forecasting for that date), agents need to try to obtain the additional information necessary to formulate their plans. However, with a complete set of markets, the individual return of this activity would be very low. There would be a trade-off between completeness and information available on the markets. Moreover, the assumption of complete markets at a given date excludes the concept of innovation from the AD economy (the First Theorem is no longer valid when there is innovation).

7 Lack of competition: when there is imperfect information, the market tends to the Chamberlin's imperfect competition and not to the competitive structure. There are several reasons: consumers' search for products is costly and therefore, it is not automatic that a small increase in the price makes the producer lose all the customers; where there are fixed costs, there is a tendency towards monopoly and the information costs are of this type (e.g. research and development (R&D) costs). Firms' demand curves can therefore be downward sloping, and some of these deviations for the entire economy can be relevant: the social marginal cost can be higher than the price.

8 The informative noise produced by the market: when a firm perceives that the consumer has to bear search costs, there can be an incentive to discriminate according to price. The increase in price dispersion is a 'noise' produced by the market and represents an inefficiency connected with its functioning.

Concluding, Stiglitz's criticism of the First Theorem leads to the discovering of 'market failures' that are more diffuse and radical than the traditional externalities, public goods and monopoly. Beyond the formalization and the proof of the theorem (that, as such, is 'true'), the traditional interpretation cannot be sustained, and the view of the theoretical foundation of Public Economics and Welfare Analysis changes perspective. It is no more a problem of management of local 'market failures'; it is about acting to provide rules and institutions without which the economic activity, and in particular the market, is never socially efficient.

2.8 Critical analysis of the Second Theorem

While for the First Theorem the most relevant interpretive issue is that about the meaning of efficiency of the equilibrium, for the Second Theorem the crucial issue is about the possibility of separating redistribution and 'market' equilibria. Remember, however, that some standard formulations of the Second Theorem do not include explicit references to the government's instruments. The theorem simply tells that it is possible to find a price vector supporting each Walrasian equilibrium corresponding to a Pareto optimum. However, it does not indicate the mechanism through which this reallocation of endowments can be implemented (as, on the other hand, it does not tell which are the criteria of equity that should make one Pareto optimum preferable to another).

When these criteria are exogenously given, i.e. a specific Social Welfare Function, one can ask how the government could operate through the Second Theorem, i.e. through a solution decentralized by price signals. What is intended exactly by a decentralized solution in this context? As argued below, there are different possibilities and different degrees of decentralization.

One of the possibilities of moving the economy is the use of arbitrary changes in agents' initial endowments, lump-sum taxes/transfers in kind, performed until the endowment vector leading to the desired Pareto optimum is found. This procedure should be, in turn, opportunely modelled to obtain the desired result, under the assumption of the government's perfect information about agents' endowments. For example, the assumption that the available aggregate endowments allow one to reach the particular desired equilibrium should be introduced axiomatically. Axiom A.12 is probably not enough (transfer-ability of initial endowments at zero cost); something more is needed with respect to the consistency and composition of the stock of AD goods that are used in order to perform the transfer.

In this respect, since the standard AD economy is a non-monetary economy, the lump-sum mechanism consists in the expropriation of given goods from given agents and their attribution to other agents (binding these operations to a zero-sum). However, how could this be done for working ability? See above, footnote 12.

The alternative interpretation (see Hindriks and Myles 2006) is a specification of taxes in terms of the *numéraire*, so that each agent pays with the goods he actually has. This assumes, obviously, there is already a given price vector that can be used to value taxes and transfers. It is also intuitive that this vector can only be the one (if unique) that supports the Walrasian equilibrium corresponding to the desired Pareto optimum; therefore here, the possibility of decentralizing is a peculiar one. The government has since the beginning solved the system of equations determining the equilibrium prices to calculate the exact amount of taxes and subsidies needed to reach the desired Walrasian equilibrium before trade is actually open. See Appendix 2.1 for a further discussion of lump-sum transfers.

Secondly, there is no reason to claim that this mechanism is unique. As what is needed to be done is to modify the balance constraint of each agent, in the standard model the government can act through alternative mechanisms. For example, non-uniform taxes can be introduced on firms' profits, which, as ownership shares are known, allow one to obtain a lump-sum income redistribution. The same property shares (endogenous ownership rights) can, in principle, be redistributed. A combination of these three mechanisms can be made. However, without additional assumptions on the social costs of each of these mechanisms, or of the informative structure, or of the effective consistency of initial endowments, ownership rights and profits, one cannot say which one is more efficient.

Given the Second Theorem, instruments such as quantity rations and distortive taxation (both direct and indirect) are not virtually available for the government. However, when the informative structures and the functioning of the exchanges are better specified, it seems likely that a certain degree of price distortion is necessary or may simply be better than alternative mechanisms.

Two groups of remarks can be made here. The first is again about the informative structure of the model. The second goes beyond.

In the first group, again referring to Stiglitz (1994), the following problems are included:

1   As the potential income depends on personal endowments, to a certain extent, the taxes should use observable magnitudes as a tax base, e.g. exchanges, even if some of them are not directly observable by the government or are a proxy of non-observable ones. In this context, there is a certain necessary degree of distortion and inequality (or the desire of reducing it), which has a social cost. Efficiency and redistribution are not separable.

2   The distribution of initial endowments can affect the incentive structure: for example, if all the land belongs to a unique social class and sharecropping contracts are diffused, this corresponds to a 50 per cent 'tax' on the sharecropper work. In general, contracts between agents with different endowments can lead to a variety of equilibria with respect to risk-sharing and output; therefore, even in this case, efficiency and equity are not so neatly separable.

3   With economies of scale, excessive equality in resource endowments can be inefficient.

4   The theorems of Greenwald and Stiglitz (1986) (see Box 2.2) can also be viewed as theorems of non-decentrability, with the implication that corrective taxes and proper regulations can be unambiguously desirable (including the use of non-linear taxes, if necessary).

5   Several aspects of the discussion of the First Theorem are relevant for the discussion of the Second Theorem: in particular, the issue of the fundamental non-convexities of production processes when there are information costs; the diffused externalities due to interrelations in agents' behaviours; the tendency towards monopolistic competition.

Box 2.2 Information and inefficiency of markets

Economies in which there are incomplete markets and imperfect information are not, in general, constrained Pareto efficient. Households maximize utility subject to the budget constraint:

$$u^h\left(x^h, z^h\right), h = 1, \ldots, H$$

$$\text{s.t.}$$

$$x_1^h + q\bar{x}^h \leq \ell^h + \sum_j d_j^h \pi^j$$

where:

$x^h = \left(x_1^h, \overline{x}^h\right)$ is the consumption vector of h, where x_1^h is the *numéraire* good;

z^h is a vector of N^h other variables affecting utility (e.g. levels of pollution, average quality of goods,…);

q is a vector of consumers' prices;

π^j are profits of firms j;

d_j^h = fractional holding of household h of firm j;

ℓ^h = lump-sum government transfer to household h.

Firms maximize profits: $\pi^j = y_1^j + p\overline{y}^j$ s.t. $y_1^j - G^j\left(\overline{y}^j, z^j\right) \leq 0$, where:

$y^j = \left(y_1^j, \overline{y}^j\right)$ = production vector;

p = producers' prices;

G^j = production function;

z^j = vector of other N^j variables affecting firm j analogously defined to z^h.

The government produces nothing, collects taxes, distributes proceeds and receives net income:

$$R \equiv t\overline{x} - \sum_h \ell^h$$

where $t \equiv q - p$ and $\overline{x} = \sum_h \overline{x}^h$. Assume there exists an initial equilibrium with no taxes and $\ell^h = 0$ for all h. At this equilibrium $p = q$ and $\overline{x}(q, \ell, z) - \sum_j \overline{y}^j(p, z) = 0$.

A necessary (but not sufficient) condition for a Pareto optimum is that the following program:

$$
\begin{cases}
\displaystyle \max_{t,\ell} R \equiv t\overline{x} - \sum_h \ell^h \\[2mm]
\text{s.t.} \\[1mm]
\displaystyle \ell^h + \sum_j d_j^h \pi^j = E^h\left(q, z^h, \overline{u}^h\right)
\end{cases}
$$

has a solution at $t = 0$.

To see when the solution to the problem is $t = 0$, the constraint can be differentiated:

$$\frac{d\ell^h}{dt} + \sum_j d_j^h\left(\pi_z^j \frac{dz^j}{dt} + \pi_p^j \frac{dp}{dt}\right) = E_q^h \frac{dq}{dt} + E_z^h \frac{dz^h}{dt}.$$

Thus, it can be demonstrated that the total compensating payments that the government must make to satisfy the constraint amount to:

$$\sum_h \frac{d\ell^h}{dt} = \overline{x} - \left(\sum_j \pi_z^j \frac{dz^j}{dt} - \sum_h E_z^h \frac{dz^h}{dt} \right).$$

Differentiating the objective function with respect to t:

$$\frac{dR}{dt} = \overline{x} + \frac{d\overline{x}}{dt}t - \sum_h \frac{d\ell^h}{dt} \Rightarrow \frac{dR}{dt} = \frac{d\overline{x}}{dt}t + \left(\Pi^t - B^t \right),$$

where $\Pi^t \equiv \sum_j \pi_z^j \dfrac{dz^j}{dt}$ and $B^t \equiv \sum_h E_z^h \dfrac{dz^h}{dt}$.

For the initial equilibrium to be Pareto optimal, $\dfrac{dR}{dt}$ must be zero at $t = 0$, which implies $\dfrac{dR}{dt} = \left(\Pi^t - B^t \right) = 0$. Thus, Pareto optimality depends on the absence of any z that change with taxes and affect profits or household utilities. The defining characteristics, however, of non-pecuniary externalities are that they enter utility or profit functions in the form of z variables. Except under special conditions, the presence of these externalities will make the initial equilibrium inefficient and guarantee the existence of welfare-improving tax measures.

Source: Adapted from Greenwald and Stiglitz (1986).

2.9 The government rediscovered in second-best economies

According to McKenzie (1987):

> Just as the [general equilibrium] model does not accommodate monopoly easily, government does not fit in well. A chief difficulty arises from its compulsory features which allow it to extract resources by force rather than by voluntary agreement.
>
> (McKenzie 1987: 510)

If in the model of the economy the government is explicitly introduced with a Social Welfare Function (SWF), according to which different Pareto optima are evaluated, it is then possible to note that the SWF, *per se*, is not necessarily a Paretian concept. In fact, the SWF allows one to define as 'welfare superior', or socially preferable, an allocation with respect to another one, notwithstanding at least one subject is harmed, for example, by the lump-sum tax needed to pass from one Walrasian equilibrium to the other. This problem was already known by Pareto himself, who – as mentioned in the previous chapter – maintained explicitly that his concept of economic optimality was not applicable when the state is introduced as an economic agent in the social equilibrium.

Therefore, it is necessary to evaluate with a non-Paretian criterion different Pareto-efficient points.[19]

If the government cannot use optimal (personalized) lump-sum transfers to obtain a given Pareto point, and desires to implement redistributive policies, or to produce public goods financed with distortive taxes, or to compensate externalities with subsidies on prices of some goods, or to introduce compulsory insurance mechanisms when there are risks that are not insurable through the market, then in all these cases, and others, the government should revert to 'second-best' policies.

As shown later, this definition of second best is often as restrictive as the one of first best discussed above. What is a second-best in an AD economy?

The first-order conditions of optimality for an AD economy that is characterized by differentiable functions and functions with other adequate formal properties, imply (i) the equality of the marginal rates of substitutions for each pair of consumption goods, (ii) the equality between the marginal rates of transformation between goods, and (iii) the coincidence of these rates with the relative prices, given a *numéraire*.

A simple reformulation of the traditional second-best problem is as follows.

Given an AD economy in a Walrasian equilibrium E with a vector of equilibrium prices p^*, let us introduce a new constraint on the price of a specific good $\tilde{i}$ (with $i = 1, ..., I$). $\tilde{p}$ is the vector made of the distorted price of $\tilde{i}$, and the other $(N - 1)$ prices are p^*. Then, in general, there exists a vector $p^{**} \neq \tilde{p}$ such that equilibrium E^{**} exists and this equilibrium is second-best Pareto efficient, while in general the equilibrium $\tilde{E}$ for $\tilde{p}$ is not Pareto-efficient.[20]

What the above conjecture says is that if, for example, a regulator imposes a price–cap on the supply of electricity to households, even if all the other prices are undisturbed, the resulting equilibrium will not be a Walrasian one, as there will be excess demand on one side of the market. Thus, Pareto inefficiency is introduced in the economy. It may be the case (this is the conjectural aspect of the story) that, however, if another regulator manipulates one or another price elsewhere, the combined distortions are such that the overall adjustments allow the markets to be cleared, attaining a new Walrasian equilibrium, hence Pareto efficiency again. This would be a second best.

It is clear that this conjecture is difficult to demonstrate 'in general', nor can rules for p^{**} be found without specifying the model. For example, it could be, and has been maintained (Mishan 1969), that if a market is characterized by appropriated formal characteristics isolating it from the other $I - 1$ markets, it could still be convenient to use the old prices for $I - 1$ markets (or in some of them). Everything depends on the characteristics of the constraint and on the behaviour functions.[21]

In this perspective, a general theory of the second-best, indicating a set of uniform rules enabling one to treat AD economies unable to reach P-efficient positions due to distorted prices, does not exist.

The huge literature, originated by Lipsey and Lancaster (1956) and McManus (1959), failed to lead to a general result, but it uncovered a simple intuition:

> The general theorem for second best optimum claims that if in a general equilibrium system a constraint impeding the reach of one of the Paretian conditions is introduced, other Paretian conditions, even if still reachable, in general are no more desirable.
>
> (Lipsey and Lancaster 1956: 11)

Lipsey and Lancaster (1956) consider a constraint on prices. A quantity constraint would also be an appropriate example.[22] Governments can act on quantities, e.g. imposing minima or maxima on the use of resources and factors, or even more binding constraints as compulsory quotas on foreign trade, production or consumption.

The main differences between a Lipsey–Lancaster-type constraint on prices and the quantity constraints is that the equilibrium, determined after the introduction of the constraint, whatever the other public policies and agents' reaction, is such that for one or more activities agents' demanded quantities, net of initial endowments, are not equal to supplied quantities.

In this sense, some equilibria – considered in the next chapter – have been called non-Walrasian equilibria or, in a less precise but maybe more suggestive way, disequilibria.

This definition of equilibrium also has an impact on the distinction between second-best policies and policies of reform. In the first case, given an evaluation criterion of social welfare, which is either the Paretian efficiency or a non-Paretian criterion, the economist, having considered price and quantity distortions of the economy under analysis, determines the optimal value of the policy instrument. In the second case, the economist observes the current value of the instruments and determines which small changes in those values can increase social welfare, taking into consideration the evaluation criterion adopted.

In this much wider context, the second-best approach implies the design of a model of the economy in which, apart from functions of agents' behaviour and the SWF, there are both constraints of technical feasibility, budget constraints and additional exogenous constraints that restrict the range of variation of some variables. In the second-best Walrasian equilibrium, these are exclusively price constraints, whereas in a non-Walrasian equilibrium they can be both price and non-price constraints.

For an economy in disequilibrium, the optimization of controllable price distortions is not enough; it is also necessary to establish, e.g. when there is involuntary rationing on the labour market, which are the optimal controls of quantity on specified markets. Alternatively, it will be necessary to act through simultaneous combinations of price interventions through distortionary taxation and on quantities through rationing. This is shown in the next chapter.[23]

2.10 Further reading

For those readers who want to explore more in-depth the discussion on the theorems, this section suggests a small list of introductory references. The concept of equilibrium in contemporary economics is different and wider, than the one implicit in earlier frameworks of analysis, including the notion that Adam Smith may have had in mind, as shown by Milgate (1979, 1987); see also Donzelli (2007, 2008), not to mention the misleading analogy with equilibrium in mechanics by Pareto (Donzelli 1997).

For a review of non-Walrasian equilibria (in some cases labelled 'disequilibria' or 'rationing equilibria'), see the excellent book by Backhouse and Boianovsky (2013). Albert and Hahnel (2017) also present a good review of the traditional welfare theory, its evolution and recent interpretations.

On the origin of the two theorems, see Feldman (1987). Proofs of the theorems are given in many forms, but an applied economist would be happy with the simple presentation in Varian (1992, 2014).[24] Arrow and Hahn (1971) is still the reference text for those who are interested in the standard framework. Bowles (2004) is a heterodox advanced textbook in the theory of microeconomics that discusses at length how behaviour, institutions, and evolutionary games should change the Walras–Pareto perspective. In the concluding chapter, Bowles offers a neat synopsis of the core assumptions of the Walrasian frame, set against what the author labels 'evolutionary social sciences'.

Public Economics textbooks are less detailed on the two theorems but are usually more explicit than texts in microeconomic theory when drawing policy implications. Leach (2003) is a good example of critical distance:

> The theorems are interesting exactly because they do not describe our economies.
>
> (Leach 2003: 36)

However, he interprets them in terms of 'ideal market economy', which is different from what this chapter suggests. A very good and accessible critical discussion of the Second Theorem is provided by Hindriks and Myles (2006, Chapter 12).

Acocella (2005) restates the second-best theory (Lipsey and Lancaster 1956). For a fine presentation of its origins, see Streissler and Neudeck (1986). They link this concept to the evolution of the role of constraints in optimization. Bator (1958) on the 'Anatomy of market failure' is a classical paper that is still worth reading. For market failures and unemployment, see Greenwald and Stiglitz (1988), and Shapiro and Stiglitz (1984). The latter article shows why, if information is asymmetric, an equilibrium with unemployment arises.

Additional materials about some concepts briefly touched in this chapter are mentioned here. Roberts (1987) is a concise (and critical in terms of empirical relevance) reference to Lindahl equilibrium and related pseudo-prices. Planning mechanisms and their relation to the theorems are discussed by Vohra (1987); see his list of references on this now neglected topic. For a systematic introduction, see Heal (1973). This book offers a systematic treatment of quantity planning, based on previous theoretical papers by the same author (the core ones published in the *Review of Economic Studies*). Picard (1993) surveys disequilibrium ideas in contemporary economics (and their implications for macroeconomics). About rationing, Neary (1987) writes that:

> Within a utility-maximizing framework it may be noted that rationing necessarily imposes a welfare loss. This consideration underlies the instinctive preference by most economists for the use of the price system as an allocation mechanism rather than direct controls, a preference which is supported by the two fundamental theorems of Welfare Economics. Nevertheless, in situations where the conditions for the two Theorems do not obtain, it may be possible to give a second-best justification for rationing.
>
> (Neary 1987: 96)

For a more general discussion of non-Walrasian equilibria, see Benassy (1993, 2006) and Backhouse and Boianovsky (2013). Koutsougeras and Ziros (2015) develop a version of the second welfare theorem to address the decentralization of a Pareto-optimal allocation when markets are non-Walrasian.

Debreu (1959) is probably responsible for the axiomatization of the theory, following the 'Bourbakist' mathematical perspective of the author. Geanakoplos (1987) offers a critical view on the limitations of the Arrow–Debreu model. Qizilbash (2005) suggests that the First Theorem would survive some violations of the basic axioms of agents' rationality (incommensurability). This is just one out of the many examples attempting to show the resilience of the fundamental theorems to the introduction of a bit of realism in their axiomatic structure. This literature has had, however, little impact on Applied Welfare Economics, which – when properly understood – tends to move away from the Walras–Pareto setting, as it allows scope for planning, rationing, and direct control of the economy by governments through public production and supporting second-best policies. Blaug (2007) is a good reference on the history of the theorems: he also explains why there is no perfect competition in the current meaning in Adam Smith's work, while the concept is due to Cournot; and lump-sum taxation to Hotelling.

Clower (1995), in his very entertaining paper on 'Axiomatics in economics', writes:

> I find no logical flaw in any aspect of the Arrow-Debreu theory; I argue, however that as foundation for applied economics, Arrow-Debreu theory is empirically vacuous and conceptually incoherent.
>
> (Clower 1995: 317)

2.11 Summary of Chapter 2

- An Arrow–Debreu economy is a highly abstract analytical device based on a long list of axioms needed to simplify the very complex features of real-world economic arrangements.
- Based on these axioms, and on the concept of Walrasian equilibrium and Pareto optimality, the two fundamental theorems of Welfare Economics have been stated and proved in several ways by different authors over more than one century.
- Under a Walrasian equilibrium, demand and supply of each good are equal.
- Under Pareto optimality, it is impossible to change the allocation of goods without harming at least one agent.
- The First Theorem states that a Walrasian equilibrium is Pareto-efficient and the Second Theorem states that any Pareto optimal allocation can be supported by a vector of prices such that a Walrasian equilibrium is ensured.
- A 'second best' is an arrangement such that personalized lump-sum transfers are unfeasible, and the government must use distortionary taxation while still aiming at Pareto efficiency under these constraints. In general, some authors have suggested that if an inefficiency arises in one market, it is no more desirable to stick to the efficient allocations elsewhere, as second-best optimality would require one to introduce countervailing departures from efficiency in other markets.
- A marginal reform is a change from the existing situation in the direction of a second best. It is usually seen as less demanding in terms of information than 'jumping' to the second best.
- The First Theorem has been interpreted by several authors as a demonstration of the optimality of competitive markets. Other authors, however, have remarked that the theorem can also be viewed as supporting market socialism or even centralized planning. This is because the theorem *per se* says nothing about the mechanisms that would lead to equilibrium from any starting point.
- The Second Theorem has often been interpreted as saying that if different Pareto points are feasible, then the government can lead the economy from one point to

another through lump-sum transfers of agent's endowments allowing markets to achieve once again a Walrasian equilibrium. Thus, redistribution policy can be separated from efficiency. Several authors have questioned this view, either because lump-sum transfers are unfeasible or because they are less efficient than directly allocating goods (rationing).

- Joseph Stiglitz has criticized both theorems because they assume perfect information, and this is highly unrealistic or even illogical.
- Moreover, some of the axioms are particularly troubling in terms of realism and in some cases even in mutual consistency.
- A more fundamental critique of the fundamental theorems is that it is not self-evident that the Pareto criterion is socially desirable, as it would be compatible with extreme inequality. Moreover, to actually use the lump-sum transfers as for the Second Theorem, the government should rank different Pareto points through a non-Paretian Social Welfare Function.
- If the government is not restricted to selecting Pareto points that are associated with Walrasian equilibria as in the First Theorem, it could aim at picking up non-Walrasian equilibria as socially preferred allocations.
- Economic models with non-Paretian governments and non-Walrasian equilibria are wider, more realistic and more appealing for Applied Welfare Economics than the Walras–Pareto traditional frame. The latter should be considered as an abstract reference point, and not as a guide for economic policymaking.
- Shadow prices are the solutions of the optimization program of the economy. There are potentially as many sets of shadow prices as there are SWFs and constraints on the equilibria. Shadow prices should not be confused with observable market prices or even with prices arising from supply-demand equilibrium.

End chapter questions

1　Consider an Arrow–Debreu economy (AD) given by $E \equiv \{I, H, X, J, Y, U, d, e, p, G, W, t, \ell, \bar{x}, \bar{y}\}$, where all variables are defined as in Section 2.2.

   a　Discuss in which cases the axiomatic structure of this economy may fail in general equilibrium analysis. Refer to concepts such as Walrasian equilibrium and Pareto-efficiency and consider the existence of non-Walrasian equilibria.

   b　Discuss the features of this economy when $I, H, J, X, Y, U, W, d, e, G$ are exogenous and $x, y, \bar{x}, \bar{y}, p, t, \ell$ are endogenous. How does the interpretation of the model's result change when, for example: (i) p is exogenous (ii) J is endogenous?

   c　Can the government allow Walrasian equilibrium when there are quantity constraints on the demand and supply functions?

2　Briefly discuss the most relevant critics of the two fundamental welfare theorems by providing meaningful examples. What are the main Stiglitz's critiques on the first fundamental theorem? And the most relevant issues for the interpretation of the second theorem?

3　How do lump-sum taxes and subsidies relate to first-best and second-best policies? What is the difference between policies of reform and second-best policies?

Appendix 2.1

Policies based on the Second Theorem

Lump-sum transfers

A lump-sum tax or subsidy is defined as a fiscal measure independent from the agents' behaviour, such that there is no possibility for them to modify the amount of the transfer through a specific action. This does not mean the lump-sum fiscal measures are neutral because the agents' behaviour would not be modified by the tax: the behaviour is actually modified, but there are no substitution effects, as there are only income effects.

Income effects are often the objective of a government applying this kind of policy: for example, giving incentives to people to work more or less, according to the individual level of *ex-post* welfare with respect to the *ex-ante* level (see Atkinson and Stiglitz 1980; Hindriks and Myles 2006), or modifying the interpersonal allocation of consumption.

An economy able to move along the utility possibility frontier, having the chance of continuously passing from one P-efficient position to another through the use of lump-sum transfers, is called a 'first-best' context in the literature. The terminology is quite peculiar and analytically misleading, as it may give the idea of the best of all possible worlds, which is not what it means. In particular, nothing says that, from the individual point of view or that of the group (or the government point of view with a non-Paretian Social Welfare Function), there are no better allocations than those of first-best.

This is a totally different problem concerning the discussion on the practical difficulties of implementing first-best policies. Turning to these difficulties, a crucial problem is the informative one. In an AD economy, there is nothing that characterizes the position of agents in production and exchange activities, except for their preferences, rights d_j^h and their initial endowments e_i^h.

The reason why a discussion of lump-sum taxes usually refers restrictively to 'admissible' characteristics, such as personal wealth and working ability in particular, and not to others such as gender, race, age, health status, social class at birth, is because the latter characteristics are not deemed to be easily inserted in the model.

If, however, in general disequilibrium[25] involuntary unemployment of a Keynesian type or a classical type is rationed through discrimination based on qualitative agents' characteristics, such as race or gender, agents' indistinguish-ability under this respect in a 'welfaristic' Social Welfare Function is a serious limit to the possibility of providing normative directions with respect to specific reforms (e.g. gender balance actions).

In the two-dimensional space of utility possibilities, suppose that two social groups of otherwise identical individuals exist, for example, Black and White (or Male and Female, or any other pair of socially relevant characteristics) with fixed labour supply. The government wants a social system with more equality between Whites and Blacks.

To obtain this, one has to move from allocation X to position Y. In Y, the possibility of first-best intervention is blocked if it is unknown whether the hth individual is White (W) or Black (B).[26]

But suppose that these features are easily observable and that the current educational level roughly represents the earning capacity of type B and type W individuals. For example, all the Whites are illiterate while all the Blacks have a degree. Then there are only two types of income, $w^B l^B$ and $w^W l^W$ (where w is wage and l is labour supply), and the application of a tax on income of graduates is equal to applying a lump-sum tax on earning capacity.[27]

This may be an argument in favour of rationing policies. However, if labour demand and supply depends (also) on the White–Black characteristic, but this characteristic is not fiscally 'admissible', even if observable, it is not possible to implement the desired lump-sum transfers aimed at redistributing welfare between White and Black. Then, as an alternative, it is possible to impose compulsory quotas of employment to the Whites, or reserved places in the universities, etc. Governments and employers do this on a large scale (also with age, gender, disabilities as other typical observables, and special provisions for some types).

These reserved quotas, of course, create rationing, i.e. demand or supply excess, on the labour market (or on the university education market), and they do not allow the persistence of Walrasian equilibrium or P-efficiency. However, they could still be preferable according to other social welfare criteria.

Eventually, with lump-sum taxation, there may be perverse distributional effects under a utilitarian Social Welfare Function to be maximized, with the high-skilled ending up after taxation with lower welfare than the low-skilled (Hindriks and Myles 2006).

Notes

1 See Atkinson and Stiglitz (1980). For an analogous but more elaborate version, see Laffont (1988); for a more rigorous formulation, see Guesnerie (1980) or Mas-Colell *et al.* (1995).

2 See, for other examples, Lectures on Microeconomic Theory by Malinvaud (1972), Arrow and Hahn (1971), Varian (1992). For a perspective of history of ideas, see Weintraub (1974, 1985) and Kornai (1971). See also the review by McKenzie (1987).

3 The authors cited, however, are usually more cautious in developing the interpretation and they introduce from the beginning a certain number of clarifications and distinctions.

4 Hindriks and Myles (2006), after the standard presentation in the preliminary chapters, later on are critical of the theorems. See also Guesnerie (1980), Laffont (1988) and Starret (1989).

5 There is no explicit government role in the AD frame. What is done here and in Chapter 3 is to introduce it explicitly and discuss the implications of different assumptions.

6 In the presentation of the axioms, Geanakoplos (1987) and Cornwall (1984) are freely followed. An alternative axiomatic approach is the one by McKenzie (1987).

7 To give an example of this fact, a discussion of the differences between the numéraire in E and money (nominal and real) in observable economies and their implications for the interpretation of the two fundamental theorems can be useful. If an index 1 is attributed to the numéraire-good, i.e. gold, so that $p_1 = 1$, then the $(N-1)$ dimensional vector of all the other prices can be univocally defined; x_1, y_1, ℓ_1 etc. can in turn be interpreted in a very natural way as units of gold consumed, produced or taxed away. Suppose for a while that (under particular conditions not discussed here) there is a demand and a supply of gold to be used as money (i.e. as a reserve value or for transaction purposes): then it is claimed that there is 'private money' in the model. Similarly, it can be imagined that private paper money (or even electronic money) exists, based on gold or on whatever good or basket of goods. The interest rate i should be univocally determined by the relationship between the prices of the numéraire good with different time indexes. Therefore, there is no specific role for G with

respect to supply of money. In order to create public money and the related government's or central bank's monopoly of emission, additional assumptions are needed, for example, uncertainty of future states of the world, which cannot be contracted through private insurance. In the AD frame, the absence of public money is an example of what standard assumptions cannot capture if the role of government is not explicitly considered. In the rest of this book, however, the role of money in the determination of the overall state of the economy is not considered, and when a currency is mentioned as a unit of account, euro for example, the fact that in the real world it is more than a yardstick is ignored.

8   Equivalently: a system of (linear) equations is over-determined when there are more equations than unknowns; hence, in matrix form, there are more rows than columns. It is well known that these systems may have zero, some or infinite solutions according to linear dependency of the constraints. Thus, finding a unique solution for prices implies some special conditions.

9   This would imply that the second theorem result in general cannot be achieved, except when the lump-sum exogenous taxes are optimal.

10 'We think of a commodity as a good or service completely specified by its characteristics [...]. Often identical goods at different locations may trade at different prices, entering differently in preferences' (Starr 1997: 69).

11 Some definitions are here reminded: Convexity of a set S of n-vectors is defined by: $(1 - \lambda)x\lambda x' \in S$ and $x \in S$, $x' \in S$, and $\lambda \in [0, 1]$. Suppose now that f is a function of many variables defined on the convex set S. Then concavity of the f function is defined by y the property: $f\lfloor(1-\lambda)x+\lambda x'\rfloor \geq (1-\lambda)f(x)+\lambda f(x')$. Convexity in turn is defined as: $f\lfloor(1-\lambda)x+\lambda x'\rfloor \leq (1-\lambda)f(x)+\lambda f(x')$. Strict concavity of a function is defined when $f\lfloor(1-\lambda)x+\lambda x'\rfloor > (1-\lambda)f(x)+\lambda f(x')$. Strict convexity is defined when $f\lfloor(1-\lambda)x+\lambda x'\rfloor < (1-\lambda)f(x)+\lambda f(x')$. The function f defined on a convex set S is quasi-concave if all upper level sets off are convex. That is, $U_a = \{x \in S : f(x) \geq a\}$ is convex for every value of a. The multivariate function f defined on a convex set S is quasi-convex if every $U_a = \{x \in S : f(x) \leq a\}$ is convex for every value of a. Concave functions are quasi-concave and convex functions are quasi-convex. The reciprocal may or may not be true. The multivariate function f defined on a convex set S is strictly quasi-concave when it is true that for all $x \in S$, all $x' \in S$ with $x' \neq x$, and all $\lambda \in (0, 1)$: if $f(x) \geq f(x')$ then $f\lfloor(1-\lambda)x+\lambda x'\rfloor > f(x')$.

12 This is admitted in a footnote by Starr (1977: 146, footnote 1): 'Note that this may require an implausible redistribution of labour endowments'.

13 The assumption that endowments are only in terms of labour has its own problems; see below in the main text. There are other problems related to the implications on budget constraints and demand functions of subsidies on some goods in the endowment. These cannot be discussed here.

14 See page 40, Section 2.1 citation from Atkinson and Stiglitz (1980) of the First Theorem, and the fact that the term 'competitive' there could possibly be deleted.

15 For the literature that discusses efficiency of non-Walrasian equilibria in a pure exchange economy, see Backhouse and Boianovski (2013).

16 In this chapter the relationship between Nash and Walras equilibrium is not discussed. This issue is not elaborated on here, but it should be clear from the above discussion why the concepts are different.

17 'The market takes place at a single instant, prior to the rest of economic activity. We think at the market meeting, demand being expressed, equilibrium achieved, and allocations decided, all prior to actual consumption and production taking place' (Starr 1997: 69).

18 Some of these issues are discussed by Kornai (1971) in his book *Anti-Equilibrium*.

19 Then why should one be particularly interested in these points? Is the presence of other points possible, representing different equilibria and socially preferable? Moreover, if the aim of the government is fully represented through the SWF, and it is accepted as given per se, no matter its specification, why should the reach of the Walrasian equilibrium be considered an exogenous condition? It is actually difficult to find a compelling logical, normative or

realistic motivation for the hidden axiom which imposes to that imposes the agents to close of closing their transactions only at Walrasian equilibrium prices. If the government could find non-Walrasian equilibria, in which some agents are rationed, and evaluate them as socially superior under its own SWF, why should it skip these equilibria as the aim of its policies when it has the tools (e.g. quantity constraints) to push the economy in that direction?.

20 This formulation is different from the one by Lipsey and Lancaster (1956), but it could be retained as similar in its intuition.

21 It could well be that the additional constraint will anyway allow a Pareto-efficient solution. An additional constraint in a constrained optimization problem can be supported by a vector of shadow prices such that, using them, nobody could increase his/her welfare without reducing the welfare of at least another agent. In order that the conjecture on second best be always true in the formulation here reported, it should be demonstrated that in the new situation, thus after the additional constraint, the welfare of at least one individual is worse while the welfare of the others is the same as before. To demonstrate this, however, seems difficult.

22 The archetypes of these second best problems, and thus of the modern theory of optimal taxation, are three famous articles: Ramsey (1928), Little (1950) and Corlett–Hague (1953). For the fundamentals of general equilibrium of the theory of optimal taxation a classical reference is Diamond and Mirrlees (1971).

23 However, optimal provision of public goods g will not be considered explicitly.

24 Mas Colell *et al.* (1995) restates the welfare properties of general equilibrium 'with transfers' in Chapter 16, and presents more advanced material (uncertainty, non-cooperative game game-theoretic foundations, inter-temporal context, Social Welfare Functions).

25 Equilibrium without rationing.

26 Atkinson and Stiglitz (1980) note that, in some cases, a proxy can substitute relevant information. Their example is the following: if the earning capacity w^h is not taxable with lump-sum taxes, the government can collect a tax on $w^h l^h$: if the labour supply function is known, the earning capacity can be deduced from the income level. Given that incomes are observables, through them it is possible to implement a lump-sum tax on w.

27 Moreover, if labour supply functions are not homogeneous for all the Blacks and all the Whites, because, for example, they depend on further characteristics such as numerosity of the household, age, etc., then a continuum $w^h l^h$ will be observed and l^h will need to be known for each individual in order to find w^h; knowledge of the aggregate functions $l^B l^w$ is not enough to discriminate.

3 Shadow prices and the social planner

Overview

This chapter presents a conceptual framework for Applied Welfare Economics,[1] consistent with some of the ideas discussed in the previous two chapters. Chapter 1 has discussed some definitions of social welfare. Chapter 2 has offered a critical review of some interpretations of the two fundamental welfare theorems and has concluded that there are numerous possible solutions to the optimization problem of a benevolent government, given its objectives and constraints. The first-best solutions have no practical relevance, and there are several ways to consider a second-best frame.

Given a Social Welfare Function, 'shadow prices' are the second-best solutions of constrained optimization of government's planning. These are not necessarily related to observed prices delivered by market mechanisms or to any other set of observed prices, including tariffs of publicly provided services. As clarified in Chapter 2, the term 'shadow price' indicates the solution to the maximization problem of the social planner under budgetary and side constraints.

In this chapter, the term 'accounting price' is preferably used when referring to the proxy of shadow prices, estimated through different methodological shortcuts. A model for social cost-benefit analysis based on shadow prices is presented. It draws on a highly simplified version and adaptation of the Drèze and Stern (1987) CBA theory (DS), which provides a general definition of shadow prices in a second-best planning framework and summarizes much of the earlier literature.

The DS model has the following features:

- in contrast to the standard AD framework, there is an explicit role for a welfare-maximizing government, including public production of goods;
- the SWF does not need to be strictly Paretian: it can include social preferences for equity, merit goods or paternalism;
- lump-sum transfers are possible (e.g. taxes on profits) but not optimally personalized; hence, the economy is in a second-best environment;
- non-Walrasian equilibria are allowed through the introduction of quantity constraints;
- there is a clear distinction between observable prices and other signals, shadow prices and information available to the social planner;
- there is no need to assume that governments are able to adopt optimal production plans: they can make errors or be constrained in terms of information and policy adoption;

DOI: 10.4324/9781003191377-4

- the government itself can be decentralized in the form of a multilevel federation or hierarchy;
- a simple CBA rule emerges, with practical implications for projects and policy evaluation.

The presentation is still abstract; the notation is mostly consistent with that of the previous chapter where, however, the Walras–Pareto setting, *de facto*, preempted the role of government. Some of the ideas arising from the model are used in the rest of the book as a benchmark to understand how distant some CBA practices are from theory. In fact, as explained in this chapter, some earlier traditions of CBA based on partial equilibrium, consumer and producer surplus, and their variants (separation of equity from efficiency, implicit SWF of a Paretian type, etc.) are often helpful in specific cases and contexts, without generalized validity.

The structure of the chapter is as follows. After a section of introductory remarks (3.1), the next section presents a sketch of the theory. The DS model is then applied to a simple second-best economy (Section 3.3), and its extension to policy reforms is discussed (Section 3.4). The chapter ends with a section (3.5) on the multi-government setting and with some remarks on the efficiency of using shadow prices compared to computable general equilibrium models (3.6). There is then a Further Reading section and an appendix about some of the DS results.

3.1 Introductory remarks

To begin the discussion, we consider a closed Walrasian economy where the relevant SWF is its GDP expressed as the sum of agents' individual expenditures. Let us assume a Bentham context, with welfare weights equal to one for all agents. Prices are optimal by assumption, as they equal the individual marginal utility of each good given a *numéraire*, plus marginal costs.

This situation can be described as:

$$\text{GDP} = p_1 x_1 + p_2 x_2 + \ldots + p_I x_I. \tag{3.1}$$

The vector $x = (x_1, \ldots, x_I)$ is formed by all consumers' plans, good by good of H individuals: $x_1 = \left(x_1^1, \ldots, x_1^h, \ldots, x_1^H\right); x_2 = \left(x_2^1, \ldots, x_2^h, \ldots, x_2^H\right)$; etc.

At this stage, it is not important to discuss how equilibrium prices were determined. One can imagine that the social planner imposed trading at those prices, or those prices are the result of a Walrasian *tâtonnement* mechanism, or we can assume that there is no trade at all, as the social planner rationed quantities optimally based on the solution of the optimization program; hence, those prices are no more than conversion factors relating quantities, as discussed in Chapter 1.

Then, the question at this stage is the following: what is the marginal social value of increasing the availability in the economy of good i by an arbitrary small amount? We can think, for example, of an incremental technological innovation that offers something more of the x_i good for the same amount of inputs previously employed. Now a small change, say dx_i, in a given state of the world, occurs as, for instance, the acquisition of a piece of new knowledge. As this occurs in a Bentham setting where individual welfare equals income, it is not important to know who gain this additional consumption arising from the increased productivity. The intuition is straightforward: the marginal social value of the change is exactly p_i, i.e. the price around the previous equilibrium (more generally, the social value will be the price times the private marginal utility of income). Indeed agents before the innovation valued as p_i their consumption of one unit of x_i; they now receive an additional small quantity of it; thus, the individual utility of this change is conveyed by p_i.

Let us consider the first derivative of GDP around its previous optimal value: $\frac{\partial \text{GDP}}{\partial x_i} = \frac{\partial px(\cdot)}{\partial x_i} = p_i$ as parametric prices imply $\frac{\partial p_{i_1}}{\partial x_{i_2}} = 0 \forall i_1, i_2$ (two different goods), where px, in simplified vector notation, is the inner product of fixed prices and quantities for all H individuals, i.e. income or equivalent consumption.

In other words, in this special context, the social value of a small enough bit of good i is the value of the increase of GDP, and this is exactly the (relative) price assigned by the government (or by perfectly competitive markets, or by an optimizing computer) to that good. As prices are parametric, this boils down to a partial equilibrium context. Readers are invited to think about a more general context where cross-elasticities of demand to prices of other goods are different from zero, at least for some goods, remembering that prices are here assumed to be the optimal ones, occurring before the small increase in the availability of one good.

One may wonder whether this is the end of the story, given the possible interrelations of quantities and prices through general equilibrium adjustments, i.e. when partial cross-derivatives of SWF, with respect to quantity changes, are different from zero. In this very simple context, the innovation is small enough that the increased availability of the ith good does not change relative prices (in this perspective, equilibrium prices are fixed). Hence, the answer is: yes, this is the end of the story. If we know the equilibrium prices of a Walrasian economy and if its SWF is of the GDP type, we do not need to know anything else to make welfare calculations. A small project increases net output, GDP responds by a proportional increase evaluated at the previous equilibrium prices, and this is all.

This seems to be in contrast to the need to calculate consumer's and producer's surpluses or other welfare measures, as presented in Welfare Economics textbooks (see Box 3.1). However, this is not the case, as prices are assumed to be the 'right' ones for welfare calculations, i.e. are *shadow prices*, and these, by assumption, will take care of any general equilibrium adjustments.

Box 3.1 Compensating and equivalent variation; consumer's surplus

Consider a discrete change in a policy regime in a one-consumer equivalent economy. Suppose there are two budgets, (p^0, m^0) and (p', m'), that measure observable prices (p) and income (m) a given consumer would face under two different policy regimes, where the first one is the status quo and the second one is a proposed change. The change in welfare is simply measured by the difference between indirect utilities in the two scenarios: $v(p', m') - v(p^0, m^0)$.

If the difference in utility is positive, then the policy change will improve welfare, whereas if it is negative, this policy is not worth doing.

However, in some cases, it is convenient to have monetary measures of changes in consumer welfare.

Let us define $\mu(q; p, m)$ as the amount of income the consumer needs at prices q to reach the same utility he/she has when prices are p and income is m. Then, the difference in welfare generated by the policy can be measured in monetary terms $\mu(q'; p', m') - \mu(q^0; p^0, m^0)$.

Thus, three measures for the utility difference can be defined according to the base prices q considered: equivalent variation, compensating variation, and consumer's surplus.

- *Equivalent variation (EV)* uses current prices $q = p^0$ as the base and asks what income change, at the current prices, would be equivalent to the proposed change in terms of its impact on utility:

$$\text{EV} = \mu\left(p^0; p', m'\right) - \mu\left(p^0; p^0, m^0\right) = \mu\left(p^0; p', m'\right) - \mu^0.$$

- *Compensating variation (CV)* uses the new prices $q = p'$ as the base and asks what income change would be necessary to compensate the consumer for the price change:

$$\text{CV} = \mu\left(p'; p', m'\right) - \mu\left(p'; p^0, m^0\right) = \mu' - \mu\left(p'; p^0, m^0\right).$$

- *Consumer's surplus (CS)* is a measure of the welfare change. Assume that $x(p)$ is the uncompensated demand for some good as a function of its price. Consumer's surplus associated with a price movement from p^0 to p' is defined as $\text{CS} = \int_{p^0}^{p'} x(t)\, dt$. This expression identifies the area to the left of the uncompensated demand curve bounded by the two prices.

There are problems of path-dependency with consumer surplus when more than one parameter changes (except when utility is quasi-linear). When utility is quasi-linear, i.e. linear in *numéraire*, indifference curves are 'parallel' and the EV, CV, and CS coincide. In many practical circumstances, the relationships between these measures and price indexes are such that an observable price change is a sufficient proxy for the welfare change, but only if the price is representative of the marginal social welfare of the good. This, however, is not true in general because of interrelations between prices and because of the SWF. This is why shadow prices are needed.

The above-mentioned welfare measures apply to discrete projects, whereas marginal projects or policies are considered in the rest of the chapter.[2] Shadow prices for large projects are not covered; see Starret (1989).

Source: Author, adapted from Varian (1992).

The advantage of not considering, market by market, demand and supply adjustments in welfare calculations is obvious, as once the shadow price is calculated, this is a 'parameter' for the social planner. Nothing more is needed for the applied welfare economist who wants to evaluate the impact of a new project or a public policy reform. However, the problem is that real-world economies are sub-optimal (as discussed in Chapter 2); hence, observed prices are often different from shadow prices, which remain unknown. This does not mean that the empirics of Welfare Economics are impossible. The following Chapters 4 and 5 will present some empirical strategies. However, before discussing the empirical issues, we need to go into the details of the theory of shadow prices from the viewpoint of the social planner.

3.2 A model for project and policy evaluation

What follows is a restatement of the DS framework with many simplifications and some adaptations. The notation is mostly consistent with Chapter 2 and with Drèze and Stern (1987, 1990). We consider a closed economy (differently from DS).[3] The following definitions are used:

Individuals are $h = (1, \ldots, H)$ consumers, workers, taxpayers, and shareholders. Some individuals may combine these four aspects; others may be just consumers, or consumers–workers–taxpayers with no shareholding, or consumers–taxpayers–shareholders, or other combinations. Workers are negative consumers of their leisure time. Individuals earn different net income according to how much they work, their abilities, their salary, the dividends they earn through their shareholdings, the tax they pay or public transfer they receive (negative taxes). Individuals have well-defined preferences, are welfare maximizers (altruism, if it exists, is embodied in the SWF), and, given prices, make their consumption decisions (x). There is no saving. Some agents may be rationed, meaning that, at the observed prices, they cannot consume what their income would allow them to do (unemployment can be considered as a rationing equilibrium; see Chapter 5 on shadow wages). For their net demand, see below.

Private firms (indexed by j) are profit maximizers on behalf of their shareholders. Given their technologies, prices of inputs and outputs, they determine their net supply y and earn profits π gross of taxes. Their net demand to the public sector is the difference between their total demand and their demand to private agents, i.e. other private firms and workers. They respond to signals. Firms fully or partly owned by governments but not under their direct control (i.e. not included in the production plan of the public sector) are considered private.

Public firms are production units fully controlled by governments. Given their technology, they are assumed to efficiently produce what requested by their principal. Profits, if positive, are cashed by the Treasury as the owner or through taxation of regulated firms. Transfers cover losses. Privately owned firms fully controlled by the government are considered public ones.

Signal (s) is the generic name given to a variable that influences private agents' behaviour. Signals may include producer prices, direct or indirect tax rates, shareholding rights, rations on production or consumption of specific goods, transfers, and any other variable needed to model the behaviour of private agents. Some of these variables are endogenous, meaning that their value is determined by optimization. Others are exogenous or parameters $(\bar{s})$. Depending on whether signals are assumed endogenous or exogenous, a different planning solution is obtained.

Individual welfare depends either directly on private consumption or indirectly on signals. Public production enters only indirectly in individual welfare.[4]

An *environment* is determined by the vector of all signals $s = (\ldots, s_k, \ldots)$ of dimension $k = 1, \ldots, K$. Aggregate net demands are given by $E = E(s)$. Private agents adjust their behaviour, hence their net demand, to the economic environment. This is similar to Section 2.3 in the previous chapter, with a slightly different notation to simplify the presentation.

Observed prices are expressed in terms of a national currency (or otherwise by an appropriate convention). They are determined in different ways: some are market prices, where some markets are competitive, others imperfect; other prices are set directly by planners (i.e. fixed tariffs). A common feature of prices is that they are non-negative: p are producer prices, q are consumer prices.

The *social planner* is a unit of government with a specific SWF such as $W\left(U^h\right)$ or $V\left(v^h\right)$ embodying all the objectives of the government. These functions include as arguments individual direct $\left(U^h\left(\cdot\right)\right)$ or indirect utility $\left(V^h\left(\cdot\right)\right)$, but in principle, they could also include other non-welfaristic variables, such as merit goods. Each unit of government is a welfare maximizer.

Production plan: let us define $z = (\ldots, z_i, \ldots)$ as the net supply of the public sector, a production plan of dimension I, where i is the index for commodities (including time, space, and state of the world). The components of z can be zero or negative (i.e. net demand from the public sector to the private sector).

Small Project is a marginal change dz, in the net supply of goods by the public sector (private firms fully controlled are considered to be in the public sector). The feasibility condition is given by $(z + dz) \in Z$. Starting from an arbitrary position, the project slightly increases the production plan, for example, adding a bed in a hospital.[5]

Policy is a rule (ϕ) that associates a state of the economy with a (public) production plan. Appropriate signals (s), e.g. rations or taxes, have to be provided to incentivize people to adopt the desired behaviour (see below). A feasible policy is such that (a) first, the scarcity or resource constraints are met, or in other words, net private demands are equal to public production; and second (b), the planner can select appropriate signals within its opportunity set. The latter means that the change in signals is needed to implement a legally or politically feasible production plan. Some government levels can face just one predetermined policy.

The *scarcity constraint* is given by a system of equations $E(s) - z = 0$. If private net demand is greater than the public production plan, i.e. $E(s) > z$, there is a shortage of public products or *congestion*. This can happen because the signals are such that private agents could and would demand some public sector goods which are not produced. This situation is referred to as *unintended rationing*. In the discussion below, however, the scarcity constraint holds with strict equality: the supply of public goods is equal to the demand generated by the environment. In some cases, the planner is not free to set the signal at the desired level for solving the optimization plan, i.e. the planner has a side constraint $s \in S$, where S is the opportunity set of the planner. For example, this can happen with direct taxation: the government has an upper bound in the tax rate because of political constraints. Another example is a municipality constrained by a superior level of government.

Shadow price is the net impact (v) on the SWF of a unit increase of an input or output i and it is evaluated around the optimum. We assume that a first-order condition is enough for the evaluation.[6] Shadow prices of the economy 'before' the project cannot be used to evaluate the project when it would change the structure of the economy (for large projects, see Box 3.1).

Cost-benefit analysis (CBA) is the assessment of a decision in terms of its welfare impact (positive, negative, null). The CBA test involves accepting only projects that make profits at shadow prices.

Having in mind this framework, a government takes decisions about:

- production plan (e.g. how many places in a school, etc.);
- a policy rule (for each production plan, a set of signals supporting it. Note that it is generally possible to have more than one policy option supporting a production plan, e.g. transfers, tickets, taxes, etc.);
- the adoption of shadow prices, i.e. the solution to the maximization problem;
- the approval of projects;
- the approval of policy reforms.

The units of a government need to implement their production plans, meaning the quantity of the service to be provided, each under its own competencies. Therefore, the planner is just an office that wants to optimize a SWF under scarcity constraints and additional constraints.[7] The question arises whether the planner may not further increase social welfare by a change in the vector of levels of public output.[8] The answer is that, while any planner should try to optimize its choices, the production plan may be sub-optimal for several reasons, for example, because the regional planner must comply with some national legislation (i.e. environmental regulations) or for other political and managerial constraints, or for lack of information.

The social planner's problem is about finding $s*$ as a solution of:

$$\begin{cases} \max_{s} V(s) \\ \text{s.t.} \\ E(s) - z = 0 \end{cases} \tag{3.2}$$

(without, for simplicity, considering here constraints on signals). Signals influence only the private production plans, not the public ones. In this sense, z is an *arbitrary* parameter and captures the unique role of the government in forcing the economy to produce and consume outside the voluntary exchange. In this perspective, the social planner's decision about the production plan is outside the Walrasian frame, and if $V(s)$ is non-Paretian, then we are also outside the standard 'Two Theorems' world in its 'free market' interpretation.

Policy optimization in the DS context implies exactly the same evaluation process as the determination of shadow prices. If the benevolent social planner has to accommodate a production plan, it will select the combination of taxes, rations, prices, etc., under its control that has the least adverse social impact. If some of these variables are out of control, i.e. are exogenous parameters, the study of reforms can be pursued with a similar approach (e.g. regulatory impact analysis).[9]

As mentioned, a feasible policy in the DS frame is a function $s = \phi(z)$. It associates a production plan z with a vector of signals, such that the scarcity constraints are met:

$$s_k = \phi_k(z) \quad \forall k = 1, \dots, K \tag{3.3}$$

subject to

$$E_i(s) - z_i = 0 \ \forall i = 1, \ldots, I. \tag{3.4}$$

Once such a policy is specified, social welfare is a function of z:

$$V = V[\phi(z)]. \tag{3.5}$$

In other words, an environment s is associated with each production plan z. The environment determines the state of the economy E and the level of (indirect) social welfare V. The discretionary production plan z supported by the policy $\phi(z)$ generates the social welfare through its impact on signals. The aim of CBA is to evaluate any project dz. To do this, shadow prices have to be used to value inputs and outputs.[10]

In the DS framework, shadow prices v are defined as the impact on social welfare of a change in the public provision of a good, given an optimal supporting policy. If this change is small (in a technical sense), shadow prices v are defined as the first partial derivatives of the SWF around the optimum with respect to each of the goods considered[11],

$$v_i = \frac{\partial V}{\partial s} \frac{\partial \phi}{\partial z_i} \ \forall i = 1, \ldots, I. \tag{3.6}$$

Given $\phi(z)$, consider the differential of social welfare[12],

$$dV = \frac{\partial V}{\partial s} \frac{\partial \Phi}{\partial z} dz, \tag{3.7}$$

where:

$$\frac{\partial V}{\partial s} = \left(\ldots, \frac{\partial V}{\partial s_k}, \ldots \right) \text{ a vector in } R^k, \tag{3.8}$$

$$\frac{\partial \Phi}{\partial z} = \left(\ldots, \frac{\partial \Phi_k}{\partial z_i}, \ldots \right) \text{ a matrix } I \times K \text{ with } I \leq K. \tag{3.9}$$

The dimension of the z row vector, as mentioned, is I, while the dimension of the signals is K. If the two dimensions are the same, and under certain formal conditions, the policy is fully determined by constraints, and ϕ collapses to the vector s.[13] The project is to be accepted if $dV > 0$, i.e. if there is a welfare improvement.[14] This is our CBA test in the DS frame.

Consider, for example, a project for a new bridge dz_i (and nothing else changes in the production plan). According to this approach, $vdz_i > 0$ increases welfare when inputs/costs (labour, materials) and outputs/benefits (passengers' travel time, etc.) are evaluated at shadow prices v, and net benefits (shadow profits) are positive.

While the DS theory is quite general, its application is often difficult, and intelligent shortcuts are needed. Observed prices can be distorted, but estimated shadow prices v can be wrong. A good understanding of both issues is the key to successful evaluation. Chapters 4 and 5 are about finding shortcuts to compute shadow prices.

In many cases, these shortcuts are not different from the current CBA practice in different fields, but, in some cases, it would be important to have a general definition of what a 'good enough' accounting price should be to estimate the unknown 'true' shadow price.

3.3 A second-best economy in the DS frame

This section aims at translating the above general CBA model into something more specific, even if purely illustrative. The notation is the same as in Section 3.2.

As optimal lump-sum taxes and transfers are not available, consumers pay distortionary taxes that create a difference between production and consumption prices: $t = q - p$. Given the constraints on lump-sum taxation, commodity taxes need to be optimally chosen by the planner. This is an unrealistic assumption, but a convenient one to fix some ideas; see below. A household's lump-sum income is the sum of government transfers and the share of profits of firms owned by the household (as in Chapter 2):

$$m^h \equiv r^h + \sum_j d_j^h \pi^j, \tag{3.10}$$

where r^h are government's lump-sum taxes or transfers and d_j^h is household h's profit (π) share in firm j. The profit tax can be expressed as:

$$\zeta_j = 1 - \sum_h d_j^h, \tag{3.11}$$

that is, the share of firm j owned by the government.

The taxation of profits and/or the initial allocation of shares are such that first best cannot be achieved, as discussed in Chapter 2. Moreover, commodities can be rationed: lower and upper bounds on consumption or rations are indicated by $\bar{x}^h = \left(\bar{x}_-^h, \bar{x}_+^h \right)$. Rationing policy is constrained, and first best cannot be achieved by it, i.e. first-best quantity planning is impossible.[15]

Consumers choose the optimal consumption plan, denoted by $x^h \left(q, \bar{x}^h, m^h \right)$, maximizing their individual utility subject to their budget constraint and given the prices distorted by indirect taxation and rations. The consumer's optimization problem can be stated as:

$$\begin{cases} \max_{x^h} U^h \left(x^h \right) \\ \\ \text{s.t.} \\ \\ qx^h = r^h + \sum_j d_j^h \pi^j \\ \\ \bar{x}_-^h \leq x^h \leq \bar{x}_+^h \end{cases} \tag{3.12}$$

The aggregate net consumption vector is the sum across all households h of the h's consumption plan: $x = \sum_h x^h$ with $x^h \in X^h$.

Analogously, producers choose the optimal net supply vector $y^j\left(p,\overline{y}^j\right)$, i.e. the supply vector that maximizes profits given the technological constraints and rations on supply $\left(\overline{y}_-^j,\overline{y}_+^j\right)$. Production rationing is again not the first best.

The producer's problem can be stated as:

$$
\begin{cases}
\max_{y^j} \Pi^j \equiv \left(py^j\right) \\
\quad\text{s.t.} \\
\quad y^j \in Y^j \\
\quad \overline{y}_-^j \leq y^j \leq \overline{y}_+^j
\end{cases}
\tag{3.13}
$$

where $y = \sum_j y^j$ is the aggregate production plan, p are producer prices, $\overline{y}$ are rations on output, with upper and lower bounds, and y^j is the set of feasible production plans given the technological options.

The social planner's problem includes a set of signals s and a SWF. The signals can now be explicitly divided into endogenous or control variables and a set of fixed parameters $\overline{s}$. The latter will be considered in Section 3.4. The list of endogenous signals for this economy can be expressed as a subset of dimension K of the following variables: $\left(p_i\right),\left(r^h\right),\left(\overline{x}_1^h\right),\left(\overline{y}^j\right),\left(d_j^h\right)$.

The private sector's net excess demand is given by net consumption less net supply:

$$
E\left(s\right) \equiv \sum_h x^h\left(p+t,\overline{x}^h,m^h\right) - \sum_j y^j\left(p,\overline{y}^j\right).
\tag{3.14}
$$

The planner's objective function is an indirect function of exogenous and endogenous signals and is indicated by:

$$
V\left(s\right) = V\left(\ldots,V^h\left(q,\overline{x}^h,m^h\right),\ldots\right),
\tag{3.15}
$$

where $V(s)$ is determined by indirect utilities $V^h(s)$, without loss of generality, instead of considering $U^h\left(x^h\right)$.

The planning problem (3.2) can now be restated, ignoring side constraints on signals:

$$
\begin{cases}
\max_s V\left(\ldots,V^h\left(q,\overline{x}^h,m^h\right),\ldots\right) \\
\quad\text{s.t.} \\
\quad x - y - z = 0
\end{cases}
\tag{3.16}
$$

From the first-order conditions (henceforth, FOCs) of this problem, Drèze and Stern (1987, 1990) derive the optimal policy rule or shadow pricing rule for the economy (see Box 3.2 and Appendix 3.1).

Box 3.2 Shadow prices and Lagrangian multipliers

To solve the constrained optimization problem (3.16)

$$\begin{cases} \max_{s} V(s) \\ \text{s.t.} \\ E(s) - z = 0 \end{cases}$$

consider the Lagrangian: $L(s; z; \lambda) \equiv V(s) - \lambda[E(s) - z]$, where $\lambda \equiv (\ldots, \lambda_i, \ldots)$ is a vector of I multipliers. Some signals $s = \bar{s}$ are exogenous and will be ignored here (see Section 3.4). The FOCs for the optimization problem (omitting corner solutions) are:

$$\frac{\partial L}{\partial s} = \frac{\partial V(s)}{\partial s} - \lambda \frac{\partial E(s)}{\partial s} = 0,$$

$$\frac{\partial L}{\partial \lambda} = E(s) - z = 0.$$

Hence, the Lagrange multiplier vector is $\lambda = \dfrac{\partial V(s)}{\partial s}\left[\dfrac{\partial E(s)}{\partial s}\right]^{-1} = \dfrac{\partial L}{\partial z}$.

A small change of z, a project dz, relaxes the related constraint, hence $dV = \lambda dz$. To see that λ_i is the appropriate computation of the shadow price for good i, recall that the definition of shadow price, at the optimum $V(s)$ (see Section 3.2), is $v_i = \dfrac{\partial V}{\partial s}\dfrac{\partial \Phi(z)}{\partial z_i} \forall i$.

As $V(\cdot)$, the objective function, implicitly depends on the production plan z, which is a parameter, consider the maximum SWF $V^*(z) = \max_s V(s; z)$. By definition, this is $V^*(z) = V[s^*(z); z]$ where $s = s^* = \arg\max V(s; z)$, i.e. the optimal environment supporting the arbitrary z plan.

The generalized envelope theorem (where 'generalized' here means that constraints are included; see, e.g., Simon and Blume 1994/2002, Vol. II, Section 9.2) states that under certain properties of the relevant functions:

$$\frac{\partial V^*(z)}{\partial z_i} = \frac{\partial L(s; z)}{\partial z_i}\Big|_{s=s^*(z)} \forall i$$

and $s = 1, \ldots, k, \ldots, K$.

The above-mentioned definition of v_i holds if the optimal policy is selected. This implies:

$$v_i \equiv \frac{\partial V(s)}{\partial s}\frac{\partial \Phi(z)}{\partial z_i} = \frac{\partial V^*(z)}{\partial z_i}.$$

As $\lambda_i = \dfrac{\partial L}{\partial z_i}$, it is true that $\lambda_i = v_i \forall i$. This formal property holds only if the optimization problem is in the (problem 3.2) form. As important remark is that if $s_k \neq s_k^*$ for some $k, v_i = \lambda_i$ is no longer a valid condition for a CBA test of the project dz, as any feasible $dz \geq 0$ would support $dV > 0$ when associated with a small change $dz \geq 0$, as discussed in Section 3.5. When constraints are in the form of a disequality, Kuhn–Tucker multipliers should be considered.

Source: Adapted from Drèze and Stern (1987).

3.4 Policy reforms and shadow prices

The purpose of this section is to show how to use CBA to evaluate policy reforms instead of projects. As mentioned, there are two types of signals: endogenous (s) and exogenous or parameters $\bar{s}$. The main question is what will happen if this parameter changes. The DS approach is to simulate something exogenous as if it was endogenous to see how social welfare could be improved. The underlying assumption is that demand depends separately on s and $\bar{s}$.[16]

The FOC for the constrained planning problem with $V(s; \bar{s})$ leads now to:

$$\frac{\partial V^*}{\partial \bar{s}} = \frac{\partial L}{\partial \bar{s}_k} = \frac{\partial V}{\partial \bar{s}_k} - \lambda \frac{\partial E}{\partial \bar{s}_k} = 0. \tag{3.17}$$

A change in social welfare is again decomposed into two elements:

- the direct impact of the reform on social welfare (e.g. of a previously exogenous tax rate);
- the general equilibrium impact on net private demand evaluated with shadow prices.

It is clear that $dV = 0$ at the optimum as the social benefit of the reform equals its social cost. As an illustration, consider the case of the abolition of a local property tax. This reform increases the first term (social benefit) and also increases the second (social cost). If $E(\cdot) = x - y$ increases, additional resources in the economy are being consumed, and this represents a cost for the whole economy. Additional inputs are then needed: there is an opportunity cost, which can be evaluated through shadow prices. The direct effect is captured by the first term (benefit less property taxes) since prices affect indirect utilities in the SWF: $V^h = V^h(p + t, m)$ and t decreases. Therefore, the direct effect is a positive welfare benefit. The other effect is represented by a welfare cost: in order to sustain the positive welfare effect, the economy must consume additional resources.

To further illustrate the evaluation of a reform, we can consider the case of a poor country and the effect of softening a consumption tax on rice (see Box 3.3).

In general, the marginal social value (MSV) of any change in the signals can be decomposed into:

- a direct benefit;
- a social cost (since we are consuming scarce resources, there is an opportunity cost).

Box 3.3 Illustrative case

The world price of rice (p) can be considered as exogenous or predetermined by the global market. If the government decides to decrease the tax rate t_i on rice, the price paid by consumers decreases as $p + t = q$. Given the marginal value of income, then $\dfrac{\partial V(\cdot)}{\partial q_i}$ can be estimated through Roy's identity, which states that the Marshallian demand $x(\cdot)$ of a good at the optimum is given by taking the ratio of the marginal utility of price to the marginal utility of income. The individual's benefit is captured by this effect.

To match this change, there will be an increase in private demand for rice. To meet the scarcity constraint $E(s) - z = 0$, in general equilibrium (possibly with rationing somewhere), the government must cut its provision of some other goods. There is now less government revenue, and to match budgetary constraints (see Walras's Law in Chapter 2), hence it is possible that some public production must be cut (maybe healthcare). The general equilibrium effect on all the vectors of consumption is given by this second term: $-\lambda \dfrac{\partial E}{\partial t_i}$.

At the optimum, the reform is carried on until the point where the social cost equals the social benefit of reducing taxation. Hence, DS defines $\dfrac{\partial L(\cdot)}{\partial t_i}$ as the marginal social value of implementing a tax reform on good i.

Source: Authors.

Why does computing the shadow prices of goods and selecting the optimal policies amount to the same conceptual mechanism in the DS setting?

Consider again the shadow prices and FOC for the following problem (a restatement of the system of equations 3.16):

$$
\begin{cases}
\max_{s_k} W = W\left(\ldots, V^h\left(q_i, \bar{x}_i^h, m^h\right), \ldots\right) \forall k, \forall h, \forall i \\
\text{s.t.} \\
\sum_h x^h\left(q, \bar{x}^h, m^h\right) - \sum_j y^j\left(p, \bar{y}^j\right) - z = 0
\end{cases}
\tag{3.18}
$$

The Lagrangian is:

$$
L = W\left[V^h\left(q, \bar{x}^h, m^h\right)\right] - \lambda\left[\sum_h x^h\left(q, \bar{x}^h, m^h\right) - \sum_j y^j\left(p, \bar{y}^j\right) - z\right]
\tag{3.19}
$$

with

$$\text{MSV}_{s_k} \equiv \frac{\partial L}{\partial s_k}. \tag{3.20}$$

The relationship between the MSV of signals and shadow prices is now apparent. Consider the example of lump-sum transfers (for instance, subsidies to disabled citizens) and remember that:

$$m^h \equiv r^h + \sum_j d_j^h \Pi^j. \tag{3.21}$$

The first derivative of the above Lagrangian (3.19) with respect to r^h is:

$$\text{MSV}_{r^h} \equiv \frac{\partial L}{\partial r^h} = \frac{\partial W}{\partial V^h} \frac{\partial V^h}{\partial m^h} \frac{\partial m^h}{\partial r^h} - \nu \left(\frac{\partial x^h}{\partial m^h} \frac{\partial m^h}{\partial r^h} \right). \tag{3.22}$$

Note that $\dfrac{\partial m^h}{\partial m^h} = 1$ by the definition of m as for (3.21). Thus, simply, the FOC would be:

$$\text{MSV}_{r^h} = \beta^h - \nu \frac{\partial x^h}{\partial m^h} = 0, \tag{3.23}$$

where the welfare weights (see Chapter 1) are:

$$\beta^h \equiv \frac{\partial W}{\partial V^h} \frac{\partial V^h}{\partial m^h} \tag{3.24}$$

and, at the optimum, this equality holds from (3.23):

$$\beta^h = \nu_1 \frac{\partial x_1^h}{\partial m^h} + \nu_2 \frac{\partial x_2^h}{\partial m^h} + \cdots + \nu_I \frac{\partial x_I^h}{\partial m^h} \; \forall h. \tag{3.25}$$

Here, β^h is the welfare weight (see Chapter 7), or the social marginal utility of h's income, and the vector $\nu \dfrac{\partial x^h}{\partial m^h}$ is the social cost of h's additional consumption due to the increase in income (the inner product of two vectors of dimension I).

At the optimum, the MSV of any signal should be zero for optimal policies. Then, by the previous equation and the system of all equations solving (3.18), you can compute the complete vector of shadow prices of consumption goods x. Some of the DS results for other MSVs are shown in Appendix 3.1.

If the government has different signals under its control, social welfare optimization implies the simultaneous solution of a set of equations such that MSV = 0 for all these instruments, and the obtained shadow prices must be the solution vector of such a system. In this perspective, getting the solutions in terms of shadow prices of goods or in terms of policy instruments (i.e. signals under the control of the planner), implies solving the same problem. Drèze and Stern (1990) also show that the welfare calculations can be done equivalently in terms of a shadow revenue, i.e. government revenue at shadow prices. At an optimum, the marginal change in shadow revenue and that of social welfare sum exactly to zero.

Conversely, if the government does not pick up the optimal policies, the shadow prices will be the 'wrong' ones, an issue often overlooked in partial equilibrium CBA.[17] Obviously, when the government has no choice $(I = K)$, it is optimizing in a trivial sense. But when there is a choice and the wrong policy reform is selected, this will distort the shadow prices and cost-benefit analysis.

3.5 Multi-government setting[18]

The abstract setting discussed above is now turned into a more realistic and inform alone. In this way, we can also summarize some elements of the previous discussion and introduce some practical issues that will be tackled in the next chapters. The considered economy includes six types of agents: individuals, private and public firms, regional (or local) governments, national governments, and one supra-national planner such as the European Commission (EC) or the United States (US) Federal Government.

These agents have preferences and react to observable signals, such as prices, taxes, and rations. Some of these signals are under the control of the regional government, others under the control of different levels of government; others are exogenous for all planners. For example, for a small open economy, some prices are given from international markets, and governments cannot change them (even if they can add taxes or subsidies on internationally traded goods).

Decentralization in this context means that each level of government computes its own set of shadow prices on the basis of its own preferences and constraints and uses them to evaluate changes in the state of the world. A public production project, for example, is the instruction given to a public enterprise to increase the supply of a certain service. A tax reform is a change in the rate of taxation on a production factor or consumption. A regulatory change is often a change in a ration, e.g. the admissible pollution rate in a production process, and so on.

What follows is a non-technical and highly selective adaptation of the DS framework to a multi-government setting. The economy, as mentioned above, is described explicitly as an array of governments and other social actors, plus a supra-national body. Thus, there are different planners.

Let us focus on governments, i.e. social planners. They are like a set of institutions with specific SWFs embodying the objective of their government level. The SWF includes individual (direct or indirect) utility but in principle could also include other non-welfaristic variables, such as specific merit goods. In this very broad meaning, each government is a welfare optimizer and budget constrained.

This multi-government setting is particularly interesting because it is more realistic than the earlier framework for planning in the Barone–Lange–Taylor tradition (Stiglitz 1994), where there is just one social planner. In that traditional framework, the planner has all the relevant information and powers, including the power to set *ad personam* optimal lump-sum taxation. In principle, it can either implement a command economy based on full control of quantities of inputs and outputs or decentralize the same Pareto-efficient equilibrium through a complete set of shadow prices and then let the agent react to those signals.[19]

With multiple governments, it may be the case that each of them has some powers, but not all, on the same areas of the economy. Regional governments, for example, may levy some types of taxes (e.g. some taxes on land) but not others (e.g. Value Added

Tax). They may be in charge of the provision of some services, e.g. health, while other services are beyond their competencies, e.g. defence.

Thus, the regional government may wish to pursue a production plan or a marginal change of it (i.e. a public sector project) for the public provision of certain services. To do so, it needs to disturb the economy, e.g. raise taxes on land use or hire workers in urban waste management, etc. This relationship between the public provision of services and the signals under the control of the planner is a policy function in the above-mentioned DS definition.

Regional or local governments, in some cases, may have only one policy option.

National governments usually have a wider policy opportunity set than regional ones, but not necessarily a wider production plan. For instance, some countries have widely decentralized the provision of education, health, transport, environment, and other functions to regional governments while retaining larger tax powers. As a result, a system of transfers is needed to finance the public provision of services at the regional level.

The supra-national social planner is now introduced. This planner, similarly to the national and regional governments, has a SWF, a budget constraint and side constraints. Around the world, there are several supranational organizations that have a quasi-governmental status, but the interest here is particularly on the European Commission.[20]

In this context, as in the previous discussion, planning has three different dimensions that may arise in each government layer: determination of the production plan, policy selection, and calculation of shadow prices.

First, regions and Member States need to establish their production plans, each for its own competencies. A production plan here refers to the quantity of the service to be provided by firms under the control of the government (publicly owned, private, or public–private partnership). Examples are the quantity of urban public transport or waste collection per year or water supply of a given quality. At any point in time, such a production plan exists and can be observed.

The next step is policy selection. As there is a function that associates a new production plan with a vector of signals under the control of the planner, there may be more than one option open to the government. A significant advantage of the DS framework is that policy optimization implies exactly the same evaluation process of determining shadow prices. The intuition is simple. If the planner has to finance a production plan, it will select the combination of taxes, rations, prices, etc., under its control with the most favourable social impact. If some of these variables are out of control (exogenous parameters), the study of reforms can be pursued with a similar approach, as stated in Section 3.4.

The third area of planning is the calculation of shadow prices. These have been defined in Section 3.2 as the social opportunity cost of a marginal increase in the provision of one good in the public production plan. Thus, there are as many shadow prices as the dimension of the vector of goods and their inputs (which are negative supplies).

In an ideal world, the planner determines the optimal production plan (e.g. the needed stock of highways) and selects the optimal feasible policy to sustain this plan (e.g. taxes on fuel); then it computes the shadow price of the highway service, which may be different from the observed toll of zero, or free access to the highway. However, as mentioned, the production plan cannot be optimal, but still, we assume the social planner is benevolent, meaning that it does not select sub-optimal policies or projects to get a personal benefit.

After the planning is settled, that social cost-benefit analysis, or project evaluation plays its role. A new highway project is proposed in the region. A policy for financing highways should be decided at the appropriate government level. Then, it is necessary to evaluate whether that new highway is a welfare improving project compared with the do-nothing alternative, i.e. to stay with the existing stock of highways. To do so, one can either explicitly measure the net social welfare impact of the increased service (the with-without change of the world, usually a difficult task), or use the shadow prices.

There is one shadow price to measure the output of the service (something like the equivalent passenger per mile per year), and some shadow prices for the inputs, such as labour and land. All that one needs to do is to use these shadow prices in the accounting for the project (including the consideration of any externality) and use the most straightforward benefit-cost test: if the highway project is profitable at shadow prices, it means that it increases the social welfare exactly by that amount, and the project is approved. If the project has very limited shadow profits or incurs shadow losses (whatever its financial income forecasts), the project is rejected.

What happens in the multi-government setting? In the DS framework, there is no all-powerful government. Each layer of the social planner has limited powers but is assumed to be consistent in planning and evaluation. The regional government has its own SWF and transport policy and its own specific constraints in the implementation of a transport plan. It will then evaluate the highway project on the basis of its own set of shadow prices.

In the DS framework, this is the end of the story. Each government unit makes its own project evaluation based on its objectives, policy opportunity set, and constraints, including those constraints arising from decisions of higher-level government.

In the multi-government context, however, the evaluation problem may become nested in different ways. First, one lower level of government may need approval by another level of government, for example, national, and second may ask for supra-national co-financing. There are then three planning and evaluating bodies that must cooperate in some way, and one may think that because they face different objectives, policy mix, and constraints, they will compute different shadow prices for the same good. Is this complex environment leading to intractable problems? This, of course, maybe the case if, for example, two of the three players evaluate the project positively, each on the basis of its own shadow prices, and the third one rejects it because its evaluation is negative. Florio (2007) discusses informally possible compromise solutions, for instance, lexicographic ordering.[21]

In this framework, the roles of planners and evaluators are conceptually quite different. Planners should carefully describe the SWF of the government, the signals available as control variables, the signals outside the area of control, the scarcity, and additional constraints. Then, having set the objective function and all constraints, they will calculate the first-order conditions of the constrained optimization problem. This necessitates calculating the derivative of the Lagrange function of each control variable, i.e. the marginal social value of the control variable, and deriving the shadow price rule by setting the MSV to zero. In practice, shortcuts will be used (see Chapter 4). The planners will then ask the evaluators to use these shadow prices in appraising specific public projects, to perform the cost-benefit test on them, and then to select projects suitable for approval. Interestingly, by doing so, the optimal signal is also picked up. Thus there are two possible interpretations of the optimization process: either the government establishes the optimal signals after having solved the problem and imposes them on the agents. Alternatively, the government manipulates the economy in such a way that a new demand-supply ('market' for short) clearing equilibrium[22] is compatible with the optimal signals.

In the multi-government setting described above, the supra-national, the national and regional governments each hire their own evaluators. The information on shadow prices relevant to each planner is available to all evaluating teams. Thus, if the decision process is nested through mechanisms of co-funding and/or authorization, implemented projects will be only those passing simultaneously or in sequence three CBA tests. In this case, each evaluator needs just to be consistent in using its own shadow prices.

At this stage, let us still suppose that information on estimated shadow prices and CBA evaluations for individual projects is available to all players. Having said this, the use of shadow prices by evaluators is relatively straightforward. Evaluators (and the public firms) are 'price-takers', exactly like firms in a competitive environment. They calculate shadow profits or losses and suggest a decision based on what basically is an accounting job.

Evaluators will typically be interested in a relatively small set of shadow prices:

- the shadow prices of other major inputs and outputs (see Chapter 4);
- the standard conversion factor for internationally traded goods (*ibidem*);
- the marginal cost of public funds or other parameters related to specific distortions (*ibidem*);
- the shadow wage rate, i.e. the social value of labour (see Chapter 5);
- given a *numéraire*, the social discount rate, i.e. the shadow price of such unit of account over time (see Chapter 6);
- welfare weights to account for distribution issues (see Chapter 7).

This needs detailed information on specific market conditions.

Hence, the information needed to implement the DS framework is considerable, and it is not surprising that it has never been fully used in practice. If the model, for example, is framed as a (non) cooperative game involving different levels of governments, the solutions of such a game might be quite different from those arising in the DS frame.[23]

Three major departures from the DS framework can be observed in the real CBA world. First, planners use shortcuts to estimate shadow prices, i.e. they recur to general, simple rules, that in some cases, may be shown to be robust to different planning environments. Drèze and Stern (1987) themselves discuss sympathetically such shortcuts and their relative merits. Chapter 4 deals with some of these rules.

Moreover, planners' and evaluators' roles are often confused, i.e. project evaluators calculate shadow prices, because planners do not provide them with their calculations but with rather general rules. As a result, inconsistent shadow pricing is more probable. The real-world state of the art in evaluation is discussed in Chapter 9.

Third, and most damaging, policies are always sub-optimal in some cases because the quality of government is poor. It has been shown that this distorts all welfare calculations. See Del Bo and Florio (2012) for a discussion on why corruption or capture of policymaking is more dangerous than the corruption of managers and mismanagement of public production.

3.6 Why use shadow prices?

An alternative to shadow prices in estimating the welfare impact of a project or a policy reform is to use a computable general equilibrium (CGE) model of the economy. With this model, in principle, we can observe the state of the world 'before' the change, then alter the situation by introducing the project or a policy into the model, run the model, and simulate the state of the economy 'after the change'. A SWF would translate the before–after scenarios into a welfare change. If the net effect of the 'after–before' change is positive, a CBA test is passed.

This procedure does not involve the estimation of shadow prices. So why estimate accounting prices as possibly imperfect empirical proxies of shadow prices instead of just running a CGE model? There are several reasons, some of them discussed by Stern (1987):

- a good and up-to-date CGE model simply does not exist for many economies;
- the level of disaggregation of these models is often inadequate to deal with specific policies or projects (say, tax on wine or the investment of public enterprise in natural gas);
- policymakers would be interested to know the welfare impact of a change on specific social targets, e.g. households of a certain region or ethnic group;
- a CGE model is usually rather rigid in its implicit or explicit assumptions, whereas social planners need to explore several scenarios of policy reforms and project options.

In contrast, as shown in the following chapters, accounting prices are – albeit imperfect proxies of shadow prices – estimated through relatively simple procedures. In a sense, it is more cost-effective to work having in mind shadow prices than having in mind the intricacies of a CGE, which in some cases is a 'black box' that incorporates a number of assumptions about input-output coefficients, market forms, elasticities of substitution among goods, etc.

The effectiveness comparison between working with shadow prices and with CGE models is obvious when shadow prices are thought to be close to production prices (Diamond and Mirrlees 1971), consumption prices, world prices, long-run marginal costs (at shadow prices), or linear combinations of these observable prices. This is the topic of the next chapter.

3.7 Further reading

The DS setting is best understood as the outcome of the insights of optimal taxation theory (Diamond and Mirrlees 1971; Mirrlees 1976) and the theory of second best and reform (Guesnerie 1995); see Myles (1995), Drèze (1995), and Kaplow (2010). Coady (2006) reviews partial equilibrium, 'limited' general equilibrium and general equilibrium approaches to price reforms. Newbery and Stern (1987) offer several insights on tax reforms in developing countries, evaluated by the CBA theory discussed in this chapter.

On second-best see Hoff (1994). Ahmad *et al.* (1988) give a complete set of estimated shadow prices for a developing country (Pakistan). Johansson (1984) gives an early treatment of CBA under disequilibrium, and Papps (1993) under price controls. Malinvaud and Nabli (1997) discuss the scope and role of government planning in market economies and suggest that there still is a role for it. Van Der Burg (1996) discusses the relationship between CBA and macroeconomic policy.

More recent topics of CBA or use of shadow prices in a general equilibrium setting are mentioned, for example, by Kaplow (1996), Arrow *et al.* (2004), Stern (2011), Coady and Drèze (2002), Schroyen (2010), Swales (2009), Coady and Harris (2004), and Tsuneki (2002). Weymark (2005) extends the seminal idea by Diamond and Mirrlees (1971) that in some cases, producer prices are the appropriate shadow prices for public firms. See also Johansson (2010) for a restatement of CBA and taxation issues.

The literature on Applied Welfare Economics in a general equilibrium setting is relatively less wide than the partial equilibrium approach to CBA. An example of the latter is Just *et al.* (2004), a book that presents a number of variations and applications around the concept of consumer, producer and factor owner surplus (see Willig 1976). The presentation is mostly graphical or based on simple algebra, and the examples often mention agricultural policy in the US. Another good example of CBA presentation is Boardman *et al.* (2018), an excellent book in a partial equilibrium setting. This is not the preferred theoretical approach in this book; in practice, consumer surplus, willingness-to-pay and other notions based on using actual prices instead of shadow prices (or their proxies) are often helpful. See also Boardman *et al.* (2018) for a discussion of this subject and for a concise review of many shadow pricing issues.

An example of a textbook using the general equilibrium approach to Applied Welfare Economics is Jones (2005). Jones, however, uses an approach derived from a Harberger-type CBA, which differs from the DS frame in several ways. The two most important differences are, first, the treatment of policy distortions, that in the conventional Harberger-type CBA are circumvented by assuming that lump-sum transfers are feasible; second, the distributional issues are dealt with in a separate way in this approach, whereas they are included in the DS definition of shadow prices (see Drèze 1998). Jones (2005), however, discusses 'revised' shadow prices, which try to capture the additional welfare fact arising from a second-best policy setting. Londero (2003), Dinwiddy and Teal (1996), and the book edited by Layard and Glaister (1994) are also recommended reading. More recently, a personal selection would include De Rus (2010), Weiss and Potts (2012), the readings (more than 80 collected papers) in three volumes edited by Schmitz and Zerbe (2009), Ray (1984), and Gramlich (1994). The classic book by Little and Mirrlees (1974) is still worth reading. On the difference between partial and general equilibrium evaluations, see Johansson and Kriström (2018). Other CBA texts will be suggested in the next chapters.

3.8 Summary of Chapter 3

- The government, by assumption, wants to maximize social welfare, and there may be different levels of government.
- There are public firms implementing an arbitrary production plan decided by the government (possibly, but not necessarily, optimally).
- Consumers maximize individual welfare, while private firms maximize profits.
- A closed economy is in equilibrium with rationing when the excess demand of the private sector is matched by the net supply of the public sector, and quantity constraints, resource constraints and any additional constraints are met.

- The shadow price is defined as the change of social welfare around the optimum of the unit increase of supply of one good.
- Given some parameters, including the production plan of the public sector, prices, taxes, rations and any signal influencing the agent's behaviour must be optimally selected by the government to achieve the maximum social welfare.
- Project evaluation is based on a simple CBA test: any project that makes a profit at shadow prices should be accepted because it increases social welfare.
- The same applies to reforms (of taxes, subsidies, etc.): any change that increases social welfare should be approved, and at the optimum, no further change is desirable.
- Under certain conditions, shadow prices can be computed as Lagrange multipliers of a constrained planning problem.
- In a multi-government setting, each government should determine its SWF, production plans, optimal policies and shadow prices. If different layers of government cooperate, compromise solutions should be found, as the shadow prices for evaluating projects and reforms may or may not converge.

End chapter questions

1 What are the main characteristics of the DS model, and how does it differ from the AD model?
2 What are shadow prices? Please describe the main caveats in their estimation. Under which conditions, shadow prices can be computed as Lagrange multipliers of a constrained planning problem?
3 Please describe how a dependent social planner operates within a multilevel government, determines a production plan, selects a policy, and calculates shadow prices.
4 What is a cost-benefit analysis test?
5 Why is it often advisable to use accounting prices as imperfect empirical proxies of shadow prices instead of running a computable general equilibrium model?

Appendix 3.1

Some results from Drèze and Stern (1987)[24]

Some of the DS results relating to the MSV of selected signals are reported below, with some brief explanations. The following DS results are considered: prices, indirect taxes, change in production constraint. All of them are derived by the FOC of problem 3.18. The details are in Drèze and Stern (1987).

Marginal social value of producer prices

If the government can set producer prices, or equivalently if prices are endogenous and such as to clear markets, the FOC of 3.19, using the equality of shadow prices and Lagrange multipliers (by the envelope theorem), is:

$$
\begin{aligned}
\text{MSV}_{p_i} = \sum_h & \left(\frac{\partial W}{\partial V^h} \frac{\partial V^h}{\partial q_i} \frac{\partial q_i}{\partial p_i} + \frac{\partial W}{\partial V^h} \frac{\partial V^h}{\partial m^h} \sum_j d_j^h \frac{\partial \Pi^j}{\partial p_i} \right) \\
& - v \sum_h \left(\frac{\partial x^h}{\partial q_i} \frac{\partial q_i}{\partial p_i} + \frac{\partial x^h}{\partial m^h} \sum_j d_j^h \frac{\partial \Pi^j}{\partial p_i} \right) - \sum_j \left(\frac{\partial y^j}{\partial p_i} \right).
\end{aligned}
\tag{A3.1}
$$

As $q = p + t$ and $\dfrac{\partial q}{\partial p} = 1$, after rearranging:

$$
\begin{aligned}
\text{MSV}_{p_i} = & \sum_h \frac{\partial W}{\partial V^h} \frac{\partial V^h}{\partial q_i} + v \sum_j \frac{\partial y^j}{\partial p_i} - v \sum_h \frac{\partial x^h}{\partial q_i} + \\
& \sum_h \sum_j \left[\left(\frac{\partial W}{\partial V^h} \frac{\partial V^h}{\partial m^h} - v \frac{\partial x^h}{\partial m^h} \right) d_j^h \frac{\partial \Pi^j}{\partial p_i} \right].
\end{aligned}
\tag{A3.2}
$$

Using Roy's identity (which states that the Marshallian demand of a good at the optimum is given by taking the ratio of the marginal utility of price to the marginal utility of income)

$$
x^h(p,m) = - \frac{\dfrac{\partial V^h(p,m)}{\partial q_i}}{\dfrac{\partial V^h(p,m)}{\partial m^h}},
\tag{A3.3}
$$

it follows that:

$$\frac{\partial V^h}{\partial q_i} = -x^h \frac{\partial V^h}{\partial m^h}. \tag{A3.4}$$

Moreover, the definition of $b^h = \beta^h - v \dfrac{\partial x^h}{\partial m^h}$ (see equations 3.23 and 3.24), where

$\beta^h \equiv \dfrac{\partial W}{\partial V^h} \dfrac{\partial V^h}{\partial m^h}$, is used to obtain:

$$\text{MSV}_{p_i} = -\sum_h \frac{\partial W}{\partial V^h} \frac{\partial V^h}{\partial m^h} x_i^h + v \sum_j \frac{\partial y^j}{\partial p_i} - v \sum_h \frac{\partial x^h}{\partial q_i} + \sum_h \sum_j \left(b^h d_j^h \frac{\partial \Pi^j}{\partial p_i} \right). \tag{A3.5}$$

This explains the DS result (Drèze and Stern 1987, equation 2.63, page 945):

$$\text{MSV}_{p_i} = -\sum_h \beta^h x_i^h - v \left(\frac{\partial x}{\partial q_i} - \frac{\partial y}{\partial p_i} \right) + \sum_h \sum_j \left(b^h d_j^h \frac{\partial \Pi^j}{\partial p_i} \right) = 0. \tag{A3.6}$$

Recalling the vector definition of x and y and rearranging:

$$v = \left[\sum_h \sum_j \left(b^h d_j^h \frac{\partial \Pi^j}{\partial p} \right) - \sum_h \beta^h x^h \right] \left(\frac{\partial x}{\partial q_i} - \frac{\partial y}{\partial p_i} \right)^{-1}. \tag{A3.7}$$

This is a system of I equations with I unknown variables: $v = (v_1, \ldots, v_i, \ldots, v_I)$; see also Box 3.2. In an empirical perspective, to compute the vector of shadow prices v, after setting the MSV at zero, in principle, all the other terms are observable, given some SWF parameters. The first term on the right-hand side is the social value of profits change (across all firms and shareholders and goods), the second term in parentheses is the social value for consumers of changes in producer prices, while the last term is the net effect of consumption and production responses to price change, i.e. the social cost of meeting the additional consumption (signs are to be determined for price increases and decreases). It can be shown (DS, page 946) that the shadow price of each good will be higher when its distributive impact is high (also taking into account complementary and substitute goods). In other words, the marginal social benefit of producing a good that is mainly consumed by the poor and produced by the rich is higher than the other way round.

Marginal social value of commodity taxes

The government can select optimal taxes as policy instruments, or taxes are endogenous. The FOC of 3.19 is:

$$\text{MSV}_{t_i} = \sum_h \left(\frac{\partial W}{\partial V^h} \frac{\partial V^h}{\partial q_i} \frac{\partial q_i}{\partial t_i} \right) - v \sum_h \left(\frac{\partial x^h}{\partial q_i} \frac{\partial q_i}{\partial t_i} \right). \tag{A3.8}$$

Note that $\dfrac{\partial q_i}{\partial t_i} = 1$. Moreover, using Roy's identity to substitute $\dfrac{\partial V^h}{\partial q_i}$, then:

$$\text{MSV}_{t_i} = -\sum_h \left(\frac{\partial W}{\partial V^h} \frac{\partial V^h}{\partial m^h} x^h \right) - v \sum_h \left(\frac{\partial x^h}{\partial q_i} \right), \tag{A3.9}$$

$$\text{MSV}_{t_i} = -\sum_h \beta^h x^h - v \frac{\partial x}{\partial q_i},$$

and hence, setting MSV to zero,

$$v = -\left(\sum_h \beta^h x^h \right) \left(\frac{\partial x}{\partial q_i} \right)^{-1}. \tag{A3.10}$$

It follows, given the DS framework, that $\text{MSV}_{t_i} = \text{MSV}_{p_i} = 0$ (i.e. the shadow prices are the common solution of the two systems of equations), which implies the following important result (building on earlier Diamond–Mirrlees results):

> Thus, in this model, when both p_i and t_i are control variables (e.g. the ith commodity is optimally taxed, and exchanged at a market-clearing price) and unrestricted, the shadow price of the ith good reduces to its marginal social cost (suitably averaged over firms), corrected by a distributional term: the latter follows a simple inverse-elasticity rule, and vanishes if profits are fully or optimally taxed.
>
> (Drèze and Stern 1987: 951)

Marginal social value of a production constraint

$$\text{MSV}_{\overline{y}_i^j} = \sum_h \left(\frac{\partial W}{\partial V^h} \frac{\partial V^h}{\partial m^h} d_j^h \frac{\partial \Pi^j}{\partial \overline{y}_i^j} \right) - v \left(\sum_h \frac{\partial x^h}{\partial m^h} d_j^h \frac{\partial \Pi^j}{\partial \overline{y}_i^j} - \frac{\partial y^j}{\partial \overline{y}_i^j} \right). \tag{A3.11}$$

Rearranging, and setting to zero:

$$\sum_h \left[\left(\beta^h - v \frac{\partial x^h}{\partial m^h} \right) d_j^h \frac{\partial \Pi^j}{\partial \overline{y}_i^j} \right] + v \left(\frac{\partial y^j}{\partial \overline{y}_i^j} \right) = 0. \tag{A3.12}$$

Finally, using the definition of b^h,

$$v = -\sum_h \left(\beta^h d_j^h \frac{\partial \Pi^j}{\partial \overline{y}_i^j} \right) \left(\frac{\partial y^j}{\partial \overline{y}_i^j} \right)^{-1}. \tag{A3.13}$$

Notes

1 The chapter draws from Drèze and Stern (1990), Stern (1990), Drèze (1998), Coady and Drèze (2002). For Section 3.5 it also draws from Florio (2007) and Del Bo and Florio (2012).

2 A marginal policy or project does not change the underlying growth rate of the economy.

3 See Chapter 4 for foreign trade.

4 Having, for example, more publicly provided transport would meet the excess demand of transport and thus influence individual welfare, including effects on markets other than transport.

5 This would imply changing just one item zj, with all the others at zero change. In general, however, some public sector inputs will change along with the output.

6 For second-order conditions, see, for example, Simon and Blume (1994/2002), Vol. 2, Section 9.3.

7 All functions are supposed to be continuously differentiable and well-behaved.

8 The optimal production plan z* is the solution of:
$$\begin{cases} \max\limits \\ zV*(z) \\ \text{s.t.} \\ z \in Z \end{cases}$$
assuming convexity of $z : v * z* = \max\limits_{z \in Z} v * z$, where shadow prices are $v* = \partial V*/\partial z$ at z*.

9 See Section 3.5 for a discussion of policy optimization.

10 There are as many shadow prices as the dimension of the vector of goods (tangibles and intangibles) provided by the private and public sector and their inputs (which are negative supplies).

11 Lower case vi is used to avoid confusion; the meaning is that of a first derivative of V.

12 Local governments in some cases may have only one policy option: for example, the only way to increase the provision of some transport services may be through a tariff such that the firm has a balanced budget (the Boiteux case). This is a very simple planning situation. When there is just one policy option, the matrix ø(z) collapses to a vector coincident with s, e.g. only one set of public tariffs, indirect taxes and rations etc. can support the production plan z.

13 In this case a marginal change of z is functionally linked to a marginal change of s, and the government has no freedom to pick up a policy from a menu.

14 The analogy with the example in Section 3.1 is simple: if GDP is the SWF and actual prices capture the general equilibrium effects, a project that increases GDP is socially beneficial, whoever gets the additional income.

15 Thus, it is outside both the Walras–Pareto and the Barone–Lange–Taylor settings.

16 If this does not hold, the story becomes more complex, and this will not be discussed here. Drèze and Stern discuss side constraints such that these relations arise. Side constraints involve additional terms in the Lagrange function, i.e. additional Lagrange multipliers.

17 The idea that an optimal policy function is needed to properly define shadow prices has received limited attention in the CBA literature. In discussing some conditions that may justify the role of public enterprises, Del Bo and Florio (2012) argue that public provision is socially beneficial (thus passing a social cost-benefit test at shadow prices) under a benevolent government and symmetric information, or, as an alternative, even when the social planner is not fully benevolent but is such that it cannot profit from policy design. On the contrary, when the government is not (fully) benevolent and information is asymmetric, sub-optimal policy adoption may also lead to inconsistency in project selection.

18 A wider discussion on multi-government setting is in Florio (2007).

19 This point was taken, for example, by Maurice Dobb (1955) in his theory of market socialism. See Coco and Fedeli (2014) for a discussion of market socialism.

20 The EC is however only one part of the EU architecture, which includes the European Council, the various Councils of Ministries, the European Parliament and some EU judiciary institutions and consultative bodies, including one representing the regions (the Regions Committee).

21 The interplay of planners can be modelled, for example, through a bottom-up lexicographic approach. This means that when co-funding or licensing decisions involve different planners, selected projects are those that are mutually compatible, i.e. simultaneously passing a CBA test. Hence, the regional planner will select its policies and compute shadow prices, and will propose to national or supra-national planners only those projects that will pass its cost-benefit tests.

22 In fact, as there are possibly binding rations, the equilibrium is not of the Walrasian type described in Chapter 2.
23 This remark is due to Per-Olov Johansson, in private correspondence with the author. It may also be the case that some of the Arrow impossibility theorems apply to this context, and this explains why in practice decentralized government planning needs some convergence mechanisms, e.g. semi-structured hierarchy.
24 This appendix is by Massimo Florio, Elisa Borghi, and Chiara Del Bo.

Part Two

Empirics

4 The social cost of goods

Overview[1]

This chapter moves from the abstract framework of Chapter 3 to a more applied setting. The chapter describes how financial costs and revenues and social costs and benefits can be assessed through a financial and economic analysis respectively. Figure 4.1 describes the different steps for carrying out a project evaluation. The important relationship between financial performance, financial sustainability, and economic performance is analyzed in Section 4.1 by discussing and justifying the necessity to consider observed prices as a first step in the assessment of the economic value of a project. The chapter then illustrates the steps that have to be taken to move from financial performance results to economic performance estimates (Section 4.2) and presents, in an empirical perspective, the approaches typically used to proxy shadow prices in real-world economies. An overview of the ideas and approaches for accounting price calculation and a taxonomy of the goods for which accounting prices are estimated (distinguishing between tradable and non-tradable, minor and major, inputs and outputs) are given in Section 4.3, while further analysis is made in the following sections. In particular:

- Section 4.4 deals with the Little–Mirrlees method of using border prices as proxies of shadow prices of traded and tradable goods;
- in Section 4.5, two alternative methods for the valuation of minor non-traded and non-tradable goods are discussed, namely the standard conversion factor and the shadow exchange rate;
- Section 4.6 explains the long-run marginal cost approach used for major non-tradable project inputs; and
- finally, Section 4.7 depicts different empirical approaches to the estimation of the willingness-to-pay.

The shadow price of labour and the shadow price of capital and public funds are discussed respectively in Chapters 5 and 6.

Most of the chapter will maintain a practical perspective, with the support of several examples illustrating empirical applications of the analyzed methodologies. The concluding section (4.8) suggests a list for further reading. Appendix 4.1 at the end of the chapter illustrates how to compute the financial performance indicators, while Appendix 4.2 provides numerical and simplified examples of financial and economic analysis, to show how rules and notions discussed in these sections apply in practice.

DOI: 10.4324/9781003191377-6

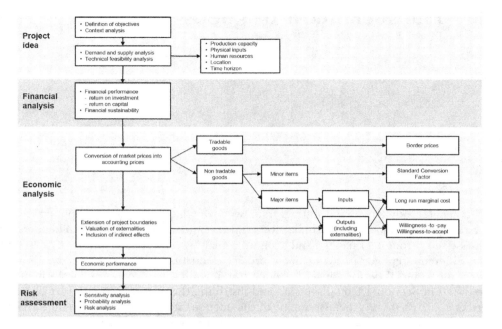

Figure 4.1 Structure of project evaluation.
Source: Authors' elaboration, based on Saerbeck (1990), Florio (2003) and European Commission (2014).

4.1 Observed prices and financial analysis

As is illustrated in Figure 4.1, the necessary condition to carry out a cost-benefit analysis is to have an already well-defined, even if preliminary, project idea, which will serve as the unit of analysis of the CBA exercise. This should clearly identify the content of the investment, including all its essential features and components, its objectives, i.e. the (net) benefits that can be attained by the project, and the social, political, institutional, and economic context in which the investment is integrated. On this basis, the current and forecast demand of the project can be analyzed and quantified. The purpose is to make a hypothesis on the demand quantities that the project could presumably capture, which could then be compared with an analysis of the current and future supply and validated through a technical feasibility analysis showing the available technological options. This information is essential to determine the project's productive capacity size, its location, the physical inputs, and personnel required and, subsequently, to estimate the investment and maintenance cost of the intervention, the future operating costs, as well as possible revenues.

Data provided by the demand and technical feasibility analyses are collected and organized in the financial analysis, in which monetary values based on observed prices are attached to each outflow and inflow item of the project. The timeframe of expected costs and revenues involved in the project's implementation, and thus the number of years for which inflows and outflows are forecast, depends on the expected economic life of the project. The financial analysis is preparatory to the economic analysis, in which financial flows measured at observed prices are converted into economic flows at accounting/shadow prices.

Besides identifying the monetary flows generated by an investment and providing the data for building up the tables of economic analysis (as explained in Section 4.2), there are other reasons for considering the financial analysis as a necessary step in the appraisal of an investment's performance. By assessing the financial performance, through the calculation of the financial return on the whole investment or on capital, and financial sustainability, the financial analysis allows one to determine whether the investment project (or policy) is able to generate a sufficient inflow to cover the outflows, or, conversely, if it runs a risk of liquidity and insolvency. Maintaining a positive cash flow during the whole project's time horizon is deemed important for both private and public investments to be successfully implemented and produce their effects.

Even when public sector projects are not specifically intended to earn income, the financial sources of income and revenues and the expected costs have to be accurately forecast so as to guarantee the best timing of cash proceeds and payments and the efficiency of the project/policy financial administration. The erroneous prediction of costs or revenues may cause budgetary imbalances, which, in turn, provoke destructive consequences on the investment implementation. For instance, a not-for-profit business incubator centre, for which operating revenues are not enough to cover the operating cost and recover the initial investment, may at a certain moment have to stop providing its services to enterprises, unless other sources of financing are found. As another example, a hospital which does not receive enough public and private contributions to sustain its construction is unlikely to be completed and start operations on time. Hence, financial and economic performance is directly related, since the former affects the possibility of the project to generate effects of a socio-economic nature.

For this reason, any analyst interested in evaluating the impact of a certain project on economic welfare usually starts by verifying that the project is feasible from a financial standpoint. As a general rule, if the project or programme foresees any type of financial revenues (tariffs, fees, sale of products and services, etc.), these should at least cover the operation outflows. If no inflows can be expected, or these are not enough to cover operating costs, financial analysis should be accompanied by a financial plan envisaging any source of financing that will allow one to cover the outflows.[2]

Finally, the financial analysis is a valuable instrument to set the 'right' volume of public grant to be committed to a welfare-improving project. By analyzing the balance between sources of financing, operating revenues and outflows, the governmental decision about whether investing public funds in the project and how much to allocate can be taken on the basis of the investment's financial profitability and the private profitability after the public grant. It is often preferred by government agencies that the former results are negative, and the latter moderately positive: this would give the project's owner a proper incentive to invest, without incurring the risk of generating undue private benefits.[3]

In practice, for the determination of the project's financial performance, the financial analysis may consist of the calculation of (i) the financial return on investment, (ii) the financial return on capital and (iii) financial sustainability. Unlike standard company accounting, the financial analysis does not apply the accrual basis of accounting but the cash method. Inflows and outflows are not considered when revenues are earned and expenses incurred, even without any payment actually being made, but only when they effectively occur, i.e. when revenues are received and expenses paid.[4]

Another fundamental rule is to calculate the financial (but also economic) return according to the 'incremental' method, meaning that the differences in the outflows and inflows referred to the project under assessment and a counterfactual without-the-project situation have to be considered. This approach allows one to evaluate the net revenues and benefits accrued by the sole project, after considering those that would have been produced even if the project was not implemented (see more details in Box 4.1). Appendix 4.1 discusses more extensively how to measure financial performance and sustainability.

While the practice of assessing the financial performance and sustainability of an investment is more common for physical investment projects, in principle proper financial analysis could also be carried out for policy reforms. As an illustrative example, public subsidies allocated by a public agency, or by financial intermediaries on behalf of it, to stimulate an increase of enterprises' investment can be considered in fact as financial cash outflows, and additional tax revenues raised from new business investments and profits would represent financial inflows. On the basis of these data, the financial profitability of the investment could be estimated. When all financial sources are considered,

---

Box 4.1 The incremental nature of the cost-benefit analysis

When assessing the total effect of a project on the state of the economy, the economy 'with' the project often needs to be compared with the economy 'without' it. This rule aims at ensuring that only the effects produced by a project are evaluated, net of those that would have been generated even without the project implementation. See, however, Section 3.6.

In practice, both financial profitability and economic analyses are carried out in two situations/scenarios: in the project, and in the without-the-project situation. In the former one, investment costs sustained to implement the new project, the operating costs and revenues related to the project and any external cost or benefit valued in monetary terms are considered. In the latter, financial investment management cost as well as revenues and other inflows related to works that have to be made in any case in order to maintain the existent structure at the current efficiency levels, are described and quantified on the basis of the demand-supply analysis.

When there is a pre-existing infrastructure or economic activity in which the project takes place, the without-the-project scenario includes actual flows of the business-as-usual (BAU) or do-minimum situation. Under the BAU scenario the current financial and economic flows are assumed to remain the same in the future. Under the do-minimum scenario, instead, an assumption is made on the future evolution of current trends, by considering small adaptation investments that will be needed in order to maintain the project's functionality and/or avoid serious deterioration and/or comply with legal standards and rules.[5] On the other hand, when the project takes place in a context with no pre-existing infrastructure or economic activity (as it is in the case of greenfield investments), the incremental scenario coincides with the with-the-project situation, since the counterfactual has cash flows equal to zero.

Finally, the balance with-without the project situation is computed, so as to analyze the present value of the net cash flow of the inflows and outflows additionally generated by the project.

Source: Authors.

including any transfer from other public administrations, the policy's financial sustainability could also be assessed. Policies to support human capital or research can also be dealt with.

4.2 Accounting prices and economic analysis

As presented, the financial analysis is focused on ascertaining net cash flows which are produced by an investment project (return on investment) or by injecting a certain amount of capital in the project (return on capital) and on estimating their net present value. On the other hand, the economic analysis is focused on showing the project's contribution to economic welfare, on a regional, national or even wider level. In general terms, while the perspective of the investor and private entrepreneur is limited to the results of the financial analysis, the economic analysis is an exercise usually implemented for public investments, or for private investments that apply for public financing.

When implementing an economic analysis, the perspective moves from monetary flows gathered from observed prices to the social CBA framework, in which shadow prices represent the relevant prices for determining the project's welfare impact on public investment decisions. Actually, these prices are defined precisely to capture the net costs and benefits of increases or decreases in public supplies. The return on the investment valued through shadow prices may differ even significantly from financial profitability estimated at market prices. This depends on the degree of distortion in the economy, which drives a wedge between market and shadow prices. The main reasons for price distortions are duties and quotas, private monopoly (leading to market prices higher than the marginal cost), public monopoly (market prices being lower or higher[6] than marginal costs), regulated tariffs and externalities.

As shown in Figure 4.1, the economic analysis can be considered as composed of three steps: the conversion of market prices into accounting prices, the extension of project boundaries to include externalities and indirect effects, and the assessment of economic performance. They are presented in the following paragraphs.

4.2.1 *Conversion of market prices to shadow prices*

For the purpose of financial analysis, market prices represent a relevant signal for the investor when assessing the project's financial performance, even when the investor is a public sector agent. However, they may be no longer relevant when the aim is to assess the project's contribution to economic welfare. Hence, the starting point for evaluating the project's welfare effect consists in converting all observable inflows and outflows considered when appraising the financial performance into shadow values reflecting the opportunity cost of resources. In particular, the appraiser should consider the financial flows included in the tables for the evaluation of the financial return on investment.

This operation allows one to depurate costs and revenues from any element of distortion generated by taxes and subsidies. The former could be imposed, for example, on real estate, trade, profits and wages; the latter can apply to employment (e.g. subsidies to enterprises hiring women, migrants, or other socially disadvantaged groups) or to production.

As a general rule, the economic price of goods (outputs) should be corrected for all indirect taxes and subsidies. In some cases, the producer prices are considered appropriate proxies of the marginal cost of goods, thus reflecting their opportunity cost better than consumer prices (on the ground of Diamond and Mirrlees 1971). Instead, prices of input factors (such as labour) are usually considered gross of direct taxes, because these actually enter the cost borne by the firms and their total output. In fact, the estimation of the social cost of labour follows specific rules, which are explained in Chapter 5.

It could be justifiable to include indirect taxes and subsidies only when these represent mechanisms to fully 'internalize' certain externalities and thus have an economic value. This is the case, for example, of taxes on CO_2 emissions levied to discourage the generation of pollution, or subsidies to producers of energy from renewable sources, given to encourage the generation of clean energy.

Other possible price distortions are rigid exchange rates, duties on imports and oligopoly price setting. These do not represent signals of the economic value of goods but are driven by different economic or political logics. Correcting for these distortions means identifying the marginal social value of resources, which in the economic analysis are substituted for the prices determined by inefficient markets. Shadow prices could also be set in such a way as to incorporate the government's social distributional preferences. The use of weights to reflect different welfare distributional effects is discussed in Chapter 7.

4.2.2 Extension of project boundaries: externalities and indirect effects

Once all costs and revenues identified in the financial analysis are transformed into accounting values, the second step of the economic analysis consists in including in the appraisal those additional impacts that are relevant for society but have not been considered from the financial perspective. Two types of external impacts can be identified and assessed by the project examiner: (i) positive and negative externalities, and (ii) relevant indirect effects occurring in secondary markets and not included in accounting prices.

Externalities are the effects of production or consumption on third parties not involved in the production and consumption processes and for which there is no compensation. Pollution caused by a factory and hampering the well-being of people living near the factory, without any sort of monetary compensation (even in the form of public taxes or subsidies), is a typical example of negative externality. However, a very large number of possible externalities, both positive and negative, exists, imposing social costs or producing benefits which are not reflected in the private marginal costs of goods. Even though externalities may be easily identified, their valuation can be difficult, particularly when external effects take place in the long run. The most common approach, in practice to assign monetary values to externalities is based on the willingness-to-pay estimation (see Section 4.7).

As for indirect effects, these are defined as quantity or price changes occurring in secondary markets not directly affected by the project or policy. These could be, for instance, an increase in tourism's added value due to the construction of a new motorway improving the region's accessibility, or reduced demand for parking places and petrol because of improved railway transport.

In a partial equilibrium setting, the measurement of indirect effects is fully reflected in the surplus change occurring in the primary market, valued at shadow prices, under the assumption that the secondary markets are not distorted. In these cases, impacts on efficient secondary markets are deemed to be irrelevant and thus should be ignored. Conversely, when secondary markets are distorted by taxes, subsidies, externalities or other factors, and hence their prices do not equal social marginal costs, the use of partial

Box 4.2 Economic effects of externalities

In this book, the theory of externality is not extensively dealt with (see 'Further reading'). However, the way in which externalities disturb the partial equilibrium setting and how this determines a divergence between market prices and social shadow values is briefly recalled here.

Negative or positive externalities respectively impose a social cost or produce a benefit to society which is not captured by the marginal private costs. The figure below illustrates the deadweight loss (triangular area ABC) produced by negative externalities occurring when producing a good. The externality makes the social marginal cost of the good higher than the marginal private cost reflected by the market. The deadweight loss reflects the fact that market prices do not take into account the overall social cost of production so that too much output is produced. As a result, marginal social costs p^* exceed marginal social benefits, as shown by the demand curve and measured by the consumer's marginal willingness-to-pay p for the good.

Similar mechanisms could be highlighted when positive externalities are considered, provided that in this case, the marginal social value of goods would be higher than the marginal private value, or, alternatively, that the marginal social cost would be lower than the private one.

In general equilibrium, change in prices in one market (ξ) are assumed to influence quantities in other markets (σ): $\partial q_\sigma / \partial p_\xi \neq 0$. Thus, the effect on other markets should be considered and included and p^* will change accordingly.

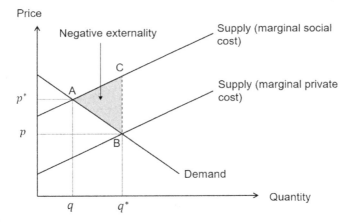

Figure Box 4.2 Social cost of a negative externality.
Source: Authors' elaboration, based on Boardman *et al.* (2018).

equilibrium 'shadow prices' in the primary markets is not enough to capture indirect effects. Boardman *et al.* (2018) maintain that, even though in principle effects occurring in distorted secondary markets should be valued, in practice they can often be neglected on the ground of their limited magnitude. Actually, they argue that to produce significant changes in secondary markets, very large price or quantity changes in the primary market are necessary, which is not the case for most investments.

Even if partial equilibrium assumptions are particularly convenient for the purpose of quantitative analysis, it cannot be neglected that indirect impacts may in fact be significant, generating an impact that could lead to significant variation of social well-being. Just as an example, in the transport infrastructure sector, the following indirect (or wider) economic effects are often produced by an improvement of the transport network: effects on the density of economic activities (agglomeration effect); effects on the labour market, by influencing the participation rate of people; effects on competition; and effects on productivity (DtF 2016).

A general equilibrium framework *à la* Drèze–Stern, through the solution of the maximization problem for the social planner, would allow one to compute shadow prices that incorporate both direct and indirect effects on the economy. Yet the partial equilibrium approach is still largely applied in the practice of economic evaluation of many investments, such as in the transport sector. A partial equilibrium analysis treats the sector of the economy or market or infrastructure of immediate interest as operating in isolation from the rest of the economy, omitting the indirect effects.

In short, to evaluate the economic effects of an investment, additional inflows and outflows have to be added to cost and revenue items considered in the financial analysis and valued at their accounting prices. These must reflect all positive and negative external effects which are not captured by the market (and not already accounted for by shadow prices) and indirect effects produced in secondary markets.

The purpose of valuing all relevant externalities and indirect effects is to estimate the total economic value (TEV) of a project or of a policy. This concept, which was initially used in the environmental economic context (Daily 1997; OECD 1999; Turner 1999), refers to the social value derived from having a natural resource, an infrastructure or a service compared to not having it. The TEV is the sum of two main components: the use value and the non-use value of a good/service; each of them includes subcomponents with their own specificities.

In particular, the use value refers to the social value people have from actually using a good or potentially using it (respectively 'actual' and 'optional' use values). For example, when the willingness-to-pay of a number of households for reducing air pollution in their city is estimated, it is referring to the actual use value for the good 'clean air'. Instead, when valuing the increased quality of life derived from cleaner sea water as perceived by people who could potentially use new bathing beaches, it is referring in fact to the value of potential use of the good 'clean water'.

The non-use value refers to the shadow price of maintaining some goods (such as a waterfall, a park, etc.) in existence, even if currently there is no actual or possible use. Each individual could be assumed to place a value not only on the well-being produced by the good's existence on himself/herself ('existence value'), but also on well-being caused to other individuals by the availability of that good, either in the same generation ('altruism value') or in future generations ('bequest value').

It is worth stressing that all these conceptually different values are usually taken into account not only when identifying and valuing the project's market and non-market effects, but also when calculating specific parameters for the analysis, such as the social discount rate and welfare weights. Actually, as explained in other parts of this book, both these types of parameters could also be set in a such a way as to reflect bequest and altruism values to individuals and society.

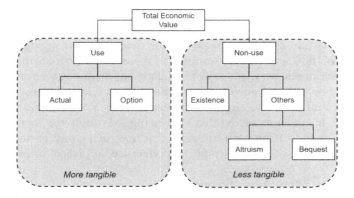

Figure 4.2 The composition of Total Economic Value.
Source: Authors' elaboration of Pearce *et al.* (2006).

4.2.3 Assessing the economic performance

After the correction of price distortions and the inclusion of all possible social effects in the project analysis, the investment's economic performance can be calculated through the use of the following indicators:

- the economic net present value (ENPV), defined as the difference between the discounted total social benefits (including shadow operating revenues, shadow residual value, positive externalities and any positive indirect effects) and costs (shadow investments, shadow operating costs, negative externalities and relevant negative indirect effects);
- the economic internal rate of return (EIRR), which is the social discount rate that produces a zero value for the ENPV;
- the benefit-cost (B/C) ratio, i.e. the ratio between discounted economic benefits and costs.

The formulas for the calculation of the ENPV and EIRR are the same as those applied for the estimation of the financial performance indicators (FNPV and FIRR) and presented in Appendix 4.1, in which monetary flows of costs and revenues and the financial discount rate are substituted by economic flows of costs and benefits and a suitable social discount rate.

Discounting the net cash flow of future years is needed to allow aggregation of flows taking place in different periods. Different methods of discounting exist. Those normally used in the economic analysis are more widely discussed in Chapter 6, while the most commonly used mechanism of discounting is concisely presented in Box 4.3.

A B/C ratio greater than one indicates that a project's benefits are higher than its costs. Like the EIRR, the B/C ratio is independent of the project size, but has the limitation that it could be affected by considering a given flow as either a benefit or a cost reduction.[8]

The highest the economic return is, the largest are the benefits achieved net of costs and negative externalities. An investment project with a negative economic return uses too much of socially valuable resources to achieve too modest benefits for society.

Box 4.3 Discounting the future

The fact that flows take place in different periods of time determines an aggregation issue: can the net cash flow at time t be summed to the net cash flow at time
$t + 1$? Even when constant prices are used, so as to exclude an inflationary effect,
the utility of spending or obtaining 1 euro today is higher than 1 euro tomorrow,
for different reasons: first of all, there might be forecast errors which increase
along with time; second, it can be expected that well-being (or simply the monetary income) is a function increasing with time and that marginal consumption
or utility is decreasing; or again, there may simply be preference for present utility
rather than future.

The aggregation of data referred to different periods of time can be solved
by applying to future inflows and outflows suitable weighting coefficients which
decrease (or discount) the value of flows over time. The most common method
of discounting is to use a coefficient based on the financial or social discount rate
(depending on whether a financial or an economic analysis is implemented) which
exponentially declines with time. The formula for this discount coefficient (d) is d_t
$= (1 + r)^{-t}$, where t is time, ranging between 0 and T (the total number of periods),
and r is the financial or social discount rate (which is generally positive).

If B_t is the balance of inflows and outflows, the net present value of the investment
is obtained as the sum of the series of B_t weighted by the discount coefficients d_t:

$$\text{NPV} = \sum_{t=0}^{n} d_t B_t = \frac{B_0}{(1+r)^0} + \frac{B_1}{(1+r)^1} + \cdots + \frac{B^T}{(1+r)^{nT}}$$ [7]

An equivalent equation is the following:

$$\text{NPV} = \sum_{t=0}^{T} d_t I_t - \sum_{t=0}^{T} d_t O_t$$

where I_t are inflows and O_t are outflows. These formulas suggest that a flow will
be more discounted (i.e. lower) the higher the discount rate i and the more distant
the year at which the flow to be discounted takes place.

Source: Authors

The results of the economic analysis are particularly relevant for a publicly funded
project, since they may influence public authorities' decisions about the allocation of
public expenditure. A benevolent government should be reluctant to sink a capital grant
in a project with low or negative social returns, which would divert precious resources
away from an alternative, more valuable use.

The different steps of the financial and economic analysis could also be used
to compare different projects. In principle, many different options may be implemented for reaching a desired socio-economic objective, and through the option
analysis, it is possible to inspect which is the best one among the different alternatives by financially and economically evaluating them within the CBA incremental

framework. For instance, the economic net benefits achieved through different routes or technologies may be considered in transport projects; the impact of alternative locations of water treatment infrastructures could be assessed; improvements of the existing technologies instead of the construction of new power plants could be compared.

Appendix 4.2 illustrates a numeric example of economic analysis. The next section moves on, presenting the main methodologies applied in the empirics of cost-benefit analysis to calculate the accounting prices.

4.3 Empirical approaches for guessing accounting prices

The Drèze–Stern theoretical model for CBA shows that a general equilibrium optimal planning problem needs to be solved to obtain shadow prices that reflect all the changes provoked by an investment project or policy in the economy. As stressed in Section 3.6 of Chapter 3, one way to solve this problem would require one to use, *inter alia*, a multi-sectorial database with data of inputs and outputs of the economy, which allows one to identify the effects of any change in the quantity or price of a certain good on all other sectors of the economy.

Such data could be provided in principle by an input–output table, a national quantitative economic tool suitable for sectorial and project investment planning purposes. The input–output analysis takes into account all interdependences of the economic sectors and can be used to take resource allocation decisions concerning the creation of new productive capacity. The tables indicate the contribution (in absolute and/or percentage terms) that both primary factors (such as labour, capital, foreign exchange, taxes and subsidies) and outputs produced in each sector of the economy make toward the total market value of outputs produced in all other sectors, by entering their production processes as inputs. This method of analysis gives the opportunity, through the solution of a set of simultaneous equations, to derive the conversion factors, and hence shadow prices, of all national non-tradable products.[9]

Some economists argue that the use of the input–output method provides the most appropriate way of systematically estimating a set of shadow prices, the main advantage being that, once input–output tables have been set up, they can be modified according to changing circumstances, thus allowing one to recalculate the conversion factors. However, it has to be acknowledged that these estimates are typically not updated as often as changes in the economic and policy setting occur. Other issues limiting the effectiveness of input–output tables are represented by the level of data disaggregation, which in most cases is insufficient to derive project-specific estimates, or the lack of some categories of inputs and outputs in the national tables which instead arise in the assessed project (such as externalities).

In order to overcome the shortcomings related to the input–output approach and, more generally, the dimensionality difficulty that arises when empirically applying the general equilibrium problem, different 'shortcut' methods have been developed and are used in practice.[10] As shown in Figure 4.1 at the beginning of this chapter, there is no unique way of calculating shadow prices that fits all types of market and non-market goods. Instead, several approaches exist, and each of them could be more or less suitable for certain typologies of goods and sectors.

In order to apply the most appropriate method, a first important discrimination is whether the good is tradable or not in international markets. The general shortcut for internationally tradable goods, such as most agricultural and manufactured commodities, is often (but not always) to use their border price. This rule is presented in Section 4.4.

As far as non-tradable goods are concerned, a different approach is used depending on the event of considering minor items or major items. For minor items, i.e. those inputs and outputs that represent a relatively limited share of the total project inflows or outflows, thus having only minor influence on results of analysis, a 'standard conversion' factor can be used. From a theoretical perspective, the standard conversion factor is consistent with the border price rule for traded goods. This method is discussed in Section 4.5.

Accounting prices for non-traded major inputs or outputs depend on the effect that a demand or supply change for that good has on social welfare; these effects, in turn, depend on how the market adjusts to those demand or supply changes. In particular, for inputs and outputs whose use would lead to an increase in production (such as cost of construction, building materials, internal transport and non-traded public utilities on the input side, and revenues from the sale of goods on the output side), their opportunity cost has to be estimated through the long-run marginal cost of producing extra items of that good (see Section 4.6).

When the use of an input will not result in increased production but in a reduction of consumption by alternative users, the willingness-to-pay or willingness-to-accept has to be estimated by reference to their value, rather than to their cost. The accounting price in these cases is the price that alternative users would be willing to pay to consume that good. The willingness-to-pay approach (which is presented in Section 4.7) is applied also to value non-traded outputs, both actually sold or non-sold ones, like externalities.

When significant difficulties are encountered in the valuation of major items, a possible shortcut approach could be to break them down into their main subcomponents. In this way, the appraiser will disentangle the traded components for which the border price rule applies, the minor non-traded components for which the standard conversion factor is used, and the remaining major non-traded items which are valued either through the long-run marginal cost or the willingness-to-pay. The latter items, in turn, could further be broken down into their respective components and the procedure could continue in the same way until the appraiser is able to estimate all the subcomponents of the major input or output.

Labour constitutes an exception to this scheme, since it is valued differently from other non-traded inputs. In line with Drèze and Stern (1987), the marginal social cost of employment is estimated as the net welfare change determined by total increased consumption on the cost side, and by the sum of the benefits for individuals of that consumption on the benefit side. Chapter 5 is dedicated to this topic.

4.4 The border price rule for tradable goods

The border price rule is often used to proxy the shadow prices of internationally marketable goods. It is gathered from the Little and Mirrlees (1974) approach to project evaluation. Although such an approach was conceived for developing economies, where markets are deemed to be much more distorted than in developed countries, similar rules are also relevant to national economy.

The Little–Mirrlees approach measures costs and benefits in terms of international prices (border prices) and is based on the estimation of the trade opportunity cost of goods. The underlying assumption is that the next best alternative to self-production is import and the next best alternative to self-consumption is export. Thus, international prices reflect the economic cost of imported goods and the economic benefit of exported goods better than domestic prices, since these are more likely to be distorted by duties and subsidies, inefficient transport, administrative regulations, etc.

According to the border price rule, the shadow price of tradable goods i, v_i, is given by its world price (or marginal cost) $p_{f,i}$ multiplied by the marginal social value of foreign exchange v_f:

$$v_i = v_f p_{f,i}. \tag{4.1}$$

Hence, the effect of an increase in the availability of an extra unit of good in the economy can be treated simply as a reduction in net imports and an increase in foreign exchange earnings (the theoretical underpinnings of this approach can be derived from the Drèze–Stern theoretical model using an open economy setting where foreign exchange is treated as a separate good).

The rule implies empirically that the best guess of the economic value of exported outputs is represented by the FOB (free on board, before insurance and freight charges) prices, while the value of imported inputs is represented by CIF (cost, insurance and freight) prices. The rule has some advantages: first of all, it is relatively easy to apply and it holds good by good; second, if world prices are taken as parameters (i.e. exogenous), shadow prices can be calculated without knowing the exact structure of the economy; third, in principle, the rule applies to all goods that are tradable, provided that an international market exists, regardless of whether they are actually traded or internally produced and consumed.

However, the Little–Mirrlees rule does not apply to goods that are non-tradable by nature, for which no international markets exist: these are, for example, most transport services, land, local transport and some other public utilities, construction, maintenance services, and labour. In order to value them, one could try to break down these goods and services into their inputs, and these inputs into their respective inputs, and so on, in order to identify traded and non-traded sub-components. For the former, the border price could be considered, while for the latter other methods should be used to estimate their opportunity cost through a standard conversion factor for minor items, or the long-term marginal cost and the willingness-to-pay for others.[11]

The main assumption for using the border price as shadow price of commodity i in a country, is that the world price of that commodity is not affected by variations in demand and supply in the national market where the investment project is implemented. This assumption is generally considered to hold in relatively small countries. Yet particularly large investment projects could in fact influence national trade flows: when this happens, shadow prices of imports could be better proxied by their marginal cost and shadow prices of exports by marginal revenues. The Little and Mirrlees rule is not applicable even to large countries, where domestic market changes can affect international markets.[12]

To sum up, border prices often represent the appropriate shadow price of tradable goods and tradable sub-components of non-tradable goods. This approach allows one to identify the economic value of goods and it is particularly justifiable when there are market imperfections which distort domestic market prices. As argued by Potts (2012a), divergences between world and national market prices of tradable goods have been reduced in most countries by extensive liberalization policies and rapid technological changes. However, the price dispersion of some goods and services is still a fact not only in developing but also in developed countries. For example, there is still no effective single market for electricity in the EU.[13] When intra-country price dispersion for some internationally tradable goods is so large, it is more appropriate to estimate the border prices at their respective national borders, regardless of the distinction between developing and developed countries.[14]

4.5 The Standard Conversion Factor

Before going into the discussion of specific methodologies to value the relevant economic cost and benefit items, this section deals with minor non-tradable items. These are goods for which information on their cost structure is generally unavailable; input–output tables also are often not detailed enough to trace the chain of all non-traded and traded inputs that enter their production process. Little and Mirrlees (1974) propose a general adjustment method for the calculation of shadow prices of this kind of goods, which consists in estimating the so-called Standard Conversion Factor (SCF). Following the definition of conversion factors as the ratio between shadow prices and market prices, the SCF is defined as:

$$\text{SCF} = \frac{M + X}{(M + T_M - S_M) + (X - T_X + S_X)}, \tag{4.2}$$

where:

- M is the total value of import at accounting prices, i.e. CIF prices;
- X is the total value of export at accounting prices, i.e. FOB prices;
- T_M and T_X are the value of duties on import and export, respectively;
- S_M and S_X are the value of subsidies on import and export, respectively.[15]

As the formula suggests, the SCF is a proxy of the average distance between world prices (at the numerator) and domestic prices (at the denominator). If the country has no taxes or subsidies on international trade, then the SCF is equal to one. The assumption that domestic prices are distorted only by taxes and subsidies, thus excluding any other possible factor of distortion such as inefficient transport and handling costs, monopolies etc., is clearly a simplification, which however, guarantees easy applicability of the method.

The definition of the SCF is consistent with the border price rule for traded goods. Actually, they are both based on the choice of considering units of foreign exchange as *numéraire* of the economic analysis. More specifically, Little and Mirrlees (1974) propose as *numéraire* present uncommitted social income measured in terms of convertible foreign exchange of constant purchasing power. This means that the value of domestic resources is adjusted in terms of foreign exchange at the official exchange rate, while units of foreign resources are left unchanged.[16]

A different approach aimed at making traded and non-traded goods commensurable, which was proposed by Dasgupta, Marglin, and Sen (1972) and Squire and van der Tak (1975), consists in converting all foreign resources into domestic units using the foreign exchange rate. Both approaches capture the same market distortions, with the main difference being the *numéraire*.[17]

4.6 The long-run marginal cost

The accounting price of non-tradable inputs and outputs, for which an increase in demand results in increased production, can be measured by the marginal social cost of production. As already mentioned, this method can be applied when the cost structure is known or can be easily identified.

The marginal social cost of a good is the accounting price of the inputs required to produce an extra unit of the good, less the social value of the extra profit (see Box 4.4). It measures the cost of increasing the production by one additional unit, or the cost saved by reducing the production by one unit of output, holding the production levels of all other goods and services constant. According to the standard economic theory, in the absence of externalities and other market distortions, setting prices at the marginal cost allows one to maximize economic welfare, since prices would reflect the costs involved in providing an additional unit of output.

The marginal social cost could be estimated through the use of input–output tables, through which the cost of any non-traded good is broken down into its components, in terms of both foreign exchange and reward to domestic factors of production. More frequently, given the already mentioned empirical difficulties in using the I/O tables for project analysis, it relies on sector- or project-specific calculations about the incremental operating and capital costs necessary to increase productive capacity.[18]

Since marginal costs are typically unstable in the short term, due to their dependence on the level of productive capacity, the long-run marginal costs (LRMCs) are considered the most appropriate basis for cost-reflecting pricing.[19] In particular, while short-run marginal costs only refer to changes in operating cost, LRMCs generally consider both operating and capital costs.

Saunders, Warford, and Mann (1977) argue that it is not possible to establish a precise and complete set of rules for marginal cost estimation which could be followed in all circumstances, since these are strictly related to the degree of elasticity of demand, the typologies of prevailing cost and the level of capital indivisibility. Nevertheless, it is possible to state that LRMCs are often less than average total costs due to substantial fixed costs and economies of scale which characterize many activities.

In general terms, the LRMC that should be taken into account in valuing an input or output should include, on the operating and capital side, only the actual extra cost of creating the increased capacity required to meet the needs of the project. It is possible that not all costs necessary for production will need to be incurred to allow increased supply: for instance, some existing capital facilities may be able to cope with new productive capacity. Only the extra costs should be taken into account, i.e. the marginal costs.

Box 4.4 The long-run marginal cost (LRMC) rule in the Drèze–Stern framework

Drèze and Stern (1987, 1990) derive the LRMC rule by examining the particular form of expressing shadow prices when the existence of binding producer rations $\bar{y}_i$ is assumed. The first-order condition for the optimization of the Social Welfare Function (see Chapter 3, particularly Appendix A3.1), subject to the scarcity constraint, is:

$$\frac{\partial L}{\partial \bar{y}_i} = v \frac{\partial y}{\partial \bar{y}_i} + b \frac{\partial \pi}{\partial \bar{y}_i},$$
(A)

where b stands for the sum of the marginal social value of transfers to households (b^h) weighted by the share of households' shares in the firms' profit d_j^h:

$$b \equiv \sum_h d_j^h b^h.$$
(B)

An easy way to interpret equation (A) is to consider $\bar{y}_i$ as the amount of inputs required by the firm to produce the output i. Hence, a marginal increase of $\bar{y}_i$ generates a twofold effect: an increase in the output ∂y, valued at shadow prices v, and an increase in the firms' profits for selling the extra output. Given that $\frac{\partial y}{\partial \bar{y}_i}$ is equal to 1 (a unit increase in the required output determines a proportional unit increase in the overall production vector), Drèze and Stern show that equation (A) can be rewritten as:

$$\frac{\partial L}{\partial \bar{y}_i} = v_i - \text{MSC}_i + b(p_i - \text{MC}_i),$$
(C)

where MSC_i is the marginal social cost of good i, i.e. the value at shadow prices of a marginal change in the production vector, and MC_i is the marginal private cost of i, i.e. the value at market prices p_i of the inputs required to produce an extra unit of good i. This means that the shadow price of good i is its marginal social cost, corrected by the marginal social value of the profit effects.

Setting (C) equal to zero will lead to the expression for the shadow price:

$$v_i = \text{MSC}_i - b(p_i - \text{MC}_i)$$
(D)

This rule is straightforward since it does not have to take (directly) consumers into account, but only the social cost of production and profit changes.

Source: Adapted from Drèze and Stern (1990).

Furthermore, the project analyst should consider that marginal cost pricing is a forward-looking concept, meaning that it should be based on the expected development in asset prices and demand. Hence, when calculating the LRMC, the costs associated with the existing system should be considered only as long as they allow one to estimate the future cost structure.[20]

Box 4.5 An example: calculation of the long-run marginal cost in the water sector

The LRMC approach can be used to determine the water supply tariff in a way that ensures sufficient revenue to fully cover the financial costs associated with maintaining and enhancing the water supply and distribution system. London Economics (1997) highlights that average cost pricing would be acceptable only upon the conditions that there are no economies of scale, the water company is on its optimal expansion path, all costs are accounted for, with no double counting, and accounting measures of profit reflect the economic depreciation of assets.

The long-run marginal cost should take into account the increase in pumping and treatment costs led by an increase in consumption, as well as the costs associated with the provision of new water resources, treatment capacity and reinforcement of the water main, which may occur in the long run.

More specifically, the following cost categories are generally considered:

- Capital costs: they are based on the unit cost of the resource required in the future, calculated as the annualized capital and operating costs of the resources divided by its capacity. Capital costs should include also investment costs aimed at improving the water quality and the water supply system performance (e.g. by reducing losses, improving reliability, etc.).
- Treatment costs: they can be estimated through the unit cost of the relevant treatment process.
- Distribution costs: they include the costs of installing and maintaining the connection from the customer's property to the main and the specific costs related to the pumping head, dams, the lengths of mains required, the soil types, desalination (depending on how water is gathered). When these costs depend on the volume of water distributed, as is often the case, it is appropriate to distinguish between small and large users (such as industrial and household consumers).
- The costs of supplying a customer, which include the cost of meter-reading, billing, keeping customer records and dealing with enquiries and other administrative costs.

In calculating the LRMC, one may decide to consider not only the financial costs related to the water supply and distribution service, but the total economic value of water.

Source: Adapted from London Economics (1997).

4.7 Willingness-to-pay

4.7.1 Definition and scope of application

The concept of willingness-to-pay is often associated with the valuation of project outputs. It entails the estimation of the total value of benefits and costs generated by a project by summing the maximum amount people would be willing to pay to gain outcomes that they view as desirable, or, alternatively, the maximum amounts that people would be willing to pay to avoid outcomes they view as undesirable. The category of outputs may include both goods and services actually sold on the market, and externalities. In the former case, even if a tariff is paid by consumers, this could be distorted and would not reflect either the total cost of production or any additional social benefit and cost entailed in the production of that good or service. A typical example is public or publicly provided goods, such as health care or public transport, for which a subsidized tariff is paid by users. In similar situations, the WTP provides a better estimate of the social value of the good than the observed tariff.

The importance of using the WTP approach is even more evident when externalities, for which no monetary compensation is paid, are produced by the project. The general rule for externalities is that they have to be 'internalized', i.e. valued in monetary terms (where money is the *numéraire*) and brought into the economic analysis of the project. This allows one to value total welfare improvement taking into account welfare changes in all gainers and losers of a project.

For both positive and negative externalities, the WTP often provides a reference estimate of their social value.

WTP can also be used when valuing inputs entering the project's production process, where its use in the project leads to an adjustment in the net demand of other consumers of that good. In order to better understand why the long-run marginal cost cannot be applied in this case, consider the following example. Take a project input, such as a machine to be used in the construction phase, and assume it is non-tradable. In a theoretical framework, assume also that the machine is produced by one firm which is not able or willing to increase the supply of that good in order to meet the increase in demand, maybe because the firm is already operating at full capacity. The machine, then, could be obtained only by contracting with another agent which already owns it.

The economic value of the good will not be estimated as the long-run marginal cost to produce that good, because in fact there has been no effect on marginal production, but on its opportunity cost.

It is clear that this holds only in efficient markets. In most real-world situations, market distortions make the purchase price not fully reflective of the real economic value of the good. This could happen, for instance, if there is only one seller on the market who has the power to set the price (monopoly), or if the seller is aware of a deficiency in the good and does not inform the buyer, in order to set the price in his own favour (information asymmetry). The maximum amount of money the buyer would be willing to pay to get the good is therefore the most appropriate way to estimate the economic value of that good. As an alternative approach, taking the opposite perspective, the minimum amount of money the seller would be willing to accept to give away the good, which is the willingness-to-accept (WTA), could be considered.

Another major input whose consumption does not drive a change in production, but in demand of that good, is land. Land is a type of good that is required, either directly or indirectly, in the production of all goods, but it cannot be manufactured or reproduced. Supply can be considered fixed because it cannot be significantly expanded. Thus, demand is the only determinant of land's market price, which is equal to the present value of land rental, purchase or expropriation, net of land taxes. In most cases, this value reflects the economic value of land, which includes considerations about its utility, desirability and scarcity. However, as argued by Londero (2003), the use of land could be associated with significant external effects which are not captured by the market.

Londero provides the example of a wooded hillside overlooking an urban area, which represents a natural beauty landscape influencing the utility of citizens other than the landowner. The total economic value of the land, then, would differ from the market price at which the land is bought or rented. Instead, the willingness-to-pay could provide more reliable estimates of welfare gains or losses.

In principle, the equilibrium value of willingness-to-pay and willingness-to-accept are equivalent, with the former generally being used to value benefits, and the latter used for costs. Yet it has been empirically shown that the imperfect rationality of individuals leads to estimates of WTA higher than the equivalent WTP. This is because people tend to demand higher monetary compensation to give up goods they have, than the price they say they would be willing to pay to buy the same good they do not have. The next sections will mainly refer to the concept of WTP, which is that most widely used in the practice of CBA.

Because of the fact that in non-competitive markets the WTP does not coincide with observed market prices, appropriate techniques have to be adopted to empirically estimate it. The literature provides several approaches to empirical applications, which can be categorized into two main groups:[21]

- approaches based on revealed preferences;
- approaches based on stated preferences.

Box 4.6 The willingness-to-pay approach in the Drèze–Stern framework

Drèze and Stern (1990) prove that the marginal willingness-to-pay for good i by household h is the ratio between the marginal utility of the good and the marginal utility of income. The basic assumption is that a change in consumption of each good does not affect the marginal rates of substitution (hence, all goods are separable from the others): this is important in order to analyze the effect that a change in the production of a certain good has on the consumption of the same good.

Define b^h as $b^h \equiv \beta^h - v \dfrac{\partial x^h}{\partial m^h}$, as from equation (3.23) in Chapter 3. This is the marginal social value of an income lump-sum transfer m to household h. It is measured as the social marginal utility of income (or welfare weight) of the household minus the cost at shadow prices v of meeting the extra consumption by the household arising from the extra income m^h.

It can be demonstrated (see Neary and Roberts 1980) that the first-order condition of the optimization problem for optimum consumer rations $\bar{x}_i^h$ leads to the following definition of shadow price $v_i : v_i = \beta^h p_i^h - b^h q_i$. The social welfare increase associated with the extra production of a good can be interpreted as a gain in the marginal social utility due to a consumption increase measured in terms of the household's willingness-to-pay (first term) measured at producer prices p_i, net of the cost of paying the extra item (second term) measured at market (consumer) prices q_i.

Source: Adapted from Drèze and Stern (1990).

WTP estimates could be either directly applied to value inputs or outputs of the project under evaluation, or, after suitable adaptation, transferred to other contexts and used to value externalities of other similar projects. This is the so-called 'benefit transfer' or 'value transfer' approach. Each approach is presented in the following sub-sections.

4.7.2 Revealed preferences approaches

The revealed preferences approaches can be used to estimate the value of a non-market good whose social vale is correlated with the value of another good for which there is a market. In other words, they are used to unveil the social value of non-market effects by observing behaviour and purchases made in actual markets, instead of eliciting people's preferences as through stated preferences approaches. An appealing feature of these methods, which makes them generally followed in the first place by a project analyst, is that they are based on actual decisions made by individuals, which reveal some information on the implicit price of a related non-market good. As a shortcoming, the behavioural assumptions made for applying these methods are generally difficult to test in practice.

Revealed preference approaches are a family of different methods. The following list is proposed, including the methods that are mostly used in practice:

- travel cost;
- hedonic pricing;
- averting or defensive behaviour;
- cost of illness.

They are examined one by one below.

The travel cost method consists in evaluating a good through the full travel cost incurred to consume it, on the basis that the travel and the good under valuation are complementary. The method is especially used to value recreational sites.

By considering the cost of trips (fuel, air ticket, etc.), the cost of accommodation, the number of visits to the site over the same period of time, and the value of time spent in travelling, the analyst is able to derive the market demand curve and, hence, to estimate the average willingness-to-pay for a visit.

The applicability of the travel time method encounters several limitations, the most recurrent one being multi-purpose trips, i.e. the fact that certain trips are made for different reasons, and it is not always possible to properly apportion the cost of travel by each purpose involved. Another problem is that the travel cost method allows one to estimate the WTP for the entire site, rather than a specific feature of it, and this may make it problematic to estimate the value of a change in one attribute of a multi-dimensional good. Boardman *et al.* (2018) also point to the possibility that the travel cost variable is not exogenous but endogenous. This is due to the fact that people who expect to make many visits to an area (e.g. to the seaside) choose to live in a neighbourhood zone, thus simultaneously determining the number of trips and price for these trips. Finally, attention should be paid to avoiding endogenous stratification, determined by the higher probability of surveying visitors who more frequently visit the site.

With the hedonic price method, the focus is on the observation of behaviour in markets of goods related to the ones under evaluation. Typically observed markets are the property and labour markets. The rationale for the basis of this method is that price differentials between otherwise identical houses or jobs that differ in their exposure levels to non-market goods and bads (such as pollution or job security) reveal information

---

Box 4.7 Valuing recreation through the travel cost method

The economic value associated with the direct use individuals make of natural assets could be estimated through the travel cost method. An example of empirical estimation of the recreational value of ecosystems is provided by Mendes and Proença (2005), who proved that the Portuguese Peneda-Gerê National Park is able to produce a significant social benefit, which could justify the allocation of more public resources to eco-tourism activities.

Starting from the generic economic definition that the marginal recreational value of an ecosystem is equal to the amount visitors would pay to enjoy recreation and leisure activities, the authors estimated the relationship between the costs incurred by travellers to a site and the number of trips taken. During the 1994 summer peak-period months, questionnaires were distributed to Portuguese citizens over 18 years of age who were visiting the park at that time for visits equal to or longer than 24 hours. Information was gathered about the number of days of stay, income, geographical origin, the cost of the trip, transportation mode and various demographic characteristics. The demand of recreation per trip has been modelled as a function of the cost incurred, available income and individual characteristics (plus an independent error term). The consumer surplus of the representative visitor per average day of stay has been derived by integrating the recreation demand function over the relevant cost change. From here, the value of willingness-to-pay has been estimated through the formula proposed by Grogger and Carson (1991) and Englin and Shonkwiler (1995).

Results show one recreation day was valued at EUR 124 (2005 prices) for the average representative visitor of the sample. Considering that approximately 12,000 visitors camp in the park every year, this generates a recreation value per day of visit of EUR 1,488,000.

Source: Adapted from Mendes and Proença (2005).

---

about the willingness-to-pay of individuals for such goods or for the reduction of bads. For example, the presence of a green area inside a city is likely to positively influence the price of houses located nearby. Therefore, a model can be built to capture the effects of a change in the non-market good on prices in a related market. Typically, the hedonic price method consists of two steps. First, estimating the hedonic price function, i.e. the relationship between an asset price (or wage) and all the attributes that affect its value. From this, the marginal effect of each attribute on the value of the asset (or wage) is derived while controlling for the other variables that can affect the value. Second, estimating the WTP for the attributes after controlling for a vector of factors such as income, socioeconomic background, and tastes.

The main problem associated with this methodology could be multi-collinearity among the goods influencing market prices, i.e. that certain non-market goods could move in tandem, making it difficult to single out the independent effect of each of them on market goods (Day 2001; OECD, 2018). Second, market price could be not fully reflective of the total economic value of a non-market good, maybe because agents lack information on certain externalities (e.g. about the level of air pollution) or because individual perceptions are distorted.

A method often used to value negative externalities is the averting or defensive behaviour method. It assumes that individuals can insulate themselves from a non-market bad by adopting costly behaviours (such as restrictions on normal behaviour) to avoid it, or by buying market goods to 'defend' themselves or mitigate any actual or potential negative effect. The economic value of these behaviours or purchases is assumed to represent an implicit price for the non-market bad. With the averting or defensive behaviour method, the value of a non-market item could be estimated by observing price variations not only in market but also non-market goods (such as time) that are consumed in order to avert a given effect.

Box 4.8 Valuing urban air quality through the hedonic price method

Murty and Gulati (2004) set up a hedonic prices model to estimate the environmental benefits from the reduced exposure of people to air pollution. It could be assumed that individuals try to minimize exposure to pollution by an appropriate choice of house location, depending on house rent or price. A survey was conducted in 2004 on a sample population, selected in two Indian cities (Hyderabad and Secunderabad). In total, 1,250 households with different income levels and living within 1-km radius of the 20 existing air pollution monitoring stations have been considered. In order to estimate the household marginal WTP for high quality air, the authors examined the relationship between property prices and air pollution, taking also into account the structural characteristics of houses (such as use of air conditioners, number of rooms, ventilation, etc.), of the neighbourhood (the distance from the market or industries, or the closeness to a park), and socio-economic characteristics of households (such as education and income level).

The marginal WTP of a representative household for the reduction of one microgram of pollutant in the two cities is valued at Rupee 220.67 (approximately EUR 3). The annual welfare increase to a typical household from the reduction of pollutant levels from the level recorded at the time of the survey to the safe level set by the government is estimated as Rupee 4,449.72 (approximately EUR 62).

According to Chau *et al.* (2006), air pollution measures should be better estimated at micro level, rather than district or metropolitan level, because air quality significantly varies even within the same district in very densely populated areas. Bearing in mind this consideration, the authors estimated the air quality of each individual apartment in Hong Kong through computational fluid dynamics techniques, validating their simulation with field measurements. A hedonic price model was then constructed, assuming that property prices are a function of different property attributes, including the apartment-specific air pollution level. Other considered attributes were the building age and size, the floor level and the individual apartment size. Models to different specifications produced the same conclusion: air pollution has a significant negative impact on property prices, implying that buyers are willing to pay more for a less polluted environment. In particular, an increase of 0.1 $\mu g/m^3$ in suspended particulates lowers property prices by 1.28 per cent (semi-log ordinary least squared model), and the relationship is non-linear.

Source: Adapted from Murty and Gulati (2004), Chau *et al.* (2006).

One could consider, for example, soundproof house windows, which are sold especially in areas where the level of noise is high (e.g. because of being located near an industrial site or a congested road): an increase in the level of noise will influence the market for windows, since individuals will be more keen to replace their windows with more efficient ones. The price of windows is then a proxy of the value of the gains obtained in reducing noise. This method can be used also to value the benefit of protecting natural biodiversity, by considering the costs and resources put in place by both the public and the private sector to prevent the risk of species becoming extinct (e.g. the opening of natural reserves, communication campaigns, etc.). A further, and more detailed, example is presented in Box 4.9.

Like other approaches, this methodology entails some problems that could make its empirical application difficult. First, the gains allowed by defensive expenditure may not fully compensate for the welfare loss caused by the non-market bad: hence, the total value of the bad that individuals want to avoid is generally higher than the defensive expenditure undertaken. Second, this method assumes that people immediately adjust to the externality, whereas this could not be the case and individuals could feel the effects of the negative externality before intervening to mitigate them. This should be taken into due account to make sure that all effects of an externality are valued. A third problem arises when a certain averting behaviour or expenditure has benefits as well as remedying one bad: for example, buying double-glazed soundproof windows also

---

Box 4.9 Valuing the reliability of water supply through the defensive expenditure method

Before the water distribution network in the city of Palermo (Italy) was substantially renovated during the 1990s, for a long time the population had been suffering from severe water shortages and the water was rationed during the day. Citizens coped with this shortage by collecting water in domestic tanks operated with electric pumps, in order to compensate for the low service pressure. After implementation of the project, which involved the partial substitution of the water distribution network, water managed to be supplied 24 hours per day at high pressure, making domestic tanks no longer needed. The European Commission evaluated the impact of this intervention by estimating the monetary value of the social benefit deriving from the improved service delivery in terms of cost avoided of maintaining and operating the electric pumps. The purchase of tanks and pumps can be considered a defensive expenditure people undertook to limit the negative effects of water shortage. Thus, an improvement of water supply naturally leads to a reduction in that expenditure.

The evaluators estimated the cost related to purchase and maintenance of electric pumps, the electric power needed for their functioning, and maintenance costs sustained by users for the self-provision of water during the rationing periods for different types of users, i.e. households, apartment blocks and non-domestic users. For about 73,000 users supplied by the renovated network, the net present value of the service costs avoided over the 2003–2027 period is estimated at almost EUR 67 million (2011 prices).

Source: European Commission (2012).

positively affects energy conservation inside the house. In similar cases, the additional costs should be apportioned and attributed to the different benefits gained.

It is worth clarifying that the averting or defensive behaviour method is not directly related to the notion of avoided cost often referred to in CBA. The former is a technique to proxy the shadow prices of non-market costs. The latter, conversely, has to do with the incremental nature of CBA, according to which a benefit can be assessed in terms of the cost occurring in the counterfactual (with-out-the-project) scenario which is instead avoided in the do-project situation.

Like the 'averting behaviour or expenditure' technique, the 'cost of illness' method is based on expenditures made in response to non-market impacts. In particular, it considers the cost of medical services used to counteract negative effects on health and is widely used by policy makers when deciding which diseases need to be addressed first by health care policy.

The project analyst could decide whether to examine the expenditure pattern of private individuals or to focus on public health expenditure decisions. While the former approach allows one to value individual preferences for reduced morbidity and mortality, the latter could reflect additional dimensions of a social, political and ethical nature.

In addition to the direct monetary cost of medical care, the costs related to lost output due to illness or death are also part of the evaluation. In general, the social cost associated with a disease can be estimated as the sum of increased expenditures on medical services and the social cost due to decreased productivity or loss of earnings. Also death represents a cost to society, as it reduces a valuable economic resource such as human capital, in addition to the suffering of the survivors. As is more extensively described in Box 4.10, the technique that is generally applied to estimate the reduced productivity and the social cost of death is based on the reduced streams of earnings of the individual. Box 1.11 instead presents an example.

Like the defensive method, the cost of illness approach could underestimate the real social cost of illness or death, for example, by not taking into account the pain and suffering during acute illness. An additional major difficulty is to correctly identify the relationship between exposure to a health risk and actual physical impacts.

Box 4.10 The value of statistical life (VSL)

Notwithstanding that attaching a monetary value to human life could be seen as an unpleasant or ethically questionable task, the notion of value of statistical life has a practical relevance in many fields: insurance, education, health care, environmental pollution affecting human health, and transport, when the cost associated with accidents and fatalities has to be estimated.

Valuation of life in economic terms dates back to the contribution of Dublin and Lotka (1946) and is associated with the probability of death (hence the term 'statistical life'). The most established and frequently used methodology to estimate the value of human life is the human capital approach, which calculates the present discounted value of lifetime earnings. Researchers generally find that the value of lifetime earnings varies significantly by age and gender, with younger people and females having relatively lower values of time than elder people and males. Estimates are dependent also on the discount rate used: the higher the rate, the lower the value of time, because of the higher reduction of future earnings value (Wendy *et al.* 2004). Boardman *et al.* (2018) points out that the fundamental problem with the human capital approach is that it ignores individuals' WTP to reduce their own mortality and morbidity risks.

Other studies had recourse to different methodologies to estimate the value of life, such as hedonic pricing (observing the insurance premiums for fatal accidents) or averting expenditure (examining the purchase of life-saving devices, such as safety belts or earthquake-proof houses). Beyond market-based techniques, contingent valuation methods can also be used to estimate the VSL by posing hypothetical choices in surveys (see further in Section 4.7.2).

The literature reveals a very large range in the VSL values as indicated by various meta-analysis conducted by different authors. To mention some examples: Viscusi and Aldy (2003) predicted a mean VSL for the US population ranged between USD 7.6 million and USD 10.5 million (2016 prices); OECD (2012) calculated a base mean of USD 3.0 million for all OECD countries and USD 3.6 million for the European Union (expressed in purchasing power parity 2005 prices); Viscusi and Masterman (2017), estimated international income-adjusted VSL for 189 countries and using income classifications from the World Bank, they also calculated average VSLs in lower income, lower-middle income, upper-middle income, and upper income countries to be USD 107,000, USD 420,000, USD 1.2 million, and USD 6.4 million, respectively. Recommended VSL values are also provided by policymakers in many countries. As many health interventions increase the life spans by some given years, the value of life year (VLY) is sometimes more useful than the VSL. VLY is usually derived from an estimate of the VSL. Taking an indicative individual VSL, the VLY is the constant annual amount that, over the person's remaining life span, has a discounted value equal to her VSL. As an alternative, it is possible to calculate the VSL for a person with a given age as the discounted sum of the value of the remaining life-years.

Source: Adapted from different sources.

4.7.3 Stated preferences approaches

When costs and benefits cannot be inferred simply by observing existing market demand curves, their values could be deduced by directly asking people to express the maximum amount of money they would be willing to pay for a hypothetical change in the quantity or quality of a good through surveys.

The most used method to elicit individual preferences, in monetary terms, consists in implementing a contingent valuation. This term derives from the fact that the estimates of economic value obtained are contingent upon the features of the hypothetical scenario posed in the survey. Contingent valuation was first used by Davis (1964) in estimating the benefits of an outdoor recreation such as hunting. It entails the following five steps:

1 Preparation of a questionnaire;
2 Selection of a sample of respondents from a population;
3 Submission of the questionnaire;
4 Econometric processing of the data to estimate the respondents' WTP;
5 Inference of results to the entire population.

Various types of questionnaires could be used in this context. Respondents may be asked to state the WTP by simply answering an open-ended question such as 'What is the maximum amount of money you would be willing to pay to reduce the number of road accidents?'. Alternatively, questionnaires could contain dichotomous choices in which the price for a certain good is suggested by the interviewer and respondents are asked to state whether they would pay that price or not. A more sophisticated method consists in asking respondents whether they would be willing to pay a specified amount for the good; if the answer is affirmative, the interviewer repeats the question by slightly increasing the price until the respondent expresses unwillingness to pay the amount specified. In contrast, if the answer is negative a lower bid is offered (see Box 4.11).

Box 4.11 A contingent valuation experiment about future particle accelerators at CERN

For the first time, Florio and Giffoni (2020) applied contingent valuation to study the public good value of scientific research. Specifically, they elicited willingness of citizens to pay for the European Organization for Nuclear Research (CERN)'s future investments. The contingent valuation experiment on social attitudes about CERN future accelerators was designed as a survey of a representative sample of French citizens between 18 and 74 years old. After informing respondents about the progress in fundamental physics that particle accelerators have permitted so far, respondents were given two realistic investment scenarios with a well-defined asset to be valued (i.e. continuing research with new projects in particle accelerators as described by the investment "Scenario A" versus the non-investment "Scenario B") and a plausible time horizon within which the investments are expected to be operational. Respondents were asked to pay for the investment necessary for "Scenario A" through a tax increase to make explicit the fact that only government funds enable CERN to continue its research activity. The elicitation format employed in this study is the double-bounded dichotomous choice. In this framing, the bid level offered in the follow-up questions is higher than the offered bid in the initial payment if the answer to the initial payment question is "yes"; in contrast, if the answer is "no", a lower bid is offered. The double-bounded dichotomous choice format yields four answers paths: "yes-yes" (both answers are "yes"); "yes-no" (a "yes" followed by a "no"); "no-yes" (a "no" followed by a "yes"); and "no-no" (both answers are "no"). Moreover, in order to further detect lower or upper bounds of individual WTP, a third follow-up question on the maximum WTP is asked. Whatever the path followed by respondents, closed-ended questions were asked to justify the declared WTP and identify protest answers.

The analysis of the survey results suggests that with any of the estimated model (the double-bounded dichotomous choice model, the spike model, and the non-parametric model based on the maximum WTP stated by respondents), citizens' WTP is in excess of what they implicitly pay to CERN as taxes: in 2017, the per capita implicit tax contribution of French adults to CERN was EUR 2.7 per year against an estimated WTP range of 3.97–16.93. Moreover, the survey revealed that willingness of citizens to pay is correlated with education, income, age, and crucially previous awareness, attitudes and interest in science.

Authors based on Florio and Giffoni (2020).

In spite of being widely used to estimate, both, use and non-use values of the total economic value of a good, the contingent valuation method has drawbacks. There are several factors that could contribute to distorting the results. Non-neutral surveys, in which either the questions or the interviewers are biased, could influence respondents to deviate from their true preferences. Other problems are associated with the probability that respondents do not fully understand the scenario or what the good in question is, or that they are not willing to attach a monetary value to certain goods (for example the value of a human life). Additionally, Carson and Groves (2007) point out that increase in the provision of a public good for which only voluntary contribution is asked is generally overvalued; this is because respondents have an incentive to free-ride in order to increase the chances of provision of the desired good without having to pay for it.

An alternative method to uncover individuals' estimates for specific attributes of non-market goods, consists in asking a sample of the population to choose or rank different combinations of attributes of the same good, where price is included as an attribute. For example, respondents may be asked to state their preference options regarding a transport project, choosing between a number of alternatives characterized, for example, by different levels in terms of time saving, prices to the users and construction time. Depending on their preferences about these dimensions, each respondent will select one option, or rank different options, thus uncovering his or her preference in terms of willingness-to-pay for the whole good.

The underlying assumption is that the total utility of each consumer h for different options o can be decomposed into utilities for single attributes, plus a residual error, capturing other socio-economic and demographic characteristics of respondents. Consumers' preferences for goods are modelled through a statistical analysis of the survey's results, so as to estimate the probability that the utility associated with a particular option exceeds the utility associated with other options, and to obtain parameter estimates for each of the identified attributes which contribute to form total utility. The WTP is then estimated as a ratio between the coefficient of each attribute (b_1 and b_2) by the coefficient for price (b_3):

$$U_{ho} = b_1 \left(\text{const.time}\right)_{ho} + b_2 \left(\text{timesaving}\right)_{ho} + b_3 \left(\text{price}\right)_{ho} + e_{ho} \tag{4.3}$$

This method is called discrete choice experiments (which is part of the choice modelling approach). A review from Mahieu *et al.* (2014) shows that, in the last decade, it is becoming more popular than contingent valuation. Among problems and weaknesses affecting this approach, there are the larger samples to be collected in order to ensure statistical robustness of the experiment; difficulty of respondents to select an option or rank choices when too many attributes have to be considered; and the increase in the error term e_{ho} of the utility function when one relevant attribute is not included, thus making the WTP estimates less precise.

Box 4.12 Estimation of the value of time through stated preferences (choice modelling method)

The value of time is an important notion in transport planning when the effect of changes in travel time on social well-being needs to be analyzed. Similarly to other valuable non-market commodities, willingness-to-pay of individuals for time saving provides an estimate of the social value of this particular good.

Several studies have been conducted to estimate the value of time, showing this is a volatile measure that depends on a wide range of parameters which are specific to countries, times and individuals. A possible methodology to estimate the value of time using stated preferences, in particular choice modelling, has been proposed by Antoniou and Matsoukis (2007). In December 2005 the authors administered a survey to a random sample of 289 people travelling between the cities of Agrinio and Patras (Greece), which are 84 km apart. The survey included questions about the socio-economic characteristics of respondents, such as the level of education, type of profession and whether or not respondents were car owners. In further questions, respondents were asked to indicate their preference, on a seven-point rating scale, about ten scenarios, characterized by different combinations of transport modes (only car trips, only bus trips, mix of car and bus), travel costs (from EUR 6 to 10) and travel times (between 60 and 120 minutes).

The average value of time, estimated through the generalized linear mixed effects model, which allows one to capture unobserved heterogeneity among respondents, is EUR 5.99 per hour. Self-employed travellers, people with higher education level, elders and car owners assign the highest value to time, compared to private or public employees, students, unemployed, youngsters and people owning no car. Moreover, individuals who travel the most for leisure put a higher value on time (EUR 6.27), since this is perceived as higher quality time.

Source: Adapted from Antoniou and Matsoukis (2007).

4.7.4 Benefit transfer approach

Surveys and statistical analysis are the main instruments to carry out the above-mentioned stated preference or revealed preference approaches. Primary studies are, however, expensive and time consuming. Hence analysts may wish to extrapolate the results of existing surveys and transfer them to different populations and contexts. This is what the benefit transfer (or value transfer) approach is about. It values non-market goods by plugging in unit values of the same goods which have already been estimated for another context through *ad hoc* contingent valuations, hedonic prices, travel cost methods, or others. Plug-in values may preferably undergo an adjustment process in order to take into account the technical, socio-economic, geographic and temporal specificities of the project under evaluation. This ensures that results remain valid also in the context for which the values were not originally estimated.

The variable to which plug-in values are typically adapted is per capita income, on the ground of the fact that most non-market goods (e.g. environmental protection, safety, recreation) could be valued the highest as income rises. OECD (2018) suggest the following formula:

$$\text{WTP}_2 = \text{WTP}_1 \left[\frac{Y_2}{Y_1} \right]^E \tag{4.4}$$

where:

- Y_1 is per capita income in context 1, in which the existing value has been calculated;
- Y_2 is per capita income in context 2, to which the existing value has to be transferred;

- WTP$_1$ and WTP$_2$ are the willingness-to-pay values for each of the two contexts;
- ε is the income elasticity of WTP, measuring the unit increase in WTP due to a unit increase of income.

Box 4.13 Valuing the WTP for waste water treatment through the benefit transfer method

The benefit transfer method was used to value the willingness-to-pay for the construction of nine waste water treatment plants in eight municipalities of Ría de Vigo (Spain). The infrastructure project was implemented between 1995 and 2000 and its long-term effects have been analyzed by the European Commission (2012). The project improved the quality of life of beneficiaries, thanks to the possibility of enjoying cleaner water and more numerous bathing beaches. Considering that the total economic value of increased well-being is not fully reflected by the tariff that households pay for the new and more effective waste water service, evaluators considered it more appropriate to estimate the WTP of the beneficiaries through the benefit transfer method. The WTP has been estimated on the basis of the WTP values referred to other waste water treatment projects selected in the literature (US Environmental Protection Agency 2000a, 2000b, 2000c; Källstrøm 2010).

The benefit transfer procedure consisted of the following four steps:

1 Selection of studies concerned with the most similar types of projects to the one under assessment: only studies about waste water treatment projects implemented in coastal areas and in which the sewerage system was already in place, like Ría de Vigo, have been considered. Moreover, the evaluators discarded all studies of projects that had not been completed or did not achieve any improvement to the quality of the water basin.

2 Selection of the most similar socio-economic context: studies were selected in countries falling under the classification of very highly and highly developed countries, according to the UNDP Human Development Index 2011. These first two steps allowed the researchers to identify 28 studies of projects in different countries of the world.

3 Adjustment for per capita GDP: the WTP values referred to each of the selected studies have been divided by national per capita GDP, which was taken as a proxy of the differences in per capita income.

4 Calculation of WTP for the project in Ría de Vigo: the average WTP for the studies considered, weighted by GDP, has been in turn weighted by Spanish per capita GDP to obtain the willingness-to-pay for the improvement of the water basin in Ría de Vigo. This amounts to EUR 88.11 per household (2011 prices).

The methodology described here implicitly assumes the income elasticity ε of WTP equal to 1, meaning that the ratio of WTP valued in each of the 28 reference countries and in Ría de Vigo is equivalent to the ratio of per capita GDP at the different sites. A sensitivity test of the WTP to different assumptions of the elasticity term has been carried out, letting elasticity vary between 0.4 and 1.3. The test has shown that the WTP is not linearly dependent on elasticity but follows a parabolic shape. The minimum WTP is EUR 87.61, corresponding to an elasticity of approximately 0.85.

Source: European Commission (2012).

4.8 Further reading

The method of discounted cash flow for both financial and economic analysis is presented in numerous books, such as Alfred and Evans (1971), Ross (1995) and Hall (2000). A useful text to clarify the relationship between financial and economic return rate is Duvigneau and Prasad (1984). Sell (1991) can be recommended for a clear introduction to the mechanisms of economic and financial evaluation of development projects. Those who would like to know about the 'history' of financial analysis could read Vailhen (1998): a discussion of both the original objectives and the current uses of financial analysis can be found there. Another valuable work on the financial appraisal of investment is Merret and Sykes (1963).

As far as economic analysis is concerned, authors explaining the use of this type of project/policy evaluation from different perspectives include Squire and van der Tak (1975), Dasgupta, Marglin, and Sen (1972), Samuelson (1947), Powers (1981), Overseas Development Administration (1988), Perkins (1994), and Curry and Weiss (2000). An important theme about project analysis which this chapter did not enter is inflation and, particularly, how to deal with inflation when estimating cash flows in nominal terms. On this subject see Ward, Deren, and D'Silva (1991).

The literature on shadow price estimation is enormous. Besides the already mentioned Little and Mirrlees (1974), the reference texts on the rationale for distinguishing between traded and non-traded goods in the determination of shadow prices, and the issue of classifications changing over time, are Dasgupta *et al.* (1972), and Bell and Devarajan (1983).

In this chapter, most formulas utilized to estimate shadow prices have been skipped. Some of them, particularly those related to the shadow price of foreign exchange, land and produced goods, are provided by Londero (2003). The theoretical underpinnings of the effects of externalities and public goods on market equilibrium can be found in Brent (2006). Much more about willingness-to-pay theory in relation to the Hicksian compensated demand curve and the Marshallian demand curve is in the book by Just, Hueth, and Schmitz (2004).

On a more empirical ground, a helpful introduction to the calculation of shadow prices using input–output tables is found in Weiss (1988), while Londero (2003) and Potts (2012a) show how to use this approach in empirical cases. Boardman *et al.* (2018) is a comprehensive textbook for the valuation of impacts, entering in the details of most methodologies presented, such as contingent valuation. The book also discusses how to derive shadow prices from secondary (i.e. non-survey) sources for a variety of goods, including life, crime, time, recreation, nature, water, noise, and air pollution. A comprehensive bibliography of studies about contingent valuation is offered by Carson (2011).

Three pricing methodologies based on the LRMC (i.e. the marginal incremental costs, the average incremental costs and the long-run incremental costs methods) are examined in detail by Marsden Jacob Associates (2004). The authors also review the international experience in valuing the LRMC in a specific sector, that of water supply, and present a hypothetical case study involving the increase of capacity of a water treatment plant in order to meet forecast demand. A vast part of the literature examining how to estimate the economic value of non-market goods focuses on the environmental sector. Interesting readings are OECD (2018), Anand (2012), Freeman (2003), Haab *et al.* (2002), Dixon *et al.* (1994), Johansson (1993), and Hanley and Spash (1993). Additional specific references for estimating the willingness-to-pay of determined goods can be retrieved from the Environmental Valuation Reference Inventory (EVRI).

4.9 Summary of Chapter 4

- The financial analysis is the first necessary step in project (but also policy) evaluation. It is followed by the economic analysis, which consists in computing the economic net present value and internal rate of return when all economic costs and benefits are taken into account. It requires that distorted market prices are converted to shadow (or accounting) prices and that the values of externalities and indirect effects are considered.
- Different methods are in place to estimate the economic value of costs and benefits. They depend mainly on the type of goods. The border price rule is often applied to proxy the shadow prices of internationally marketable goods and it relies on the consideration that the FOB and CIF prices represent the economic value of exported and imported goods respectively.
- A standard conversion factor can be applied to convert the price of minor items from any possible distortion. It is computed as a proxy of the average distance between world prices and domestic prices due to taxes, duties and subsidies on imports and exports.
- The long-run marginal cost is the most appropriate proxy of shadow prices of non-tradable inputs for which an increase in demand results in an increase in production. The long-run marginal cost is determined by considering both the operating and capital costs to meet the current and expected needs of the project.
- The willingness-to-pay approach provides the social value of the remaining outputs and inputs, including externalities and goods for which no market price is set. It can be calculated by relying on individual preferences, expressed in monetary terms and stated through *ad hoc* surveys (contingent valuation) or 'choice modelling' valuation. Alternatively, preferences can be unveiled by observing actual behaviour and purchases that can be related to the non-market good under evaluation. The following methods are ascribable to this approach: the travel cost, the hedonic price, the averting or defensive behaviour and the cost of illness.
- The WTP can also be valued by plugging in WTP values that have been previously estimated for a similar project in a different context, after proper adjustment. This is the so-called 'benefit transfer' approach.

Questions

- Imagine that a project uses a locally produced, but potentially importable, input that has an artificially inflated price because of high import tariffs. What approach would be the most appropriate to proxy the shadow prices? Why?
- If a lake becomes used for bathing thanks to a remediation project, how do you value the benefit? Is it correct to consider the use-value associated with it and leave out the non-use value?
- If all the citizens of a given area use bottled water in order to compensate for the bad quality of tap water, is it reasonable to believe that a project aimed at improving the tap water quality in the given area will provide health benefit?
- Imagine a group of 100,000 people faces a 1 per cent risk of dying aged 30 to 40, and a public intervention could eliminate this risk. More specifically, the intervention could be described as preventing 1,000 fatalities. These unknown 1,000 people whose early deaths are prevented would each gain, on average, 45 years of life expectancy. What is the benefit of the intervention if the monetary value for a statistical life-year is EUR 50,000?
- Which method would use to value a private hospital room relative to a shared room?

Appendix 4.1
Financial analysis

The financial return on investment

Financial performance can be calculated in terms of return on investment or return on capital. The former will tell if a project is profitable in the long term regardless of the way it is financed, the latter if the project will produce a net return for the investors compared to an alternative use of their equity capital.

For the calculation of the financial return on investment, items to be considered are the flows of total investments, operating costs and revenues. The flow of total investments includes the following:

- Fixed investments: these refer to the incremental cash disbursements for cost of capital assets (land acquisition, civil works, equipment etc.) at the moment they are actually paid by the project promoter with own funds or other sources of financing. They could include both initial investments and relevant replacement and renewal costs of capital assets occurring in the time horizon considered, which make it possible to restore the value of the project and guarantee its full functionality.
- Start-up costs: these are costs for licensing, tests, tendering, preparatory studies, consulting services, research and development and all those costs which have economic effects accruing beyond the period in which the relative disbursements are made. Because the cash accounting method applies, these costs are included in the period in which the expenses actually occur.[22]
- Changes in net working capital: they represent the increase over one period of time in the difference between current assets (including receivables, stocks, cash and other net short-term liquidity) and current liabilities (including short-term debts to suppliers). Increments of net working capital are generally sizeable at the beginning of project life, when stocks and other components need to be built up for the first time, and subsequently they will stabilize or might even diminish.

The flow of operating costs includes the direct production cost, administrative and general expenditures, ordinary periodic and planned maintenance costs, sales and distribution expenditures. The flow of operating revenues comprises revenues obtained by the project's owner from the sale of goods and services, which are determined by the forecasts of the quantities of services provided and their prices. At the last year of the project's period of life, the residual value of fixed investment is included as an inflow. This represents the present value at the last year of any net future revenue that the project would be able to generate because its economic life is not completely exhausted. It is generally estimated by calculating the market value of fixed assets as they were to be sold at the end of the time horizon considered.[23]

The financial return on capital

A different approach is followed when computing the financial return on capital. In this case, financial profitability is calculated only for some project stakeholders, such as a specific group of investors, or even a single public or private investor. The return on capital is calculated on the basis of the sole inflows and outflows that are referred to the selected investor.

On the basis of this definition, the estimation of the financial return on capital will include as inflows the operating revenues (the same as for the calculus of the financial return on investment), while outflow items comprise the following:

- capital contributions of those stakeholder(s) from the perspective of whom the analysis is carried out (which are used to pay fixed investment, start–up costs and changes in net working capital);
- operating costs (like revenues, these are the same as for the computation of the financial return on investment);
- the loans granted by third parties to the investor, considered at the time at which they are reimbursed;
- the related interest on loans.

Financial performance indicators

The financial return on investment and capital is calculated by means of two indicators: the financial net present value (FNPV) and the financial internal rate of return (FIRR).[24] The former, expressed in monetary terms, is defined by the sum of the yearly difference between outflows and inflows, suitably discounted. A positive (incremental or marginal) FNPV is interpreted as a positive return on the investment, which derives from total discounted inflows which exceed total discounted outflows. On the other hand, if the marginal FNPV is negative, it is because the investment, over its whole period of life, is not able to raise enough revenues to cover the total investment and operating discounted costs involved. Such a project produces a loss in financial terms compared to its counterfactual scenario.

As to the financial internal rate of return (FIRR), this is defined as the discount rate that produces a zero FNPV and it measures the capacity of the net revenues to remunerate the investment costs. For each internal rate of return lower than the established discount rate i, the project is not worthwhile. This definition implies that:

$$\text{NPV} = \sum_{t=0}^{n} \frac{B_t}{(1+\text{IRR})^t} = 0, \tag{A4.1}$$

where B_t is the balance between inflows and outflows at time t and IRR is the internal rate of return.[25]

The advantage of using the IRR is that it is a pure number, thus making it easier to compare projects of different financial scales. Yet, as spotted by Ley (2007) and Boardman *et al.* (2018), the IRR may be misleading in several situations:

- If the sign of the net cash flow changes more than once over the project's lifespan, there may be multiple IRRs for a single project which would make the financing decision rule impossible. This is the case for projects with very large cash outflow both at the beginning and at the end of the project.[26]
- Depending on the time horizon and the size of capital outlay, the IRR tends to be higher with projects having a short life. For this reason, it can be more properly used to compare projects with the same time horizon.
- The IRR cannot be calculated when time-varying discount rates are used (see Chapter 6 for declining discounting).
- It also cannot be calculated if the project shows negative net cash flows over its lifespan (i.e. the project is not revenue-generating).
- Lastly, unlike the NPV, the IRR contains no relevant information about the economic value of an investment project.

Financial sustainability

Besides the financial performance of the investment or capital, the possibility that the project will incur the risk of running out of cash in the future should also be considered and minimized. The capacity of financial sources to cover the expenditures year-by-year is addressed through the sustainability analysis. Differently from financial return, the calculation of financial sustainability does not require an incremental approach.

Financial sustainability is verified when the cumulated net cash flow is positive or at least equal to zero for each of the years considered in the time horizon. The analysis is carried out by considering as incoming flows not only operating revenues, but also any other sources of financing, including public contributions, national private capital or other resources, such as loans. On the other side, outgoing flows are related to investment costs, operating costs, but also to reimbursement and interest on loans, interests paid, taxes and other disbursements (such as dividends, retirement bonuses, etc.).

If the cumulated net cash flow is negative even in one year only, the project is defined as not financially sustainable. The project promoter should then find a more suitable combination of revenues and capital finance to ensure the coverage of costs in each year of the time horizon.

Dealing with taxes in the financial analysis

From the perspective of the private investor, what is typically more relevant is the project's profitability net of taxes. However, in principle, the financial net present value of investment and capital could be computed both gross and net of taxes. As for indirect taxes which are recoverable by the investor, such as value added tax (VAT), this cost is ultimately sustained by other parties (usually the final consumer), thus is not a real outflow for the investor. Whenever indirect taxes are not recoverable, these should be included as outflows in the estimation of the financial return on investment and capital. As to financial sustainability, all taxes paid by the investor should be accounted for (including VAT) at the moment they are paid, and, if this is the case, at the moment they are recovered.

Appendix 4.2
An example of financial and economic analysis

A simplified example of how the financial and economic analyses are to be carried out can provide helpful clarifications on the different inflow and outflow items to be considered and on how results can be interpreted.

A small project is considered, for example, an industrial investment, with a time horizon of only ten years. Investment costs occur in the first two years, while the project starts operations in year 3 and reaches its full regime at year 5. Hence, operating costs and revenues stabilize from year 5. At the last year of the horizon, the project maintains a residual value which is included as an inflow.[27] Data are expressed in constant thousand Euro terms.

Table A4.1 shows the calculation of the return on investment, which is negative: at a discount rate of 5 per cent, the financial net present value amounts to EUR −28,640 and the financial rate of return to −4 per cent.

In order to estimate the financial sustainability of the project, total financial sources that contribute to finance the project are added to operating revenues. It is assumed that the project is financed by three sources: the contribution from the private company in charge of running the project, national public contribution and an EU grant. Private funding derives from equity and a loan, which the investor reimburses in six years (from year 2 to year 7) and on which it pays some interests. In the example illustrated in Table A4.2, financial resources are allocated at years 1 and 2 and they equal the investment and operating costs, but also the loan reimbursement and interest and taxes paid by the private investor. Note that the residual value is not included, as it does not represent a real financial flow.

A proper timing of outflows and inflows ensures a positive accumulated net cash flow over the time horizon. Different loan conditions or lower financial sources could make the project financially unsustainable.

Table A4.3 is about the financial return on capital. The analysis is carried out from the perspective of the private investor, whose total financial contribution amounts to EUR 110,000. This is paid through equity (EUR 50,000), allocated in years 1 and 2, and a loan (EUR 60,000), which is reimbursed starting from year 2. The relatively lower investment costs sustained by the private investor allow him to gain a financial return from the project. In this case, the net present value amounts to EUR 19,570 and the internal rate of return to 17 per cent.

The first step to assess the economic performance of a project is to start from the outflows and inflows considered for the assessment of the financial return on investment: the total operating revenues and costs, the total investment costs and the residual value of the investment. These flows need to be valued at their accounting prices and

Table A4.1 Illustrative table for the calculation of the return on investment (EUR thousand)

Item	Year									
	1	2	3	4	5	6	7	8	9	10
Total operating revenues	0	0	30	50	80	80	80	80	80	80
Residual value of fixed investments	0	0	0	0	0	0	0	0	0	10
Total inflows	**0**	**0**	**30**	**50**	**80**	**80**	**80**	**80**	**80**	**90**
Total investment costs	70	70	0	0	0	0	0	0	0	0
Total operating costs	0	0	5	10	20	20	20	20	20	20
Total outflows	**70**	**70**	**5**	**10**	**20**	**20**	**20**	**20**	**20**	**20**
Net cash flow	−70	−70	25	40	60	60	60	60	60	70
Net cash flow discounted at a 5% financial discount rate	−66.67	−63.49	21.60	32.91	47.01	44.77	42.64	40.61	38.68	42.97
FNPV of the investment	−28.64									
FIRR of the investment	−4%									

Source: Authors.

Table A4.2 Illustrative table for the calculation of financial sustainability (EUR thousand)

Item	Year									
	1	2	3	4	5	6	7	8	9	10
Total operating revenues	0	0	30	50	80	80	80	80	80	80
Total financial sources	72	82.5	0	0	0	0	0	0	0	0
Total inflows	**72**	**82.5**	**30**	**50**	**80**	**80**	**80**	**80**	**80**	**80**
Total investment costs	70	70	0	0	0	0	0	0	0	0
Loan reimbursement	0	10	10	10	10	10	10	0	0	0
Interest on loan	0	0.5	0.5	0.5	0.5	0.5	0.5	0	0	0
Taxes	2	2	2	2	2	2	2	2	2	2
Total operating costs	0	0	5	10	20	20	20	20	20	20
Total outflows	**72**	**82.5**	**17.5**	**22.5**	**32.5**	**32.5**	**32.5**	**22.0**	**22.0**	**22.0**
Net cash flow	**0**	**0**	**12.5**	**27.5**	**47.5**	**47.5**	**47.5**	**58.0**	**58.0**	**58.0**
Accumulated cash flow	0	0	12.5	40.0	87.5	135	182.5	241.0	299.0	357.0

Source: Authors.

for this purpose suitable conversion factors (CFs) are estimated. If the conversion factor is greater than one, then the actual price is lower than the shadow price, whereas if the conversion factor is lower than one, then the actual price is higher than the shadow price. That is, given the shadow price, $v = k \cdot p$, where p are observed prices and k is the conversion factor, we find three cases:

- $k = 1 \Leftrightarrow v = p$;
- $k > 1 \Leftrightarrow v > p$;
- $k < 1 \Leftrightarrow < p$.

In this simplified example, specific conversion factors are applied to the main categories of costs, including, as far as investment costs are concerned, labour, equipment, civil

Table A4.3 Illustrative table for the calculation of the return on private capital (EUR thousand)

Item	Year									
	1	2	3	4	5	6	7	8	9	10
Total operating revenues	0	0	30	50	80	80	80	80	80	80
Residual value of fixed investments	0	0	0	0	0	0	0	0	0	10
Total inflows	**0**	**0**	**30**	**50**	**80**	**80**	**80**	**80**	**80**	**90**
Private contribution (equity)	25	25	0	0	0	0	0	0	0	0
Loan reimbursement	0	10	10	10	10	10	10	0	0	0
Interest on loans	0	0.5	0.5	0.5	0.5	0.5	0.5	0	0	0
Total operating costs	0	0	5	10	20	20	20	20	20	20
Total outflows	**25**	**35.5**	**15.5**	**20.5**	**30.5**	**30.5**	**30.5**	**20.0**	**20.0**	**20.0**
Net cash flow	**−25**	**−35.5**	**14.5**	**29.5**	**49.5**	**49.5**	**49.5**	**60.0**	**60.0**	**70.0**
Net cash flow discounted at a 5% financial discount rate	−23.81	−32.20	12.53	24.27	38.78	36.94	35.18	40.61	38.68	42.97
FNPV of private capital	19.57									
FIRR of private capital	17 %									

Source: Authors.

works and licences, and, for operating costs, labour, energy and raw materials. In the real world, a more detailed taxonomy of cost items could be considered, by distinguishing, for example, skilled labour from non-skilled labour. The following conversion factors have been applied:

- 0.8 for labour cost, that might have been estimated as shown in Chapter 5;
- 0.9 for equipment, energy and raw materials, estimated, for example, according to the border price rule;
- 1.0 for the licences and civil works, assuming that their prices fully reflect their economic value. A conversion factor equal to 1 applies also to the residual value of fixed investment (e.g. buildings).

Secondarily, externalities that are not already captured by accounting prices are valued and included as additional rows in the tables. It is assumed that the project generates negative externalities during the construction phase (these may be noise and air pollution) amounting to EUR 5,000 in years 1 and 2.

The tariff paid by consumers and contributing to produce the operating revenues does not reflect the social value of the service provided by the investment. For this reason, a willingness-to-pay has been estimated (e.g. through a contingent valuation). Since the WTP results higher than the tariff actually paid, the social value of operating revenues is higher than financial revenues.

The resulting economic net present value, estimated at a social discount rate of 3.5 per cent, is positive and equal to EUR 11,840; the economic internal rate of return is 7 per cent; the benefit/cost ratio, i.e. the ratio between the discounted total inflows

(EUR 537.62 thousand) and the discounted total outflows (EUR 219.13 thousand), is 2.45.

In order to better interpret the results of the analysis hereby presented, the following observations can be made:

- despite not generating a positive financial return, from a social perspective the project has a positive welfare effect;
- the positive economic net present value justifies the investment of public grants from national and EU authorities;
- the positive return on private capital justifies the involvement of the private investor in the project.

Table A4.4 Illustrative table for the calculation of the economic performance (EUR thousand)

Item	CF	Year									
		1	2	3	4	5	6	7	8	9	10
Willingness-to-pay		0	0	36	60	96	96	96	96	96	96
Residual value of fixed investments	1	0	0	0	0	0	0	0	0	0	10
Total inflows		**0**	**0**	**36**	**60**	**96**	**96**	**96**	**96**	**96**	**106**
Labour	0.8	21.6	24	0	0	0	0	0	0	0	0
Equipment	0.9	9	27	0	0	0	0	0	0	0	0
Civil works	1	30	10	0	0	0	0	0	0	0	0
Licences	1	3	0	0	0	0	0	0	0	0	0
Total investment costs		63.6	61	0	0	0	0	0	0	0	0
Labour	0.8	0	0	1.6	3.2	6.4	6.4	6.4	6.4	6.4	6.4
Energy	0.9	0	0	1.8	3.6	7.2	7.2	7.2	7.2	7.2	7.2
Raw materials	0.9	0	0	0.9	1.8	3.6	3.6	3.6	3.6	3.6	3.6
Total operating costs		0	0	4.3	8.6	17.2	17.2	17.2	17.2	17.2	17.2
Negative externality	5	5	0	0	0	0	0	0	0	0	
Total outflows		**68.6**	**66**	**4.3**	**8.6**	**17.2**	**17.2**	**17.2**	**17.2**	**17.2**	**17.2**
Net cash flow		−68.6	−66	31.7	51.4	78.8	78.8	78.8	78.8	78.8	88.8
Net cash flow discounted at a 3.5% social discount rate		−66.28	−61.61	28.59	44.79	66.35	64.10	61.94	59.84	57.82	62.95
ENPV of the investment		11.84									
EIRR of the investment		7%									
B/C ratio		2.45									

Source: Authors.

Notes

1 This chapter is with Emanuela Sirtori.
2 This is particularly important when a public contribution to the investment is required. Actually, the results of the financial analysis are elements to be considered also when deciding about the justification of public intervention. A project that does not produce positive financial returns may still be likely to receive public contribution if this will ensure the financial sustainability of the project, thus giving it the possibility to produce positive economic effects.

On the contrary, a government may be less inclined to allocate additional public financing to a project that is financially sustainable and profitable with the already available resources.

3 The latter situation would imply an inefficient allocation of public funds, as the same effect could be reached with a lower grant (e.g. the grant that would give a return just marginally above the investor's opportunity cost of capital).

4 This issue would require an extensive discussion, which is, however, skipped in this book. A comprehensive book for non-expert accountants is Pinson (2007).

5 When the objective of a project is specifically to ensure compliance with legislation (e.g. waste water treatment plants to fulfil rules requiring a certain quality of water), the counter-factual scenario could be an alternative investment that still satisfies the minimum legislative requirements. Another possibility is to consider as counterfactual the BAU or do-minimum scenario, including also the financial and social costs attached to the missed compliance with regulations (e.g. payment of fees, limitation of recreational and bathing activities and fishing due to bad quality water, with the resulting lost revenues, etc.).

6 Some public monopolies are regulated at average costs, which are above marginal costs.

7 This formula can be written also in a continuous variation: $\text{NPV} = \int_{t=0}^{\infty} (1+i)^{-t} b(t) dt$, where $b(t)$ is the rate of flowing cash given in money time, which is nil $(b(t) = 0)$ when the investment is over.

8 For instance, one of the possible benefits attached to the construction of a new incinerator plant for urban waste is the avoidance of costs of building and operating a new landfill to collect the same volume of waste. This item can either be included on the benefit side of the do-project scenario, or on the cost side of the do-minimum scenario, thus reducing the incremental costs of the project. The benefit-cost ratio computed in each of the two cases would be different, because of different total inflows and outflows.

9 For an illustrative application of the input-output method to derive conversion factors, see Potts (2002) and Londero (2003). The I/O table has been used also by Ahmad and Stern (1984, 1990) to assess the impact of marginal changes in taxes on the demand of commodity goods, through the computation of shadow prices.

10 Some of them draw from partial equilibrium approaches.

11 The Little and Mirrlees approach has been developed under the assumption that trade is always a feasible option to the national planner (for those goods for which there is an international market). However, the border price rule may not apply in contexts where the planner has no possibility to determine its own trade policy. This is the case, for example, of exogenous quota or legal barriers being set at national or any other higher level of government, without any possibility for the local planner to change them. Hence, if foreign trade does not represent an alternative solution to domestic consumption and production, because no control on the trade policy is in place, the value of tradable goods should be estimated on the basis of the long-run marginal cost of production or the willingness to pay, as for other non-tradable goods.

12 In the context of a 'big country', it can be assumed that the world price of the commodity depends on the quantity traded. In other words, a binding side constraint is added to the planner's problem, which is the following: $p_d = p_f \psi(\overline{y}_i^F) + \overline{t}_i$, where p_d is internal price, p_f is the international price, $\psi(\overline{y}_i^F)$ is a function of the net import level, and $\overline{t}_i$ is an exogenous tariff imposed on good i. With this constraint, the FOC becomes: $\dfrac{\partial L}{\partial \overline{y}_i^F} = v_i + v_f \dfrac{\partial y_f^F}{\partial \overline{y}_i^F} + \mu p_f \dfrac{\delta \psi}{\partial \overline{y}_i^F} = 0$, where μ, the Lagrange multiplier, is the shadow price related to the fact that the country is able to affect international prices. In the case of a big country, for which prices are not parameters, the procedure of Little and Mirrlees cannot be applied, due to the additional side constraint. The only case in which the border price rule could still be used is when the tariff is optimal, i.e. $\mu = 0$.

13 See also Florio (2013) for an analysis of price trends in the EU network industries (telecommunications, electricity and natural gas).

14 Sticking to the electricity example, some handbooks of applied cost-benefit analysis still regard electricity as a non-traded good. Yet, this depends on the characteristics of the market.

In most EU countries, for example, electricity can in fact be considered a traded good, even if not fully internationally traded. Anyway, if there is an interconnector, the price of power in the bordering market can be taken as a reference if this represents the next best alternative of domestic production.

15 Rationing of export and import should also be considered.

16 Sometimes project analysts apply a double conversion factor on goods expressed at their market price: the Standard Conversion Factor to correct for the currency distortions, and a specific conversion factor to capture any other market distortion related to the good. This procedure, which is backed by the Drèze and Stern theory, can be applied only if the specific conversion factor does not already fully incorporate the distortions of the currency market.

17 According to this approach, units of domestic resources are the *numéraire* against which all goods, both traded and non-traded, are valued. When there are distortions in the capital and currency market, a shadow exchange rate (SER) has to be used. The SER measures the extent to which local prices of goods exceed the world prices and is the inverse of the SCF. In deciding which of the two approaches to use, the degree of distortion of the currency market should be considered. In the EU Member States, for example, in which there is full currency convertibility and capital flow mobility, the European Commission (2014) recommends using the Little and Mirrlees border price and the SCF rule, since in principle there is no difference between the official exchange rate and the shadow exchange rate.

18 Note that the incremental capital cost per unit of output is equal to the average cost of the existing productive plant only upon the condition that the long-run cost is constant and the assumption that the plant operates in a completely static world.

19 The long-run marginal cost plays an important role in determining the most efficient price for third-party access to infrastructure or services, or in the identification and measurement of cross-subsidization (Marsden Jacob Associates 2004).

20 As Kahn (1988) pointed out: "Marginal costs look to the future, not to the past: it is only future costs for which additional production can be causally responsible; it is only future costs that can be saved if that production is not undertaken" (Kahn 1988: 98).

21 The latest version of the UK Green Book refers identifies a third method: the 'Subjective wellbeing Approach'. This approach uses direct wellbeing based responses (in existing data or from research by questionnaire) to estimate relative prices of non-market goods. One of the limitations of this method has to do with the bias occurring when individuals adjust their wellbeing scores in order to give more socially desirable responses. Furthermore, people generally tend to value their present wellbeing on the basis of their past, rather than current, experiences. See the discussion on happiness in Chapter 1.

22 The decision of which year to consider as starting point of the analysis is particularly relevant for projects involving a very long time for preliminary studies, or land acquisition, or other start-up activities. In principle, all the start-up costs directly connected to the project assessed should be included in the analysis.

23 When different stakeholders are involved in the project's implementation, e.g. as owners, investors or operators, it is appropriate to carry on a consolidated analysis for all parties involved and to estimate the profitability of the investment regardless of the actual return to specific different stakeholders.

24 The FNPV and FRR are generally considered the most synthetic, coherent and easy-to-use indicators for financial analysis. Other indicators, still based on the cash flow approach and which may provide additional information for the evaluation of investment performance, are the Inflows–Outflows ratio (i.e. the ratio between the net present value of total inflows and the net present value of total outflows) and the Discounted Payback Period (defined as the necessary number of years at which cumulated discounted net positive flows generated by the investments equal the negative discounted flows occurred in the initial years to start the project).

25 The financial rate of return of private capital (equity) is generally expected to be higher than the financial rate of return of the project, because the public contribution reduces the total investment cost.

26 E.g. nuclear power plants with final decommissioning costs, or projects with high replacement and renewal costs.

27 Alternatively, it could be included as an outflow with opposite sign.

5 The social cost of labour

Overview[1]

According to cost-benefit analysis theory, the shadow wage rate (SWR) is the social opportunity cost of labour and may differ from the observed wage because of distortions in both the labour market and the product market. In practice, appropriate conversion factors (CFs) are used to translate observed market wages into shadow wages. As the conversion factor is defined as the ratio between the shadow wage and the observed market wage, if the shadow wage is lower than the market wage, the social profitability of the public project is greater than its financial profitability. For many infrastructure projects, ignoring this correction may lead to an underestimation of the social benefits of public investment. The same would be true for policy reforms leading to significant job creation (or destruction).

Section 5.1 reviews earlier theoretical and empirical literature dealing with the definition of the opportunity cost of labour and the computation of shadow wage rates. Shadow wages differ across countries and regions due to underlying spatial economic, demographic, and labour market structures. One reason for the difficulty of translating shadow wage theory into practice is the heavy information burden for evaluators, who are often required to use project-specific micro-data, such as surveys of reservation wages or firm-level marginal productivity.

A framework for the empirical computation of shadow wages and conversion factors at the regional level, accounting for structural characteristics and labour market conditions, is presented in Section 5.3. This approach is explicitly based on well-established CBA theory, particularly on a combination of the Little and Mirrlees (1974) and the Drèze and Stern (1987, 1990) frameworks (Section 5.2). The derived empirical formulae are implementable with regional and national statistical data, moving away from the more precise but cumbersome and costly approaches based on project-specific micro-data.

After the analytical underpinning and the conceptual model at the basis of the empirical methodology have been set out, the shadow wage rates and the corresponding conversion factors are computed with data on European regions in 2007. The empirical findings highlight a substantial degree of SWR variability between European regions, with important implications for public project evaluation and for the allocation of the EU Structural Funds. The final section (5.5) suggests some further reading.

DOI: 10.4324/9781003191377-7

5.1 Earlier literature on the social opportunity cost of labour

5.1.1 Theoretical contributions

A project that uses labour as an input must normally consider this fact as a social cost, in the same way as financial analysis considers the wage paid as a financial outflow. In principle, the social opportunity cost of additional project employment is either the value, given a *numéraire*, of the marginal product of labour in the economy, or the worker's subjective disutility of effort. In principle, the two measures would coincide for an equilibrium labour market, and would be equal to the observable market wage. Nevertheless, even under full employment and in a competitive labour market, the market wage may differ from the shadow wage because of the social cost of displacing workers from one activity to another and because of price distortions in other markets. Moreover, labour markets are often far from being in equilibrium, and close with unemployment and/or migration.

The definition and calculation of the shadow wage rate has been an important research topic in Applied Welfare Economics since the 1950s and 1960s. The CBA literature offers different shadow wage formulae based on different hypotheses on labour market conditions, and sometimes on capital and product markets as well. This makes comparisons across results often difficult. In this section a concise picture of early contributions and recent findings on the social cost of labour are provided. See, inter alia, Little (1961), Sen (1966, 1972), Harberger (1971a), Lal (1973), Little and Mirrlees (1974), and Sah and Stiglitz (1985). More recently, shadow wages have been discussed, inter alia, by Potts (2002), Londero (2003), de Rus (2010), Haveman and Farrow (2011), Weiss and Potts (2012), Haveman and Weim (2015), and Johansson and Kriström (2020).

In one of the earliest contributions, Lewis (1954) argued that the shadow wage is equal to the lost output from the former employment, i.e. the value of the marginal product of the sector of provenance (that will be the one with the lowest wages at the end of the vacancy-replacement chain, e.g. agriculture). He proposed a simple closed economy model in which society maximizes aggregate output, and consumption of different workers is given equal social weight by the government. Within this framework, the unemployed do not receive any subsidy and neither employment *per se* nor leisure is given social value,[2] implying the lack of a term capturing the disutility of effort. The project displaces some workers and hires some unemployed, in a proportion that represents the share of employed and unemployed in the economy. Being the model based on the notion of output loss, with high unemployment or marginal productivity in the previous occupation equal to zero, the new job created has no real effect on other sectors of the economy.

A seminal contribution to the shadow wage theory was given by Little and Mirrlees (1974). The authors, drawing from their previous guidelines of the Organization for Economic Cooperation and Development (OECD) for project appraisal in developing economies, justify the use of shadow prices because of the presence of real wage rigidity in the formal sector of the economy, which exaggerates the social cost of employment. Specifically, they identify four main sources of distortion. First, even if actual wages were equal to the value of the marginal product of labour at market prices, the former may be distorted by taxes and subsidies; hence consumption at shadow prices may be greater or less than that at market prices. Second, labour in the rural sector receives subsidies.[3] Third, in the formal sector there are minimum wage requirements because of government regulation or unionization that may distort the market. Finally, in some sectors, high wages may correspond to even higher productivity and consumption, and transferring labour from the rural sector to the urban or formal sector may entail some costs.

Some of these sources of distortion are considered by Roberts (1982) in his economic model for governmental expenditure with Keynesian unemployment, which leads to somewhat surprising results. He shows that in an economy with labour rationing, wage rigidity, flexible prices for goods, savings and money balances, one public good, lump sum transfers, profit and indirect taxation, the shadow wage can even be *negative* under very high unemployment. Actually, in a context where the government may have a monetary policy, and public production can be financed either by money, indirect or lump taxes, the sign of the shadow wage is reversed if both the reservation wage[4] and the marginal propensity to consume are high: a public good production at shadow prices is the more desirable the more it is unprofitable at producer prices.

Another example showing how general equilibrium models of shadow wage rates tend to be very complex is provided by Johansson (1982). He proposes a model of a small open economy with three private firms, producing three goods (one exported, one imported, one non-traded), one public firm offering a non-traded good, labour and money. This setting potentially generates 24 rationing equilibria (for each good there may be either excess demand or supply, given the $N - 1$ conditions constraining the remaining market). Johansson offers welfare measures, hence shadow prices, for four cases based on Malinvaud (1977): Walrasian equilibrium, 'orthodox' Keynesian unemployment (characterized by wage rigidity and price flexibility), fixed-price Keynesian unemployment (with excess supply in both product and labour markets and widespread price rigidity, except for the exchange rate), and classical unemployment (with excess labour supply combined with excess demand for goods). Welfare measures are shown to be different in the four cases.

Another strand of SWR literature stemmed from the works by Harris and Todaro (1970) and Harberger (1971a), which consider the role of trade and migration. The basic Harris and Todaro framework is described by a two-sector static model, with internal trade and unemployment. The main idea is that workers in the rural sector with lower productivity (i.e. income) migrate to the urban sector, despite unemployment, until the urban expected wage equals the rural certain wage. In this context, the proportion of employed in the total labour force represents the probability of being hired. The main conclusion therefore is that the shadow wage will equal the market wage if the unemployment rate remains unchanged.

An early analysis of a two-sector model, with a traditional agriculture sector and the government project sector, is given by Warr (1973). Fitzgerald (1976) introduces a petty urban service sector, and defines a more complex saving cost concept. Mazumdar (1976) proposes a different migration equation that allows for different methods of financing the period of urban job research (e.g. income support by rural family or self-financing with informal activities in the urban sector). The dynamic equilibrium obtained is shown to be a particular form of the Little and Mirrlees solution. The result, with stringent conditions, could theoretically give a shadow wage greater than the market wage.[5]

This setting has been further extended in the Sah and Stiglitz (1985) contribution, which presents a general equilibrium model for shadow wages in developing countries. Shadow wages are influenced by the structure of industrial and agricultural sectors, by the nature of the international trade environment and by the equilibrating mechanism of the model. The derived relationship between shadow wages and market wages can be adapted to various technological and institutional frameworks which are country-specific.

Another interesting extension to the Harris and Todaro model was proposed by economists aiming at a conceptually relevant formula for efficient regional employment policies in Canada. Boadway and Flatters (1981), and later on Wilson (1993), describe poor regions as those with fixed wages and unemployment while rich regions are characterized by full employment and self-adjusting productivity. The shadow wage in these models includes output loss along with changes in the imputed value of leisure and migration costs from taking workers from the labour market.

It is apparent from this brief and very selective review of theoretical literature that it is not possible to compute shadow wages, and thus infer the social cost of labour, without a model of the underlying labour market. Such a model should include at least a simple theory of wage determination and migration: actually, unemployment *per se* may not be sufficient to guarantee a shadow wage lower than the market wage, because of migration phenomena.

5.1.2 Empirical contributions

Actual estimation and practical applications of shadow pricing in general, and particularly of the SWR, have in fact been limited, as critically discussed, for example, by Squire (1998) or Little and Mirrlees (1974).

When the shadow wage is simply seen as the marginal productivity of labour, as in earlier theories, it can be directly estimated using a production function. Cobb–Douglas specifications are often used in models estimating the labour supply of members of agricultural households, especially in developing economies. A very good example of this approach is by Jacoby (1993), who uses data on 1,034 households in 1985–1986 from the Peruvian highlands region and finds that testing the equality between wages and marginal product leads to estimates of the conversion factor between 0.37 and 0.58. Other empirical studies are mentioned in Box 5.1.

Box 5.1 Some empirical results from the literature

Among the papers that provide estimates of shadow wages for developing countries, Skoufias (1994) can be mentioned. He considers data from six villages in India for the rainy season crop-cycle of the calendar years 1975–1979. This leads to an estimated total of 675 farmers/year in 166 households and a conversion factor of 0.83 for males and 0.63 for female workers. Abdulai and Regmi's (2000) analysis is based on a cross-sectional survey of 280 farm households in Nepal from May 1996 to April 1997. Eight villages were selected, representing the three agro-climatic zones of the country, and the authors estimate a conversion factor of 0.414. In a study on child labour, Menon *et al.* (2005) estimate the shadow wage using a cost function that treats household labour as a quasi-fixed factor, using data from the Nepal Living Standards Survey (1996) along with additional estimations carried out on a sample of 2,380 farm households. Their main results are that, considering families with working children, the adults' shadow wage is

---

below the market wage, implying a conversion factor well below unity. Using data from the 2010 Nepal Living Standard Survey Phase III of 2,022 households, Nepal and Nelson (2015) estimate the shadow wage by gender for Nepalese agricultural households. A very comprehensive computation of shadow prices for Colombia is offered by Londero (2003), who considers skilled and unskilled labour, foreign labour, administrative and professional jobs, and differences in the level of benefits, with conversion factors ranging from 0.41 (administrative labour with high benefits) to 1.0 (for foreign employees). Using data from rice producers in Cote d'Ivoire, Barrett, Sherlund, and Adesina (2008) illustrate a method for estimating structural labour supply models in the presence of unobservable wages and deviations of households' marginal revenue product of self-employed labour from their shadow wage.

Source: Authors.

When turning to developed economies, the focus of the analysis usually shifts towards the effects of inter-regional migration and the presence of different categories of workers. An empirical application specific to the Irish economy is given by Honohan (1998). The author's equation for the shadow wage, broadly based on the Harris and Todaro frame, is:

$$w^* = \frac{w_a}{(1-u)} = w_m, \tag{5.1}$$

where w^* is the shadow wage or opportunity cost of the extra job, w_a is the labour productivity in the agricultural sector, w_m is the urban economy wage rate, and u is the unemployment rate. The creation of an extra job in the urban sector will induce $\frac{1}{1-u}$ migrants to move (just enough to restore the equilibrium unemployment rate), where the opportunity cost of an extra job is equal to the loss of output of these migrants. Irish unemployment was very high at the time and this might justify a low shadow wage. In fact, the estimated impact of job creation on unemployment was consistent with conversion factors of at most 80 per cent. Other empirical studies are mentioned in Box 5.2.

Box 5.2 Some empirical results from the literature

Picazo-Tadeo and Reig-Martinez (2005) compute shadow wages for family labour in the Spanish agricultural sector by exploiting the duality between input distances and cost functions. With data on citrus farms in the Valencia area, taken from the 1997 Survey on Input Use by Farms, the authors estimate a conversion factor of family labour of around 0.68. De Borger (1993) uses data from Belgian Railroads operations (1959–1986) to estimate a log-linear specification of the shadow wage formula that includes a variable to grasp the influence of politics on the public enterprise and its employment policy. The main result is that the mean of conversion factors over time is 0.72. Following the same line, Saleh (2004) uses sectoral employment and data from the Australian Bureau of Statistics. The main results are that conversion factors differ across sectors and range between 0.94 for Intermediate Clerical, Sales and Service workers and 1.01 for Elementary Clerical, Sales and Service workers. Using data for Mexico, Guillermo-Peon and Harberger (2012) illustrate a detailed procedure to estimate the social opportunity cost of labour in real-world cases. Resting on a general equilibrium model of a tax-distorted but otherwise perfectly competitive economy and using data on market wages and countries' fiscal regimes, Lang and Riess (2019) estimates shadow wages for 33 OECD countries. These estimates are national parameters, which can be applied to all projects in a country.

Source: Authors.

It should be apparent that, in the vast majority of the contributions reviewed, highly project-specific micro-data were often needed to compute shadow wages and corresponding conversion factors.[6] This is a clear disadvantage when considering the fact that governments need to evaluate hundreds or thousands of investment projects every year. Therefore, several countries have developed national guidelines and recommendations for applied CBA which include considerations of the social cost of labour. Examples of official guidelines for investment appraisal include HM Treasury (2020a) in the UK, the Australian Guide to cost-benefit analysis (NSW Treasury 2017), and the Guide to Social Cost-Benefit Analysis (2015) published by the New Zealand Treasury.

5.2 A conceptual model for the social cost of labour

The review of the literature shows that there is wide consensus about the broad definition of the SWR as the marginal social opportunity cost of labour. This section focuses on the Little and Mirrlees (LM) framework for the estimation of the SWR, whose formula has become quite popular among CBA practitioners in empirical applications. The aim is to provide a simple baseline shadow wage equation that lends itself to empirical estimation through national and regional statistical data, as shown in the next section. In what follows, the SWR formulae that were proposed by Little and Mirrlees are recalled. With respect to the original formulation, notation is slightly adapted for ease of comparison with the Dréze–Stern model.

In the original Little–Mirrlees contribution, by focusing on developing countries, the core idea was framed in a context where there are two sectors: the modern/urban one and the informal/rural one. The labour markets in the two contexts are different, because, in the former, labour conditions are fairly regulated, for example, because of minimum wage legislation, unionization and other institutions. In contrast, in the latter, there is a much less regulated labour market, self-employment in small rural firms, hidden unemployment, etc. Also, the price structure in the two environments is different.

Using a slightly different notation to that in other chapters of this book, in line with Del Bo *et al.* (2011), c_1 denotes the before-project average consumption of the rural worker, some of which (possibly through a series of interrelated effects) is transferred to the urban context because of the new job opportunity given by the public project; c_2 is the new consumption level of the worker after the project is launched and has hired its employees;

d is the cost of urbanization related to migration of the worker from the countryside (including transport costs to provide food, accommodation and other goods/services in the new urban location); e is any cost-saving associated with the new employment (e.g. saving of unemployment benefits by the government); $L\left(\dfrac{\partial c}{\partial L}\right)$ is the side effect of increased employment (L) on consumption (c) of existing employees, for example, because of increased unionization. Also, m_1 and m_2 are defined as the value of the marginal productivity of the rural worker and urban worker, respectively, at shadow prices.

Following Little and Mirrlees, the social planner wants to maximize a Social Welfare Function (SWF), where consumption is the welfare metric.[7] $V(c_1)$ and $V(c_2)$ are the welfare levels associated with c_1 and c_2, respectively. Little and Mirrlees associate 'welfare weights' with each consumption level. Thus the welfare weights in the SWF are simply $v(c_1) = dV(\cdot)/dc\big|_{c_1}$ and $v(c_2) = dV(\cdot)/dc\big|_{c_2}$, respectively, related to consumption levels c_1 and c_2.

The assumption of iso-elasticity of the SWF leads to welfare weights that are equal to: $v(c_1) = (c_0/c_1)^{\eta}$ and $v(c_2) = (c_0/c_2)^{\eta}$, where $\eta = |(c/v)(\partial v/\partial c)|$ is the constant elasticity of the marginal utility of consumption, and c_0 is defined as the 'base' or 'critical' level of consumption. This is the level of consumption for which one euro of transfer to the poor from the government budget is welfare equivalent to any other optimal use of uncommitted social income, such as investment.

The more detailed LM formula is (Little and Mirrlees 1974: 273):

$$\text{SWR} = \left[c_2 + d - e + L\left(\frac{\partial c}{\partial L}\right)\right] - \left[V(c_2) - V(c_1) + v(c_1)(c_1 - m_1) + v(c_2) L\left(\frac{\partial c}{\partial L}\right)\right] \quad (5.2)$$

The interpretation of the formula is as follows. The first term in brackets on the right-hand side is the total consumption impact of additional employment. It is a social cost, as the economy has to commit resources to support the new employee's consumption ($c_2 + d$) and this also has some effects on taxpayers, since they now have to pay less unemployment benefits ($-e$), and on other workers as well, in the form of a pecuniary externality $L(\partial c/\partial L)$. The second term in brackets on the right-hand side is the welfare change related to consumption: the new employees previously could only enjoy the consumption level c_1, whereas they now consume $c_2 > c_1$. Thus there is an increase in the social welfare level: their relatives in the rural households were sharing with them the consumption level c_1, which is assumed to be greater than the value of the marginal productivity of the displaced worker m_1 (as supposedly within the rural households food and any compensation is equally distributed among members of the family, and not according to individual productivity); finally, there is the welfare impact of increased wages/consumption on other workers (because of less unemployment), evaluated at the c_2 level of consumption.

All the c and m variables are expressed at shadow prices, meaning that consumption and production are evaluated at prices that, in turn, reflect the social value of goods, for example, after appropriate corrections for price distortions. Thus, the intuition is simple: the marginal social cost of employment is the net welfare change determined by total increased consumption, on the cost side, and by the sum of benefits for individuals of that consumption on the benefit side, evaluated through the appropriate welfare weights.

Assuming that wages are inelastic to marginal changes in employment, that $v(c)$ is continuous and differentiable in the $(c_1 - c_2)$ interval, and using the mean value theorem of calculus,[8] equation (5.2) can be simplified to:

$$\text{SWR} = [c_2 + d - e] - \left[v(c^*)(c_2 - c_1) + v(c_1)(c_1 - m_1)\right] \tag{5.3}$$

If $v(c^*)$ is locally close to $v(c_1)$, which is reasonable if the rural origin and the urban destination are near each other, a more manageable (and popular) version of the Little–Mirrlees formula for the SWR is obtained (Little and Mirrlees 1974: 270):

$$\text{SWR} = c' - \left(\frac{1}{s}\right)(c_2 - m_2) \tag{5.4}$$

where $c' = c_2 + d - e$.

A new variable appears in equation (5.4): S, defined as the ratio between the social value of public investment and that of private consumption ('value of uncommitted government income, measured in terms of consumption committed through employment').[9] Thus, taking the inverse of S, Little and Mirrlees translate current consumption into its investment value. Clearly, the fact that S is greater than unity suggests that the present social value of future net consumption generated by public investment is greater than the social value of current consumption. In general, LM would expect that $S > 1$, because private investment is constrained, and this justifies the role of public investment in the first place.

The net effect $(c_2 - m_1)$ represents the benefit of moving the worker and arises from the aggregation of the benefit to the displaced worker $(c_2 - c_1)$ and to the rural household $(c_1 - m_1)$. This however must be translated in terms of public investment equivalent, or the LM *numéraire*: uncommitted social income. This is achieved by the $(1/s)$ term. Thus, the greater the priority of investment relative to consumption, the greater is s, and the closer is the SWR to c', the total consumption impact of additional employment. The only step needed to go from (5.2) to (5.4) is to justify the equality between the welfare weight of consumption and the inverse of the social value of investment. In fact, if the social planner is benevolent and allocates public expenditure optimally, the social marginal value of public investment should be welfare equivalent to other socially valuable uses of government expenditure, notably transfers to the poor. There is thus, in principle, a close relationship between $1/s$ and the 'base' level of private consumption (c_0), which in turn is related to the income level that would justify either tax exemption or an income subsidy.[10]

Little and Mirrlees state that once s is known, c_0 can be calculated.[11] However, in practice, the estimation of the parameter s would need a complex inter-temporal analysis of the national or local economy to establish the priority of investment over different consumption levels.

5.3 The shadow wage rate and labour market conditions

5.3.1 Simplifying the Little–Mirrlees formula for the SWR

Building on the Little and Mirrlees analytical setting, and also on the Drèze and Stern theory (1987), this section derives a baseline equation that, under certain simplifying assumptions, is a reasonable approximation of the shadow wage rate (SWR) in different regional labour market conditions. More details on the derivation of SWRs from the Drèze and Stern model are provided by Del Bo *et al.* (2011).

In order to solve the difficulty of estimating the parameter s to be entered in the Little–Mirrlees equation (5.4), the inverse conceptual relationship can be used and $1/s$ can be replaced by a welfare weight. As a practical approach to the estimation of $v(c^*)$, this being the interest on the spatial dimension of the EU, the households by regions are then aggregated, and per-capita incomes are simply used instead of consumption levels. In this context, the $v(c^*)$ welfare weight can be interpreted as a 'regional welfare weight' (see Evans *et al.* 2005; Kula 2007 and Chapter 7). Then, the estimate in the h-region will take the generic form:

$$v\left(c^{*h}\right) \approx \beta^h \equiv \left(\frac{Y^0}{Y^h}\right)^{\eta}$$

(5.5)

where the superscript h represents the average consumer in the region h, β^h is the welfare weight of the average consumer in region h, Y^h is income, Y^0 is the critical consumption/income in a reference area and η is the (constant) elasticity of social welfare to private income/consumption. Thus, the direct Social Welfare Function of LM, $V(c)$, has been turned into an indirect one.

Moreover, to further simplify, it is assumed that $c_2 = c'$, i.e. the urbanization cost d is considered as fully balanced by the fiscal benefits e, for example, because of less subsidies to the rural poor or less unemployment subsidies in the urban context; m is interpreted in a generic form as the value of labour in the previous use at shadow prices; and, given the LM assumption that private savings of workers are negligible, it is concluded that $c_2 = w_2$, where w is the consumption value of the wage. Then, by simple algebra from (5.4), this generic expression for the shadow wage rate in region h can be derived:

$$\text{SWR}^h = \beta^h m_1{}^{\eta} + \left(1 - \beta^h\right) w_2{}^{\eta}$$

(5.6)

In other words, under the above-mentioned hypotheses, the net social cost of labour in the regional economy is a welfare-weighted linear combination of the previous (*ex-ante*) and the current (post-project) social value of the new job opportunity.[12] According to region-specific structural characteristics, the value of marginal productivity in the previous occupation, m, varies depending upon which category the workers displaced by the project come from,[13] and different cases for the computation of shadow wages could be considered, which are described in detail below.

5.3.2 Empirical formulae

Before turning to further empirical estimation issues, it is shown how the simplified LM formula (5.6) is flexible and can be adapted to different regional labour markets by simply changing the variable in the first term (see Del Bo *et al.* 2011 for further details). In fact, as mentioned, the LM framework was proposed for the urban/rural divide. However, this equation is more general and can be adapted to encompass different labour market structures using the more general DS setting.

In the DS setting, three labour market conditions are rigorously derived in a general equilibrium framework using different hypotheses about the balancing mechanism of the market. These three regimes can be labelled Fairly Socially Efficient, Quasi-Keynesian Unemployment and Dual Labour markets. Additionally, the latter labour market system could be split into two cases: Rural Labour Dualism and Urban Labour Dualism. Box 5.3 provides a synthetic overview of the specific features of each labour market, which are then more extensively discussed.

5.3.2.1 Fairly Socially Efficient case

The first type of labour market is labelled the Fairly Socially Efficient (FSE) case, where labour is paid nearly its marginal value and unemployment is frictional. Formally, if labour supplies are fixed, and thus inelastic to wages, the market wage is a market-clearing variable, and will respond to the change in labour demand by the public sector. Therefore, the shadow price of labour, SWR_{FSE}, is given by the marginal social product of labour that has been displaced by the project, corrected by a distributional term.

Box 5.3 The four labour market conditions

1   Fairly Socially Efficient (FSE)
    In an efficient labour market, labour is paid almost its marginal value and there is only frictional unemployment. Shadow wage rates are equivalent to market wages, apart from a distributional factor. This type of labour market condition is typically found in high income, urbanized areas, characterized by high immigration inflows and low unemployment rates.

2   Quasi-Keynesian Unemployment (QKU)
    This labour market is characterized by a situation of high unemployment, both in the short and long run, reflecting a structural condition of wage rigidity. Shadow wages are thus related to the difference between the workers' reservation wage (in the form, e.g., of unemployment benefits) and the welfare-weighted market wage. These conditions can be found in areas of high unemployment and relatively low income.

3   Rural Labour Dualism (RLD)
    A dual rural labour market is characterized by the presence of a widespread informal market in a predominantly rural, low-income area with high emigration rates. Excess supply is absorbed in the dual rural market and shadow wage rates reflect this situation. The shadow wage rate is the welfare-weighted difference between wages in the informal agricultural sector (thus net of tax) and market in the manufacturing sector.

4   Urban Labour Dualism (ULD)
    Urban areas can also be characterized by the presence of an informal labour market. Urban labour dualism can describe the situation in urban areas characterized by high unemployment and positive immigration flows, suggesting the existence of an unofficial labour market. The shadow wage rate is thus a welfare-weighted difference between wages in the informal official manufacturing sector, which differ due to the tax wedge.

    Source: Authors.

The sign of the latter will depend upon the relative welfare impact of rents going to employees and shareholders (which in general are different social groups).

The analytical formulation for the vector shadow wage rates in competitive labour markets, using the DS framework but with some convenient changes in notation, is[14]:

$$SWR_{FSE} = m_2 + D, \tag{5.7}$$

where m_2 is the vector of marginal social product of labour, whose elements are the values taken by productivity in each region in FSE markets, and D reflects the distributional effect of a rise in wages due to the creation of new employment, through an inverse elasticity rule. If the interest is more on interregional income and welfare disparities than on intra-regional comparisons, D can be set equal to 0.

The empirical counterpart of SWR_{FSE} is:

$$SWR_{FSE} = \frac{w_2}{NPC}, \tag{5.8}$$

where w_2 represents the vector of market wages rate in the FSE manufacturing sector, and NPC a nominal protection factor to account for country-wide price distortions. The $1/NPC$ factor is our shortcut way to express wages in terms of shadow prices, and w_2 is a proxy of wages in a competitive labour market. As SWRs are obtained by multiplying the market wage by a conversion factor, in economies that are undistorted and where the distributional effects can be ignored, the vector of conversion factors (CFs) is equal to the inverse of nominal protection coefficient, i.e. $CF_{FSE} = 1/NPC$. Hence, in this case, the shadow wage in region h is estimated as the prevailing regional manufacturing average wage, corrected by the general price distortion indicator (NPC).[15]

5.3.2.2 Quasi-Keynesian Unemployment

In the case that unemployment is involuntary and there is wage rigidity – a situation labelled as Quasi-Keynesian Unemployment (QKU) – the workers hired by the public project will likely have been previously unemployed. Thus, it is not the wage that will clear the market, but a softening in the rationing of labour supply. In this situation, the increase in employment due to the public project reduces leisure time, which has a value expressed by the reservation wage. The formula for the shadow wage in the DS framework is the sum of the welfare-weighted reservation wage and the marginal social value of the increase in income that goes to the newly hired:

$$SWR_{QKU} = \beta r_w - b w_2, \tag{5.9}$$

where β is the vector of regional welfare weight, r_w is the vector of the reservation wage, and b is the vector of the marginal social value of a lump-sum transfer to consumers in QKU markets.

A proxy for b could simply be $b = (\beta - 1)$, as all worker's income is spent on consumption goods.[16] This leads, by substitution, to the empirical formula to be estimated:

$$SWR_{QKU} = \beta r_w + (1 - \beta) \frac{w_2}{NPC}. \tag{5.10}$$

If region h has a high welfare weight, i.e. the average household is poor, the social cost of labour is certainly less than the market wage. In this $\beta^h > 1$ because of the assumption that β is defined as $\beta^h \equiv (Y_0/Y^h)\eta$ for all $\eta > 0$ and the reservation wage is lower than the market wage, $r_w < w_2\eta$.[17] Moreover, while there is a vast literature in labour economics that tries to estimate reservation wages based on survey micro-data, the reservation wage value should be considered as simply equal to what the worker could have spent when unemployed, i.e. the value of the unemployment benefit. Thus, according to this shortcut formula, the cost to the economy of hiring an unemployed person is equal to the unemployment benefit, plus the additional consumption, minus the social benefit of this consumption. Differently from equation (5.2), but more or less similarly to equation (5.4), the complex side effects on public finance due to a decrease in unemployment are ignored here, and the focus is only on the consumption side of the story.[18]

5.3.2.3 Rural Labour Dualism and Urban Labour Dualism

In the DS setting, as in the LM framework, the dualistic labour market is characterized by the fact that there is excess labour supply that is absorbed in the informal market. Therefore the shadow wage is the value of the foregone marginal social product in the informal sector (i.e. labour productivity at shadow prices) minus the social value of the increase of income to the household in the informal sector, which is expressed in terms of the difference between the wage rate and the marginal product of labour, MP_l, evaluated at market prices (hence different from m):

$$SWR_{RLD,ULD} = m - b(w_2 - MP_l). \tag{5.11}$$

A proxy for the consumption/wage level of workers in the informal sector, in either the urban or the rural context, is the net-of-tax wage rate because people accept working underground, i.e. without paying taxes or social contributions.

In the case of significant migration flows, if the region is predominantly rural, the Rural Labour Dualism (RLD) case as in Little and Mirrlees applies. As workers employed by the project were previously employed in the agricultural sector, it is assumed that in RLD markets:

$$m_{RLD} = w_1(1-t), \tag{5.12}$$

where w_1 is the average regional agricultural wage rate and $(1 - t)$ represents the benefit/tax wedge on wages in the sector. Therefore, the empirical formula for the shadow wage rate in the RLD case is:

$$SWR_{RLD} = \beta \frac{w_1(1-t)}{NPC_1} + (1-\beta)\frac{w_2}{NPC}. \tag{5.13}$$

If the region is instead highly urbanized, the existence of non-negligible net immigration flows suggests that, even if unemployment is high, there might be labour opportunities in the unofficial urban labour market. This regime is labelled the Urban Labour Dualism (ULD) market. This situation is similar to QKU, but it differs from it because it is assumed that the new employee will be drawn from a combination of formal and informal employment in the urban context, whereas under QKU a fraction of workers were fully unemployed and their leisure time was valued as the reservation wage. Under ULD, the new employment comes ultimately from the urban informal market.

The DS formulation would possibly be similar to the one in the previous case, but here the earnings in the 'black' labour market are assumed to be roughly equal to the market wage net of benefits and taxes, i.e.:

$$m_{ULD} = w_2 (1-t). \tag{5.14}$$

The equation is thus:

$$SWR_{ULD} = \beta \frac{w_2 (1-t)}{NPC} + (1-\beta) \frac{w_2}{NPC}. \tag{5.15}$$

Box 5.3 sums up the four empirical shadow wage rate formulae adapted to four different regional market conditions and derived from a simplified Little–Mirrlees model. Obviously, project evaluators who have additional information can try and implement more complex formulae. An advantage of this approach, however, is its applicability to easily available data across regions of the European Union, as described in the next section.

Box 5.4 The four empirical shadow wage rate formulae

1 Fairly Socially Efficient (FSE)

$$SWR_{FSE} = \frac{w_2}{NPC},$$

where w_2 is the average regional market wage in the manufacturing sector and NPC is the Nominal Protection Coefficient.

2 Quasi-Keynesian Unemployment (QKU)

$$SWR_{QKU} = \beta r_w + (1-\beta) \frac{w_2}{NPC},$$

where β is the regional welfare weight, r_w is the reservation wage, w_2 is the average regional market wage in the manufacturing sector, and NPC is the Nominal Protection Coefficient.

3 Rural Labor Dualism (RLD)

$$SWR_{RLD} = \beta \frac{w_1 (1-t)}{NPC_1} + (1-\beta) \frac{w_2}{NPC},$$

where β is the regional welfare weight, w_1 is the average regional market wage in the agricultural sector, t is the average regional tax rate for the average taxpayer, w_2 is the average regional market wage in the manufacturing sector, NPC_1 is the region-specific protection coefficient for the agricultural sector, and NPC is the Nominal Protection Coefficient.

---

4   Urban Labour Dualism (ULD)

$$\mathrm{SWR}_{\mathrm{ULD}} = \beta \frac{w_2(1-t)}{\mathrm{NPC}} + (1-\beta)\frac{w_2}{\mathrm{NPC}},$$

where β is the regional welfare weight, w_1 is the average regional market wage in the agricultural sector, t is the average regional tax rate for the average taxpayer, w_2 is the average regional market wage in the manufacturing sector, NPC_1 is the region-specific protection coefficient for the agricultural sector, and NPC is the Nominal Protection Coefficient.

Source: Authors.

5.4 Empirical estimation of shadow prices for EU regions

5.4.1 Data and methods

Shadow prices have been estimated for the 266 NUTS2[19] regions of the EU27 in 2007 by applying the empirical formulae derived in Section 5.3.2. It is assumed that workers may be employed either in the agricultural or in the manufacturing sector, which correspond to sectors 1 and 2 in the previous notation. It has been decided to use wages in manufacturing, which is typically producing tradables, while the service sector includes government and other non-traded services.

Various data sources have been used, including Cambridge Econometrics, Eurostat, ESPON, OECD, and ILO. The main variables on regional economic performance are per capita GDP in Purchasing Power Standard levels, the rate of unemployment, and the rate of long-term unemployment (Eurostat). Demographic and geographic data include total and active population (Cambridge Econometrics) and the annual net migration flows (ESPON).[20] Regional earnings data, also provided by Cambridge Econometrics, are per employee and sector-specific (agriculture, energy and manufacturing, construction, market, non-market services). Average and marginal tax rates (Eurostat and OECD) and the unemployment benefit (Eurostat) are at the country level. Rurality is measured as the share of workers employed in the agricultural sector (Eurostat).

The marginal and average tax rates for an average taxpayer (respectively, t' and t) have then been used to compute the country-specific elasticity of marginal utility on income:

$$\eta_k = \ln(1-t'_k)/\ln(1-t_k), \tag{5.16}$$

where k indicates the country (see Stern 1977). Following the general LM formulation and Kula (2007), the vector of η is an input in the computation of the regional welfare weight vector, β^h, based on the ratio between the national poverty thresholds (expressed as 60 per cent of the median per capita GDP in EU countries), Y^0, and the region's average per capita income, Y^h, where again here h stands for a NUTS2 region:

$$\beta^h = \left(\frac{Y^0}{Y^h}\right)^{\eta}. \tag{5.17}$$

To account for price distortions, which are especially relevant for agricultural prices in the EU due to the Common Agricultural Policy, the EU27 average producer Nominal Protection Coefficient (NPC_{EU}) provided by OECD (2010) has been considered. This coefficient is used to compute the region-specific protection coefficient indices for the agricultural sector (NPC_1) and the whole economy (NPC), and it allows one to explicitly take into account the fact that price distortions may cause market wages to diverge from the opportunity cost of labour (e.g. Sah and Stiglitz 1985). The NPC_1 is defined as NPC_{EU} weighted by the ratio of the gross value added in agriculture over the gross value added in the whole economy:

$$NPC_1 = NPC_{EU}\left(\frac{GVA_1}{GVA}\right) \tag{5.18}$$

The nominal protection coefficient in the agricultural sector reflects the relative importance of the agricultural sector in the economy. Assuming that there is no trade distortion due to producer protection policies in non-agricultural sectors, the NPC is defined as:

$$NPC = NPC_{EU}\left(\frac{GVA_1}{GVA}\right) + \frac{GVA - GVA_1}{GVA}. \tag{5.19}$$

5.4.2 Estimation of the SWRs

Following the framework presented in Section 5.3, in order to compute appropriate SWRs for each EU region, these should first be classified into four groups corresponding to different labour market conditions (FSE, QKU, ULD, and RLD). For this purpose, a partitioning clustering procedure has been used. This is a statistical methodology for data analysis that assigns a set of observations into subsets, called clusters. Observations in the same cluster are similar in some sense, minimizing the effects of the researcher's subjective choices in the classification process.[21]

The cluster analysis was performed along five dimensions:

- average income levels (regional per capita GDP in parity purchasing powers);
- short-term regional unemployment rate;
- long-term regional unemployment rate;
- rurality (measured as the share of workers employed in the agricultural sector);
- migration (defined as the difference between in-migration and out-migration as a percentage of the total population).

All these variables were standardized before inclusion in the clustering algorithm.

Using the formulae described in Section 5.3 (equations 5.8, 5.10, 5.13, and 5.15), the shadow wages and the corresponding conversion factors (i.e. the ratio between shadow and market wage) have therefore been computed for each region.

Table 5.1 shows summary statistics for the SWR in the four groups of regions, as defined with regard to the main variables of interest.[22] The highest shadow wage is, as expected, found in regions classified as fairly efficient (FSE), with an average value of EUR 45,240, for which an average conversion factor with a value equal to 1 is computed. The second highest average shadow wage (EUR 27,140) is that of highly urban regions (ULD), and the conversion factor is on average 0.80, with a standard deviation equal to 0.08. Regions classified as quasi-Keynesian (QKU) have a lower average shadow wage (EUR 12,111) with a conversion factor on average equal to 0.54,[23] with a large standard error equal to 0.16. Finally, the lowest shadow wages and conversion factors (average values of EUR 5,217 and 0.62, respectively) are found, as expected, in regions with a rural–labour dualism.

Table 5.1 Summary statistics of shadow wages and conversion factors by cluster

Variable	Observations	Mean	Std. Dev.	Min	Max
FSE: cluster 1					
Shadow wages	63	45,239.47	10,738.99	13,871.10	66,528.37
Conversion factors	63	1.00	0.00	0.99	1
ULD: cluster2					
Shadow wages	129	27,143.10	10,265.68	3,255.30	50,486.03
Conversion factors	129	0.80	0.08	0.61	0.97
QKU: cluster3					
Shadow wages	52	12,111.14	8,858.47	3,494.42	53,107.76
Conversion factors	52	0.54	0.16	0.23	0.89
RLD: cluster4					
Shadow wages	22	5,216.78	3,350.83	1,590.88	1,3928.63
Conversion factors	22	0.62	0.13	0.36	0.84

Source: Del Bo *et al.* (2011) calculations on Eurostat and Cambridge Econometrics data.

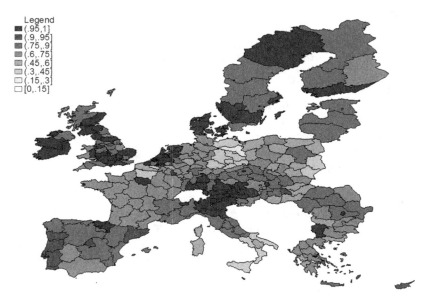

Figure 5.1 Distribution of conversion factors across NUTS2 regions.
Source: Del Bo *et al.* (2011) elaboration on Eurostat and Cambridge Economics data.

Figure 5.1 presents a graphical representation of conversion factors by regions. They are characterized by large variability in some countries, especially in Italy, Germany, and Spain.

These shadow wages reflect region-specific labour market conditions, following the taxonomy obtained through the cluster analysis based on relative GDP, unemployment, rurality, and migration. Results can be regarded as preliminary. Further research on this line can test whether including some other variables can improve the results.[24]

One of the advantages of this approach for empirical estimation of SWRs is the easy applicability of the formulae derived from the literature on shadow prices in a general equilibrium setting, in the Little–Mirrlees and Drèze–Stern traditions. Another strength is that it formally takes account of the different conditions of the labour market in terms of GDP, unemployment rates (both short- and long-term), migration flows, and rurality. The fact that it relies on official statistics, which are easily accessible and regularly updated, is another benefit which could compensate the cost of a less precise computation of the shadow wage rate.

5.5 Further reading

For an overview of the shadow wage concept and a call for the use of empirical methods to estimate conversion factors to be used in project appraisal, like the one described in this chapter, see Potts (2012b). With a specific focus on rural development, Horbulyk (2001) presents a critical overview of existing methods aimed at estimating the social opportunity cost of labour. Guillermo-Peon and Harberger (2012) present a methodology based on dualism and migration with an application to Mexico, and derive estimates of the social opportunity cost of labour for 21 different occupations in 32 labour market areas. Bartik (2012) considers the employment benefits of job creation following public investment. The author suggests framing employment benefits by looking at how the labour market responds to supply and demand shocks, and concludes by suggesting a methodology which links greater employment benefits of new job creation in labour markets with high unemployment rates.

Other theoretical contributions in the vein of general equilibrium Public Economics include Marchand *et al.* (1984), who study the interrelations between the shadow wage rate and the social discount rate. They consider an economy with one consumer, two consumption goods offered by a competitive public sector, leisure, and a benevolent government. There is wage rigidity and involuntary unemployment, and the interest rate is flexible. Expanding public expenditures financed by lump-sum taxes gradually close the gap between shadow and market wages. However, if there is displacement of private investment and employment, the social discount rate may be greater than the interest rate. Moreover, with distortionary taxation, for example, profit taxation, there is both rationing in the labour market and a wedge between the gross and net of tax cost of capital. This work is an example of the complex interrelation between the SWR and other ingredients of cost-benefit analysis, even in a very simple economic model, and it shows the limitation of the typical partial equilibrium approaches.

Burgess (1989) considers the relationship between the social opportunity cost of capital in the private sector and the gross-of-tax return to capital when tax-induced labour market distortions cause the prevailing market wage to exceed the social opportunity cost of labour (shadow wage). The main finding is that only part of the excess of the market wage over the social opportunity cost of labour should be attributed to the private sector if public investment can be considered as an input in the private sector's production processes, thus implying that the social opportunity cost of capital is a function of the marginal product of capital in the private sector and of the wedge between the market and shadow wage.

A recent article by Johansson and Kriström (2020) consider the discrete shift from unemployment to (full) employment. According to authors, such discrete shifts are more realistic than considering a marginal change in the employment constraint faced by an unemployed or rather an underemployed. The article provides guidance how to estimate the social cost of recruiting otherwise unemployed to a project. It is shown that the social cost is overestimated by using the private reservation wage. Moreover, they demonstrate that the common practice of adding different cost concepts (time, unemployment benefits, the monetary value of health changes, and so on) is flawed.

5.6 Summary of Chapter 5

- Market wages do not necessarily reflect the true social opportunity cost of labour. Shadow wages must be estimated by considering the factors that may imply a wedge between observed market wages and the opportunity cost of labour. Possible sources of distortion are taxes and subsidies in the labour market and minimum or maximum wage requirements.
- Conversion factors translate observed market wages into shadow wages, reflecting the social cost of labour, and are an essential input in evaluating public investment projects by means of CBA.
- The shadow wage is of paramount relevance for public project evaluation, but practitioners often had difficulties in estimating it because of information constraints. As the review of the literature has shown, shadow prices have been generally estimated through survey data on reservation wages, firm-level data on marginal productivity of rural firms, household's consumption spending and its distribution across income groups, etc. This approach, however, being based on project-specific micro-data, can be regarded as cumbersome and costly.
- In order to respond to the need for computable 'shortcut' shadow wage formulae a new simple framework for the empirical computation of shadow wages and conversion factors at the regional level has been developed by Del Bo *et al.* (2011) and presented in this chapter, accounting for structural characteristics and labour market conditions.
- A combination of the Little and Mirrlees (1974) and Drèze and Stern (1987) frameworks allows one to derive shadow wage rate formulae for different labour market cases. Four labour market conditions can be identified. These are labelled as Fairly Socially Efficient, Quasi-Keynesian Unemployment, Rural Labour Dualism, and Urban Labour Dualism.
- The derived formulae have been used to empirically estimate the shadow wage rates of EU regions. This methodology relies on official aggregate statistics at the regional level, overcoming the issue of previous methodologies based on project-specific data, and provides estimates for regional shadow wage rates and corresponding conversion factors which can be used in project evaluation.

End of chapter questions

- What types of distortions are believed to drive a wedge between market and shadow wages?
- What are the disadvantages of estimating shadow wages from project-specific micro-data?
- What is the reservation wage? What are the alternative methods for estimating reservation wage?
- Consider a conversion factor for labour equal to 0.8. What is the interpretation of such conversion factor? How can it be practically used in a Cost-Benefit Analysis?
- A proposed government project would require the hiring of 100 low-skilled workers. Such workers will be picked among unemployed persons. The project offers a wage of EUR 10 per hour. Imagine the hourly shadow wage is EUR 6. What is the implication from a Cost-benefit analysis perspective? What if the hourly shadow wage would be EUR 11?

Notes

1 This chapter is with Chiara del Bo and Carlo Fiorio and draws from the published paper by Del Bo, Fiorio and Florio (2011).
2 For a different view on this issue, see Brent (1991b).
3 Little and Mirrlees (1974) consider rural sector but subsidies exist also in other sectors of modern economies.
4 Reservation wage is defined as the lowest wage rate at which a worker would be willing to accept a particular job.
5 On this issue, see also Gupta (1986).
6 Londero (2003), Saleh (2004) and Lang and Riess (2019) constitute an exception.
7 Alternatively, following Drèze–Stern, one may define the SWF using indirect utilities of consumers, hence defining $V(\cdot)$ over incomes and prices (see Del Bo *et al.* 2011).
8 The mean value theorem allows us to write: $V(c_2) - V(c_1) = \int_{c_1}^{c_2} v(c)\,dc = v(c^*)(c_2 - c_1)$, where $c_1 < c^* < c_2$.
9 Little and Mirrlees (1974: 270).
10 Little and Mirrlees (1974: 243) and following.
11 In the original notation, b was used instead of c_0 (Little and Mirrlees 1974: 265).
12 In principle, weaker assumptions could be made on savings, and a part of w could be 'taken away' from the consumption costs and benefits, or a term on urbanization costs could be added, etc. However, this would not alter the results in a significant manner in the context of European regions.
13 From a formal perspective, m is here the marginal productivity of labour, which in the empirical computation will be proxied by the sector-specific average market wage. A further direction of research is to compute, especially in the case of rural–urban dualism, the value of the marginal productivity of labour.
14 Formal proofs and derivations for this and the subsequent formulae are provided in Del Bo *et al.* (2011).
15 By ignoring the distributional impact in this case, the SWR is probably slightly overstated as compared with DS. A possible extension of the research could be to find a shortcut way to include a distributional correction even when the labour market is socially efficient.
16 In this model, this fact trivially derives from the definition of b that includes the social cost of consumption, and from the fact that income equals consumption expenditure.
17 This formula probably understates the SWR because a more complete analysis should consider as a benefit only the difference between the observed wage and the unemployment subsidy. At the same time, in some countries, the reservation wage can be higher than the unemployment benefit.

18 Under distortionary taxation there may be an additional saving because of the social cost of public funds previously committed to unemployment subsidies.

19 The NUTS classification (nomenclature of territorial units for statistics) is a system for dividing the economic territory of the EU for statistical and socio-economic purposes. The NUTS2 level refers to basic regions of the EU Member States for the application of regional policies.

20 Migration data is derived from ESPON's annual net migration at NUTS3 level between 2001 and 2005 and is defined as the difference between in-migration and out-migration as a percentage of the total population. This information has been aggregated at the NUTS2 level using each NUTS3's population share in 2003 (median year of the interval).

21 Clustering methods can be divided into two broad categories, hierarchical and partitional clustering, each with a wide range of subtypes, including the type of clustering algorithm and the distance measure adopted to identify similarities among observations. For a discussion on clustering methods where the number of clusters is set *a priori*, see Kaufman and Rousseeuw (1990). Del Bo *et al.* (2011) used the 'partitioning around metoids' function, setting to four the medoids for the algorithm.

22 A detailed list of regions and corresponding conversion factors is available upon request.

23 In the RLD case, the marginal productivity in the agricultural sector (and consequently the conversion factor) might have been overestimated. If agricultural production is characterized by decreasing returns to scale, average productivity will be lower than marginal productivity and the correction for the tax wedge may be insufficient to capture this effect. Little and Mirrlees (1974: 277) in fact suggest taking half the average productivity as a reasonable approximation of marginal productivity in agriculture. Applying this short cut to the EU data, however, leaves results substantially unaltered.

24 For example, the intra-regional distributive effects can be included in this frame.

6 The social cost of capital

Overview[1]

Discounting enables one to express future monetary or socio-economic effects in terms of present values when inter-temporal decisions are to be taken. It is both deliberately used by policy makers, economists, or financial analysts and unconsciously used by every individual whenever the time-horizon of an investment decision exceeds a single period. In the context of cost-benefit analysis, this allows for directly comparing net benefits expressed in terms of their net present values, and, subsequently, for aggregating them to obtain a single measure of the project value (the net present value).

Both financial and economic flows need to be discounted in order to estimate the investment's profitability indicators. For financial flows, project analysts use the financial discount rate to reflect the opportunity cost of capital to the perspective of the financial investor(s), and for economic flows they use the social discount rate, capturing the inter-temporal opportunity cost of capital to the whole of society.

After a brief introduction to the rationale for discounting (Section 6.1), this chapter deals with the different existing approaches to estimating the social discount rate, as well as the important implications for present and future generations deriving from using one discount rate instead of another (Sections 6.2 and 6.3 on declining discount rates). An overview of the social discount rates applied in several countries worldwide is provided and country-specific social discount rates for some EU Member States are empirically estimated (Section 6.4). To conclude, some remarks on the shadow price of public funds and on the conceptual differences between the inter-temporal opportunity cost of capital and the marginal cost of public funds are made (Section 6.5). Some further reading on this topic is suggested (Section 6.6).

6.1 Rationale for discounting

A fundamental question is why it is necessary to discount the future. There are two main reasons put forward in the literature,[2] both of which derive from empirical observations. The first is that the employment of resources has an opportunity cost, meaning that resources committed to a project could be employed in another return-generating investment. Thus, to induce investment, the expected return from the investment should be at least as high as the opportunity cost of funding. This consideration applies both to financial returns for investors and to social returns in the perspective of the economy as a whole, even if the parameters involved are usually different, as discussed below.

DOI: 10.4324/9781003191377-8

The second reason for discounting future costs and benefits is that consumers generally prefer to receive the same amount of goods and services sooner rather than later. This happens both because individuals expect an increasing level of consumption over time; thus, in the future, marginal utility of consumption decreases, and because individuals have a pure time preference, due to impatience, myopia and the risk of not being alive in the future. Available experimental evidence from both economics and psychology supports this view.[3]

In a theoretical perspective, Samuelson (1937) suggested a discounted utility function based on the idea that, during any period of time, an individual maximizes the sum of his future utilities and therefore has to discount future utilities in order to reduce them to comparable magnitudes to today's. A zero discount rate implies that equal weights are given by the agent to the utilities occurring to him at any point in time, i.e. that today's and future consumption are indifferent from the utility point of view. A positive discount rate, on the other hand, indicates a preference for current over future consumption, whereas the opposite is true if the discount rate is negative. In this sense, every discount rate entails a judgement concerning the future, which affects the weight attributed to future benefits or costs. A relatively high discount rate gives a small weight to benefits or costs that occur further in the future, thus weakening projects with back-end loaded benefits and strengthening the case for projects with front-end loaded benefits (Boardman *et al.* 2018).

The individual discount rate, in this context, coincides with the concept of a pure rate of time preference, which is generally positive. This is due, as mentioned, to the impatience of individuals and the preference of immediate over future consumption. Impatience is also related to their level of wealth. In calculating the net present value, a poor person discounts future income more than a rich. Actually, if an individual is poor, the fact that in some distant future he will be richer is less important, as he has more urgency now and therefore puts more weight on today's consumption. Put another way, the opportunity cost of differing consumption is higher for a poor individual. This highlights that there is a relationship between inter-temporal discount, which is captured by the discount rate, and inter-individual discounting, which is reflected in the use of appropriate welfare weights to compare across individuals.[4]

When the perspective moves from individuals to policy makers, a discount rate other than the individuals' pure rate of time preference should be used. Caplin and Leahy (2004) state that the social discount rate should be lower than the private one, although still positive, given that benevolent policy makers should be more patient than private agents and should attach greater value to the utility of future generations. This view is further elaborated below.

6.2 Estimating the social discount rate

The social discount rate (SDR) to be used in economic analysis is the opportunity cost of capital for the whole society. Drèze and Stern (1987) define it as the rate of fall in the marginal social value of the *numéraire* against which goods are valued, and it is used to convert shadow values in different years into common units this year, or to present values.

As with the other shadow prices, the value of the SDR in principle depends upon the source of adjustments elsewhere in the economy that are needed to allow the investment. These adjustments may be decreased investments in other sectors and/or increased savings (hence less consumption). The relevant opportunity cost of capital in the former case is the rate of return of an alternative investment. This perspective is also adopted to estimate the financial discount rate. In the latter case – i.e. when the adjustment in the economy determined by the allocation of public capital is in terms of increased saving – the opportunity cost of capital is the consumption rate of interest, measuring the subjective value of present versus future consumption to the individual.

In a perfectly competitive economy and under equilibrium, the two rates coincide between them and with the financial market interest rate. However, this does not apply in practice since capital markets are in fact distorted by taxation, capital rationing, information asymmetries, and other market failures.

Different approaches have been proposed in the literature to estimate the SDR. The most popular ones are the social rate of return on private investment (SRRI)[5] and the social rate of time preference (SRTP). Other methods exist and could be used for inter-temporal discounting, although they are more rarely applied in practice. Among these, the weighted average method and the shadow price of capital approach can be mentioned. These are presented in the following sections.[6]

6.2.1 The social rate of return on private investments (SRRI)

A traditional approach suggests that public investment displaces private investment and, for this reason, the SDR should reflect the marginal social opportunity cost of the latter. The rationale is simply that private investment generates future income, and then valuable consumption in the future. This leads to a SDR equal to the marginal social opportunity cost of funds in the private sector. In other words, according to this approach, the returns from the public investment should be at least as big as one that could be obtained from a private investment. If this were not the case, there would be an inefficient allocation of resources, and welfare could be increased by reallocation of funds, away from public to private investments.

Boardman *et al.* (2018) argue that probably the best proxy for the marginal rate of return on private investment is the real before-tax rate of return on corporate bonds. The reason why one should look at the marginal, not the average return on private investment is because of diminishing returns of scale of project portfolios, which imply that rational investors conclude the most profitable deals first, so that returns are decreasing in the number of projects.

As is pointed out by many economists (Arrow and Lind 1970; Barrett *et al.* 1999 and the already mentioned Boardman *et al.* 2018), the SRRI approach tends to be biased toward high estimates of the SDR. First of all, externalities, monopoly, rationing, incomplete information and other market failures distort private investment returns and may generate private investment returns higher than the social ones. Second, the observed private return on investments usually includes a risk premium. This is however not to be included in the SDR because society as a whole, or the government, has a much larger portfolio than any private investor and consequently is able to exploit risk pooling.

By being typically based on observed returns in the private financial markets, one additional concern about the empirical estimation of the SRRI is market volatility and the role of persisting asset bubbles (the global crisis that started around 2008 is a clear reminder of this recurrent fact). Average long-term series stock exchange returns may correct this bias, but overall the results will be much higher than the returns to consumers under the social time preference approach.

Dasgupta, Marglin, and Sen (1972) note that the marginal opportunity cost of capital can be used to estimate the SDR only when the total amount of capital available for investment in the economy is fixed. Such a context would justify the assumption that one euro of public investment displaces one euro of private investment. Yet, when the amount of capital is not fixed and agents satisfy, at least partially, the capital needed for financing public projects by postponing their current consumption, then the return required by consumers is less than the marginal rate of return on private investment. This would lead to a social discount rate that is lower than the marginal opportunity cost of capital for the economy. When consumption is postponed, a better estimate for the SDR is provided by the social rate of time preference approach (see below).

6.2.2 The social rate of time preference (SRTP)

The social rate of time preference is the rate at which society is willing to postpone a unit of current consumption in exchange for more future consumption. The presumptions of this approach are two. First, that funds for government projects ultimately come from the reduced consumption of individuals (Boardman *et al.* 2018). Second,

---

Box 6.1 The financial discount rate

The idea that the opportunity cost of funds is valued as the loss of income from an alternative project applies also to the estimation of the financial discount rate, which is used to discount monetary inflows and outflows in the financial analysis of a project. When investors, both private and public, commit capital to a project, they have an implicit cost that derives from sacrificing a return on another project. The financial discount rate takes into account the time value of money, i.e. the idea that money available now is worth more than the same amount of money in the future because it could be earning interest, and the risk or uncertainty of the anticipated future cash flow, which might be less than expected.

Different approaches are proposed by the academic literature to value the financial discount rate. One approach consists in estimating the actual cost of capital, by considering the marginal direct cost of public funds. This is proxied by the real return on government bonds, or the long-term real interest rate on commercial loans (if the project needs private finance), or a weighted average of the two rates. In spite of its simplicity, this approach might be misleading, in that the best alternative project could earn much more than the actual interest rate on public or private loans. Another way to derive the financial discount rate is to consider the return lost from the best investment alternative to determine a maximum limit value for the discount rate. In this case, the alternative to the project income is the marginal return on an appropriate financial portfolio. A third approach implies using a specific interest rate or a rate of return from a well-established issuer of securities in a widely traded currency. A multiplier to this minimum benchmark could then be applied, by virtue of the assumption that project investors have relatively higher experience, which makes them able to obtain higher than average returns.[7]

Source: Authors.

government should consider the welfare of both current and future generations and solve an optimal planning programme based on individual preferences for consumption and additional parameters.

A possible candidate for estimating the social marginal rate of time preference is to look at the return on holding government bonds or other low-risk marketable securities. Yet, various criticisms can be raised concerning this method. The most important one is that it is not obvious how to aggregate different individual marginal rates of time preferences into a single social marginal rate of time preference. Individuals have different saving and borrowing preferences, to which different return rates are attached: because consumer borrowing rates exceed saving rates and because reducing the debt is not a taxed operation. The result is that consumers who save by reducing their debt earn a higher real after-tax return than other savers.

Another way to estimate the SRTP is based on a formula obtained from the Ramsey growth model. It is as follows:

$$\text{SRTP} = \rho + \varepsilon \cdot g, \tag{6.1}$$

where ρ is the pure rate of time preference, i.e. the rate at which society discounts the utility of future generations, ε is the elasticity of the marginal utility of consumption, i.e. the percentage change in individuals' marginal utility corresponding to each percentage change in consumption, and g is the expected growth rate of per capita consumption or other welfare-related variable (e.g. income).[8] The two components of this formula – one related to time preference and the other related to consumption growth – reflect the two possible reasons why future consumption may have a lower value than in the present. First, because of uncertainty about the future, which leads to a preference for present income; second, because of the probability of people becoming richer in the future: if per capita consumption is growing, then the value of additional consumption in each year in the future declines at a rate related to the rate of growth of per capita consumption and the elasticity of diminishing marginal utility of consumption.

Each term of the formula is discussed in more detail below.

The pure rate of time preference term, in turn, can be decomposed into two terms, one related to individuals' impatience and myopia and the other related to the risk of death or extinction of the human race. Impatience refers to the observation that individuals favour present over future consumption and this is reflected in a positive value of ρ.

The other component of the pure rate of pure time preference, the risk of death, is often simply taken as the ratio of total deaths to total population (Pearce and Ulph 1995). It is important to stress that the risk of death from a societal perspective is, however, not the same as the risk of death of an individual. Actually, the latter can be expected to be much higher than the one for a generation as a whole. This is due to the fact that it would take a global catastrophe to extinguish all human life, whose probability of occurrence is obviously much less than the probability of a single human person dying.

The elasticity of the marginal utility with respect to consumption captures dynamics of consumption over time. Suppose that the economy is growing, outside the steady state; then per capita consumption grows. In the future, the representative consumer is richer. How does this income effect enter into social preferences for time? The elasticity parameter captures the fact that if tomorrow the representative consumer is a bit richer, marginal utility of consumption is decreasing over time. If the parameter takes a neutral value, a future increase in consumption by one Euro adds exactly one Euro to social welfare. If instead $\varepsilon < 1$ consumers attach a lower utility to marginal increase in consumption. If $\varepsilon > 1$, when consumption increases by one unit, social welfare increases by more than one. And, as already mentioned, the poorer consumers are now, the more interested they are in present consumption growth.

This parameter can be viewed either from an individual's or a social perspective. While, from the former perspective, the elasticity indicates how an individual would like to allocate consumption over time, from the latter, it reflects how consumption should be transferred across different generations. Here, ε can be seen as a planning parameter for the social planner in that it reveals his preference for income inequality aversion.

The last component of the Ramsey equation is the expected rate of growth in real per capita consumption. Pearce and Ulph (1995) propose to use very long-run growth rates of real per capita consumption to estimate future growth. This method allows one to solve two problems that may occur if g is assessed on the basis of actual growth data of the very recent past. First, if individuals were to substitute leisure for consumption, recent data may lead to an understatement of g. Second, if real per capita consumption failed to reflect eventual rising social costs arising from consumption, g might be overestimated.

As to the point of view of inter-generational equity, this means that if future generations are expected to be wealthier than the ones of today, and thus, if consumption rises over time, this would result in an increase of the discount rate in order to shift the priority to the poorer current generation.

To conclude this analysis, the SRTP allows the government to consider the welfare of future and current generations simultaneously and to determine the optimal planning programme, based on individual preferences for consumption and additional parameters. The problem with this approach, which makes empirical estimation of the SDR difficult, is that e and ρ are essentially value judgments. Nevertheless, some empirical short cuts have been developed (see Section 6.4).

It is important to mention that some authors regard zero as the only ethically defensible value for the social rate of time preference (e.g. Pigou 1912; Ramsey 1928; Broome 1992), stating that, from a utilitarian and impartial point of view, good at one time cannot be different from a good at another. A positive value would signify that future generations are made worse off only due to the fact they are born at a later point in time, which would be unacceptable from the point of view of society as a whole.

However, most Welfare Economics literature based on empirical evidence agrees that a modest rate of time preference is justified and more realistic. Moreover, a practical implication of using a zero discount rate, as highlighted by Pearce et al. (2003), would be that in the presence of positive interest rates the current generation would have greater incentive to save and invest, given that the value of future consumption will be higher. These future benefits would then always outweigh the current costs of forgone consumption and would consequently result in the impoverishment of the current generation. This would be true for every generation still to come, which would sacrifice its own consumption for the benefit of the next one. This argument gives an ethical reason for the adoption of a positive rate of pure time preference.

6.2.3 The weighted average method[9]

While the SRRI takes into account the crowding out effect on private investment and fails to take into account the displacement of private consumption, the SRTP approach disregards the displacement effect that public projects might have on private investment and focusses on the consumption side. To solve the dilemma between consideration of returns to consumers/savers or to private investors, the SDR could be estimated by a weighted average of the investment rate of return and the net return to savers:

$$\text{SDR} = i\left(\Delta D/\Delta I\right) + q\left(\Delta S/\Delta I\right), \tag{6.2}$$

where i is the marginal rate of return of investment, proxied by the pre-tax rate of return of private investments; q is the net-of-tax return rate to the saver; ΔD is the decrease of investment elsewhere; ΔS is the increase in savings; and ΔI is the capital expenditure needed to implement the project. In the case of an open economy, these two are sometimes combined with the rate of return on funds borrowed from foreigners.

Depending on further assumptions and specifications, the SDR can take various forms. In a closed economy, it can be equal to the SRRI if the supply of funds is perfectly inelastic, and therefore only private investments are displaced, but not consumption, whereas it can be equal to the SRTP if the demand of funds is perfectly inelastic. Thus, it is realistic to assume that a value lying in between these two extremes is more probable.

While the general principle of considering the different sources of the project opportunity cost is consistent with the concept of shadow price, the same critique of the SRRI applies to the weighted average approach. Private returns, either on domestic or foreign investments, may be bad signals of the social opportunity costs. Another problem with this method lies in the determination of appropriate weights to be attached to the two rates, which should reflect the proportions of funds from the respective source. Finally, a further criticism concerns the assumption that benefits are consumed immediately and are not reinvested so as to generate future consumption and increasing social value. Ignoring the higher social value of project benefits that are reinvested instead of immediately consumed induces a bias of the approach against long-term projects, consisting in over-discounting project benefits. This latter limitation is addressed by the approach based on the shadow price of capital.

6.2.4 The shadow price of capital

Under this approach, investment flows are converted into 'consumption equivalents' through the shadow price of capital. This is intended to correct for the distortions in private investment returns that have been mentioned above and which are referred to the fact that while consumption provides an immediate benefit, investment generates a stream of benefits that occur in the future. This approach considers as total costs those arising from the displacement of current private consumption, but also future consumption, which is due to the crowding out of private investment. The total benefits, on the other hand, capture not only immediate but also future consumption, which is gained from the reinvestment.

The approach has a number of variations in both theoretical and empirical literature, but it usually revolves around three steps:

i   Costs and benefits in each period are attributed either to consumption or to investment.
ii   The latter are converted into 'consumption equivalents' using the shadow price of capital.
iii Consumption equivalents and consumption-type costs and benefits flows are then discounted at the SRTP.

In its simplest version the value of the shadow price capital is:

$$SPC = SRRI/SRTP. \tag{6.3}$$

Because the SRRI is higher than the SRTP, this equation implies that the shadow price of capital (SPC) is greater than 1. Thus, displaced investment is more costly to society than displaced consumption.

The application of the shadow price of capital method is difficult in practice, as it would require information on several parameters related to investment and consumer choices, such as the marginal social cost of capital, the social rate of time preference, the depreciation rate, the marginal propensity to save, the proportion of displaced and generated consumption and private investment due to project costs and benefits. Furthermore, the dependence of the shadow price of capital on the length of project would force one to estimate it for every project. Depending on different assumptions, which vary from project to project, the value of the shadow price of capital could vary from one to infinity (Lyon 1990).

6.3 The social discount rate as a function of time

The use of a constant SDR, which implies an exponential discounting process (as presented in Chapter 4, Box 4.4), has been criticized by several authors. Ainslie and Haendel (1983) argue that constant discounting is inconsistent with individual preferences. There is some empirical support to the view that the implicit discount rate over long time horizons is lower than implicit discount rates over shorter time horizons: when facing the decision between a smaller reward soon and a larger reward later, individuals would apply a lower discount rate in the long-run. Time-inconsistent preference would justify using certainty-equivalent social interest rates that decline over time, following, for example, a hyperbolic discounting function (Laibson 1997): this is characterized by relatively high discount rates over the short term and relatively low rates over long horizons. The question here is whether the individuals are rational in implicitly using declining discount rates. It may not be justified to use a misperception of the future in the context of Applied Welfare Economics, at least in a normative perspective.

Newell and Pizer (2004) propose a declining SDR based on a different argument: the historical behaviour of interest rates. They examine the US government's real long-term bond rate over the past 200 years and simulate the future path of bond rate, which is supposed to decrease from 4 per cent to 0.5 per cent over a time horizon longer than 300 years (see Table 6.1).

Weitzman (2001) used gamma-distributed probabilities to determine the discount rate, which is a declining function of time. He conducted a survey of 2,160 economists in 48 countries, representing different fields of economics, asking what they considered to be the 'right' social discount rate. Answers ranged from −3 per cent to +27 per cent, with a mean SDR of 3.96 per cent and a standard deviation of 2.94 per cent. Under a gamma distribution, this implies that the SDR after 300 years is zero, starting from 4 per cent in the first five years (see Table 6.2). The value of this inference is however questionable, as economists are not a representative sample of the population, and an 'expert's' view is not *per se* undistorted if the survey is not targeted to economists specializing in the field.

A possible explanation for time-inconsistent preference relates to uncertainty about future interest rates. Gollier (2002a, 2002b) explores the relationship between the SDR and uncertainty in the GDP growth rate (see Table 6.3). He considers that decreasing marginal utility of consumption is related to a wealth effect, and uncertainty about income growth drives present investment, while external shocks affect GDP growth. The interaction between these two effects creates a SDR dynamics. If the risk of recession is small, the SDR decreases in time only if relative risk aversion is decreasing as well. When growth rates are assumed constant over time, the SDR is unaffected. When, however, there is a risk of recession, the wealth effect and the precautionary effect drive the dynamics in opposite ways. Suppose the expected GDP growth is positive. Then the

Table 6.1 Declining discount rates proposed by Newell and Pizer (2004)

Time period	Discount rate (per cent)
0–100 years	4
101–200 years	2
201–300 years	1
More than 300 years	0.5

Source: Newell and Pizer (2004).

Table 6.2 Declining discount rates proposed by Weitzman (2001)

Time period	Discount rate (per cent)
0–5 years	4
6–25 years	3
26–75 years	2
76–300 years	1
More than 300 years	0

Source: Weitzman (2001).

Table 6.3 Declining discount rates proposed by Gollier (2002a)

Time period	Discount rate
0–50 years	Risk-free rate observable in financial markets
51–100 years	Maximum of 5 per cent
More than 200 years	1.5 per cent

Source: Gollier (2002a).

longer the time horizon, the higher the expected consumption (positive wealth effect) and the related risk (negative precautionary effect). When the latter effect is greater than the former, long-term SDR is smaller than in a shorter time horizon.

Another reason for using a time-declining SDR relates to the fact that the values of current market rates of interest or marginal rates of time preferences reflect the preferences of individuals currently alive. These, however, fail to appropriately account for the long-term impact of their actions on the welfare of future generations. The same could be considered true for governments' actions. This consideration suggests that time-declining discount rate is particularly important for intergenerational discounting, i.e. for a project likely to affect people which are yet unborn (whether as beneficiaries or taxpayers) and, therefore, whose effect occurs over a very long time horizon (more than 50 years).

Boardman *et al.* (2018) point out that there are at least four reasons which justify the use of a declining social discount rate and these considerations become mostly relevant for intergenerational projects. A first reason is that individuals appear to be time-inconsistent, e.g. by showing a declining preference to commit on saving plans occurring farther into future. The second reason deals with evaluating projects with impact occurring far in the future, such as reforestation, measures to mitigate global warming, actions to preserve biodiversity and others. Discounting at a time-constant discount rate can pose an ethical dilemma, since benefits would be discounted more than costs of investments occurred in the initial years of the horizon. A third reason for using a time-declining SDR is because current generation may fail to account appropriately for the effects on the welfare of future generations. A fourth reason deals with the impact of uncertainty around the elements of the discount rate, mostly the future levels of growth. Boardman *et al.* (2018) suggest using a SDR declining from 3.5 per cent (before 50 years) to 0 per cent (after 300 years) for the evaluation of projects crossing generation lines (Table 6.4 below).

The choice of the discount rate makes a huge difference to policies and projects where benefits occur in the distant future, such as certain environmental and energy projects which entail long-run consequences, affecting for instance the sustainability of raw materials, preventing/reducing global warming (reduction of CO_2 emissions), nuclear waste and species extinction. The review of current practices around the world (see Section 6.4 below) confirms the use of a time-declining discount rate or a lower constant discount rate for intergenerational projects.

When considering climate change-related projects, the catastrophes in the distant future can be so devastating as to eliminate the human race, and not only all the returns

Table 6.4 Declining discount rates proposed by Boardman *et al.* (2018)

Time period	Discount rate (per cent)
0–50 years	3.5
51–100 years	2.5
101–200 years	1.5
201–300 years	0.5
More than 300 years	0

Source: Boardman *et al.* (2018).

as in ordinary projects (life chances tend to zero). Hence, some environmental scientists have suggested to include in the SRTP a factor accounting for catastrophic risk, i.e. the risk that one devastating future event, even in the distant future, may affect the return on public expenditure. The catastrophic risk of human race extinction, for example, has been taken into account in the Stern Review on the Economics of Climate Change (Stern 2006). Nicholas Stern used a particularly low SRTP, justified by a very low value for the rate of pure time preference: 0.1 per cent, against alternative empirical estimates usually ranging between 1 per cent and 3 per cent (as discussed later). See Box 6.2 for further details. Lower discount rates encourage investors to adopt projects that offer returns at distant dates (Harrison 2010).

Box 6.2 The choice of the social discount rate in the Stern Review on the Economics of Climate Change

The Stern Review on the Economics of Climate Change aims at assessing the economic impacts of climate change on global growth, by comparing the business-as-usual situation with alternative scenarios in which adaptation and mitigation measures are adopted worldwide. This represents the largest cost–benefit analysis ever attempted, as it involves as beneficiaries the whole earth's population and sets a time horizon of 200 years. The choice of which social discount rate to use is particularly important for a project like this, whose effects are enjoyed so distant in the future.

Following the UK *Green Book* guidelines (see Section 6.4 and also Chapter 9), the Stern Review adopted the SRTP approach and assumed a near-zero pure time preference (equal to 0.1 per cent), representing the possibility of extinction of the human race, while, following Ramsey (1928), the review took the impatience and myopia component equal to zero. The elasticity of the marginal utility of consumption was set at 1. The Stern Review explained that a higher value could be justified only if there was a higher distributional preference in today's society. The expected rate of future per capita growth is assumed equal to 1.3 per cent per annum, in accordance with historical data. This value captures only the growth in consumption of goods, whereas it does not take into account the use and non-use values of environment. These values, when entered into the Ramsey formula, result in an SDR of 1.4 per cent in real terms.

The SDR estimated by the Stern Review has been criticized for being too low, thus excessively magnifying the impacts in the distant future. Nordhaus (2007) and Weitzman (2007), among others, oppose the choice of nil impatience component and are in favour of attaching greater weight to the present generation. Dasgupta (2007, 2008) argues that elasticity of marginal utility of consumption should be higher in order to be consistent with more realistic saving rates. Another major criticism concerns the use of a constant rather than declining discount rate. In this regard, Gollier *et al.* (2008) claim that a declining discount rate profile can correct the insufficient representation of future generations, without denying that current generations, in fact, discount the future.

Source: Authors.

The use of declining discount rate could be another, perhaps more appropriate (Gollier 2010), solution to evaluating these types of environmental project. Newell and Pizer (2004) apply both constant and declining discount rates when evaluating the impact of climate change caused by CO_2 emissions, finding that future valuations are much higher when using declining rates: this corresponds to nearly doubling the net present value of climate mitigation effects compared to the evaluation at a constant rate (4 per cent).

6.4 Empirical estimates of the social discount rate

Significant variations in social discount rates adopted by governments exist across the world, with developing countries generally applying higher rates than developed countries. According to a review carried out by Catalano *et al.* (2022), these range between 6 and 12 per cent for the former countries, and from 3 to 8 per cent for the latter. The actual value of the SDR adopted by different countries or institutions depends, first of all, on the estimation method used and, second, on the specific underlying parameters, reflecting different perceptions of the social opportunity cost of public funds and different inter-generational ethical values.

In this section, a number of real-world examples of estimation of the social discount rate are presented. A possible estimation of the SDR in EU27 Member States using the SRTP method is also provided for illustrative purposes.

Box 6.3 The effect of economic dynamics on CBA parameters

The social discount rate is not the only parameter of a cost-benefit analysis which could be considered as time-dependent. In principle, all shadow prices, as well as welfare weights, which are usually considered as exogenous parameters in applied CBA, are functions of time. By definition, all shadow prices represent the solution to the optimization problem of an objective welfare function, given certain constraints at a given point of time. Both the objective function and the constraints are related to a particular socio-economic scenario as seen at that point. Any change in the assumptions of the considered economic model, because of new information, would lead to an adjustment of the shadow prices, in order to re-establish the optimum.

Furthermore, very large projects might contribute to change the economic setting, by affecting the individual and social preferences for investment and consumption, and other economic circumstances. Adopting measures worldwide to reduce the effects of climate change is an example of a mega-project. Other examples could be multi-national infrastructure investments in the transport or energy sector. In similar situations, large investment projects have an influence on the economic context, thus affecting the shadow price and social discount rate estimation and transforming the optimization problem into a dynamic problem. In spite of its intellectual appeal, the solution of such a dynamic model would be extremely difficult to find and no easy short cuts can be generally derived to determine time-dependent shadow prices in practice.

Source: Authors.

6.4.1 International evidence: SDRs recommended in selected countries

Table 6.5 presents the social discount rates currently used in selected countries world-wide, together with their respective theoretical foundations. This gives an overview of the variance of SDR, which can range from 2.5 per cent in France up to 12 per cent in Pakistan and India. Also, it is interesting to point out that different discount rates are used in some countries – such as in the Netherlands and New Zealand – depending on sectors/nature of projects while a declining discount rate is justified by others – such as France, Denmark, Germany, Ireland, and the United States – for intergenerational investments.

In Australia the SRRI approach is preferred to SRTP approach. Latest guidelines provided by the Office of Best Practice Regulation requires the use of an annual real discount rate of 7 per cent with sensitivity analysis conducted at a lower bound of 3 per cent and a higher bound of 10 per cent for any appraisal of regulatory proposals (Australian Government 2020).

In the 1970s and 1980s the prescribed rates in the US for most governmental agencies was 10 per cent. This rate was measured as the real, marginal, before-tax rate of return on private investment. In 1992, the Office of Management and Budget (OMB) revised this rate downward to 7 per cent (OMB 1992), still considering the marginal rate of return on private investment as a proxy of social discount rate.

For regulatory proposal, a discount rate higher than 7 per cent was suggested. In 2003, the OMB issued a further circular confirming the 7 per cent as a reference rate for regulatory analysis and adding a second rate – equal to 3 per cent – to be used use in circumstance where the regulation primarily and directly affects private consumption (OMB 2003). These rates rely on two different approaches to discounting: they represent the opportunity cost of capital (the average before-tax rate of return to private capital) and the social rate of time preference for consumers (given by the average return to ten-year government bonds). OMB (2003) also recommends a lower rate for 'intergenerational' projects and, the US Environmental Protection Agency suggests a rate of 2.5 per cent (estimated on the basis of the SRTP approach) to account for the intergenerational nature of climate damages (US Environmental Protection Agency 2013, 2018).

In the UK, the guidelines for investment appraisal by departments and executive agencies are given in the *Green Book*, published by HM Treasury in 2003 (latest update in 2022). Until the early 1980s, the Ministry of Finance used the SRRI approach, resulting in a value of 10 per cent real in 1969, which subsequently declined to around 5 per cent real in 1978. In 1989, both the time preference and the cost of capital were derived, with the outcome of a range of 4–6 per cent. A social discount rate of 6 per cent was chosen. Following the decision by HM Treasury in 2003 to adopt the SRTP approach, the social discount rate has been revised and reduced to 3.5 per cent for projects with a time horizon of less than 30 years. This value has been reconfirmed by HM Treasury in 2020. In particular, with reference to the Ramsey formula for the SRTP, the Treasury indicates that the pure time preference and the catastrophe risk give a value of around 1.5 per cent per year. The growth per capita in the UK over the period 1949–2016 is on average 2 per cent. The annual rate (g) is therefore set on around 2 per cent per year. The two rates are applied to the social rate of time preference formula, with en elasticity value of 1, which gives a real discount rate of 3.5 per cent. A lower discount rate – 1.5 per cent – is recommended for taking into account of risk to health or life effects.

The *Green Book* suggests that for projects with very long impacts, i.e. beyond 30 years, a declining schedule of discount rates should be used rather than the standard discount rate (see Table 6.5). The main rationale for declining long-term discount rates results from increasing uncertainty about the future.

In the Netherlands, the CBA guidelines – issued in 2013 – recommended a real discount rate of 5.5 per cent (derived from SRRI approach and made up of a real risk-free rate of 2.5 per cent and a general risk premium of 3 per cent) which could be reduced by up to 1.5 per cent depending on project specific macroeconomic risk factor. The overall rate has been revised from 5.5 per cent to 3 per cent by the Netherlands Discount Rate Working Group in 2015. While no rationale for implementing a declining rate is found by the working group, different rates for specific policy areas are deemed to be justified (see Table 6.5).

In Germany, the Federal Finance Ministry offers guidance on appraisal and evaluation of public investment projects. An inter-temporal model was constructed at the end of the 1980s to compute the social discount rate. The foundation of this model is a utilitarian welfare function, where the welfare is the sum of the utility over time, discounted with the pure time preference. The empirical quantification of the parameters of this model had an outcome of a social discount rate of 4 per cent real (the average interest rate on ten years' public bonds over the last 40 years is slightly higher than 3 per cent). The German government lowered its SDR from 4 per cent real in 1999 to 3 per cent real in 2004. This value has been confirmed by the German Federal Environment Agency (UBA 2012) as a reference value for short-term evaluations (up to 20 years) while a lower and constant rate – 1.5 per cent – is suggested for cross-generation evaluations

In France, a real discount rate has been set up by committees of experts, generally under guidance of the *Commissariat Général du Plan*, since 1960. The social discount rate was determined by the analysis of the marginal return of industrial capital and amounted to 9 per cent in the seventh plan, then reduced to 8 per cent real in 1985 (ninth plan). More recently, the Quinet Commission (2013) recommends a risk free discount rate of 2.5 per cent to 2070 gradually declining to 1.5 per cent beyond 2070 (the period beyond which the guidance dictates as being the residual value). To this value, a risk premium, specific to each project, should be added according to its macroeconomic sensitivity (β) and a systemic risk premium which is set to 2 per cent up to 2070 and 3 per cent beyond 2070. This choice is justified by the markets' behaviour, the macroeconomic considerations and intergenerational concerns for the long term. Overall, the Quinet Commission recommends the rate of 4.5 per cent when the macroeconomic sensitivity (β) of a project is not known.

The differences existing between the social discount rates in European countries would produce varying estimates of the net present value of a given project. For this reason, the European Commission, in its 'Guide to Cost-benefit Analysis of Investment Projects' (2014), provides a reference social discount rate for investment projects receiving EU capital funds. Based on long-term economic growth and pure time-preference rates, the Commission proposes the following indicative benchmarks for the social discount rate: 5 per cent for the Cohesion countries and 3 per cent for the others.[13]

A recent calculation of SDR carried out by Moore *et al.* (2020) on the basis of SRTP approach recommends an average value of 3.77 per cent for Latin American countries (ranging from 2.14 per cent for Paraguay to 5.83 per cent for Chile). This value is significantly lower than those currently used by government agencies in Latin American

Table 6.5 SDR recommended by selected countries and multilateral development banks

Theoretical foundation	Country	Social discount rate (real)	Source
SRRI/SOC	Australia	7 per cent with a sensitivity range from 3 per cent to 10 per cent	Australian Government (March 2020)
SRRI/SOC	Canada	8 per cent, with sensitivity test over the range 3–10 per cent	Treasury Board Secretary (2007) confirmed by Treasury Board Secretary (2020)
SRRI/SOC	Denmark	4 per cent under 35 years (given by the sum of 3 per cent risk-free rate and 1 per cent risk premium). Reduced to 3 per cent from 36 to 70 years and to 2 per cent from year 71 onwards.	Mouter (2018)
SRRI/SOC	India	12 per cent	Campos *et al.* (2015)
SRRI/SOC	Japan	4 per cent	ITF (2015)
SRRI/SOC	Norway	4 per cent under 40 years (given by the sum of 2.5 per cent risk-free rate and 1.5 per cent risk premium). Reduced to 3 per cent from 40 to 75 years and to 2 per cent from year 76 onwards.	NOU (2012)
SRRI/SOC	New Zealand	5 per cent or 6 per cent depending on the sector. (i) Default rate (for projects that are difficult to categorize including regulatory proposals, and most social sector projects): 5 per cent; (ii) office and accommodation buildings, water, energy, hospitals, hospital energy plans, road, and other transport projects: 5 per cent; (iii) telecommunications, media and technology, IT, R&D: 6 per cent).	New Zealand Government (2015) New Zealand Government (2020)
SRRI/SOC	Pakistan	12 per cent	Campos *et al.* (2015)
SRRI/SOC	The Netherland	5.5 per cent (2.5 per cent real risk-free + 3 per cent premium for macroeconomic risk) which can be reduced by up to 1.5 per cent depending on project specific macroeconomic risk factor. The overall rate has been revised from 5.5 per cent to 3 per cent by the Netherlands Discount Rate Working Group in 2015. Also, different rates for specific policy areas are suggested (3 per cent as a default rate or for investments in nature, CO_2 and health; 4.5 per cent for public physical investments/infrastructure and 5 per cent for investments in education).	CPB and PBL (2013) Netherlands Discount Rate Working Group (2015) O'Callaghan *et al.* (2018)
SRRI/SOC	Philippines	10 per cent	Moore *et al.* (2020)
SRRI/SOC and SRTP	Latin American countries	Values from Government/agencies based on SRRI/SOC approach; Argentina: 12 per cent; Bolivia: 12 per cent; Chile: 6 per cent; Colombia: 12 per cent; Costa Rica: 12 per cent; Mexico: 10 per cent; Peru: 11 per cent; Uruguay: 12 per cent. Value calculated by Moore *et al.* on the basis of the SRTP approach: average SDR of 3.77 per cent, ranging from 2.14 per cent for Paraguay to 5.83 per cent for Chile.	Moore *et al.* (2020)[10]

Theoretical foundation	Country	Social discount rate (real)	Source
SR RI/SOC and SRTP	United States	7 per cent, (SR RI) as a reference rate 3 per cent (SRTP) to be applied in circumstance where the regulation primarily and directly affects private consumption OMB (2003) recommends lower rate for 'intergenerational' projects while US EPA (2013, 2018) recommends 2.5 per cent (SRTP) to account for the intergenerational nature of climate damages. DOE suggests a real discount rate of 3 per cent for projects related to energy conservation, renewable energy resources, and water conservation.	OMB (2003) US EPA (2013, 2018) OECD (2018) Cahill and O'Connell (2018) U.S. Department of Commerce, National Institute of Standards and Technology (2013)
SRTP	European Union	5 per cent is used in cohesion countries and 3 per cent for the other member states	European Commission (2014)
SRTP	France	2.5 per cent (falling to 1.5 per cent from 2070) plus a risk premium of 2 per cent (rising to 3 per cent from 2070) multiplied by a sector specific beta value. When the macroeconomic sensitivity (β) of a project is not known, the Quinet Commission recommends the rate of 4.5 per cent	Quinet (2013) and Ni (2017)
SRTP	Germany	3 per cent for short-term period (evaluations up to 20 years). 1.5 per cent (constant) for cross-general evaluations (evaluations extending over 20 years) which should be combined with a sensitivity analysis using a discount rate of 0 per cent.	German Federal Environment Agency (UBA 2012)
SRTP	Ireland	a. 4 per cent (for projects with long time horizons a declining discount rate applies) b. Range from 2.6 per cent to 3.9 per cent for all sectors. 1.7 per cent for carbon emissions and other long-term environmental damage	a. Department of Public Expenditure and Reform (2019 and confirmed in January 2021)[11] b. Cahill and O'Connell (2018)
SRTP	Italy	3 per cent	Invitalia (2014)
SRTP	Malta	5.5 per cent	Planning and Priorities Co-ordination Division (2013)
SRTP	Sweden	3.5 per cent	ASEK Guidelines (2020)
SRTP	UK	3.5 per cent for years 0–30, 3 per cent for years 31–75, 2.5 per cent from year 76 onwards. For health projects: 1.50 per cent for years 0–30; 1.29 per cent years 31–75 and 1.07 per cent from year 76 onwards.	HM Treasury (2020a) Freeman et al. (2018)
SRTP	European Investment Bank	A value ranging from 3.5 per cent to 5.5 per cent, depending on the degree of maturity and expected growth rate of the national economy.	European Investment Bank (2013)[11]
SR RI/SOC	World Bank	10–12 per cent	Moore et al. (2020)
SR RI/SOC	African Development Bank	6 per cent for infrastructure 9 per cent for social sector projects	Moore et al. (2020)
SR RI/SOC	Inter-American Development Bank	12 per cent	Moore et al. (2020)

Source: Adapted from Catalano et al. (2022).

countries as well as by multilateral development banks (i.e., African Development Bank, Inter-American Development Bank) which are based on the SOC approach and typically range between 10 per cent and 12 per cent.

Finally, it is worth mentioning the results of a survey of over 200 experts carried out in 2015 (Drupp *et al.* 2015, 2018). A key feature of this survey is that it elicited the recommended values for the individual components of the Ramsey Rule. By aggregating experts' responses, the authors recommend a mean SDR of 2.27 per cent, with a range from 0 to 10 per cent. More than three-quarters of experts contributing to the survey are comfortable with the median social discount rate of 2 per cent, and over 90 per cent find this value in the range of 1 to 3 per cent acceptable.

6.4.2 An example of SRTP estimation

As shown, the Social Rate of Time Preference method is widely used in developed countries. The purpose of this section is to show a possible and practical way to estimate the SRTP using the Ramsey formula. In this section a coherent methodology to estimate the SDR of many European countries is applied. The evidence presented in this section draws from the estimation carried out by Catalano *et al.* (2022) which takes into account the COVID-19 pandemic effects and enlarge the sample of countries[14] for which the SDR has been computed in previous attempts (Evans 2007; Florio and Sirtori 2013, respectively on 15 and 20 Member States) In what follows, an estimation of the different parameters entering the Ramsey formula is presented.

6.4.2.1 Estimating the pure time preference (ρ)

As to the rate of pure time preference, the economic literature[15] generally estimates a value between 1 per cent (e.g. Newbery 1992; Arrow 1995; Evans 2007) and 3 per cent (Nordhaus 1993). In the Stern Review, a much lower rate is considered (0.1 per cent), due to the assumption of a nil impatience or myopia component, on the same ground as Ramsey (1928). Thus, the rate of pure time preference takes into account the sole probability of extinction of the human race, which corresponds to a probability of human extinction of 10 per cent in 100 years. More frequently, an approximate 1 per cent rate of time preferences is accepted for European countries (Evans and Sezer 2004), which also reflects the risk of catastrophe.

A possible way to proxy this factor could be to set the impatience or myopia component equal to zero, in line with Ramsey's argument mentioned above, and the life chance measure equal to the annual crude death rate of the population (number of deaths over population). For the estimation of this parameter, Catalano *et al.* (2022) rely on the most up-to-date death rate figures provided by Eurostat in year 2019.[16] These figures are overall constant across time, with an average 2019 value for EU 27 Member States of 1.04 (ranging from 0.63 in Ireland to 1.55 in Bulgaria).

6.4.2.2 Estimating the elasticity of marginal utility of consumption ($\mathcal{E}$)

Second, the SRTP approach needs an estimation of the elasticity of marginal utility of consumption. This could be assessed with a survey (such as Barsky *et al.* 1995; Amiel *et al.* 1999[17]), or it can be inferred from observation on indirect individual behaviours. People's savings, for example, can reflect their views about how much consumption they wish to transfer over time. The literature offers a large number of empirical estimates derived from modelling lifetime consumption and demand. For instance, Evans found elasticity values of 1.6 and 1.33 for UK and France respectively (Evans 2004a, 2004b); for Italy, Percoco (2008) estimated elasticity at 1.28; Kula used 1.56 for Canada, 1.89 for the US and 1.64 for India (Kula 1984, 2002).

Another approach is to consider society's judgement about how consumption should be transferred across people at different times (the 'revealed social values' approach). In this case, the elasticity tells how much more worthwhile it is to carry out transfer of income from a rich person to a poor one; or, in other words, it reflects the social planner's aversion to income inequality. This value can be revealed by using two methods. The first one consists in considering national contribution of aid allocated to the developing countries. This approach leads to an elasticity value of around 1 for developed countries.[18] The second method is based on the progressivity of national personal income tax rates, according to a model that rests on the following assumptions: income tax structure based on the principle of equal absolute sacrifice of satisfaction, and iso-elastic utility functions. The first assumption suggests that the rich should pay more in tax, according to a progressive tax system, whereas the second implies that a social planner displays constant relative risk aversion independently of scale.

Stern (1977) proposed a formula for elasticity which is in line with the second mentioned method:[19]

$$\varepsilon = \ln\left(1 - t'\right)/\ln\left(1 - t\right) \tag{6.4}$$

where t' and t are respectively the marginal and average tax rates for an average taxpayer. The results obtained for ε are sensitive to tax coverage and to the adopted definition of the average tax rate (e.g. whether employees' social contributions are included or not in the tax rates), but in general its value is above 1. Potts (2002) stresses that, in order to be consistent with other indicators of government attitudes to distributional issues, values of e should range between 0.5 and 2. More recent estimates of elasticity can be found in Gollier (2006), which suggests a value between 2 and 4 based on a thought experiment based on willingness to pay to reduce risk, in Dasgupta (2008), which prefers a value of 2 on the basis of introspection on inequality aversion, in Drupp *et al.* (2018), which obtains a mean value of 1.3 based on a survey to over 200 discounting experts, and in Groom and Maddison (2019), which finds a value ranging from 1 to 1.5 for UK use a number of techniques.

For the purpose of their estimation, Catalano *et al.* (2022) follow the tax-based model and, particularly, they calculate the elasticity – to be entered in the Ramsey formula – by relying on the formula suggested by Stern. Data are taken from the OECD Tax Database (Taxation of Wage Income 2020)[20] and refer to personal income taxation. Tax rates include central and sub-central government taxation. Country elasticity has been calculated as the mean of elasticity at different income levels, including the social security contribution paid by the employee.[21] Results of their calculation show that elasticity values for EU27 Member States[22] range from 1.00 (Hungary) and 1.98 (the Netherlands) with an average of 1.53. The elasticity estimates under the fiscal model are probably exaggerated because they consider income tax rates, while the social preference for equity should be assessed on the whole effective marginal tax rates. These are probably lower, because indirect taxation and capital taxation in most countries are not progressive.

6.4.2.3 *Estimating the expected growth rate per capita consumption (g)*

Empirical estimates for the rate of growth of per capita consumption are usually based on past performance. Pearce and Ulph (1995), in calculating the social discount rate for the United Kingdom, decided to take very long-run rates of growth in real per capita consumption in order to smooth out possible short-term distortions. Also, Evans and Sezer (2005) used the average annual growth of per capita real consumption over the three past decades (1970–2001) to estimate the actual rate, which amounts approximately to 2.3 per cent for Spain, 2.5 per cent for Italy and Greece, 2.7 per cent for Portugal and 3 per cent for Ireland. A different method to estimate g is to consider another welfare-correlated indicator as a proxy for consumption growth, such as real per capita GDP growth.

While most authors consider a simple average of past time series, as long as it is available, the disadvantage of such an approach is that it is only backwards looking, whereas expected future growth in per capita consumption also matters. Rates of per capita consumption growth higher than 4 per cent are hardly sustainable in the long run, and so it might be assumed that long-run values for g would be in the range of 0–4 per cent for most developing countries, with most countries being at the lower end of the range (Potts 2002). Moreover, when there have been major structural shocks in past times, as happened in the European transition economies, past data may be misleading because such shocks are not going to be encountered again in the future. The best approach would be to estimate a long-term development path for each economy, based on an appropriate growth model. Yet the economic collapses recorded between 2008 and 2012 as well as in 2020 due to the COVID-19 pandemic situation and the still unstable macroeconomic situation make growth forecasts very uncertain.

For the purpose of their estimation, Catalano *et al.* (2022) considered long time series of both historical data and forecast values of per capita GDP real growth. These data are provided by the International Monetary Fund (latest release issued on 6th April 2021).[23] They include a set of consolidated data and projections. Although IMF projections go until 2026, Catalano *et al.* (2022) prudentially base their calculation on forecasts until 2021. Longer projections (from 2021 to 2026) show a more positive trend of GDP which might not take into account the risk of an increasing economic crisis due to a new COVID-19 wave. While annual data have been considered for the elasticity (2020) and for the pure time preference component (2019), g has been computed as an average of values covering almost two decades (from 2002 to 2021), in order to account for different economic cycles.[24]

The simple average value of per capita GDP growth over the period considered (2002–2021) is 1.87 per cent for EU27 Member States, with values ranging from −0.40 (Italy) and 4.93 in Lithuania.

6.4.2.4 *SDR calculation basing on Ramsey formula*

With these three elements − ρ, ε, and g − Catalano *et al.* (2022) estimate the SRTP for EU27 member states,[25] as shown in Table 6.6. An average SDR of 3.43 per cent − and a median value of 2.40 per cent − is estimated with the lowest social discount rate and the highest one applying, respectively, to Italy (0.34 per cent) and Lithuania (7.67 per cent).

Table 6.6 Estimation of the SRTP in EU27 Member States

Parameter	ρ	ε	g	SRTP
Reference period for the estimation	2019	2020	2002–2021	
Austria	0.94	1.48	0.71	1.98
Belgium	0.95	1.68	0.74	2.19
Bulgaria	1.55	n/a	3.96	n/a
Croatia	1.27	n/a	1.88	n/a
Cyprus	0.71	n/a	0.70	n/a
Czech Republic	1.05	1.30	2.25	3.97
Denmark	0.93	1.44	0.76	2.03
Estonia	1.16	1.81	3.54	7.58
Finland	0.98	1.63	0.88	2.41
France	0.91	1.52	0.52	1.70
Germany	1.13	1.33	0.95	2.39
Greece	1.17	1.69	−0.22	0.80
Hungary	1.33	1.00	2.42	3.75
Ireland	0.63	1.95	3.28	7.04
Italy	1.06	1.81	−0.40	0.34
Latvia	1.45	1.33	4.34	7.24
Lithuania	1.37	1.28	4.93	7.67
Luxembourg	0.69	1.82	0.80	2.15
Malta	0.73	n/a	2.21	n/a
Netherlands	0.88	1.98	0.76	2.39
Poland	1.08	1.08	3.59	4.95
Portugal	1.09	1.62	0.47	1.86
Romania	1.34	n/a	4.54	n/a
Slovak Republic	0.98	1.32	3.46	5.55
Slovenia	0.99	1.23	1.75	3.15
Spain	0.88	1.65	0.42	1.58
Sweden	0.86	1.68	1.12	2.73
Min	**0.63**	**1.00**	**−0.40**	**0.34**
Max	**1.55**	**1.98**	**4.93**	**7.67**
Average	**1.04**	**1.53**	**1.87**	**3.43**

Source: Adapted from Catalano *et al.* (2022).

6.5 The opportunity cost of public funds

Notwithstanding that discount rates are often seen as reflecting the opportunity cost of funds, the shadow price of public funds is in fact a distinct concept. It certainly has an effect on the discount rate, but the two notions are not equivalent. Discounting is a method of aggregating costs and benefits occurring at different points in time and it reflects the opportunity cost of capital from an inter-temporal perspective. The shadow price of public funds has instead a more 'static' nature. It refers to the marginal cost of public funds (MCPF) in terms of the forgone opportunity of an alternative use of those funds.

To finance its expenditure, governments have at their disposal a wide array of taxes to levy, including commodity taxes, taxes on labour income, on the return to capital, etc. Moreover, governments may decide to increase public sector borrowing, which in turn results in a higher tax rate required to finance the interest payments on a higher public debt. Each euro raised by taxes imposes a burden on taxpayers by cutting their expenditure opportunities and interfering with their spending choices. The welfare loss incurred by society in raising additional revenues to finance government spending is the opportunity cost of public funds.

When funds are transferred from the private sector to the government by means of distortionary taxes, firms and households allocate resources in a less efficient way compared to a situation of perfectly competitive economy without government. A tax on the consumption of specific goods, for instance, distorts the equilibrium between demand and supply by driving a wedge between the marginal value of the goods to households and the marginal cost to the producer. A general tax on consumption, instead, while not distorting the choices between goods, determines a gap between wages and the purchasing power of private agents. Similar distortions occur when taxes on labour income or on interest income are levied: in the former case, the distortion manifests itself in the difference between gross (before-tax) and net (after-tax) income; in the latter, between net and gross interest rates. These taxes distort the work-leisure choices and negatively affect the level of economic activity, *ceteris paribus*.[26] This constitutes an excess burden that makes the economic cost of raising one euro in the private sector larger than one euro. Accordingly, the conversion factor for public funds is generally set higher than unity.

According to Dahlby (2008), the MCPF is the dollar that is transferred from taxpayers to the government plus the marginal excess tax burden (METB), which measures the social cost of raising an additional dollar of tax revenue. That is, MCPF = 1 + METB.[27]

In assessing the economic cost of raising public funds, Diamond and Mirrlees (1971), Stiglitz and Dasgupta (1971), Atkinson and Stern (1974), and Riess (2008) stress that government expenditure can also work in an opposite direction. Besides generating an extra cost to society, public funds have indirect benefits which contribute to boost activities that taxation *per se* reduces. Indirect welfare gains 'counteract the departure from an efficient allocation of resources caused by distorting taxes' (Riess 2008: 91). For example, a transport project aimed at reducing travel time, or an investment measure positively affecting people's health, indirectly affect the supply of labour, with positive influence on the economic activity. More recently, Bos *et al.* (2019) argues that the best pragmatic approach is to assume first that a policy measure is financed out of general tax revenues and then that the marginal excess burden of these taxes is broadly counterbalanced by the benefits of redistribution of these taxes. This pragmatic approach implies that the marginal cost of public funds equal to 1 and then no correction is needed. Boardman *et al.* (2020) contest the empirical foundation of Bos *et al.* (2019)'s argument. In Boardman *et al.* (2021) view, CBA requires the inclusion of METB except when government revenues are not affected by any of the project alternatives examined or when positive and negative changes in government revenue exactly net out or when public funds are raised via lump sum taxes or when, in practice, the scale of any changes in revenue is trivial relative to the scale of other changes in allocative efficiency.

Differences in cost-of-funds estimates depend on country-specific tax regimes, but also on differences in definition and measurement (Riess 2008). Even if estimates vary considerably, the opportunity cost of public funds appears not negligible. For a general tax change in 20 OECD countries Dahlby (2008) reports that countries can be clustered into two groups, one with MCPF around 1.5 and the other around 1.2 to 1.25. The US, Denmark and Sweden are outliers with MCPF of respectively 1.1, 3.2 and 2.2. However, in practice the opportunity cost of public funds is rarely used by governments in the context of CBA. For instance, Abelson (2020), which examined seven Official Guidelines for CBA, found that only those from New Zealand recommended routinely including METB in their analyses. Spackman (2004) explains that this shadow price would represent an extra unfamiliar complication for governmental officers, particularly if it is considered that the shadow price of public funds should be calculated for each public investment, depending on the way this is financed. The lack of consensus on the assumptions needed to derive a shadow price for public funds makes its calculation even less attractive. Lind (1990) supports the idea of ignoring the estimation of the shadow price of public funds by virtue of the growth of international financial markets and capital mobility, which makes the impact of public investment on private investment minimal. This perspective has some implications also on the method of estimating the social discount rate, implying that the social time preference approach is generally more appropriate for comparing public expenditure over time.

Harking back to the relationship between the social discount rate and the shadow price of public funds, these could be considered as two sides of the same coin. While the opportunity cost of public funds informs us about the welfare cost of transferring resources from the private sector to the government at any point of time, the social opportunity cost of capital informs us about the rate at which society can transfer resources across different points in time. A discount rate based on the social opportunity cost of capital implies that forgone opportunities are used to measure the importance of time, but the economic cost of public funds would continue to be captured exclusively by the shadow price of public funds. What links the social discount rate based on the SRRI approach and the shadow price of public funds is the displacement effect of governmental spending on private investment, which contributes to changes in the investment pattern of the economy, thus affecting both the shadow price and the discounting rate.

6.6 Further reading

Social discount rates are generally discussed in most texts on project economic analysis. Besides the already mentioned handbook by Boardman *et al.* (2018), a comprehensive and critical review of different approaches to estimating the social discount rate is provided by Price (1993), Perkins (1994), and more recently by Kazlauskienė (2015). More particularly, the use of the marginal rate of return on private investment was supported by an influential article by Harberger (1969). Feldstein (1964) explains the social time preference rate approach. Jenkins and Harberger (1994) describe the weighted cost of capital approach. The shadow price of capital approach for discounting was first suggested by Otto Eckstein (1958) and then developed by David Bradford (1975).

More details on the marginal cost of public funds and on the theoretical and empirical issues to be addressed when measuring the effects of incremental tax rate can be found in Dahlby (2008). The author shows how to measure the loss incurred by society in raising additional revenues to finance government spending, depending on the way in which additional revenues are levied: commodity taxes, excise taxes, taxes on labour income, taxes in return to capital and public sector borrowing. The marginal cost of public funds is also extensively examined by Jones (2005), who provides a theoretical foundation, in line with the Harberger approach to cost-benefit analysis, to interpret and use different measures of the marginal cost of public funds for a variety of taxes. Barrios *et al.* (2013) provides an empirical estimation of the marginal cost of public funds for EU member states, by considering two specific tax categories which are often proposed as good candidates for efficiency-enhancing tax shifting policies: labour and green taxes.

Vast literature exists about declining discount rates. Frederick, Loewenstein, and O'Donoghue (2002) and Campos *et al.* (2015) provide evidence for hyperbolic discounting as a real-world discounting approach. With reference to environmental investments, relevant contributions have been provided by Newell and Pizer (2004), Weitzman (1994) and Hepburn (2003). A discount rate for environmental quality, which assumes that the growth of environmental quality is smaller than economic growth, was suggested by Gollier (2010).

An interesting finding that is worth mentioning is in Johansson-Stenman and Sterner (2011). While the traditional literature on SDR points to the fact that social discount rates should be lower than individual rates, due to the higher risk aversion of individuals, the two authors show that this argument does not hold when the effects of 'relative consumption' are incorporated in the theory of social discounting. Having defined the social discount rate as the discounting rate used by people when they do take into account that their final consumption may affect others ('positional externalities'), and the private discount rate as the rate used when people take into account that they themselves are affected by others' consumption, but not that their consumption affects others, Johansson-Stenman and Sterner maintain that the former tends to be larger than the latter. In other words, for a positive growth rate, if the extent by which relative consumption matters increases with the consumption level, as indicated by some empirical evidence, then the social discount rate exceeds the private one.

Finally, an important debate, launched by Baumol and Quandt (1965), is about discounting under capital rationing. When governments, agencies and companies operate on a fixed budget set by third parties, the choice of discount rate for an investment project is a practical problem, due to the influence that capital rationing has on the choice of optimal investment project combinations. How the market discount rate affects the decision regarding project selection under capital rationing is discussed by Elton (1970). On the other hand, Burton and Damon (1974) find that there is no meaningful solution for the pure capital rationing problem, and therefore any attempt to interpret or calculate such results is fruitless.

6.7 Summary of Chapter 6

- Discounting enables one to express future monetary or socio-economic effects in terms of present values when inter-temporal decisions are to be taken. Reasons for discounting the future are twofold: (i) the employment of resources has an opportunity cost, since resources committed to a project could be employed in another return-generating investment; (ii) individuals have pure time preferences, meaning that they prefer to receive the same amount of goods sooner rather than later.
- The social discount rate is the inter-temporal opportunity cost of capital to the whole society. It differs from the individual discount rate, which coincides with the concept of pure rate of time preference and reflects individuals' impatience and myopia which make them attach low value to the utility of future generations. There are various approaches to estimate the SDR.
- According to the social rate of return on private investment (SRRI) approach, when public investment is considered to have a displacement effect on private investment, the social discount rate should reflect the marginal social opportunity cost of the displaced investment. A possible proxy for the marginal rate of return on private investment is the real before-tax rate of return on corporate bonds. However, this approach is generally considered biased towards high estimates of the SDR.

- When public investments determine a postponement in consumption, a better approach to estimating the SDR is based on the social rate of time preference (SRTP). In this framework, the SDR depends on the expected growth rate of per capita consumption, the elasticity of marginal utility of consumption and a pure time preference term.
- When public funds both have a crowding-out effect on private investment and displace private consumption, a weighted average of the investment rate of return and the net return to savers can be computed.
- Another approach to estimating the SDR is based on the shadow price of capital. It consists in converting all investment inflows into 'consumption equivalents' using the shadow price of capital, and then discounting them at the SRTP.
- Most economists have criticized the use of constant social discount rates on the ground of time-inconsistent individual preferences, which would justify declining discount rates. The choice between constant or time-declining SDR is particularly important when valuing projects with impact crossing generation lines, such as climate change related investments.
- Significant variations in social discount rates adopted by governments and evaluators exist across the world, depending on the country specificities, but also on the estimation method used and on the specific underlying parameters chosen.
- The SRTP approach has been applied to estimate country-specific social discount rates in EU27 member states. Among the estimated discount rates, a wide gap can be observed between the lowest one (0.34 per cent for Italy) and the highest one (7.67 per cent for Lithuania).
- While the SDR, i.e. the social opportunity cost of capital, informs about the rate at which society can transfer resources across different points in time, the marginal cost of public funds informs about the welfare loss incurred by society in raising additional revenues to finance government spending at any point of time. It typically ranges between 1.05 and 1.57.

End of chapter questions

- What is the logic behind discounting costs and benefits? Is it coherent and ethical to discount the future? Is a zero social discount rate plausible and convincing?
- What is the impact of the social discount rate on the project's viability? Does a high discount rate favour projects with benefits accruing early or later in the time horizon?
- What are the approaches to estimate the social discount rate? What are the key differences between these approaches?
- What are the main reasons for variations in social discount rate policies of various countries around the world? Why developed countries generally apply lower rates while developing countries have higher ones?
- Why is the use of time-declining discount rates advocated in the literature? Assume project A will result in net benefits of EUR 1 billion in 200 years and project B will result in net benefits of EUR 1 million in 40 years. Compute the present value of these projects using a time-constant discount rate of 3 per cent and a time-declining discount rate of 3 per cent from year 0 to year 49, 2.5 per cent from year 50 to year 99, 2 per cent from year 100 to year 200. Discuss the results.

Notes

1 This chapter is co-authored with Emanuela Sirtori and Gelsomina Catalano.

2 See, among others, Arrow and Lind (1970), Arrow *et al.* (1996) and Frederick *et al.* (2002).

3 The philosopher Derek Parfit provided an argument for such consumption impatience, by stating that an individual is aware that his own identity changes over time. Consequently, the individual would perceive his future identities, which are different from the current one, as distinct persons from himself. This logic would justify the fact of giving less weight to utilities of these other selves (Parfit 1971).

4 See in Chapter 7 how social discounting and distributional weighting can be combined, according to the notions of 'compensating discounting' and 'ideal weighting' by Thureson (2012).

5 It relies on the Social Opportunity Cost of Capital (SOC) paradigm based on the rate of return that would be expected on funds left in the private sector.

6 Another approach that can be found in the literature is based on the use of the government's long-term borrowing rate. Since public sector projects are usually risk free, due to a large portfolio of projects across which the risk can be spread, interest rates on long-term government bonds can be thought to be representative of the most risk-free rates. However, this approach is affected by two main conceptual weaknesses: first, the market value of a government bond is in fact subject to risk, with interest return being affected by changing macroeconomic conditions; second, in reality governments finance projects mostly through funding coming from taxation, while a minor share of funding public investment is from borrowing (Kula 2012).

7 Indicative estimates for the long-term annual financial rate of returns on a portfolio of different securities (considering as assets large, mid and small stocks, international stock, bonds and cash equivalent) suggested a real financial discount rate for the European Union of approximately 4 per cent, according to the European Commission (2014). The reason for adopting a unique reference financial discount rate value for EU Member States relies on two assumptions: (i) that public funds are drawn from the EU median taxpayers; (ii) and that in the long run, inflation and interest rates converge across the EU countries.

8 As stressed by Spackman (2007) and Kula (2012). See Feldstein (1965) for more details on the algebra of this equation.

9 The notation used in this chapter differ from that used in chapters 1–3 and what reported in the notation list.

10 Moore *et al.* (2020) provides a new estimation for the SDR basing on SRTP approach for the following countries: Argentina, Bolivia, Brazil, Chile, Colombia, Costa Rica, Ecuador, El Salvador, Guatemala, Honduras, Mexico, Nicaragua, Panama, Paraguay, Peru, Uruguay, Venezuela.

11 https://www.gov.ie/en/policy-information/1a0dcb-project-discount-inflation-rates/.

12 This guide is currently under review.

13 Florio (2006) explains that, while in principle the SDR may be region/country-specific, only two macro regions should be considered for the determination of the SDR of projects eligible under the EU Cohesion Fund and the European Regional Development Fund. The rationale for using different discount rates lies in the different growth rates of EU members, with average growth rates of 'Cohesion countries' being twice as great as in the rest of the European Union during the 2000–2005 period.

14 The estimation of the different parameters entering the Ramsey formula is provided for 22 countries of EU27 countries. Because of missing values on elasticity, it was not possible to calculate the SDR for the following five countries: Bulgaria, Croatia, Cyprus, Malta, and Romania.

15 See a review in Zhuang *et al.* (2007).

16 Source: Eurostat, Demographic balance and crude rates, extracted on 28.05.2020.

17 While Barsky *et al.* (1995) obtained an elasticity of approximately 5, Amiel *et al.* (1999) estimated values ranging between 0.2 and 0.8. Such a divergence is due to the different samples of population interviewed, which reflect different degrees of inequality aversion: US middle-aged people in the former case, US students in the latter.

18 OECD/DAC website.

19 This formula has been applied also by Cowell and Gardiner (1999) and Evans (2005).
20 https://www.oecd.org/tax/tax-policy/tax-database/. OECD, Part I, Table I.4 and I.5, data extracted on 14.05.2021. This publication includes marginal and average tax rates for individuals who earn 67 per cent, 100 per cent, or 167 per cent of the average wage (single with no children) and for married persons with two children at 100 per cent, 133 per cent, or 167 per cent of average wage.
21 As highlighted by Evans (2005), average elasticity is very similar to elasticity calculated at the average production wage, i.e. the average annual gross wage earnings of an adult, full-time manual worker in the manufacturing sector.
22 The value is missing for the following five countries: Bulgaria, Croatia, Cyprus, Malta, and Romania.
23 World Economic Outlook Database, April 2021. Data extracted on 14.05.2021. GDP is expressed in constant national currency per person. Data are derived by dividing constant price GDP by total population. The unit is purchasing power parity; percent change.
24 In compliance with the approach followed by Florio and Sirtori (2013).
25 The value is missing for the following five countries: Bulgaria, Croatia, Cyprus, Malta and Romania.
26 In their theory of tax reform, Ahmad and Stern (1984, 1990) consider that the government computes the marginal social cost of extra revenue arising from different taxes and, between different options, chooses the one with the lower marginal social cost.
27 Provided that METB relies on uncompensated labour supply elasticities.

7 Welfare weights and distributional impacts

Overview

One curious aspect of most CBA practice is its neglect of distributive analysis, i.e. the welfare assessment of who gets the benefit and who bears the social cost of a public project or policy. This is in contrast with the ambition of Applied Welfare Economics to look into the comprehensive socio-economic impact of public investment and policy decisions. The debate on introducing welfare weights (also called distributional weights) in the CBA, in order to take into account not only efficiency but also equity aspects, is an old one. However, the topic is still under discussion and in evolution since some questions remain unsolved. While a traditional approach to Welfare Economics has considered impossible or misguiding the inclusion of distributional effects in project and policy evaluation, a large proportion of professionals consider this aspect a significant one.

Obviously, the concern for equity is greater where the local circumstances reveal serious social unbalances that may be exacerbated or softened by relatively large projects. For instance, within developing countries where an uneven distribution of welfare exists, governments might promote pro-poor projects. The distributional issues can also appear across regions or countries. For example, the enlargement of the EU to include the new states of Eastern Europe in 2004 and 2007 may be cited in this regard as a political decision that implied an increase of income and welfare inequality across states, regions and individuals. The interest in welfare distribution has also arisen in the literature on the economics of climate change. Here, the distributional concerns regard the way in which the burden of climate change should be distributed across the stakeholders of a project in a long-run inter-temporal setting.

In this chapter, the longstanding debate on these issues in the Applied Welfare Economics literature is reviewed and different existing approaches for introducing distributional considerations in CBA are presented. Section 7.1 introduces the reasons supporting the use of equity considerations in CBA. Section 7.2 outlines the concept of welfare weights in a Drèze–Stern theoretical framework and discusses the incorporation of distributional weights in CBA. In Section 7.3 the 'distributional characteristic of goods' approach is presented. Group and regional welfare weights are then discussed in Section 7.4, and Section 7.5 illustrates two other alternative ways of bringing distributional considerations into CBA, i.e. the 'basic needs' approach and the social affordability analysis. Finally, Section 7.6 suggests further reading and possible topics for further research.

DOI: 10.4324/9781003191377-9

7.1 Why are equity considerations needed in CBA?

One traditional view of CBA, mainly associated with the contributions by Mishan (1969), Musgrave (1969), and Harberger (1972),[1] maintains that project evaluation should not be concerned with equity issues. The reasoning behind this position is that achieving a desired distribution of welfare across individuals or households should be treated by the government through taxation and subsidies, while expenditure projects should focus on efficiency in the allocation of resources. In this view, including equity considerations in CBA could imply the possibility that any project that determines a transfer of resources from relatively richer individuals to poorer ones would pass the CBA test provided the decision makers' preference for equity is high enough, regardless of the degree of efficiency (or inefficiency) of such a project. In a first-best economy, in principle this situation would not produce any problem. Actually, governments would have lump-sum taxation available as an instrument to compensate the losers, i.e. the ones who bear the costs of the project and do not get any benefits (as postulated in the Second Welfare Theorem). Yet in the real world, which is a second-best one, governments generally cannot easily offer lump-sum compensation because, for example, information issues are imperfect (as discussed in Chapter 2).

On this ground, many economists think that cost-benefit analysis of projects should not neglect to look at distributional impacts of governmental intervention (see, e.g., Stern 1977; Drèze and Stern 1987; Layard and Glaister 1994; Adler 2016; Robinson *et al.* 2016). This position is endorsed by the European Commission's Guide to CBA (2014), which indicates possible methods of deriving welfare weights and analysing distributional issues that can be brought back to some of the approaches discussed in this chapter. The UK *Green Book* on project appraisal (HM Treasury 2020a) also recommends investigating the effects of investment proposals on different sections of society. The evaluation of distributive impacts has also been officially adopted for a long time by the World Bank, even if not pursued in practice, according to Little and Mirrlees (1994). As a matter of fact, the practical experience of using welfare weights in project evaluation is limited, and not only at the World Bank. Nevertheless, the reasons for including an analysis of the distribution impact of a project are compelling.

First of all, it can be argued that, while empirical project evaluation is generally more concerned with efficiency rather than equity, equity considerations are more often taken into account by governments when assessing the potential or achieved impact of a reform (e.g. a change in regulation). In the Drèze–Stern framework, however, there is no distinction between CBA of projects and CBA of reforms. As discussed in Chapter 3, actually getting the solutions of social planner optimization problems in terms of shadow prices of goods or of other policy instruments (all signals under the control of the planner) implies solving the same problem. Hence, it is conceptually unnecessary and misleading to consider equity issues only in public interventions involving reforms but not investment projects. The structure of the Drèze–Stern shadow prices is such that welfare weights must be explicitly considered for both project and reform evaluation, since these are included in the derivative of the SWF.

Second, any kind of public investment changes welfare distribution through the associated policy function. The new projects actually displace some previous activities and create new ones, and such a reshuffling of opportunities may have equity implications. This can happen on a regional, country or wider level. In the EU, for example, taxpayers of the German region of Bavaria indirectly pay not only for the construction of new highways in the former Eastern Länder in their own country, but also for environmental projects in Cyprus, financed through EU funds.

Third, in second-best economies it cannot be assumed that the tax and transfer system always succeeds in matching any undesirable redistribution resulting from a public project with adequate compensation to losers. In fact, this is quite often simply impossible, because the latter are not specific well-identified individuals but a mere statistical entity. In some cases, identification is possible, but transaction costs are too high. In other cases, compensation to losers is possible and offered, but this is rather an exception. Box 7.1 presents the Kaldor–Hicks compensation criterion to test whether a project that generates both gainers and losers can still be regarded as Pareto efficient.

Fourth, the standard assumption of diminishing marginal utility of income implies that the utility value of a unit change in income of a poor individual is greater than that of the same unit change in income of a rich individual. As a consequence, if the objective of a project is to maximize social welfare, then a project that improves the income distribution (or provides some services to poor individuals) will be worthier than a similar project that worsens the income distribution (or provides the same services to rich people).

Finally, a society or a government can consider greater equity as an end in itself. For instance, if one of the government's targets is to increase social cohesion, equity

---

Box 7.1 The Kaldor–Hicks efficiency criterion

The contribution by Kaldor (1939) and Hicks (1939) to the Welfare Economics theory was to extend the concept of Pareto improvement, which applies when at least one person is made better off by an economic change and nobody is made worse off, to cases when there are losers. The two authors developed the idea that a project that has a net positive benefit, i.e. the total social gains from the project exceed the losses but there are also some losers, can still be considered a Pareto improvement if the gainers from the project could compensate the losers and still be better off themselves. The criterion does not require that the losers should actually be compensated; rather, it requires that the gainers should potentially be able to compensate the losers out of their gains. Actual compensation is thus regarded as a political or ethical decision.

Several critiques have been addressed to the Kaldor–Hicks criterion. The most common ones are that it takes into account only the hypothetical willingness-to-pay of the gainers in money terms and disregards the difficulties in comparing the utility of different individuals (see Chapter 2 for more on this). In particular, it ignores that an increase in marginal utility of the low-income person is higher than the decrease in marginal utility of the high-income person. Another criticism regards the so-called 'Scitovsky paradox', which occurs when the gainer from a project can compensate the loser but the loser could also then compensate the gainer for forgoing the change in allocation. This can happen when a public project is so large that it alters the relative prices of goods.

Source: Authors, based on Boadway (2016) and
Bostani and Malekpoor (2012).

considerations become one of the purposes of the project. This would be a further element pushing for considering the distributional impact of public investment.

7.2 Deriving welfare weights

As shown in Chapter 3 (Section 3.4), the marginal social value (MSV) of a lump-sum transfer r to consumer h is the difference between the social marginal utility of h's lump-sum income (β^h), i.e. the welfare weight, and the social cost $v(\partial x^h/\partial m^h)$ of h's additional consumption valued at shadow prices:

$$\text{MSV}_{rh} = \frac{\partial W}{\partial V^h}\frac{\partial V^h}{\partial m^h} - v\frac{\partial x^h}{\partial m^h} = \beta^h - v\frac{\partial x^h}{\partial m^h}. \qquad (7.1)^2$$

Welfare weights (β^h) are the partial derivative of $W(\cdot)$, the Social Welfare Function, with respect to a marginal increase of lump-sum income (marginal utility of income) of the h-th consumer $\left(\dfrac{\partial W}{\partial V^h}\dfrac{\partial V^h}{\partial m^h}\right)$. They depend on two components:

- the change in social welfare if the utility or well-being of individual h increases marginally $(\partial W/\partial V^h)$. It indicates how the person (or institution) whose social welfare preferences are being reflected ranks the utility of consumer h in their distributional preferences.

- the marginal utility of income of individual h: $\left(\partial V^h/\partial m^h\right)$. This second term reflects the assessment, by the person whose welfare preferences are being reflected, of how the utility of consumer h changes as a result of an increase in lump-sum income (Scarborough and Bennett 2012).

By considering the FOC for the optimum plan (Chapter 3), the welfare weights are built-in with the calculation of the Lagrangian multipliers, i.e. the shadow prices. Therefore, in a DS framework the general shadow prices of goods necessarily include a distribution characteristic. The magnitude of welfare weights depends on the functional form of the SWF, which in turn involves ethical judgments about how to aggregate individual utilities and reflects the willingness to trade off the utility or well-being of one individual for another.

To sum up, under the definition of shadow prices in a DS framework, efficiency and equity considerations are closely linked together in a Social Welfare Function. The shadow prices needed to evaluate projects or reforms are the marginal changes of SWF caused by changes in its arguments around the constrained optimum for the social planner. Thus, for any SWF that among its arguments includes welfare variables defined over agents (individuals, households, social groups, territorial groups, or any subsets of the society set), shadow prices reflect both equity and efficiency considerations (and additional objectives if they are included in the SWF). In other words, the shadow prices of outputs, labour, any other inputs, and the MSV of a reform as well, combine in one set of real numbers (given a unit of account) the measurement of how the SWF reacts to changes in both net production (or consumption) and welfare distribution.

According to Drèze and Stern (1987), the most straightforward way of thinking about welfare weights is to consider a small imaginary transfer between different individuals. If, for example, a marginal lump-sum transfer of α units of income to household h_1 is judged to compensate exactly (from the point of view of social welfare, and with all other signals being held constant) a loss of one unit of a lump–sum income for another household h_2, it can be inferred that:

$$\alpha \beta^{h_1} - \beta^{h_2} = 0. \tag{7.2}$$

Or, equivalently,

$$\alpha = \frac{\beta^{h_2}}{\beta^{h_1}}. \tag{7.3}$$

Generally,

> Welfare weights will depend on the values taken by signals such as price and rations. As long as all consumers face the same signals, the above procedure remains valid for marginal changes around some initial environment. When discrete changes are considered, or when different individuals face different signals (e.g. different quantity constraints) or possess different characteristics (e.g. family structure), it will be necessary to take these additional factors into account as far as possible.
>
> Drèze and Stern (1987: 960)

The estimation of welfare weights under this frame can be difficult because of lack of data. In the rest of the chapter, some practical short cuts are discussed. Readers should be warned that in some cases the validity of these short cuts is questionable, and caution is needed in using them. The theoretical frame should always be kept in mind when elaborating and interpreting data in the specific circumstances.

7.3 Estimation of distributional weights

One simple approach to the evaluation of the equity dimension of projects, but not entirely consistent with the DS framework, is a two-step approach. First, the social planner computes a set of welfare or distributional weights. Second, the evaluator uses the weights to aggregate welfare changes of individuals or groups involved in the projects.

The first step implies estimating welfare weights, and this is not a straightforward issue. A number of methods for estimating them have been discussed in the literature. For instance, Dasgupta *et al.* (1972) and Little and Mirrlees (1974) support the idea that weights should be determined from the political system. Another proposal has been that they could be estimated by the observation of marginal rates of income taxation or by an inverse optimum approach (Ahmad and Stern 1984) based on indirect taxation. Brent (1984) presents two different approaches of estimation: the 'a priori' and the imputational ones. The former specifies in advance a set of reasonable assumptions from which the weights are derived (see, e.g., for Squire and van der Tak 1975). The latter approach imputes the weights from past government decisions (see McFadden 1975, 1976; Basu 1980; Weisbrod 1986; Brent 1991a).

The applied CBA has typically approached this issue by focussing on just one dimension of individual welfare: income (or consumption). Under this view you need to guess a SWF defined over income, and assume a functional form. A popular one is the constant elasticity marginal utility function (see Chapter 1). This is consistent with the strong (and unreasonable) assumption that all individuals have the same utility function, and that this should increase with income (monotonic) but its derivative should decrease (declining marginal utility). Such a function is:

$$U^h = \frac{m^{h^{1-\varepsilon}}}{1-\varepsilon}. \tag{7.4}$$

Here, ε is the elasticity of the marginal utility of income. Similarly, the distributional weight of household h can be expressed as a function of consumption as presented in Irvin (1978), rather than income. Under the constant elasticity assumption, the welfare weight (already defined in equation 1.19 of Chapter 1) is:

$$\beta^h = \left(m^h\right)^{-\varepsilon}, \tag{7.5}$$

and the welfare weight normalized to the average target social group or to the average household $\left(\bar{\beta}^h\right)$ is:

$$\beta = \frac{\beta^h}{\bar{\beta}^h} = \left(\frac{\bar{m}}{m^h}\right)^{\varepsilon}. \tag{7.6}$$

Here, the ε parameter is the elasticity to income of the social welfare, a parameter that would reflect society's (or the social planner's) degree of aversion to inequality. For example, the normalization rule is such that for the average income earner, $\bar{\beta}^h = 1$, the hth welfare weight is a simple function of the ratio between the average income and the hth income group.

When the value of ε is one, the welfare weight is simply the inverse of the income (or consumption) level of the individual (or group). A zero elasticity implies unitary welfare weights; hence, one euro is one euro in welfare terms whoever the winner or loser is, as in the Harberger tradition (see Box 7.2, where Harberger's criticism of the use of distributional weights is briefly presented through his famous example). A more egalitarian social planner would assume $\varepsilon > 0$, so that individuals whose income level is above average will be given a weight less than unity. Vice versa, the elasticity would be between zero and one for a moderate inequality aversion.

Brent (2006) suggests 0.5 elasticity value as a benchmark, because he does not find a convincing case for progressivity either in taxation or welfare weights. This is, however, in contrast with most observable tax systems, which are progressive, and then with inference from actual governments' choices. On the basis of the structure of personal income tax rates, Evans (2005) suggests that a value for the elasticity of social welfare to income of around unity, both when forming distributional welfare weights and computing a social time preference rate (see Chapter 6) in cost-benefit studies, is often too low. The author has calculated that, on average, for developed countries ε is close to 1.4. However, a wide range of estimates for ε exists in the literature as a result of the diverse methodologies employed for its calculation. For instance, Gollier (2006) suggested a value between 2 and 4 based on a thought experiment based on willingness to pay to reduce risk, while Dasgupta (2008) prefers a value of 2 on the basis of introspection on inequality aversion.

The implication on the marginal increase of welfare of assigning different values to ε is illustrated in Table 7.1. Assume that there is a rich individual with income equal to

---

Box 7.2 Harberger's criticism of the use of distributional weights

One of the best known criticisms of distributional weights can be found in Harberger (1978, 1984), who shows that the use of high distributional weights can lead to the acceptance of highly inefficient projects. He considers a project of sending ice-cream on a camel's back across the desert from a richer oasis to a poorer one. If the poorer recipients in the receiving oasis have a social distributional weight equal to four times that of people living in the richer oasis, then the project would be accepted even if up to ¾ of the ice cream melts on the way to the poorer oasis. This example illustrates the necessity to take into account the possible efficiency loss associated with the incorporation of equity consideration in CBA. Readers are invited to discuss this example in terms of shadow prices of the ice cream against actual prices.

Source: Authors, based on Harberger (1978).

---

300 and a poor individual with income equal to 100. Assume also that both individuals are affected by a project that produces a net benefit equal to +200 to the richer and −100 to the poorer. Thus, the total net benefit of the project, 'without' any use of welfare weights,[3] would be +100. If welfare weights calculated as from equation (7.5) are applied, the total net benefit varies according to the chosen value of ε. Large values of ε result in large weights to be applied to the loss suffered by the poorer individual, and this in turn negatively affects the total net benefit of the project. As a result, the magnitude of ε determines how large the distributional adjustment will be.

One problem with the two-step approach, in spite of its attractive simplicity, is that it is often understood as implying that welfare changes of agents can be measured through the changes of their income (or consumption) and that these can in turn be computed by shadow prices and quantities as a separate exercise. The theoretical definition of shadow prices, however, is such that welfare weights are needed to compute them, as mentioned in the previous section. Consequently, using welfare weights directly on income or consumption changes should be seen as a short cut, to be applied only when one is confident that this is appropriate.

The benefits of the short cut are, however, more limited if it is considered that the standard approach to CBA boils down to computing the NPV or IRR of the project at shadow prices. In practice, the following method is used: even when shadow prices include the welfare weights, weights are taken as one and a welfare function is applied separately to these shadow prices. When shadow prices are computed including the welfare

Table 7.1 Net benefits by different values of elasticity: some examples

Degree of inequality aversion (ε)	Net benefit of the project for richer individual	Net benefit of the project for poorer individual	Total net benefit
0	200	−100	100
0.5	162	−141	21
1	132	−200	−69
2	72	−400	−328

Source: Authors.

weights, some authors (see Little and Mirrlees 1974; Squire and van der Tak 1975) call these prices social shadow prices. When the shadow prices are calculated without the welfare weights, they are sometimes called economic shadow prices. Therefore, one could distinguish between three sets of prices:

- observed prices (used in financial analysis);
- economic shadow prices with $\beta = 1$ (usually used in economic analysis);
- social shadow prices derived from welfare weights (used in the so-called 'social analysis').

7.4 The distributional characteristic of goods

Another approach to the evaluation of the equity impact of a project is that of exploiting the distributional characteristic of goods, as proposed by Feldstein (1972). The simple idea is that distributional weights can be attached to goods and factors of production instead of being given to consumers. This approach was analyzed for the first time by Boadway (1976). The idea is to give higher weights in the CBA to goods consumed or factors owned by the poor. Obviously, this requires detailed knowledge about the distributional characteristics of goods and factors as well as value judgments regarding the marginal social utilities of income of all groups of individuals.

The distributional characteristic D_i of a good i is defined by Feldstein (1972) as the weighted average of the marginal social utilities, i.e. each household's marginal social utility weighted by its consumption of good i. Following the conventional assumption of decreasing marginal social utility, this implies that the value of D_i is greater for a necessity than for a luxury good.

Suppose there are H households, that consumption of good i by household h is denoted as x_i^h and that total consumption of good i is:

$$X_i \equiv \sum_{h=1}^{H} x_i^h. \tag{7.7}$$

The distributional characteristic of good i is defined as:

$$D_i \equiv \frac{\sum_{h-1}^{H} \beta^h x_i^h}{\sum_{h=1}^{H} x_i^h} = \frac{\sum_{h=1}^{H} \beta^h x_i^h}{X_i}, \tag{7.8}$$

where β^h reflects the relative weight attached to household h and the extent to which distributional considerations are taken into account. For instance, if distributional issues are not taken into account at all (thus each household has the same welfare weight) all goods would have a distributional characteristic equal to one ($D_i = 1 \ \forall_i$). Conversely, if the concern is about equity, a higher weight would be placed on less well-off households. In this manner, the goods whose consumption is more concentrated amongst less well-off households have a relative higher value of D_i.

There are some possible sophisticated variations of this simple formula. In practice its calculation is not difficult for a small number of consumer types (e.g. those below the poverty line and the group of all the others, or by the income quartiles) and for a set of key goods or sets of goods. In the simplest case, in order to calculate the distribution characteristic of a good, the value of β^h is set equal to the marginal utility of consumption of household h, where the utility of consumption function is in the form of equation (7.4). Thus, the welfare weight (as in equation (7.5) but considering consumption instead of income) is:

$$\beta^h = \frac{\partial U^h}{\partial x^h} = x_h^{-\varepsilon}. \tag{7.9}$$

In the literature, there have been various attempts to estimate the distributional characteristic of different goods. For instance, Newbery (1995) computed the distributional characteristics of commodities from household budget survey data for Hungary and the United Kingdom and then used these values to compare the aggregate distributional characteristic against cumulative expenditure of the two countries.

Brau and Florio (2004) estimated the distributional characteristics for various products in the UK to evaluate the welfare effect of price changes in selected privatized industries. For large price variations, the authors show that under some assumptions the welfare change per unit of price change is a function of the distributional characteristic of the good, the share of expenditure of that good, the price change, and the aggregate demand elasticity.

Madden (2009) calculated the distributional characteristics of broad aggregate of goods for Ireland using, again, data from a household budget survey. Finally, calculations have also been attempted for emerging markets where household expenditure survey data are not always available. For instance, Navajas (2004) estimated the distributional characteristic of public services for Argentina and Hughes (1987) calculated those of various products for Indonesia, Thailand and Tunisia.

Table 7.2 presents the distributional characteristics of various goods for different countries. Note that those figures do not allow for comparing the distributional characteristics for a good across countries, but only within countries, because of different periods of time considered and different country consumption levels and patterns. However, it can be remarked that the goods with the highest values of distributional characteristic are those whose expenditure is more concentrated amongst poorer households. For example, in the UK railways have lower distributional characteristics than gas because the share of consumption of gas by the poor is higher than the share of consumption of railway services.

The distributional characteristic of goods in turn enters the shadow prices v_i in different ways. One simple formula, derived from the many-person Ramsey rule (see Atkinson and Stiglitz 1980: 386–393), is:

$$v_i = MC_i \frac{\varepsilon_i}{\varepsilon_i - 1 + \bar{\beta}_i D_i}, \tag{7.10}$$

where MC_i is the marginal cost, ε_i is the price elasticity of the demand for the good i, and $\bar{\beta}_i$ is the average welfare weight.

Table 7.2 Distributional characteristics for various goods ($\varepsilon = 1$)

	Argentina[a]	Ireland[b]	UK[c]	Indonesia[d]
Non-durable goods	0.73	0.30		
Clothing	0.57	0.26		
Housing	0.48	0.28		
Durable goods	0.48	0.27		
Education	0.51			
Health	0.54			
Private services	0.45			
Public services	0.67			
Food		0.31		
Tobacco		0.35		
Fuel and light		0.36		
Service		0.25		
Transport		0.26		0.61
Rail			0.87	
Bus			0.75	
Natural gas	0.86		0.90	0.39
Electricity	0.99		0.89	0.61
Telephone	0.78		0.87	
Water	0.87		0.94	
Sanitation	0.76			
Coal			0.92	1.32
Kerosene				1.00

Source: Adapted from different studies: (a) Navajas (2004), using data from household expenditure surveys 1996–1997 as published in INDEC (1999); (b) Madden (2009), using data from household budget survey 1994–1995; (c) Brau and Florio (2004), using data from the family expenditure survey 1994; (d) Eskeland and Kong (1998), using data for Jakarta from SUSENAS 1990.

Suppose, for example, that the marginal cost of a railway project is 1 euro per passenger/km; the price elasticity of railway transport is also 1; the average welfare weight across households is 1; and the distribution characteristic is 1.1 (meaning a socially important good). Hence the shadow price is here simply $MC_i/D_i = 0.91$, lower than the marginal cost.

The great advantage of this approach is that the shadow prices can be computed without any additional analysis, since the project economic return would include equity and efficiency impacts in just one figure. One drawback however is that, by simply looking at the project performance indicator, it will be perhaps less transparent who the winners and the losers are. A second problem is that for certain values of the parameters, negative shadow prices cannot be ruled out.

7.5 Group and regional welfare weights

Distributional concerns usually focus on individuals or households. Equity, however, is a broader social issue that can be defined in different ways in the political context. The SWF arguments may include partitions of the agents according to, for example, gender, religion, language, age, location (Weisbrod 1972) and any other suitable characteristics. As a matter of fact, the reasons to do so may be carefully considered, because empirical research reveals that individual income or consumption is generally the best proxy of welfare in a broad sense. In fact, when groups or regions are considered instead of individuals, the combined equity and efficiency objective of the planner, and thus the SWF form, can change in a fundamental way. The welfare weights will represent the importance given by the planner to changes in group or regional per capita income or consumption.

In many occasions, the social planner may be interested in comparing income changes between different regions or groups rather than among individuals; thus, the estimation of group or regional welfare weights is a relevant issue. Anyway, the empirical approach to the estimation of these welfare weights is the same as for the individual ones. To see whether marginal utilities differ across groups or regions, equation (7.6) can be reformulated with reference to the r-th group or region as follows:

$$\beta = \frac{\beta^r}{\overline{\beta}^r} = \left(\frac{\overline{m}}{m^r} \right)^\varepsilon, \tag{7.11}$$

where m is the average national income per capita and m^r is the group/regional income per capita. Therefore, by choosing the average income level in the community as a yardstick, the welfare effects of a project can be compared to individuals in different social groups, or in different regions.

With this approach, the estimation of the regional welfare weights boils down again to the estimation of ε, the elasticity of marginal utility of income. Box 7.3 presents a short review of the main existing approaches for the estimation of ε.

Box 7.3 Estimating the elasticity of marginal utility of income

A wide range of the literature concerning social welfare weights is dedicated to the estimation of ε. Evans (2005) provides an extensive review of the existing empirical approaches. In particular, he identifies three fundamentally different methods:

- *Direct surveys*, which consist of the elicitation of people's response to hypothetical scenarios aimed at measuring their inequality aversion (see, e.g., Barsky *et al.* 1995; Amiel *et al.* 1999) or the relationship between income and the level of happiness (Layard *et al.* 2008).
- *Indirect behavioural evidence* approach, which comprises two different methods: the 'Lifetime consumption behaviour model' interprets as the reciprocal of the inter-temporal elasticity of substitution in consumption (see Blundell *et al.* 1994); the 'Consumer demand for a preference–independent commodity model', based on the work of Fisher (1927), Frisch (1932) and Fellner (1967),[4] takes the value of ε as the ratio of the income elasticity of demand to the compensated own–price elasticity (see in this regard also Evans and Sezer 2002; Kula 2002; Evans *et al.* 2005).
- *Revealed social values* based on government spending or tax policies. For instance, Stern (1977), Cowell and Gardiner (1999) and Evans and Sezer (2004) have produced estimates of ε using income tax data. This last approach has

been used by Evans (2005) to calculate the elasticity of marginal utility of income for 20 OECD countries, 13 of which belong to the European Union. In particular, the average tax rate used by the author in the estimation of ε is the ratio of tax liability to pre-tax income after the deduction of standard tax allowances.

Source: Authors, based on Evans (2005).

As far as the estimation of regional welfare weights is concerned, Kula (2002) presents estimates for 18 Indian states and finds a national average value of e equal to 1.60. In discussing his results, the author suggests that regional welfare weights can be used in project evaluation to establish regional planning priorities:

Regional welfare weights calculated in this way may be of some help to Indian policy makers to prioritise the establishment of infrastructure and other projects in poor states. For example, the net present value of a public project considered in Rajasthan may be multiplied by 1.50 (1991/92 welfare weight for that state [...]) to improve its ranking in the overall public sector investment portfolio.

(Kula 2002: 111)

In Evans *et al.* (2005), welfare weights are calculated for the UK regions: England, Scotland, Wales, and Northern Ireland. In this study, the best estimation of the elasticity of marginal utility of income is argued to be $\varepsilon = 1.60$, but the authors also test $\varepsilon = 1$ and a median value $\varepsilon = 1.3$. Figure 7.1 illustrates their results. The authors comment on them, stressing the importance of using regional welfare weights in the EU context:

With current member countries being culturally diverse and at varying stages of development, the calculation of regional welfare weights would need additionally to take into account a range of other variables to reflect adequately social well-being in the different countries. Such variables might include health, education and environmental indicators.

(Evans *et al.* 2005: 925)

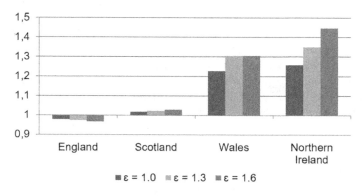

Figure 7.1 Regional welfare weights for the UK.
Source: Adapted from Evans *et al.* (2005).

Table 7.3 Regional welfare weights for Turkey ($\varepsilon = 1$)

Region	Per capita regional income, 2001 USD	Welfare weights
Marmara region	3,050	0.70
Aegean region	2,542	0.84
Mediterranean region	2,041	1.05
Black Sea region	1,694	1.27
Central Anatolia region	1,996	1.08
South-Western Anatolia region	1,217	1.76
Eastern Anatolia region	990	2.17

Source: Authors, adapted from Sezer (2007) data.

They also suggest that interregional variations of cost of life and income dispersion should be considered. In particular, they argue that countries with most income dispersion in relative terms need to have an upward adjustment to their welfare weights.

As another example, Table 7.3 considers the case of Turkey and shows the regional welfare weights computed using equation (7.11) and data provided by Sezer (2007). In 2001, Turkey had a per capita income of USD 2,146, with large gaps across its seven regions. It is clear that welfare weights are very different in various parts of the country due to these relevant regional differences.

7.6 Basic needs and social affordability

Some alternative ways of bringing equity considerations into policy or project evaluation have been developed in parallel with the idea of distributional weights. Two examples are the so-called 'basic needs' approach presented in Harberger (1984), and the social affordability analysis.

7.6.1 The basic needs approach

Though the label 'basic needs' was probably coined by Harberger (1984), this approach has ample roots in the literature concerning on the one hand the analysis of in-kind transfer and on the other hand the subject of interdependent utilities and Pareto-optimal redistribution. According to Harberger, the basic needs approach differs from the distributional weights method since it does not rely on differential weighting of the welfare of different individuals. Rather, it recognizes that, due to altruism, the utility of some individuals relies, among other things, on external benefits associated with improvements in the extent to which the basic needs (i.e. medical, educational, nutritional and housing needs) of less better-off segments of society are met. Therefore, it is not the recipient's utility that enters the donor's utility function (as in the distributional weights approach), but rather the recipient's consumption of particular goods or services like food, education, medical care, housing or attainment of certain states such as being better nourished or better educated (Harberger 1984). This can be seen in fact as a variant of paternalism, as discussed in Chapter 1, here being the rich donors', rather than the government's, preferences to be considered.

An important feature of this approach is that the donor's gratification from the increase in the consumption of a basic need by the worse-off people does not preclude someone else from being gratified as well. This means that an individual's willingness-to-pay to increase the consumption of a basic need can be vertically added to those of other donors. Thus, the market equilibrium associated with a basic need such as child nutrition can be graphically represented as in Figure 7.2. The private demand curve (equal to the marginal private benefit) of a less better-off person would lead to an equilibrium level of child nutrition equal to OP. According to the basic needs approach, social intervention is justified to bring that level up to OS. Thus, the new demand curve associated with the basic need externality reflects the marginal social benefit, i.e. both the marginal private benefit and the external benefit. The net benefit is the area *XYZ*, which is the difference between *YXWZ*, the social benefit of the externality, and *XWZ*, the loss of efficiency due to the cost of a subsidy of *WZ* to reach the social optimum level of basic needs.

According to Harberger, the great advantage of the basic needs approach is that it is totally compatible with what he regards as the three fundamental postulates[5] of Applied Welfare Economics:

1 the benefit of an incremental unit of good or service to a demander is measured by its demand price;
2 the opportunity cost of an incremental unit of good or service to a supplier is measured by his supply price;
3 when calculating social costs and benefits of a project, a policy, or a programme, one simply takes the difference between the total benefit and the total cost attributed to the various members of the relevant social unit. A dollar of benefits to one counts as much as a dollar of benefits to another.

(Harberger 1984: 456)

By contrast, the use of distributional weights entails altering the third postulate. However, the Harberger approach suffers from some shortcomings, such as the assumption that individuals are altruistic. As suggested by Duesenberry's relative income hypothesis (1949),[6] it should be considered that better-off people can also get a positive externality for having more than the others: the lower the relative income of others, the higher is the utility of income of a person (this type of utility function is discussed in Chapter 1). In this context, relative welfare matters, but in the opposite direction.

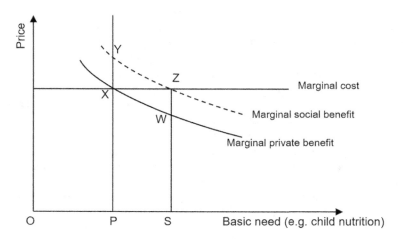

Figure 7.2 Market equilibrium of basic needs.
Source: Authors, adapted from Harberger (1984: 461).

Moreover, since this approach focuses on basic needs, it cannot be considered an alternative method to be applied to all the wide range of projects and policies for which a CBA is usually carried out. For instance, it is difficult to find a transport or telecommunication project in a developed country which has direct impact on basic needs in the usual meaning, even if the project has losers and winners, as virtually most projects have.

7.6.2 Social affordability analysis

Social affordability analysis is another shortcut approach to include distribution considerations in project evaluation. It is implemented by checking the project impact on the most disadvantaged groups, as defined by the social planner. As with the environmental impact analysis, the simple underlying idea is that it is not reasonable to assume that empirical shadow prices can in practice always do the ambitious job of giving a *numéraire*-based quantification of costs and benefits. In such cases, it would be more transparent to focus on a small set of welfare proxies and social targets and assess the expected project outcome. In other words, with the social affordability analysis, equity appears as a separate (and primary) objective and can be defined over a number of dimensions, not just income or consumption but also, for example, accessibility to services (see below). Basically, the CBA will provide an economic analysis on one side (with proxies of shadow prices that may only imperfectly capture the distributive dimension) and a distinct analysis on the impact of the project on the welfare of specific target groups (the poor, ethnical minorities, women, etc.), which is the social affordability analysis.

The concept of affordability refers to the ability of particular consumer groups to pay for a minimum level of a certain service (Fankhauser and Tepic 2007). In the literature, different approaches to measure affordability have been identified (Box 7.4); however, the most common way is to calculate the share of utility payments in total household expenditures, at national or regional level (Miniaci *et al.* 2014).

A very simple way to perform a social affordability analysis is to establish some affordability benchmarks that cannot be exceeded: for example, in a water project partly financed by an increase of tariffs, it can be set that the share of water expenditure should not exceed a threshold share of income for any household, including the poor. On the basis of the determined expenditure income thresholds, the planner will identify possible remedies (e.g. progressive tariffs, vouchers or subsidies) to ensure social affordability. Setting these benchmarks inevitably requires some value judgement. Moreover, the determination of the socially optimal expenditure/income shares should be based on two considerations: the minimum requirement of the service (e.g. under universal service obligation), prevailing prices, and an analysis of the structure of households' expenditures.

Many governments and international institutions have established indicative benchmarks in order to carry out affordability analyses for different kinds of utilities. Some of them are shown in Table 7.4.

The rationale for focussing on social affordability instead of looking at the whole distribution impact of the project is twofold. First, in many circumstances income reshuffling between top and middle income groups is less a political concern than the net impact of a project on bottom income groups. Second, project implementation may be at risk if appropriate action is not planned to compensate losers who are in bad economic conditions. For instance, when the losers of a gas service project are the low-income households, if compensation does not occur, extremely poor households could have no other choice than to stop paying for the service or avoid using it. This, in turn, damages the project's financial sustainability, reduces the net social benefits and could also lead

---

Box 7.4 Utility poverty and the measurement of affordability

Utility poverty refers to a situation where the access to utilities (e.g. energy and water supply) of disadvantaged citizens or social groups is limited or prevented, due to an insufficiently affordable service. The empirical literature on the social affordability of public services is quite wide and contains different approaches (for a review, see, e.g., CERRE 2015). The conventional way to measure affordability is to use the so-called 'affordability ratio', a crude ratio between the household total income (or total expenditure) and the expenditure on a basket of services. Alternatively, one could compute the affordability ratio by focussing on specific vulnerable groups, such as pensioners or beneficiaries of social assistance. Another approach is the 'minimum entitlement' approach, which is related to a wider definition of poverty based on standard quality of living (Fankhauser and Tepic 2007). Here the concept of affordability is closely related to what can be considered as 'essential' to ensure a socially inclusive provision.

Source: Authors.

---

to social unrest. As a result, looking for actual compensation of the poor may be more important than calculating the whole distribution impact using welfare weights and distribution characteristics in the standard Bergson–Samuelson framework.

This approach is similar to having an environmental impact analysis as a complement to standard CBA, when giving a money value to environmental risks is impossible or not appropriate. Hence the decision maker will be given the information that the project has a given expected financial and economic return, and a given expected social affordability impact, for example, in terms of number of households in the socially sensitive target that will see a worsening of their economic conditions.

Table 7.4 Benchmarks for affordability analysis (per cent)

	Electricity	*Water*	*Heating*	*Telecoms*
World Bank (2002)	10–15	3–5		
WHO (2004)	10			
IPA Energy (2003)	10		20	
UN/ECE			15	
US EPA		2.5	6	
UK government		3	10	
OECD		4		
European Commission		4		
UNDP		3		
Asian Development Bank (2003)		5		
Argentina, Venezuela and Chile government		3		
Indonesia (2006)		4		
Kenya		5		
UNCTAD				5

Source: Authors, based on CERRE (2015), Fankhauser and Tepic (2007), Florio (2013) and Smets (2009).
Note: the affordability metrics adopted by the different studies differ.

7.7 Further reading

The standard discussion of distributional objectives in modern Public Economics can be found in Atkinson and Stiglitz (1980), and in several more recent texts such as Myles (1995), Jha (1998), and Hindriks and Myles (2006). Goldfarb and Woglom (1974) argue that the decision of governments to include or exclude income distribution considerations in their investment decisions depends on two different policy selection rules, i.e. the 'efficiency rule', according to which projects that maximize income are selected, and the 'welfare rule', which explains the selection of projects that maximize social welfare. The authors investigate under which conditions each rule applies. For a recent discussion on distributional considerations in CBA, the reader can refer to three papers forming a symposium. The first is Fleurbaey and Rafeh (2016), which uses insights from welfare economics to examine how distributional weights can be introduced into benefit–cost analysis, and Robinson, the second is Adler (2016), which presents weighted CBA as practicable method for implementing an SWF, with a particular focus on two specific SWFs: the utilitarian and isoelastic/Atkinson SWFs. Finally, Robinson, Hammitt, and Zeckhauser (2016) focus specifically on the role of distributional considerations in U.S. regulatory analyses.

Commenting specifically on Adler's article, Boardman *et al.* (2020) highlight the practical difficulties to derive distributional weights. The authors observes that the analyst needs, at a minimum, to specify a utility function, to know or estimate each individual's status quo consumption and non-consumption attributes, and the change in each individual's consumption due to the policy alternative being evaluated. Under some assumptions, the analyst also has to specify a coefficient of risk aversion and the degree of inequality aversion. As a result, the authors think this approach does not represent a practicable solution for policy makers. In a similar vein, the reader may be interested in the article by Weisbach (2014). Boardman *et al.* (2020) argue that it is best to use multi-goal analysis to treat the effects of distributional impacts separately from the effects on allocative efficiency.

Somanathan (2006) advanced a new view on welfare weights. He suggests using a SWF based on two axioms: that lives should be valued equally, and that the money value of a person's life should respect its own valuation. Based on this, he suggests that if $w^h(m^h)$ is the monetary valuation by the hth individual of a given probability to reduce the loss of life, then his value of the statistical life is $w^h(y^h)/p$, where p is the reduction in the risk of death and the value of a unit of income in terms of life probability is $p/w^h(m^h)$. Because of the first axiom, the SWF in terms of p-life units is simply:

$$\text{SWF} = \sum_h \frac{m^h}{w^h\left(m^h\right)}. \tag{7.12}$$

Thus, in this function, weights are inversely proportional to the value of a statistical life for a person with income m^h. This approach in fact uses lives (multiplied by the p scalar), not money, as a *numéraire*.[7] Hammit (2021) claims that when individuals' rates of substitution between potential *numéraires* differ, the relative efficiency of different policies can be affected by the choice among them. Therefore, for the author, the analytic distinction between efficiency and equity is imperfect because the measure of efficiency depends on the *numéraire*. To better integrate concerns about distribution and efficiency, he proposes three alternative evaluation methods: a CBA using a different *numéraire* such as health units, weighted CBA, and SWFs.

Cowell and Mercader-Prats (1999) look at multiple dimensions of welfare measurement, beyond income. They review different approaches to building equivalence scales (i.e. equivalized income measures) that include non–income items such as age and disability, and conclude:

> […] it is fanciful to suppose that equivalence scale can be constructed without the introduction of fundamental value judgements. The choice of a particular equivalence scale allows one to quantify the exact differences between welfare levels of those with different levels of needs, but given the value judgement inevitable implicit in any equivalence scale, it may be more appropriate to recognise that value judgements may differ when measuring income inequality and social welfare, in the same way that this is done in other areas of measurement.
>
> (Cowell and Mercader-Prats 1999: 28)

The impossibility of avoiding value judgments in Welfare Economics is a recurrent theme. In this respect, Hammit (2021) claims that all CBA approaches (equal-weight CBA, equal-weight CBA using an alternative *numéraire*, weighted CBA, and SWF) depend on normative choices that are fundamentally equivalent judgments about how to evaluate improvements to some people and harms to others.

Finally, it is worth mentioning an approach consisting in using inter-temporal distributional weights, which has been especially developed in the context of climate change. The idea here is to attach different weights not only according to different households or groups or regions, but also to costs and benefits occurring at different times:

$$b_{i,t} = \beta_{i,t} \times \delta_{i,t}, \tag{7.13}$$

where $\beta_{i,t}$ denotes the social welfare weight and $\delta_{i,t}$ is a discount factor:

$$\delta_{i,t} = \prod_{t=t_0}^{T}\left(\frac{1}{1+r_{it}}\right), \tag{7.14}$$

with $r_{i,t}$ being the social rate of time preference $r = p + \varepsilon \cdot g$ (Chapter 6). Both the welfare weights and the ε discount factor differ between regions i and time periods t.

Thureson (2012) underlines that combination of discounting and distributional weighting can potentially be implemented in all long-term decisions where distributional weighting is used. He also points out that in equation (7.13) economic growth is double counted, both through intra-temporal weights and through discounting. He therefore proposes alternative approaches. One of these is the 'ideal weighting' method which considers only the pure time preference rate p within the discount factor:

$$b_{i,t} = \beta_{i,t} \bullet (1+p)^{-t}. \tag{7.15}$$

7.8 Summary of Chapter 7

- This chapter deals with the relationship between CBA, which focuses on efficiency, and equity, specifically in terms of distributional implications of projects and policies on income and wealth. In other words, it discusses the practical ways to account for distributional issues in CBA.

- The traditional view of CBA has excluded equity considerations. The reasoning behind this position is that achieving a desired distribution of welfare across individuals or households should be treated by taxation and subsidies, while expenditure projects should focus on efficiency. The main problem with this view is that we live in a second-best world where governments cannot offer lump-sum compensation to individuals who bear the cost of a project. Another reason for including distributional considerations in CBA is that equity can be an end in itself.

- Considering equity within the cost-benefit framework implies the specification of value judgments, which, despite their subjective nature, can be rationally and explicitly taken into account when evaluating projects.

- The way to include distributional considerations into CBA is by using welfare weights. At the theoretical level, they are the partial derivative of the welfare function with respect to a marginal increase of a lump-sum income of the hth consumer. In a DS framework, the welfare weights are built-in with the calculation of the shadow prices. However, such a calculation can be difficult to implement in practice.

- A simple approach to the evaluation of the equity dimension of projects, but not entirely consistent with the DS framework, is a two-step approach. First, the social planner computes a set of welfare weights of the form $\beta = \dfrac{\beta^h}{\bar{\beta}^h} = \left(\dfrac{\bar{m}}{m^h}\right)^\varepsilon$. Second, the evaluator uses the weights to aggregate welfare changes of individuals or groups involved in the projects.

- Another approach to consider the equity impact of a project consists in attaching distributional weights to goods and factors of production instead of individuals. The idea is to give higher weights to goods consumed or factors owned by the poor. In practice, this approach implies the calculation of the distributional characteristic of goods which in turn enters in the shadow price. Therefore, this approach is in line with the DS one. However, it does not allow a transparent identification of the project's winners and losers.

- When calculating welfare weights, the chosen value for ε, which captures the degree of inequality aversion of a society, is of paramount importance.

- Alternative ways of bringing distributional considerations in CBA have been developed alongside the idea of welfare weights. The 'basic needs' approach by Harberger and the 'social affordability analysis' are the main evolutions in this direction. The first one relies on an altruistic foundation of society which recognizes the importance that the less better-off people should achieve some minimum level of basic needs consumption such as education, nutrition and medical care.

- The social affordability analysis can be defined as checking the impact of a project on the most disadvantaged groups, as defined by the social planner. A very simple way to perform a social affordability analysis is to establish some affordability benchmarks which cannot be exceeded when deciding to implement a project.

End of chapter questions

- What are the arguments for including an analysis of the distribution impact of a project or a policy?
- What is the Kaldor–Hicks criterion or test? What is the difference between the Pareto principle and the Kaldor–Hicks criterion? What are the advantages and the disadvantages of such criterion?
- Suppose an agency has conducted the CBA for three alternative projects. The results of the CBAs are reported in the following table in millions of Euros:

Project	NPV overall	NPV Group A	NPV Group B
Project 1	2	2	0
Project 2	6	7	−1
Project 3	−1	−4	7

Consider that Group A contains households with an annual income over EUR 20,000 and Group consists of households with an annual income under EUR 20,000.

Which of the projects should be funded if one looks at the total NPV? For which of the projects might distributional considerations be an issue? Recompute the total NPV for the projects using a distributional weight of 1 for Group A and a weight of 1.5 for Group B. Which projects should be funded if these distributional weights are applied?

- How can welfare weights be derived in a DS framework?
- What is the definition of social affordability? Why and when is it relevant for project evaluation?

Notes

1 See Harberger and Jenkins (2002) for a restatement of Harberger (1972)'s approach.
2 In general, the marginal social value of a small change in any parameter or control variable can always be regarded as the difference between its direct impact on social welfare and the social cost of the net additional commodity demands it generates (see Chapter 3).
3 In fact with $\varepsilon = 0$.
4 It is commonly referred to as the FFF model.
5 It should be clear from the discussion in Chapters 1–3 why these postulates are not assumed in this book.
6 The relative income hypothesis states that the satisfaction (or utility) of an individual derived from a given consumption level depends on its relative magnitude in the society (e.g. relative to the average consumption) rather than its absolute level (Duesenberry 1949).
7 The role of *numéraire* in CBA has been discussed by Brekke (1997), Johansson (1998), Drèze (1998).

8 Risk assessment

Overview[1]

CBA at project or policy appraisal stage is a forecasting exercise.[2] It deals with the fact that investment projects or policy interventions, by sinking present resources in exchange for future expected benefits, are affected by risk and uncertainty. Uncertainty may be related to the technology used, people skills or commitment, financial resources, the economic, social, and political context and the environment (a typical example of an uncertain event is the occurrence of an unpredictable natural disaster). The uncertainty can affect the project or policy cost, leading, for example, to significant cost overruns; it can cause delays in the construction or the generation of benefits, or lower the expected revenues due to changes in the demand. The incidence of uncertainty can greatly differ from one kind of intervention to another and can affect the project or policy outcome in different ways. The capacity to identify the sources of uncertainty and mitigate the risks could play a crucial role in guaranteeing that the expected effects take place at the desired time.

This chapter focusses on the last step of the project appraisal process as it has been depicted in Figure 4.1 of Chapter 4, i.e. risk assessment. From a very general standpoint, risk assessment entails a number of procedures that consist in formally dealing with the project risk in the context of cost-benefit analysis (CBA). Even if it is true that today risk can be relatively easily dealt with by using standard methods suggested by various guidelines to CBA, this remains one of the most technically difficult parts of project appraisal.

After introducing the rationale of risk assessment (Section 8.1) and the fundamental concepts of risk and uncertainty (Section 8.2), the chapter presents the current state of the art of analysis of risk (Section 8.3). The sensitivity, probability, and risk analysis procedures are then described in detail from a methodological point of view in Sections 8.4–8.6, respectively. The chapter concludes with a section suggesting further reading (Section 8.7). Three appendices deepen some of the aspects presented, namely the types of probability distribution functions that could describe the critical variables (Appendix 8.1), the theoretical framework of Monte Carlo simulation techniques and more practical indications on how to choose the number of simulations to be performed (Appendix 8.2), and the models to generate randomized numbers for the purpose of Monte Carlo simulations (Appendix 8.3).

DOI: 10.4324/9781003191377-10

8.1 Rationale of the risk assessment

The risk assessment of a project or a policy intervention is ultimately motivated by the necessity of taking into account the uncertainty and risk characterizing the future. To this end, starting from the deterministic framework of the CBA, costs and benefits become part of a probabilistic model so that the decision maker is provided with a more complete outlook of the expected outcomes of the project under assessment.

Before describing in detail what the risk assessment procedures consist of, it is worth spending some words on the reasons why they can be considered particularly important. Perhaps the most convincing argument in support of the analysis of risk comes directly from an extensive set of empirical evidence relative to the *ex-post* analyses of investment project performances. Focussing on large-scale infrastructure projects co-financed with public-sector resources, Flyvbjerg *et al.* (2003) and Flyvbjerg (2011, 2014) highlight that there exists substantial evidence of a tendency to underestimate costs, overestimate revenues, undervalue environmental impacts, and overvalue economic development effects. Many case studies reveal that cost overruns and lower than forecasted revenues or social benefits can pose serious obstacles to the economic growth of entire areas, exactly when the project itself had been promoted as an effective vehicle for boosting economic growth and development. The problem is particularly critical for the so-called megaprojects, whose success or failure is able to affect the balance-sheet of regional or even national governments, both in the medium and the long term.

Deviations from predictions can be related to many different and sometimes concurrent causes. For instance, positive regional development effects, typically overstated by project promoters to gain political acceptance, often turn out to be hardly measurable, insignificant in their magnitude or even negative. Similar 'optimism bias' is often observed with respect to financial resources needed and environmental impacts. Another part of the story concerns the quality of the data adopted to carry out the analyses.

The aim of the present chapter is to show what can and should be done by evaluators in order to produce reliable and accurate risk assessments of project or policy proposals and, in this way, provide policy makers with a technical and sound assessment which should facilitate their decision process.

8.2 Definitions and concepts

The large variety in the terminology related to the concept of risk in a number of different areas (including, among others, process industry, nuclear and civil engineering, information and communication, transport, business and finance, health and agriculture) contributes to making it difficult for analysts and decision makers both to communicate through a common language and to exploit fruitful advancements in related areas. In this section, the most common definitions used in the context of project appraisal are recalled.

A traditional and fundamental distinction, first developed by Knight (1921), is between the concepts of uncertainty and risk. The former usually refers to events that are inherently unpredictable, for which it is impossible to forecast the probability of occurrence (e.g. Kayaloff 1988; Nevitt 1989). Even if uncertain events are unpredictable, sources of uncertainty can at least be identified, so as to be ready to react and manage them when they show up. On the other hand, risk is defined as the part of the unknown which can be embedded into a stochastic model by means of probability distributions. As such, risk can be defined as 'measurable uncertainty' (Knight 1921).

Risk assessment can be considered as the set of qualitative and quantitative methods and procedures aimed at evaluating the probability that a given project will achieve a satisfactory performance. In the applications, the term 'satisfactory' is operationalized by a predefined threshold value of the outcome of interest. The probability reflects the degree of certainty, ranging between the extreme values 1 (full certainty about the confirmation of a given prediction) and 0 (full certainty that the prediction will not be confirmed). The standard approach is to interpret probabilities as subjective estimates of objective (or 'true') probabilities, and to define them through relative frequencies. Since probabilities in this context express the expert's uncertainty about a given variable, their interpretation falls within the scope of the Bayesian analysis approach.[3]

The overall risk assessment body of procedures is traditionally split into sensitivity analysis, probability analysis and risk analysis. These three related but distinct methodological steps are illustrated in Figure 8.1, introduced in Box 8.1 and more extensively discussed in the rest of the chapter.[4]

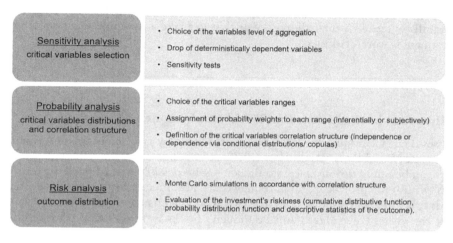

Figure 8.1 The three steps of risk assessment.
Source: Authors.

Box 8.1 Overview of the sensitivity, probability, and risk analyses

Sensitivity analysis

The goal of sensitivity analysis is to select a subset of the most relevant CBA variables affecting a predefined outcome measure (such as the ENVP or the EIRR). They are usually named *critical variables*. To this aim, two broad kinds of sensitivity tests can be adopted. First, the appraiser can inspect the impact of each input on the outcome separately (by changing each CBA 'best guess' value in absolute terms or by arbitrary percentages, one by one). Second, it is possible to build alternative scenarios, where the entire set of values is changed simultaneously. In order to carry out sensitivity tests, the appraiser must first choose the level of aggregation of the inputs and eliminate deterministically related variables, i.e. variables that are functions of others.

Probability analysis

Probability analysis consists in setting up a range of variation and assigning a marginal probability distribution function (PDF) to each critical variable previously selected. The analyst may exploit inferential techniques (where available data are statistically modelled to estimate the probability distributions) or the subjective approach (where the distributions are subjectively assigned on the basis of available information about the phenomena under assessment).

Risk analysis

In risk analysis Monte Carlo simulation methods are exploited to approximate the PDF of one or more outcome measures of interest. Each Monte Carlo iteration returns a potential state of the world – as defined by the CBA model – weighted for the probability to occur. This way of characterizing the risk of the project in probabilistic terms in turn allows the analyst to make a final judgment about the investment's overall riskiness.

Source: Authors.

8.3 Historical background: the World Bank model

Risk assessment techniques for CBA were introduced by two seminal books, both endorsed by the World Bank: Reutlinger (1970) and Pouliquen (1970). Although some differences can be found (for instance, Pouliquen – who possibly first adopted the term 'risk analysis' within the project appraisal framework – puts more effort on the description of methods from an applied standpoint), the two works can be considered on a continuum.

Over the years, Reutlinger's and Pouliquen's books were followed by a number of other influential works supported by the World Bank, which eventually shaped the World Bank model (WBM) relative to risk assessment.

The starting point of the WBM approach to risk is the awareness that the adoption of sensitivity analysis techniques – which in 1970 were already existing – is not sufficient to take into account uncertainty and risk characterizing the CBA variables (or 'inputs'). As described by Pouliquen, the sensitivity analysis that project appraisers were carrying out at that time consisted in making CBA inputs vary one at a time, by assigning each of them alternative possible values (such as the 'pessimistic', 'optimistic' or 'best' estimates) in order to evaluate the corresponding variation in the outcome of interest, for instance, the project ENPV.

Overall, the WBM advocated the necessity of a formal approach able to eliminate or minimize the arbitrariness in the analyst's judgment on the project. The proposed approach was based on the definition of the possible range of each variable and on the likelihood of occurrence of each value within this range. This procedure was called 'probability analysis', as the expert's judgment about the variables ranges and the likelihood of the variables values relative to these ranges took the form of probability distributions.

Accordingly, sensitivity analysis no longer provided a criterion to directly evaluate the project riskiness. Instead, it became a way to select (according to specific criteria that are addressed in more detail in the next section) a small subset of the large number of CBA variables on which to perform the probability analysis.

In accordance with Reutlinger and Pouliquen, the crucial step, consisting of the definition of the variables' probability distributions, can then be followed by a proper analysis of the risk associated with the project, called 'risk analysis'. The specific statistical tool proposed by Pouliquen was the Monte Carlo approach, a constellation of simulation techniques which had already been used in many other fields, such as physics and engineering applications.

Starting from the 1970s, the influence of the World Bank on the analysis of risk kept growing over time, but the adoption of the methods described above did not immediately take place. In fact, notwithstanding that the CBA approach based on shadow prices met a substantial increase in its application at the World Bank, reaching its peak in terms of number of projects evaluated in the early 1980s (Little and Mirrlees 1994), risk analysis techniques lagged behind in favour of much simpler sensitivity analysis tests (OPD/OED 1995; Balcombe and Smith 1999; Bock and Trück 2011).

Starting from the end of the 1980s, the WBM met what some authors call a 'renaissance period' (among others, Kirkpatrick 1994; Weiss 1996). This is confirmed by the World Bank itself, which during this period renewed its concern about the quality of its project portfolio through stricter rules regarding the evaluation of investments (World Bank 1994a, 1994b). At the same time, new manuals, which would have become standard resources for practitioners, gave new impulse towards a formal assessment of risk (for instance, Brent 1998). Rapid developments in computer technologies have been facilitating the implementation of Monte Carlo (and hence risk analysis) techniques, which by definition are 'computer intensive'.

As a consequence, since the 1990s research and applications in the risk analysis field have kept growing. This again happened because of the effort of the World Bank, but also thanks to other institutions, e.g. the European Commission, which made risk assessment of major projects compulsory under the EU structural and cohesion funds regulations.

8.4 Sensitivity analysis

8.4.1 Identification of the critical variables[5]

The starting point of sensitivity analysis is the CBA deterministic model relating to the financial or economic analysis of the project. As it has been pointed out in Chapter 4, this model is built by exploiting the discounted cash flow approach.

This allows one to compute the ENPV, one possible outcome measure of the project, as follows:

$$\text{ENPV} \equiv y = \sum_{t=0}^{T} \frac{B_t}{(1+r)^t}, \tag{8.1}$$

where $B_t = I_t - O_t$.

In this equation:

- $t = 0, 1, \ldots, T$ is the time period up to T, i.e. the time horizon set up within the CBA;

- I_t and O_t are the total inflows, or benefits, and the total outflows, or costs, relative to year t (at a base-year's prices);
- r is the real social discount rate.

As previously mentioned, an alternative performance indicator is provided by the EIRR, defined as the specific discount rate value $\bar{r}$ which is such that $ENPV = 0$.

Since B_t, the algebraic sum of the positive and negative cash flows related to period t, is a function of a number of inputs, it is possible to reformulate equation (8.1) in more general terms as:

$$y = g(X_1, \dots, X_T) = g(X), \tag{8.2}$$

where $= (X_1, \dots, X_t, \dots, X_T)$, $X_t = (x_{1,t}, \dots, x_{k,t})$ is the vector of k input values relative to t and $g(\cdot)$ is a generic function linking the inputs to the corresponding output value, y.[6]

The deterministic nature of CBA is evident from equation (8.2). In fact, the input matrix X consists of a set of 'most likely' values, subjectively assumed by the analyst in accordance with empirical evidence and with his/her knowledge about the project specificities. In other words, X is not subject to any kind of stochastic variability. Also, the link function $g(\cdot)$ is set up through a set of *ex-ante* assumptions, and is fixed as well.

Sensitivity analysis is the procedure aimed at selecting the inputs that significantly influence the ENPV (or other performance indices),[7] that are commonly referred to as critical variables. The selection of critical variables is oriented at reducing the complexity of the probabilistic model subsequently built into the probability analysis step. In the end, this is a practical expedient to select a subset of variables, and it is characterized by a certain degree of discretion, mainly depending on the selection criteria considered (see below).

In the framework of sensitivity analysis, the model (8.2) is used to consider the impact of each input value on the ENPV. Hence, broadly speaking, the overall procedure consists in formally inspecting to what degree $g(\cdot)$ links each input to y. Considerations of the stochastic being of X are not addressed by the sensitivity analysis and the deterministic nature of the model is not affected, unlike the approach adopted for the probability and risk analysis steps.

Table 8.1 provides some of the possible inputs that can enter the CBA model. Although the list is clearly non-exhaustive, and in general highly depends on the specific kind of investment project, it can still provide the reader with an operational idea of the 'input' or 'cash flows determinant' concept.

As a starting point, the sensitivity analysis requires the analyst to decide the level of aggregation of the possible critical variables composing the costs and benefits of the project. By 'level of aggregation' is meant the degree of detail characterizing the quantities whose impact on the discounted cash flows of the investment is to be analyzed. If the socio-economic appraisal of a project involving the construction of a road and resulting, as a benefit, in the reduction of vehicle operating costs is considered as an example, in principle it is possible to split the overall vehicle operating costs into the fuel consumption and tyre wear costs, among other components, and to test the sensitivity of CBA results to changes in each item. Alternatively, the analyst could uniquely consider variations in the vehicle operating costs, which in contrast is relatively higher aggregated.

As a general suggestion, the appraiser should start by focusing on the sources of uncertainty specifically related to any project cost or benefit (see, e.g., Table 8.1). This is often most easily done by taking into account the low-level quantities composing each grand category of cash flow. This 'low-level' attitude to defining the variables, first proposed by Pouliquen (1970) and Reutlinger (1970), is additionally motivated by two methodological considerations. First, for the purpose of the subsequent probabilistic analysis, it could be easier to formulate a subjective probabilistic opinion relative to a lower-level variable (e.g. the distribution of fuel consumption is easier to guess than the vehicle operating costs).[8] Second, by considering such quantities at a low level it is possible to identify (and drop) deterministically related variables,[9] namely those variables which are by construction a function of other critical variables. This, in turn, allows one to rule out distortions in the assessment of risk.

In the end, given the predefined threshold[10] of significance, a subjective decision has to be taken with respect to the aggregation level and, indirectly, on the final number of selected critical variables. In fact, sensitivity analysis techniques are implemented precisely to select an arbitrarily small number of significant quantities through one or more predefined formal criteria, hence reducing the scope of arbitrariness.[11]

8.4.2 Approaches to test the sensitivity of the CBA model

In the literature, different approaches to analyse the sensitivity of the CBA model have been proposed. According to some standard project appraisal manuals (such as the European Investment Bank 2013; European Commission 2014; HM Treasury 2020a), it is possible to distinguish between four broad categories of sensitivity tests:

i   Testing the extremes: this implies the consideration of extreme values (pessimistic and optimistic) and of their impact on the ENPV;
ii Testing for arbitrary changes: the best-guess values are all changed, one by one, by a predefined percentage;
iii Applying the switching value approach: finding the variable changes that turn the ENPV from being positive to being negative, or below a given threshold;
iv Carrying out a scenario analysis: combining different possible values of the critical variables.

Table 8.1 Some examples of possible critical variables in CBA

Category	Possible critical variable
Investment costs	Hourly labour cost, hourly labour productivity, cost of land, cost of expropriations, cost of rentals, useful life of equipment
Operating costs	Hourly labour cost, price of other inputs (electricity, etc.)
Operating revenues	Tariffs, prices of products and semi-finished goods
Demand and supply dynamics	Demand and supply growth rates, population growth rate, volume of traffic, etc.
Accounting prices	Conversion factors, value of time, shadow prices of goods çand services, willingness-to-pay or willingness-to-accept parameters, externality values

Source: Authors.

The first three techniques are characterized by a similar perspective, as the impact of each CBA input is assessed separately (i.e. holding all the other input values constant). In contrast, through the analysis of scenario, all the inputs are made to vary simultaneously.

In order to test the extremes of the CBA variables, the appraiser determines, for each input value of the CBA model, two alternative extreme values (pessimistic and optimistic) and computes the corresponding outcome measure. This implies that the best estimates of the inputs are changed in absolute value, one by one, choosing from those values that have some probability of proving true in the most optimistic and pessimistic circumstances. Overall, this approach allows one to evaluate to a certain extent the variability of the results. However, although the appraiser can evaluate the impact of the determinants on the ENPV, this strategy does not provide a direct way to compare the ENPV sensitivity to changes of different variables, as each input is tested by a specific percentage variation different from the others.

The above shortcoming is avoided by exploiting another sensitivity analysis strategy, consisting in changing every 'most likely' value, one by one, by the same arbitrary percentage variation. This approach requires the appraiser to choose a specific threshold of variation (in percentage terms, e.g. 1 per cent, 5 per cent, 10 per cent, 15 per cent, 20 per cent, etc.) of the outcome measure in order to define the inputs as 'critical'. The absolute percentage variation around the best estimate can be interpreted as the elasticity of the output to the specific input. In short, this sensitivity test requires one to consider three main elements:

i   The variable value around which the percentage change is considered;
ii The magnitude of the variation;
iii The final criterion to decide whether the variation in the output is sufficiently high.

As to the first point, some guides suggest focusing on a neighbourhood of the best estimate. This choice is sensible, as within the Monte Carlo simulations the extraction of critical variables will precisely converge towards their expected value, which often corresponds to the CBA 'best guess' value.[12] However, one could also consider the variations of inputs around other values, especially the 'pessimistic' and 'optimistic' ones (with respect to the project outcome). This is particularly useful for inspecting the separate effect of these variables in correspondence with the occurrence of extreme scenarios.

A second issue concerns the magnitude of the neighbourhood of variation taken into account. Instead of testing single per cent changes around the threshold, a good practice is to consider a range of percentage variation around the best estimate (or other reference values) on a continuum scale, with the lower and upper bounds being at least equal to −10 per cent and +10 per cent, respectively. This is because the inputs may impact on the project outcome non-linearly, so that the effects of critical variables may be highly dependent on the (subjectively chosen) percentage variation values. It is also worth noting that it may well be possible that the effect of the variable is not symmetric with respect to the specific reference value considered. Then, one useful way to take into account the existence of potentially non-linear and asymmetric effects of the variables is to exploit graphical methods.[13]

An exemplificative plot is provided in Figure 8.2. The labour productivity and the labour cost are linearly related to the ENPV of the project. The percentage variation of the former variable is associated with an equal percentage variation in the outcome.

On the other hand, the ENPV is strongly sensitive to the labour cost: for the entire range of variation, the percentage change in the outcome is always higher in absolute value than the percentage change in the input. Finally, the demand growth is not linearly associated with the ENPV, and its impact is asymmetric for negative and positive variations. In particular, in the case of positive variations, the outcome always changes more than the demand growth. For negative changes higher than about 6 per cent in absolute value, the outcome varies less than the demand growth.

Once the appraiser has analytically or graphically inspected the impact of the variable change, it is necessary to choose the outcome variation in correspondence to which the variable is considered critical. At first, the analyst can focus on the subset of critical variables for which the percentage ENPV variation tends to be constantly greater – for the entire range of variation – than the corresponding input variable percentage change (in accordance with this, in the previous example the labour cost could be considered as critical).[14] If the resulting number of critical variables still too high for the computational constraints, more stringent criteria should be adopted. However, this is usually not the case in the applications.

The third sensitivity analysis strategy presented, i.e. the switching value approach, consists in finding the specific value of a variable in correspondence to which the ENPV of the project is equal to 0 or, more in general, below a minimum level of acceptability. This allows the analyst to make some preliminary judgments on the riskiness of the project or on the possibility of implementing risk-preventing actions. As for other sensitivity analysis techniques mentioned above, computing the switching values allows

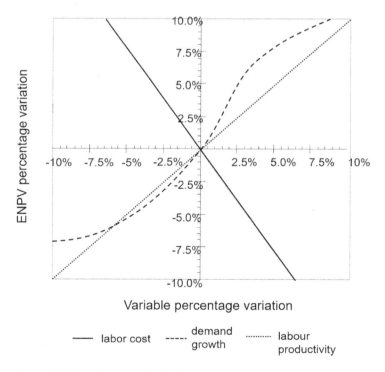

Figure 8.2 Sensitivity analysis plot.
Source: Authors.

the analyst to test the robustness of the project's outcome to individual changes in the CBA inputs.

Another possibility is to carry out a scenario analysis, also commonly named a 'what-if' analysis (Vose 2008). This is a specific technique that consists in studying the combined impact of different values of an entire set of inputs, typically the ones already defined as 'critical' through the previously exposed techniques. The preliminary step of this procedure is equivalent to the one relative to testing the extremes of single variables, but it allows one to inspect the impact of different combinations of 'optimistic' and 'pessimistic' values. In this way different 'realistic' scenarios can be built, and related performance indicators computed.[15] More specifically, the appraiser has to consider the variation of the incremental socio–economic net benefits of the project against an alternative use of available public resources.[16]

Pouliquen (1970) stresses that the scenario analysis cannot be treated as alternative to a complete risk assessment. This is because it consists in defining only some possible values for each input, whereas through risk analysis the likelihood of the values occurring is elicited for the entire range of each variable. Actually, in principle, there exists a potentially infinite number of possible scenario combinations.

Another limitation of any form of sensitivity analysis is that it does not explicitly take into account how likely or unlikely the change in the 'best guess' value of a given variable is. That is, even if changes in the estimated value of a given input highly affect the final outcome measure of interest, it is well possible that such changes will almost never take place in reality. This issue also holds when complete scenarios are built, as there is no way to ultimately interpret a potentially large number of concurrent real-world possibilities and determine which weight should be assigned to each of them.

In accordance with the original proposal made by the World Bank researchers, the standard way to address the problems related to the sensitivity analyses consists in moving towards a fully-fledged analysis of probability.

8.5 Probability analysis

8.5.1 Probability distributions of the critical variables

To establish the basis for a proper assessment of risk, assigning a specific probability distribution to each critical variable resulting from the sensitivity analysis is necessary. The probability distributions are highly dependent on the specific type of project under evaluation and they may be derived through different sources of information, including

---

Box 8.2 Testing the sensitivity of uncertain CBA parameters

Sensitivity tests are generally implemented to analyse variables whose current value is known but whose future value is uncertain, thus influencing the future costs and benefits of the project under assessment. However, they could also be adopted to test the sensitivity of CBA to some fundamental hypotheses or parameters, such as the discount rate and the unit estimates of shadow prices, among others.

Source: Authors.

experimental data, distributions found in literature and adopted in projects similar to the one under assessment, time-series or other kinds of historical data (Vose 2008).[17] The trade-off is that the quality of data to be collected is characterized by a rapidly increasing cost in terms of expense, time and effort of collection.

In addition to empirical data, the appraiser generally relies on personal experience cumulated over time or in consultation with other experts. Hence, the probability distribution for each critical variable is typically based on both empirical data and subjective beliefs about the likelihoods of occurrence of various outcomes of uncertain events. A different approach, largely used in the valuation of technological risk but less common in CBA, refers to inferential methods of analysis. These exploit historical information, using data of the past values of the variables to derive their frequency distribution (they are briefly described in Box 8.3). The two strategies are not alternative, as the empirical distribution can constitute the starting point for the final distribution subjectively set up by the expert.[18]

Although from a statistical viewpoint the 'subjective approach' is simpler than the inferential one, it still poses non-trivial methodological issues. In the literature, the process of subjectively estimating probability through expert judgment is known by the name of 'probability distribution elicitation', and has received attention especially because of its being subject to numerous biases. Additionally, meta-analysis studies have shown that it is hard to find recurrent patterns of distributional choices made by analysts of the same area (e.g. Binkowitz and Wartenberg 2001). In fact, from an applied standpoint, probability analysis is complicated by the fact that standard guidelines generally

---

Box 8.3 Inferentially estimating the probability distribution functions

A possible way to select the probability distribution functions consists in using inferential techniques aimed at statistically estimating the distributions of interest from available historical data. A first method consists in using the empirical distribution function of the variable of interest (which graphically is simply summarized by a histogram based on available data) to approximate its population counterpart (Back *et al.* 2000). No parametric assumptions are made on the shape of the distribution, which is left completely free to vary according to the data. However, it must be borne in mind that what is obtained is a marginal distribution, i.e. the distribution of the variable of interest irrespective of all the other distributions of critical variables. This does not pose any problem as long as the inputs considered are independently distributed, or as long as it is realistic to assume so.

If some correlation among two or more variables – for instance the inverse relationship linking prices to quantities – needs to be considered, parametric techniques have to be applied, the easiest one being the classical linear regression model (Berechman and Chen 2011). More sophisticated parametric modelling is also required to fit historical data.[19]

Two major problems characterize the inferential approach in the context of the probability analysis. Firstly, usually the data at hand are not sufficient to undertake robust statistical analyses of such a kind. Secondly, a trade-off is in place in parametric statistical modelling between simplicity and complex specificity.

Source: Authors.

provide limited information on the rational and reliable criteria behind the choice of the distributions.

In what follows, the standard procedure to subjectively set the marginal probability distributions of the variables is considered. According to the subjective approach, probability analysis procedure takes place in two separate stages:

i   Definition of the support of each critical variable;
ii Assignment to each of them of the discrete or continuous probability distribution functions.

Define x as a generic random variable selected within the sensitivity analysis step, and define $\tilde{x}$ as being a specific value assumed by x; the support of x is defined as the set of all the possible realizations that have a strictly positive (i.e. greater than zero) probability of being observed. Setting the stochastic variable support is equivalent to deciding the range of variation of that variable. In doing so, implicitly a decision about the discrete or continuous nature of x must be taken.

This first step is facilitated whenever there exist physical or mathematical constraints for the lower and upper bounds of the quantity considered. For instance, in the medium run firms can be expected to set prices equal to or higher than the marginal costs, quantities produced are subject to limitations relative to deterioration and storing, and so on. If no physical constraints exist, the expert can directly focus on the likelihood of the occurrence of extreme values (usually already defined within the sensitivity analysis step). This, in turn, may lead to the determination of either bounded or unbounded ranges of variables.[20]

The next step is to assign to each critical variable a probability distribution. In principle, the only constraint is given by the support previously defined, for instance the exponential distribution is defined on the left-bounded interval $(0, +\infty)$, while the normal distribution is defined on the unbounded interval $(-\infty, \infty)$. Regardless of the continuous or discrete nature of x, its PDF is referred to as to $f(x)$ in this chapter.

In the case that x is continuous, $f(x)$ takes strictly positive values on a continuous support, and the PDF is a probability density function. The area underlying $f(x)$ is interpreted as a probability, and sums to 1 over the entire (either bounded or unbounded) support of x. On the other hand, when x is discrete, its PDF is a probability mass function, and it is the sum of the punctual $f(x)$ values corresponding to its discrete support to be equal to 1.

There exists a wide number of standard probability distributions from which the evaluator can choose, with each PDF being completely specified by a specific set of distribution parameters. For instance, when the variable range is not bounded, the likelihood of the occurrence of extreme values tends to be infinitesimal and in general, but not necessarily, the most likely value corresponds to the central one. In such instances the normal distribution, which additionally requires one to assume symmetry around the expected value, is widely adopted.

An alternative distribution often used in the applications is the triangular one (Back *et al.* 2000). The main reason for its popularity is that it is completely specified by the minimum, maximum and mode parameters, which are usually already set up within the sensitivity analysis step. This facilitates the probabilistic assessment, provided that the triangular distribution is an appropriate functional form for the quantity considered.

The fact that it is possible to obtain a well-known distributional form by setting a few parameters is appealing, but it may be misleading as well. In fact, it might be difficult to correctly characterize some variables through a specific standard distribution so that the adoption of predefined functions may lead to unreliable final results. A strategy more directly linked to the idea underlying the subjective approach to probability analysis is to define a discretized version of the variable of interest in accordance with successive expert's judgments. First, the expert identifies the variable minimum and maximum values, and a uniform or rectangular distribution is built (assuming that the phenomenon is equiprobable in the closed interval). Then the area of probability is divided by the expert into two rectangles of unequal heights. Subsequently, each of the two rectangles is again divided into two rectangles, and different probabilities are assigned for the smaller sub-intervals. The process is iterated as long as there is sufficient information to refine the overall distributional form. In the end, the resulting histogram is based on the subjective perception of the probabilities associated with the subintervals constituting the entire distribution.

The above technique is useful when the likelihood of occurrence of the values can be safely assumed to be constant within each of the intervals. Clearly, in the case that the critical variable considered corresponds to a phenomenon measurable on a continuous scale, the number of sub-intervals should be relatively large in order to provide a sufficiently precise distribution. In addition, smoothing techniques may be implemented at the end of the discrete probability distribution elicitation, so that the final distribution is approximated on the continuum (see Gosling *et al.* 2012 on this subject).

An alternative strategy falling within the scope of the subjective approach consists in exploiting an expert's judgments to define the cumulative distribution function of the variable of interest. This can be easily done by asking the expert which are the cumulated probabilities in correspondence to a specific set of variables values. Again, if the necessary distribution is on a continuous scale, smoothing techniques can be implemented at the end of the elicitation step.

8.5.2 Dealing with correlations between the critical variables

In the previous section, the focus was on the $f(x)$, i.e. the marginal (or 'unconditional') distribution functions of the critical variables. However, in probability analysis a crucial issue concerns the dependence relationships which may characterize two or more of the selected inputs. Inspecting all the critical variables to highlight possible correlation patterns corresponds to trying to find quantities that are economically or physically related.

A relatively standard simplifying assumption is to consider variables as independent. Treating two inputs as independent means that any given value of the first is not affected in any way by the occurrence of any value of the second, and vice versa. If the appraiser wants to carry out analyses as simplified as possible, only the marginal distributions of variables 'truly' independent of each other should be elicited, and any kind of correlation should be ruled out from the model by selecting only one of the correlated variables. This can be a somewhat extreme oversimplification, but it is arguably better than treating correlated cash flow components (such as prices and quantities, or demand and supply growths) as if they were unrelated.

Alternatively, correlation may be accounted for by relaxing the independence assumption. Although this is an area of research where there is still extensive room for improvement, two main strategies have been proposed: the conditional distributions approach and copula methods. They are today often implemented for the assessment of private investments of various types (see, e.g., Clemen and Reilly 1999), but in principle they can be adopted without modifications also to evaluate investments relative to public sector or policy reforms.

As to the conditional distribution approach, it consists in either subjectively assuming or inferentially estimating the conditional distributions of the critical variables considered as dependent. In the former case, the conditional distributions are elicited within a purely subjective framework according to which the expert is asked to provide, for a predetermined set of values of a given variable, the corresponding values of another (correlated) variable, so that it is possible to reconstruct the resulting conditional distribution function (e.g. Clemen and Reilly 1999). The main drawback is that even in the case of just three correlation relationships the elicitation of the conditional distributions may become extremely problematic.

Alternatively, the appraiser can exploit regression techniques to estimate the correlation between two or more critical variables. For instance, it is possible to model the dependence between the price of a given good, x_p, and the quantity demanded, x_q, through a simple linear relationship. Suppose the response variable is x_p, while x_q is the only explanatory variable (i.e. x_p is regressed on x_q). Once the univariate linear model has been estimated through the available data, it is obtained precisely as $f_{x_p|x_q}(\cdot)$, the conditional distribution of the price, given the quantity demanded.

Regardless of the way it has been obtained (either subjectively or inferentially), the conditional distribution can then be exploited in the risk analysis step to simulate correlated price and quantity values (see the next section).

A different approach to modelling correlation among critical variables is to use copula methods. These require one to determine not only the marginal PDFs of the critical variables, but also specific 'copula' functions, which completely specify all the two–way correlation relationships among the selected inputs. One of the most widely adopted copula functions in applications is the normal or Gaussian copula, a special case of the t-student copula. However, other families of copulas can be adopted, especially in the case when the dependence relationships are not symmetric, or when correlations are more likely to occur for the extreme values of the variables considered and not for the central values.

Fundamental theoretical results guarantee that, whatever copula is adopted, the previously defined PDFs of the critical variables will still marginally describe the behaviour of the phenomena considered (Frees and Valdez 1998). Another important element is that the subsequent Monte Carlo simulations (see the section on risk analysis below) can be directly implemented keeping into account the copula, through common statistical software and spreadsheet add-ons.

The knowledge of advanced theoretical and applied statistical methods is crucial in order to correctly implement this technique. The most relevant issue is the choice of the specific copula type, because it ultimately affects the way the correlated random numbers are extracted in the risk analysis. Graphical methods are usually adopted to inspect the specific correlation patterns implied by alternative copulas. Then, once the copula type has been set up, the two-way relationships of dependence can be simply elicited by exploiting expert's opinion (Clemen and Reilly 1999).[21] In particular, the expert is asked to provide the probability of concordance of any two covariates, and this allows one to fully determine any copula dependency structure and hence the way the (correlated) random variables should be simulated.[22]

Box 8.4 provides additional remarks on how to model correlation though copulas. A more formal presentation of the issue of generating correlated random numbers in the framework of the risk analysis, either through conditional distributions or through copulas, is presented in Appendix 8.3.

8.6 Risk analysis

8.6.1 Monte Carlo simulations

Whatever method is used to obtain the probability distribution functions of the critical variables, the analyst can then proceed by carrying out the risk analysis step. To this end,

---

Box 8.4 Modelling correlation through copulas

For a long time, statisticians have been interested in studying the relationship among a multivariate distribution and its univariate marginal distributions. In the case of statistical independence, the former is simply equal to the product of the latter ones, but this does not hold when even just one of the variables is correlated to another one.

Considering the example in which the interest is in modelling two correlated variables, the price of a good and its demanded quantity (x_p and x_q, respectively), a copula is the function that joins or 'couples' the multivariate PDF of price and quantity to its two univariate marginal PDFs, $f(x_p)$ and $f(x_q)$.

The intuition behind copulas is that the joint behaviour of the two variables, which is fully summarized by their multivariate PDF, can be partitioned into two completely separate components. The first component consists of the two marginal PDFs, where each PDF captures all the possible sources of variation specific for the corresponding variable, irrespective of those relative to the other variable. The second component is the copula itself. It embeds any source of correlation between the price and the quantity, describing how these inputs co-vary (in terms of direction, strength, and shape of their correlation pattern) irrespective of any source of independent variation.

Copulas are particularly appealing because the entire correlation structure of any number of critical variables is summarized by a single function and, at the same time, the approach is fully compatible with the standard probability analysis procedure of eliciting the marginal PDFs of the inputs. Instead, the definition of a potentially high number of conditional distributions may rapidly become cumbersome. In addition, the conditional distributions approach does not allow the analyst to directly exploit existing information on the marginal PDFs of the correlated variables (see Appendix 8.3).

On the other hand, although the use of standard parametrized copulas is attractive, it does not judge immediately whether the phenomena under study truly behave like the specific copula prescribes. Thus, it is advisable that the analyst is used to calibrating the copula parameters, also by making judgments based on the resulting two-way correlation plots.

Source: Authors.

Monte Carlo techniques are today a standard tool for analysing the risk associated with an intervention. They allow one to aggregate the probabilities assigned to the critical variables or, using a terminology more related to Statistics, estimate the integral corresponding to the probability distribution function of the outcome of interest.

When the critical variables are independent from each other, each iteration of the Monte Carlo simulation consists in separately drawing without replacement one value of each kth critical variable from the corresponding PDF $f(x_k)$ in accordance with its predefined support (with $k = 1, ..., k$). Then the extracted critical variables values are plugged into the CBA model $y = g(X)$, which is adopted to calculate the associated outcome measure of the project. This process is repeated over a large number of iterations.

In the case where the conditional distribution approach has been adopted to model correlation among some of the critical variables, it is additionally required to explicitly exploit

---

Box 8.5 Monte Carlo method

The Monte Carlo method was invented by Enrico Fermi, the Nobel Laureate in Physics. He first used Monte Carlo algorithms in the 1930s to study neutron diffusion (Metropolis 1987). Some 15 years later the Monte Carlo technique was developed by Stanislaw Ulam and John von Neumann, two prominent scientists working at the Manhattan research project – the one which led to the production of the first atomic bomb. The name 'Monte Carlo' was coined by von Neumann referring to the gambling habits of Ulam's uncle, who used to play in a Monte Carlo casino. The idea of the statistical method came to Ulam's mind while considering the chances to win at Canfield solitaire by laying out 52 cards. In his words:

> After spending a lot of time trying to estimate them by pure combinatorial calculus, I wondered whether a more practical method than "abstract thinking" might be to lay it out say one hundred times and simply observe and count the number of successful plays.

(Eckhardt 1987: 131)

The intuition underlying Monte Carlo techniques is exactly that of repeating a given 'experiment' a large number of times in order to address mathematical and numerical problems that are otherwise hardly tractable analytically. This can be seen also through a classical example, mentioned in Sivarethinamohan (1964). Suppose the interest is on estimating the surface of a lake, S_l, which is inscribed in a squared area of known dimension S_{sq}. To achieve this aim it is possible to randomly shoot a large number (N) of cannonballs within the square, some of which will fall within the lake (N_l) while the others will fall outside the lake but inside the square ($N - N_l$). The lake surface can be estimated by use of a simple proportion: $\dfrac{S_{sq}}{S_l} = \dfrac{N - N_l}{N_l}$ Since S_{sq} is known, solving for S_l leads to $S_l = \dfrac{N_l}{N - N_l} S_{sq}$.

This example introduces two important aspects of Monte Carlo simulations. First, the lake surface is better estimated the higher the number of cannonballs shot. Second, the final approximation is reliable as long as the direction taken by the cannonballs is truly random.

Source: Authors.

their conditional distributions for simulation. For simplicity, only two correlated critical variables are taken among all the K critical variables, such as the price of a good and its demanded quantity (x_p and x_q), where $f(x_p|x_q)$ is the conditional distribution of the price given the quantity. The overall simulation procedure then consists of the following steps:

1 To separately draw one value from each of the $K - 2$ marginal distributions of the independent variables;
2 To draw a demanded quantity value $\tilde{x}_q$ from its marginal distribution: $x_q \sim f(x_q)$;
3 To generate the price from the conditional distribution: $x_p \sim f_p\left(x_p|x_q = \tilde{x}_q\right)$;
4 To plug the entire set of simulated values into $y = g(X)$ and repeat the steps a sufficiently large number of times.

If in probability analysis one or more two-way correlations have been modelled through copula methods, the copula functional form is applied to the marginal PDFs of all the K critical variables, and the entire critical variables vector is drawn from the resulting multivariate density of X, $f(X)$. See Appendix 8.3 for additional information on this.

Whatever the possible dependence structure of the critical variables, through risk analysis a large number of potential states of the world are simulated, each characterized by a specific set of input (and hence output) variables values. These scenarios are weighted for the risk associated with each input. Overall, the usefulness of the Monte Carlo approach is ultimately linked to the fact that through the law of large numbers – which implies the convergence of the ENPV empirical distribution to its 'true' counterparts – the outcome measures can be considered in probabilistic terms, and not just in deterministic ones as for the CBA assessment.[23] In other words, after a sufficiently large number of simulations, Monte Carlo asymptotic theory allows to estimate $f(y)$, the PDF of the performance measure of the project, and the first or higher moments of it (see Appendix 8.2 for a more formal presentation).

Although Monte Carlo methods rely upon the law of large numbers, it is worth while discussing what number of simulations is considered sufficiently 'large'. In general, it is not known what is the necessary finite number of iterations to approximately reach asymptotic convergence, precisely because $f(y)$ is unknown (Robert and Casella 2004, 2010). As a consequence, the criterion to define the number of iterations varies on a case-by-case basis. Although in the practice the number of simulations may often fall around 1,000, it can happen that certain variables with a high impact on the outcome and a relatively low probability of occurrence may not be sufficiently covered through this number of simulations (Helton and Davis 2003). The issue of sampling from the entire range of marginal distribution of each critical variable appears to be crucial in risk analysis, where it is important to take into account the impact of rare events (either 'catastrophic' or 'optimistic'). A useful approach is to set up a larger number of iterations and to analyse the convergence path by exploiting graphical methods (Robert and Casella 2004, 2010).[24] See Appendix 8.2 for an example.

8.6.2 Evaluation of the investment's riskiness

Once the simulation step is completed, the simulation results can then be interpreted to judge the riskiness of the project. To this purpose, the analyst can focus on the approximated probability distribution of the outcome of interest and on its cumulative distribution, whose shapes can be graphically inspected (Figures 8.3 and 8.4). The PDF of y summarizes the likelihood of occurrence of all the outcome values, while the cumulative distribution function returns the probability that the outcome is equal to or smaller than any given value belonging to the range of y.

The cumulative distribution function of y, in particular, can be directly exploited to study the cumulated probability in correspondence to some crucial cut-offs, which can be referred to as feasibility thresholds. For instance, when $y \equiv$ ENPV the interest is on the probability that the ENPV is equal to or smaller than 0. In the case that the probability $\Pr\{\text{ENPV} \leq 0\} \cong 0$, then the project can be preliminarily judged as socially desirable (since the discounted benefits are expected to be greater than the discounted

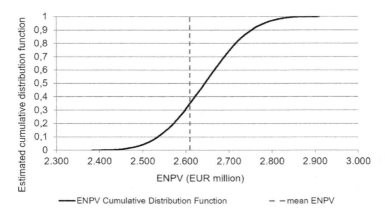

Figure 8.3 Empirical cumulative distribution function of the ENPV.
Source: Authors' elaboration, based on 6,000 Monte Carlo simulations related to an illustrative transport project.

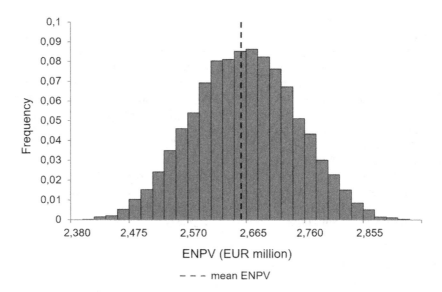

Figure 8.4 Distribution of the ENPV.
Source: Authors' elaboration, based on 6,000 Monte Carlo simulations related to an illustrative transport project.

costs). Alternatively, if $y \equiv EIRR$ the relevant cut-off is the real social discount rate r. If $Pr\{EIRR \leq 0\} \cong 0$ then the project is socially feasible, as the return on the investment is likely to be higher than the one relative to alternative uses of public resources.

Additional relevant information on the project risk is provided by various summary statistics of y and by its approximated PDF. In particular, the project can be analyzed in the following terms:

- Range of y. This consists of the window of values within which the outcome varies. In particular, the minimum and maximum values are relative to the most pessimistic and optimistic simulated scenarios. It provides a first criterion of risk, in terms of the project variability. A project characterized by a lower range of variability of its performance is preferable, *ceteris paribus*.
- Mean of y. This is the estimate of the expected value of y and is interpreted as the outcome which is expected to occur over a wide number of potential project realizations. In other words, the mean of the outcome weights the project performance for its risk. This is an important summary statistic because it provides an immediately readable synthesis indicator of the most likely discounted social value of the project.
- Standard deviation of y. This is a synthesis indicator of the variation or dispersion around the mean of y. Given the average value of the project outcome, its higher variability is related to a higher risk of the project itself (because the residual uncertainty relative to the final performance indicator is higher). In general, there does not exist a general rule to interpret the standard deviation of y as 'high' or 'low' in absolute terms. However, the standard deviations of projects of a similar kind can be compared in order to have a more in-depth information about the investment risk.
- Extreme values probabilities. The tails of the outcome distribution also provide information on the project risk. In particular, extreme values of y, associated with a negative performance of the project (and weighted for the probability to occur), provide a direct information concerning the likelihood of occurrence of particularly pessimistic scenarios in terms of the project outcome.

Once the risk assessment has been completed, the appraiser is provided with enough elements to judge the investment's riskiness and possibly to apply measures for risk mitigation. A direct criterion to decide whether the project is characterized by an acceptable level of risk is to evaluate the cumulated probability in correspondence to a predetermined performance threshold. This, however, is not always sufficient, for at least two reasons.

First, the above-mentioned performance test may be passed by considering some outcome measures, but not others. For instance, it is possible that the project is socially desirable if the focus in on the ENVP, but not when the EIRR is considered.

Second, it is not immediate to suggest a priori 'how small' the cumulated probability relative to the performance threshold should be, as this cut-off is related to a desired risk profile, which in turn depends on the project type, the socioeconomic environment and the degree of risk aversion of the social planner. The same reasoning also holds for the estimate of the expected value of the outcome and all the other relevant above-mentioned criteria to be considered in order to take the final decision. In principle, it could be decided to implement riskier projects by virtue of higher social benefits, or, on the contrary, projects with low benefits but also lower risk.

8.7 Further reading

The assessment of risk encompasses a number of different streams of literature. The reader may refer to the already mentioned textbooks on CBA such as Boardman *et al.* (2018), Brent (2006) and risk analysis such as Vose (2008), and the books by Pouliquen (1970) and Reutlinger (1970). These last two publications are strongly focused on the application of the sensitivity and risk analysis techniques, with real-world examples relating to a highway project and other typical sectors of public intervention. Some papers focused on specific risk-related problems when considering the evaluation of public investments; see for instance Arrow and Lind (1970) and Anderson (1989).

With respect to sensitivity analysis, the reader may refer to Briggs and Schulper (1995) and Merrifield (1997). The former is a review of studies of the analysis of sensitivity in economic evaluation, while the latter is focused on sensitivity analysis within the cost-benefit analysis field. The analysis of risk within CBA is also discussed by Zerbe and Dively (1994). Moreover, to have a clear idea of the analyses of probability and risk through case studies, see World Bank (1994a, 1994b). Other research papers with an applied slant have been proposed in many different fields. Salling and Leleur (2011) provide a good introduction to the separation of inherent randomness in the modelling system and the lack of knowledge. They also focus on the subjective definition of the probability distributions. The Asian Development Bank (2002) also provides some relevant information on the methodological issues covered in Sections 8.4–8.6 of the present chapter, with specific application to Development Economics.

With respect to Monte Carlo simulations, standard textbooks treating cost-benefit analysis do not cover in detail the issue of correlation among variables. However, this is an extremely active field of research in many journals that publish papers relevant to the appraisal of investment projects, especially (but not necessarily) with an engineering-related approach. Berechman and Chen (2011) focus on probability distributions, fitting methods and regression analysis to model dependence before carrying out Monte Carlo simulations. Wu and Tsang (2004) provide a complete tutorial on how to model dependency in alternative ways, also focusing on graphical methods for the subjective assessment of the correlation among variables. The already cited Clemen and Reilly (1999) also adopt copulas to subjectively set up correlations among variables. Their paper, in which an insightful case study is presented, is also characterized by a reference list for appraisers interested in modelling dependency among critical variables.

Specialized readers may find of interest the paper by Helton and Davis (2003), which proposes a rigorous covering of simulation techniques, going beyond the classical Monte Carlo method and describing one of its extensions, Latin Hypercube sampling, a simulation technique which today can be easily implemented by any standard spreadsheet-based software. The authors also take into account the issue of correlation. A very good introductory paper on the different coverage properties of the classical Monte Carlo approach and the Latin Hypercube Sampling is by Diwekar and Kalagnanam (1997). Another work reconsidering the role of the Monte Carlo method for the analysis of risk of investment projects is by Balcombe and Smith (1999). On the other hand, Haas (1999) focuses on the different ways in which model dependency can be implemented, while Durante and Sempi (2010) present a complete (and technical) review of the mathematics behind copulas. Interested readers may also consider Feller (1948) and the Smirnov tables (1948) for the large sample properties of Monte Carlo simulations.

Finally, expert opinion within the subjective approach to probability analysis is covered by Almansa and Martinez-Paz (2011), who present a method to elicit subjective probabilities when the opinion of more than one expert is available (the so-called 'Delphi method'). The references of their work may be useful to deepen this research field.

8.8 Summary of Chapter 8

- An *ex-ante* CBA exercise is typically concluded by the risk assessment procedure. Starting from the deterministic framework of the CBA, in which 'best guess' values of costs and benefits are considered, input variables become part of a probabilistic model that provides an estimate of the degree of uncertainty and risk affecting the CBA results, so that the decision maker is provided with a more complete outlook over the available investment options from which to choose.
- In project appraisal literature, a traditional distinction is made between the concepts of risk and uncertainty: risk is defined as measurable uncertainty, while uncertainty refers to unpredictable events or components of the CBA model for which it is not possible to estimate or hypothesize a probability distribution. Both of them characterize any project performance measure, such as the financial and economic internal rate of return or the net present value.
- The overall risk assessment body of procedures is split into three methodological steps: sensitivity analysis, probability analysis and risk analysis. Sensitivity analysis is the procedure aimed at selecting the inputs that significantly influence the ENPV or other performance indices. These inputs are commonly referred to as *critical variables*. In probability analysis a specific probability distribution is assigned to each variable selected within the sensitivity analysis step. Risk analysis exploits Monte Carlo simulation techniques to aggregate the probabilities assigned to the critical variables.
- In choosing the level of aggregation of the possibly critical variables within the sensitivity analysis, the literature suggests focusing on low-level quantities that compose the grand categories of cash flows. This facilitates the elicitation of the probability distribution function in the subsequent probability analysis step, making it easier to highlight deterministically related variables. However, there exists a trade-off between the level of detail of the variable considered and the likelihood that it will be considered as critical.
- When determining the thresholds of significance for considering a given variable as critical, the project appraiser can graphically inspect the impact of the variables on the CBA results over its entire range of variation. Only variables for which the variation in the output is constantly greater than the corresponding variation in the input could be selected, but alternative criteria may be set up on a case-by-case basis.
- The probability distribution functions of critical variables may be defined among standard pre-defined functional forms (e.g. normal, triangular, etc.) on the basis of experts' judgment. An alternative strategy is to start from a uniform distribution and to split it into different rectangles associated with different likelihoods of occurrence. Similar steps may be undertaken by eliciting cumulative distribution functions. Alternatively, the analyst may exploit historical information, fitting the future trend on the basis of the past values of the variables considered.
- Some critical variables may be correlated among each other. This issue should be duly taken into account in both probability and risk analysis. The usual independence

assumption may be relaxed in two ways, either by determining the conditional distributions of the correlated variables or by adopting copula function methods.

- Final considerations concern the implementation of Monte Carlo simulations as a tool to aggregate the probabilities assigned to the critical variables. The number of iterations of the Monte Carlo simulations can be set at a sufficiently high number in order to refine the probability distribution of the output. The results of the risk analysis are expressed in terms of the cumulative distribution function of the CBA result indicator and simple statistics about the CBA results.

End of chapter questions

- What is the difference between risk and uncertainty?
- What is the difference between sensitivity and risk analysis?
- The investment cost of a flood prevention project is EUR 400 million. The annual net benefit will depend on the amount of rainfall: EUR 10 million in a "normal" year, EUR 25 million in a "flood" year. Meteorological historical data indicate that over the last 50 years there have been 40 "normal" years and 10 "flood" years. Using this information as a basis of prediction, what are the net benefits of the project if the real discount rate is 3 per cent?
- What are the different approaches to test the sensitivity of a CBA model?
- What are the basics steps in performing Monte Carlo simulations?

Appendix 8.1

Distributions of probabilities

This appendix summarizes the main probability distribution functions used in the probability analysis, along with the corresponding parameters and support. In discrete cases the PDF is a probability mass function, and punctual probabilities associated with the finite set of discrete values of x sum to 1. In continuous cases the PDF is a probability density function, and the area underlying the density is equal to 1. In addition, any PDF is equal to 0 outside the support Ω.

Table A8.1 Overview of probability distribution functions

Name	Type	Parameters and support	Distribution function	Description
Uniform (rectangular)	Continuous	$-\infty < \min < \max < \infty$ $\Omega = \left[\min, \max\right]$	$f\left(x; \min, \max\right) = \dfrac{1}{\max - \min}$	It assigns equal probability to all values belonging to the support. It is usually adopted when little is known about x and few or no available data exist. It is often used as an 'uninformed' prior distribution in Bayesian analysis.
Histogram	Continuous	$-\infty < \min < a_1 < a_2 < \cdots \max < \infty$ * $\Omega = \left[\min, \max\right]$ *$a_2, a_2 \ldots$: classes cut-offs	Generalization of the uniform distribution	It can be either subjectively constructed by eliciting the variable range, number of classes and height of each class, or obtained through the observed frequencies of x relative to each class (in any case, as for any PDF, the overall histogram area sums to 1). It relies on the assumption that the probability corresponding to any given bin is constant within that bin. The step-like nature of the PDF may be modified by exploiting smoothing techniques.
Trapezoidal	Continuous	$-\infty < a < c_1 < c_2 < b < \infty$ * $\Omega = \left[a, b\right]$ *$a = \min, b = \max,$ $c_1 = \text{mode } 1, c_2 = \text{mode } 2$	$f\left(x; a, b, c_1, c_2\right) = \begin{cases} u\left(\dfrac{x-a}{c_1-a}\right) & \text{if } a \leq x < c_1 \\ u & \text{if } c_1 \leq x < c_2 \\ u\left(\dfrac{b-x}{b-c_2}\right) & \text{if } c_2 \leq x < b \end{cases}$ with $u = 2(b + c_2 - c_1 - a)^{-1}$	It can be used to model a phenomenon characterized by three stages: a first growth stage, a stability phase and a decreasing stage (triangular and uniform distributions can be seen as special cases of the trapezoidal distribution). It relies on the assumption that the growth and decay of x occur linearly. It is also founded on the assumption that two alternative modal values exist, and that all the values within them have equal probability to occur.
Weibull	Continuous	$\alpha, \beta > 0$ * $\Omega = \left[0, +\infty\right]$ *α: shape parameter; β: scale parameter	$f\left(x; \alpha, \beta\right) = \dfrac{\alpha}{\beta}\left(\dfrac{x}{\beta}\right)^{\gamma-1} \exp\left\{-\left[\left(\dfrac{x}{\beta}\right)^{\alpha}\right]\right\}$	It is an extremely flexible continuous distribution. It has been proposed to study the time until occurrence of a given event. The failure rate is a function of time. If $\alpha > 1$, the failure rate increases over time (e.g. the 'aging' process of a mechanical system). If $\alpha < 1$, the failure rate decreases over time (e.g. any phenomenon where the risk is polarized in early stages of time). When $\alpha = \beta = 1$, the Weibull becomes an exponential distribution with $\lambda = 1$, while for $\beta = 1$ and $\alpha \cong 3$ or greater, the PDF is bell-shaped and almost symmetrical (i.e. similar to a normal PDF).

Gaussian (normal)	Continuous	$$f(x;\mu,\sigma^2)=\frac{1}{\sqrt{2\pi\sigma^2}}\exp\left\{-\frac{(x-\mu)^2}{2\sigma^2}\right\}$$ $$\mu=E[x]\in(-\infty,+\infty);$$ $$\mathrm{Var}[x]=\sigma^2>0$$ $$\Omega=(-\infty,+\infty)$$	It is one of the most popular distributions for real-valued random variables. According to the central limit theorem, under mild conditions the mean (or the sum) of a large number of any independent and identically distributed random variables is approximately normally distributed, whatever their initial distribution form. A normal PDF is bell-shaped, symmetric around its mean and strictly positive over the real line.
Exponential	Continuous	$$f(x;\lambda)=\lambda\exp\{-\lambda x\}$$ $$\lambda=\frac{1}{E[x]}>0*$$ $$\Omega=[0,+\infty)$$ *λ: rate parameter	It is the continuous analogue of the geometric PDF, used to describe the time for a continuous process to change state when the instantaneous probability of changing state (the rate parameter λ) is constant over time. This implies the memorylessness property: $\mathrm{pr}(x>t+s|x>s)=\mathrm{pr}(x>t)$, $\forall t,s\in\Omega$. The exponential PDF is used, for example, to model the time to a system break, the time to the next car accident or the time until a rare event occurs. It may be well suited for highly right-skewed data bounded at 0, although the constant rate assumption can often be too restrictive.
Triangular	Continuous	$$f(x;a,b,c,d)=\begin{cases}\dfrac{2(x-a)}{(b-a)(c-a)} & \text{if } a\leq x\leq c\\[2mm]\dfrac{2(b-x)}{(b-a)(b-c)} & \text{if } c<x\leq b\end{cases}$$ $$-\infty<a<c<b<+\infty*$$ $$\Omega\in[a,b]$$ *$a=\min, b=\max,$ $c=\text{mode};$ $$E[x]=\frac{a+b+c}{3}$$ $E[x]=c$ only if x is symmetric	A common choice for subjectively describing a phenomenon when only limited data are available. Its popularity is due to the parametrization of the PDF through the x range (a and b, which have 0 probability to occur) and the 'best guess' value (the mode c). Even if the three parameters are correctly determined, it does not necessarily happen that the true variable distribution shape is triangular. According to a, b and c, the PDF can be either symmetric or right/left skewed. Alternative choices for right-skewed continuous PDFs are the beta and chi-square, which are preferable in cases where the phenomenon distributes smoothly.

(Continued)

Name	Type	Parameters and support	Distribution function	Description
Discrete	Discrete	$p_j \in (0,1)$ $\sum_j p_j = 1, j > 1$ $\Omega \in \{a_1, a_2, \ldots, a_j\}$	$f(x; p_j) = \begin{cases} p_1 & \text{if } x = a_1 \\ \vdots & \vdots \\ p_j & \text{if } x = a_j \end{cases}$	It is a very general distribution type. According to its PDF, x takes a finite set of mutually exclusive and collectively exhaustive discrete values, each of them characterized by a specific probability of occurrence. It requires a relatively high knowledge of the phenomenon considered, as the entire set of probabilities of occurrence must be either subjectively of inferentially elicited, and all the possible realizations of x must be taken into account.
Bernoulli	Discrete	$E[x] = p \in (0,1)$ $\Omega \in \{0,1\}$	$f(x; p) = p^x (1-p)^{1-x}$	This distribution is well suited to model the occurrence of a risky event which may either occur ($x = 1$) or not occur ($x = 0$). The parameter p (the 'probability of success') returns the probability that the event of interest occurs. The Bernoulli is a special case of a binomial PDF characterized by one trial only ($n = 1$).
Binomial	Discrete	$n > 0^*, p \in (0,1)$ $\Omega \in \{0,1,\ldots,n\}$ * if $n = 1$ the PDF reduces to the binomial.	$f(x; n, p) = \binom{n}{x} p^x (1-p)^{n-x}$	It is the generalization of the Bernoulli PDF, where x is modelled as the number of successes out of n independent Bernoulli trials, with p being the (constant) probability of success in each of those trials. Although the p constancy is not always met in reality, the binomial PDF can be exploited in a number of applications where the number of 'successes' is of interest (number of system failures, number of tickets sold, number of adverse events having occurred, all with respect to a given number of trials).

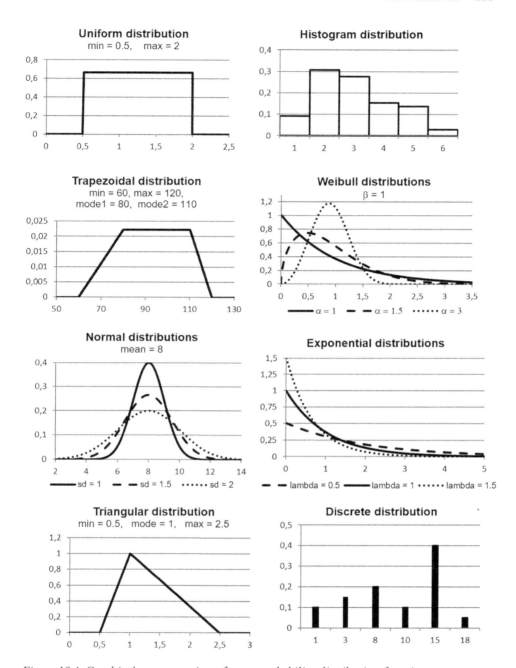

Figure A8.1 Graphical representation of some probability distribution functions.
Source: Authors.

Appendix 8.2

Monte Carlo method

Theoretical framework of the Monte Carlo method

The main goal of risk analysis is to estimate the cumulative distribution function (CDF) – or, equivalently, the probability distribution function (PDF) – of the ENPV of the project under assessment.[25] In doing so, the following notation, partly already introduced into the main body of the text, will be used:

- X: vector of K critical variables selected within the sensitivity analysis, indexed by the subscript $k = 1, ..., K$. Any critical variable XK could assume a specific value, indicated as $\tilde{x}_k$.
- $f(X)$: k-dimensional joint PDF of the vector of inputs X. The corresponding joint CDF is $F(x) \equiv \Pr\{x_1 \leq \tilde{x}_n, ..., x_k \leq \tilde{x}_k\}$.
- $y = g(X)$: the inputs (cashflow determinants) in X are linked to the outcome y (taking e.g. $y \equiv$ ENPV) through the link function $g(\cdot)$, defined by the CBA model. In general, $g(\cdot)$ is a complex function involving the present discounted value of sums and products of random variables.
- $f(x_k)$, $k = 1, ..., k$: marginal PDFs of the joint distribution $f(X)$. They constitute a quantitative representation of the uncertainty about the inputs. These density functions – or, equivalently, the marginal CDFs $F(x_k)$ – are usually established by expert's opinion.
- $F(y)$: CDF of the ENPV. The ultimate aim of the risk analysis procedure is to estimate this function, or the corresponding density function $f(y)$. In fact, both functions provide a probabilistic representation of the risk relative to y, as propagated by the risk about X through the CBA model, $g(\cdot)$.

The Monte Carlo method's objective can be considered an integration problem. In fact, it aims at approximating the CDF of the ENPV, which is the following integral[26]:

$$I = \int_{-\infty}^{\tilde{y}} f(y)\, dy = \Pr(y \leq \tilde{y}) \equiv F(\tilde{y}) \tag{A8.1}$$

where $\tilde{y}$ is any specific value belonging to the support of y (i.e. any possible realization of y). Notice that here reference is made to absolutely continuous random variables, but everything holds also in the discrete case.

As shown by Helton and Davis (2003), a fundamental further step stems from the recognition that equation (A8.1) can be equivalently rewritten as the first-order moment or expected value $E[h(y)]$:

$$I = \int_{-\infty}^{+\infty} I_{(-\infty,\tilde{y}]}(y) \cdot f(y)\, dy \equiv E\big[h(y)\big] \tag{A8.2}$$

where $I_{(-\infty,\tilde{y}]}(y) = h(y)$ is the indicator function, taking value 1 in $((-\infty,\tilde{y}])$ and 0 otherwise. Having shown that (A8.1) is equivalent to (A8.2) it is possible to exploit Monte Carlo results, which imply convergence towards expected values (Robert and Casella 2004).

The Monte Carlo approach allows one to evaluate $\hat{\imath}$, the estimate of the above integral. However, before exploiting Monte Carlo theoretical results, it is necessary to simulate a sample of size n: $(X_1, \ldots, X_n)$, where each element $X_i < f(X)$ is composed of the entire vector of critical variables ($i = 1, \ldots, n$). If the critical variables are assumed to be independent, then their realizations are separately sampled from the marginal densities $f(x_k)$.[27] Otherwise, when the variables are assumed to be correlated, it is necessary to exploit either their conditional distributions or copula methods (see Appendix 8.3).

After the simulation step, regardless of the dependence structure of the inputs, for each realization of X_i it is possible to compute the corresponding ENPV through $y_i = g(X_i)$. As usually happens in the applications, the output values are obtained through the CBA model through spreadsheet applications, even if $g(\cdot)$ is not explicitly known in close form. Notice that each set of realizations (X_i, y_i) is interpreted as a possible future state of the world, as defined through the $g(\cdot)$ model and the joint density $f(X)$.

The fundamental Monte Carlo result is justified by the 'Law of Large Numbers', which guarantees that:

$$\bar{h}_n = \frac{1}{n}\sum_{i=1}^{n} h(y_i) \rightarrow E\big[h(y)\big] \tag{A8.3}$$

where n is the number of simulations and y_i is the output value relative to the ith iteration (Robert and Casella 2004). The convergence result is extremely general: it holds for each $h(\cdot)$ function (whether it is known in close form or not), only requiring that $n \rightarrow \infty$. In particular, if $h(y) = y$ then (A8.3) implies that the average value of the output (computed over the n simulations) converges towards its population counterpart:

$$\bar{y}_n = \frac{1}{n}\sum_{i=1}^{n} y_i \rightarrow \int_{-\infty}^{+\infty} y \cdot f(y)\, dy \equiv E[y] \tag{A8.4}$$

Similarly, if $h(y) = (y - E[y])^2$ then the empirical variance of the outcome variable – used to approximate the true (unknown) variance $\mathrm{Var}[y]$ – is such that:

$$\widehat{\mathrm{Var}}[y] = \frac{1}{n}\sum_{i=1}^{n} (y_i - \bar{y}_n)^2 \rightarrow \int_{-\infty}^{+\infty} (y - E[y])^2 f(y)\, dy \equiv \mathrm{Var}[y]. \tag{A8.5}$$

Finally, to estimate the probability that the outcome is smaller than a given cut-off, say 0, it is set $h(y) = I_{(-\infty,\ 0]}(y)$, and the Monte Carlo asymptotics guarantee that:

$$\widehat{\Pr}(y \le 0) = \frac{1}{n}\sum_{i=1}^{n} I_{(-\infty,0)}(y_i) \to \int_{-\infty}^{+\infty} I_{(-\infty,0)}(y) \cdot f(y)\,dy \equiv F(0) \tag{A8.6}$$

According to (A8.6), by setting as cut-offs all the values constituting the support *of y* it is possible to reconstruct its entire estimated probability distribution function, namely the approximation of the initial integral of interest at equation (A8.1). The higher the number of simulations, the better the approximation of the integral considered.

Choice of the number of simulations

Since the Law of Large Numbers holds for $n \to \infty$, a related methodological issue is the choice of a 'sufficiently large' number of Monte Carlo simulations. In general, there is no fit-for-all rule for knowing in advance what is the number of iterations required for convergence. The standard approach is to exploit graphical methods where the $\bar{h}_n$ values are plotted against the increasing simulated sample sizes 1, 2, ..., n, with n at least equal to 1,000 or 2,000 (Robert and Casella 2004).

In Figure A8.2, the average ENVPs have been plotted against Monte Carlo sample sizes running from 1 to 6,000 (using previous notation, the convergence of $\tilde{y}_n$ towards $E[y]$ is assessed). In addition to the punctual estimates of $\bar{h}_n$, the corresponding 95 per cent normal confidence intervals have also been plotted. They provide the measure of the precision of the corresponding punctual estimates. Normal confidence intervals are theoretically justified by the Central Limit theorem, which implies, as $n \to \infty$:

$$\frac{\bar{h}_n - E\left[h(y)\right]}{\sqrt{\widehat{\text{Var}} - \left[\bar{h}_n\right]}} \to N(0,1). \tag{A8.7}$$

The convergence towards the standard normal distribution allows the analyst not only to compute normal confidence intervals, but also to construct formal convergence tests (although graphical methods could be sufficient for inspecting the simulations behaviour). Figure A8.2 shows that only after about 3,000 Monte Carlo simulations does the average ENPV stabilize, and the same holds for the width of confidence intervals. Hence, the general suggestion is to generate more than just 1,000 simulations, as today personal computers are efficient enough to produce thousands of random numbers in a relatively short time.

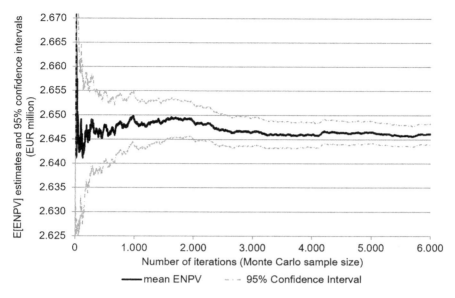

Figure A8.2 Monte Carlo convergence plot of the ENPV.

Source: Authors' elaboration, based on 6,000 Monte Carlo simulations related to an illustrative transport project.

Appendix 8.3

Generating correlated random numbers

Modelling dependence through conditional distributions

As mentioned in Appendix 8.2, at the heart of the Monte Carlo method's application lies the issue of generating random numbers. Each standard statistical software and spreadsheet application presents built-in uniform random variable generators, which allow one to simulate say d independent and identically distributed (IID) random variates according to a uniform PDF defined on (0, 1):

$$u_1,...,u_d \sim U_{(0,1)}.$$ (A8.8)

The next step is to transform the uniform random variables into X, the required vector of K (non-uniform) critical variables. To this end, the computer algorithm returns $X = h(u_1, ..., u_d) \sim f(X)$, with $h: (0, 1)^d \to R^k$.

The inversion-transform method (Devroye 2003) is the easiest approach to accomplish the above task.[28] In the simple univariate case ($K = 1$), it only requires one to define an invertible CDF for x, then it is possible to demonstrate that:

$$x = F_x^{(-1)}(u).$$ (A8.9)

In words, at each Monte Carlo iteration one uniform random variable taking values on (0, 1) is first extracted, and then its realization is plugged into the inverse of the CDF of x, hence obtaining the desired critical variable value.

In virtually any application, though, at each iteration project appraisers are interested in simulating an entire vector of random variables $X = (x_1, ..., x_K) \sim f(X)$ (with X being composed of either continuous or discrete random variables). In general, when the elements of X are independent of each other:

$$f(X) = f(x_1) \cdot ... \cdot f(x_k).$$ (A8.10)

so that in order to obtain X it is sufficient to generate $x_1 \sim f(x_1), ..., x_k \sim f(x_k)$ separately (e.g. through the inversion-transform method) and then to return the X vector.

In many applications, however, the x_ks are dependent (e.g. the price of a normal good and its demanded quantity). Suppose all the K variables are correlated. In this case the joint PDF is no longer the product of the K marginal PDFs, but:

$$f(X) = f(x_1) \cdot f(x_2|x_1) \cdot ... \cdot (x_k|x_1,...,x_{k-1}).$$ (A8.11)

A first way to simulate X is to directly exploit the marginal densities, and consists of three steps:

i   Generate $x_1 \sim f(x_1)$ (e.g. through the inversion-transform method);
ii Conditional on $x_1 = \tilde{x}_1$, generate $x_2 \sim f_2\left(x_2 | x_1 = \tilde{x}_1\right)$;
iii Continue generating a random number for each of the K components of X, conditional on the previously extracted values.

The key issue is the definition of up to $K - 1$ conditional distributions (one for each variable correlated with at least another one), which may become difficult and extremely inefficient even when the number of correlated variables is moderately large.[29] In addition, and contrary to copula methods, even if information about the marginal densities $f(x_k)$ of the correlated variables is available it cannot be exploited to compute $f(X)$ (see equation (A8.11), where only the $f(x_1)$ marginal density is included).

Modelling dependence through copulas

An increasingly popular alternative strategy to allow dependence between the simulated components of X is the adoption of copulas. Copulas are particularly appealing because they do not require one to define conditional distributions, and are suitable for applications where expert's opinion about the dependency structure of X is crucial, namely in risk analysis.

By definition, a copula C is a K-dimensional CDF defined on $[0, 1]^K$ and with uniform marginals. In other words, a copula is a joint CDF $C: [0, K]^k \rightarrow [0, 1]$ of K dependent uniform random variables $u_1,\ldots,u_K \sim U_{(0,1)}$:

$$C\left(u_1,\ldots,u_k\right) \equiv \Pr\left\{u_1 < u_1,\ldots,u_k < u_k\right\}. \tag{A8.12}$$

The crucial difference with respect to the uniform random variables in (A8.8) is that variables are not IID, but correlated. In particular, the correlation structure of $u_1, \ldots, u_K$ is provided by the specific copula functional form.

The fundamental Sklar's theorem (Sklar 1959) proves that any joint CDF $F(x_1, \ldots, x_k)$ can always be represented as a function of its marginal CDFs and of C, which describes the dependence part of $F(\cdot)$:

$$F_x\left(x_1,\ldots,x_k\right) = C\left(F\left(x_1\right),\ldots,F\left(x_k\right)\right). \tag{A8.13}$$

The result is very general, holding for X either continuous or discrete (when X is continuous C is unique). It only requires that the K marginal CDFs are invertible, as the proof of the theorem relies on the inverse-transform method; see Ruschendorf (2009).

Sklar's theorem admits a fundamental converse implication (Durante and Sempi 2010), which is crucial for the purpose of modelling the dependency structure of X: if $F(x_1)$, ..., $F(x_K)$ are univariate CDFs and C is any K-variate copula, then $F(x_1, \ldots, x_K)$ as defined in (A8.13) is a K-dimensional CDF with margins $F(x_1)$, ..., $F(x_K)$.

This implies that, having set up the K-dimensional distribution of the uniform random vector U (i.e. the copula function) and the marginal F_k, the vector of interest is $X = (F^{-1}(u_1) \ldots F^{-1}(u_k))$, distributed in accordance with $F(\cdot) = C(F(x_1), \ldots, (x_K))$, and has the previously defined margins $F(x_1)$, ..., $F(x_k)$.

The underlying idea is that through the copulas it is possible to simulate a vector of dependent uniform random variables U. Then the inverse-transform result is exploited to generate the final X vector, for which the dependence structure is preserved. At the same time, Sklar's theorem guarantees that the correlated random numbers finally obtained are marginally distributed in accordance with the marginal distributions initially defined.

Regardless of the specific copula functional form, the dependence structure among the random variables is introduced through the Kendall's coefficient τ (a rank correlation measure) or alternative copula parameters which are one-to-one functions of τ. For instance, the dependency structure of elliptical copulas (the normal and t-student ones) is defined through the correlation matrix $\Sigma_{(K \times K)}$, composed by the Person's correlation coefficients ρ_{kl} relative to each pair of x_k and x_k ($k, l = 1, \dots, K$). They are such that

$$\rho_{kl} = \sin\left(\frac{\pi}{2}\tau_{kl}\right);$$ see the discussion by Wang in the paper by Frees and Valdez (1998)

and a less technical presentation though a CBA case study by Clemen and Reilly (1999).

Notes

1 This chapter is co-authored with Stefano Lombardi.

2 Pure *ex-post* evaluations implemented at the end of the project's time horizon are rare. The rationale and some methodological indications to perform an *ex-post* evaluation are discussed in Chapter 11.

3 However, Aven *et al.* (2004) stressed that in practice no Bayesian methods are adopted to update, through empirical data, the probability distributions subjectively assumed. Hence, strictly speaking, risk assessment procedures, and particularly the probability analysis, based on the so-called subjective approach (see Section 8.5) do not necessarily exploit Bayesian inferential methods, even if it would always be possible to do that through repeated assessments.

4 It should be noted that, according to the above terminology, a distinction is made here between risk assessment procedures and risk analysis, which is only the last step in risk assessment. In other literature, however, the two terms are sometimes treated as interchangeable.

5 The notation used in this chapter differ from that used in chapters 1–3 and what reported in the notation list.

6 According to the notation adopted in this chapter, upper-case letters denote vectors or, more generally, matrices of input values, while lower-case letters denote single elements belonging to a given matrix. This notation is different from the simplified notation used elsewhere in this book.

7 For the sake of simplicity, in the rest of the chapter the analysis is referred to the ENPV only.

8 There may be cases, however, in which it could be more sensible to focus on more aggregated quantities, provided that the assumption of independence of critical variables is not violated. For instance, the probability of an investment cost change associated with the tender phase could be estimated with reference to the total or a macro-aggregate of investment costs.

9 By assuming the independence of the critical variables, each input may take any given value (in accordance with its range and probability distribution function) irrespective of the values taken by the other inputs (i.e. for any input there exists no deterministic or probabilistic constraint due to other inputs).

10 In this regard, the European Commission recommends the appraiser to consider as critical those variables for which an absolute variation of 1 per cent around the best estimate gives rise to a corresponding variation of not less than 1 percentage point in the NPV (European Commission 2014).

11 In some cases, it may happen that no single variable presents a sufficiently strong influence on the outcome. In these cases, the standard sensitivity analysis procedure is of little help, and alternative *ad hoc* methods of selecting variables should be implemented (for instance based

on recurrent patterns relative to projects similar to the one under assessment). However, in practice this does not happen often.

12 More precisely, the simulations always converge towards the expected value (or 'mean') of the critical variable distribution, which in general is set to be equal to the CBA 'best estimate' value (this is the case, for instance, of the normal distribution). However, attention must be paid when the distribution of the critical variable is not directly defined through its expected value. For instance, in standard statistical and spreadsheet software the triangular distribution is completely specified by the minimum, maximum and mode values. The latter is equal to the expected value only if the distribution is symmetric around the mode. Otherwise, when the triangular distribution is skewed, the Monte Carlo simulations tend to converge to a value different from the mode. Since the mode is a one-to-one function of the expected value, this problem can be solved by first setting the expected value (and not the mode) equal to the CBA 'best estimate', and then by computing the corresponding mode in order to define the distribution.

13 This can be straightforwardly implemented by any spreadsheet software and built-in add-ons.

14 It may also be useful to focus on the critical variables whose impact on the outcome is linear, which may still constitute a relevant part of the ones selected.

15 The scenario analysis must not be confused with the option analysis (see Chapter 4), as the former consists in evaluating different states of the world associated with the implementation of the same project, while the latter consists in systematically comparing concurrent project options.

16 Determining whether the variation in a critical variable positively or negatively affects the CBA results, thus making it suitable to be included in the optimistic or pessimistic scenario, should preferably not rely solely on the results of the project analysis. The incremental results, calculated as the difference between the project's cash flows and the cash flow of the counterfactual, should instead be considered. Actually, a variation in a critical variable could affect both the project and the without-the-project cash flows, leading to an opposite change in the marginal results with respect to the sole do-project performance.

17 In addition to the data specifically characterizing the project, the analyst can exploit meta-analysis techniques. This systematic approach to using all the available empirical evidence, in general, can also be useful in order to augment the generalizability of results. However, it is also time- and resource-intensive.

18 The Bayesian inferential approach provides a feasible way of linking these approaches. Personal experience and available information can be adopted to set prior distributions. Then, as data become available over time, they can be adopted for updating the initial distributions through the Bayes theorem. This has been relatively recently suggested by the World Bank (e.g. Ouchi 2004).

19 To this end, time-series statistical models can be exploited to take into account autocorrelation (the correlation between values of the same variable across different time periods).

20 In particular, if the range is considered as bounded, it is immediate to determine its extremes equal to 'pessimistic' and 'optimistic' values previously elicited.

21 However, inferential methods can be fruitfully adopted as an alternative to the subjective approach. By fitting available data through different copulas it is possible to determine which one provides a better predictive performance. At the same time, for any given copula type, the parameters quantifying the dependency relationships among the critical variables are estimated (instead of being subjectively assumed). Semi-parametric and non-parametric copula functions may also be inferentially constructed.

22 The probability of concordance between any two covariates x_1 and x_2 is defined as the conditional probability $P_{1,2} = \Pr\{x_1 < \tilde{x}_1 | x_2 < \tilde{x}_2\}$, where $\tilde{x}_1$ and $\tilde{x}_2$ are two independent copies of x_1 and x_2 respectively. $P_{1,2}$ can be elicited by simply asking: 'suppose that two independent copies of x_1 and x_2 are extracted, given that for the second variable it is observed that $x_2 < \tilde{x}_2$, what is the average probability that also $x_1 < \tilde{x}_1$?'. Once the copula type and all the two-way probabilities of concordance have been set up, the dependent random variables can be extracted from the resulting copula functional form.

23 This is a direct consequence of using random variables in the right-hand side of equation (8.2) instead of deterministically setting up their values. By doing so, also the left-hand side of the equation is now a random variable distributed according to an (unknown) PDF.

24 In addition, simulation techniques alternative to the classical Monte Carlo method, such as Latin Hypercube Sampling or Stratified Sampling, may be exploited to better simulate events with a low likelihood of occurrence (Helton and Davis 2003).

25 Note that the following reasoning may be extended to alternative performance indices, such as the economic internal rate of return (EIRR).

26 The integral is considered over $(-\infty, \tilde{y})$. This is necessary when y varies on an unbounded support, i.e. $y \in (-\infty, \infty)$, but is also correct if y is left bounded in $\min_y$ (the lowest y value in correspondence of which $f(y) > 0$). In this last case, starting from $-\infty$ the integral is by definition equal to 0 until $y = \min_y$. Then the area underlying f(y) starts to be greater than

$$0, \text{ so that: } I = \int_{-\infty}^{\tilde{y}} f(y)\,dy = \int_{-\infty}^{\min_y} f(y)\,dy + \int_{\min_y}^{\tilde{y}} f(y)\,dy = \int_{\min_y}^{\tilde{y}} f(y)\,dy.$$

27 In fact, if the independence assumption holds, the joint distribution of the critical variables is simply the product of its marginal distributions, namely: $f = f(x_1) \dots f(x_k)$. On the contrary, when the variables are correlated, it holds: $f(X) = f(x_1)\, f(x_2|x_1) \dots f(x_k|x_1, \dots, x_{k-1})$. Hence, in this last case it is necessary to exploit the conditional distributions in order to generate an entire vector of random variables.

28 Alternative random numbers simulation methods (such as the acceptance-rejection algorithm) may be far more efficient; see Devroye (2003) and Robert and Casella (2004).

29 In fact, as the dimension of X increases the number of probability assessments keeps growing. As a consequence, in order to carry out feasible marginal and conditional analyses, in the applications it is common to assume independence between many of the variables at hand, an a priori practice that clearly fails to address the issue of dependency (Kroese *et al.* 2011).

Part Three

Experience

9 International evaluation practices

Overview[1]

This chapter reviews some cost-benefit analysis (CBA) traditions, guidelines, and practices developed by international organizations and national governments. The first section (9.1) presents some features of the CBA traditions in the United Kingdom (UK), France, and the United States of America (US), whose national governments have developed considerable experience in the evaluation of public investments. As is shown, this tradition can deviate, even substantially, from the evaluation practice of international organizations.

The CBA appraisal practice of public investments in the European Commission is discussed in Section 9.2. This is based on the *Guide to Cost-benefit Analysis of Investment Projects*, and the latest Economic Analysis Vademecum (EAV) adopted respectively in 2014 and 2021 by Directorate-General for Regional and Urban Policy (DG Regio) as the main tools to appraise infrastructure investments to be financed with EU budget. The role played by evaluation through CBA in multilateral development banks, such as the World Bank (WB) and the European Investment Bank (EIB), is then presented in Section 9.3 in order to outline when it intervenes into the project's life cycle and how it supports the decision-making and financing processes. While describing rules, guidelines and procedures, the review points out to what extent these are actually implemented by the various institutions, and the possible deviations from theory.

A brief list of suggested further readings is in Section 9.4.

9.1 National traditions and operative guidelines

9.1.1 United Kingdom

In the UK, HM Treasury (hereafter the Treasury) is the key institution in programming public expenditure. It receives proposals for expenditure from different government departments and presents them to Parliament in the form of 'Estimates'. It is the only department holding authority for public expenditure so as to keep central control over the allocation of resources between governmental departments.

How to perform evaluations in the public sector in the UK is a well-structured procedure, as the result of a long tradition. Each department carries out its evaluations according to the general guidelines issued by the Treasury. Since 2003, the key relevant document is the *Green Book* (see HM Treasury 2020a for latest edition) which explains how policies, programmes, and projects must be evaluated. It does not define rigid procedures to be followed, but a general and flexible approach for the analysis of public investments and

DOI: 10.4324/9781003191377-12

other socio-economic proposals. Thus, instructions are not binding; rather, they are intended as guidelines that reflect the moral suasion that comes from the strong position of the Treasury in the system of financial delegations to spending departments. The *Green Book* is complemented by other HM Treasury guidance[2] and supplementary documents focused on specific topics[3] which apply to all public policies, programmes, and projects.

In the UK, appraisal and evaluation are conceived as integral and continuous aspects of a broad policy cycle that the *Green Book* formalizes in the acronym ROAMEF: Rationale, Objectives, Appraisal, Monitoring, Evaluation and Feedback. While the appraisal is the *ex-ante* analysis in which a potentially wide range of hypotheses are compared, the evaluation is the interim or *ex-post* analysis where the outturn of a programme, policy, or project is assessed against what it was expected to achieve. The latter analysis is designed to ensure that lessons learnt are fed back into the decision-making process. The key appraisal steps, as pointed out by the latest edition of the *Green Book* (HM Treasury 2020a), are the following:

i   Preparing the strategic case: defines what should be appraised, quantifies the present situation and Business as Usual (the BAU) and identifies the SMART objectives[4];
ii Carrying out a long-list appraisal: considers how best to achieve the SMART objectives, assess alternative options through the lens of public service provision, selects a viable shortlist for a further detailed appraisal;
iii Carrying out a short-list appraisal: estimates the expected costs and benefits and considers possible trade-offs. Social Cost-Benefit Analysis or Social Cost Effectiveness Analysis (CEA) is mobilized for this purpose.
iv Identifying the preferred options: basing on the detailed analysis at the shortlist appraisal stage, it involves determining which option provides the best balance of costs, benefits, risks and unmonetizable factors thus optimizing value for money.

Box 9.1 UK architecture for public expenditure decisions

The Treasury's task is to ensure that public funds are spent on activities that provide the greatest benefits to society in the most efficient way. The Treasury exercises this control in a strategic manner by giving wide delegations (i.e. authorizations), up to given defined levels, for public money spending. In particular, each government department is provided with a mandate that spells out a typology of eligible expenditure, financial levels, reference to overall total public expenditure (as agreed in the estimates submitted to Parliament) and timing for undertaking revisions of planned expenditures.

Most important is that, once approval from Parliament is granted and funds allocated to different departments, the public investment projects contained in the programmes must be evaluated by the economic and financial division of each department, under the supervision of the Accounting Officer, who is appointed by the Treasury Officer of Accounts. Moreover, each department is required to produce to Parliament annual departmental reports, setting out the government's spending plans, initiatives, and achievements (including progress against Public Services Agreements' targets).[5]

Source: Authors.

Florio (1990) discusses the British approach to project appraisal to select investments under budget constraints, while discussing the role and status of CBA in the 1980s. Although the issue of controlling quantity and quality of public expenditure was quite strong at that time, he observes that CBA was playing a minor role, with spending departments adopting a heterogeneous blend of appraisal techniques. This resulted in inconsistencies in selecting investments and limited government control over the setting of objectives by departments.

The picture has, however, evolved since then, also thanks to the extensive application of the *Green Book*. Beria *et al.* (2012) confirm that, almost two decades after Florio's review, the British approach to evaluation is more deeply rooted in CBA. This analysis is performed systematically, and consistently, for the appraisal of any important public investment, and is seen as the most significant instrument that government has at its disposal to make the best decisions about resource allocation and risk minimization. Beria *et al.* also point out that, differently from the Nordic European traditions, CBA in the UK is used for approving or rejecting the financing decision of single project schemes (similarly to the Italian and French approaches), and not at planning level in order to rank priorities (such as in the Netherlands or Germany).

That said, it is clear that the *Green Book* was not an ending point, but rather a starting one, as new frontiers in project appraisal are being pushed up. Andersson (2018) reports that the *Green Book* has played a key role in creating a cost-benefit analysis culture in UK policy making across different fields.

The *Green Book* shares the overall logic of continuous evaluation during the project life cycle, as summarized by the ROAMEF. It relies on the following broad ideas: the legitimacy of public intervention to address market failures, the concept of social opportunity cost of inputs and outputs, the need to consider different options from the beginning of the project's appraisal, the need to value as far as possible costs and benefits, the concept of discounting, a consideration of distributional impact, as well as a wide discussion of risk and uncertainty.

A peculiarity of the UK *Green Book* concerns the use of shadow prices: it does not recommend the use of shadow prices, unless there is there is no market price for costs and benefits to society. This is particularly important for environmental, social and health effects. In particular, the *Green Book* reads as follows:

> The costs of using assets and resources are defined by the value which reflects the best alternative use a good or service could be put to – its opportunity cost. Market prices are usually the starting point for estimating opportunity costs. Where market prices are not suitable or available non-market valuation techniques can be used.
>
> (HM Treasury 2020a: 42)

This position is qualified in a following statement:

> Market prices will not represent total costs and benefits where a market is distorted because of restricted competition, such as a monopoly in supply (only one seller), or monopsony in purchasing (only one buyer). If this is the case valuation may be required and discussion is advised between the responsible organisation and their approving authority, or HM Treasury in the case of major expenditure.
>
> (HM Treasury 2020a: 59)

A further feature concerns the treatment of the opportunity cost of labour, which is just mentioned in the main text of the *Green Book* as follows:

> The opportunity cost of labour should include the total value of the output produced by employees. This is the cost of employees' time, based on Full Time Equivalent (FTE) costs and includes pension costs, National Insurance, allowances, benefits and basic salary.
>
> (HM Treasury 2020a: 57)

Wider economic benefits are considered by the *Green Book* (Abelson 2020). Specifically, it opens the door to including significant productivity/agglomeration benefits related to infrastructure over and above-user benefits.

> Productivity effects should be included in the calculation of UK costs and benefits where they can be objectively demonstrated. Productivity effects may arise from movement to more or less productive jobs, changes in the structure of the economy, benefits from dynamic clustering or agglomeration (benefits that arise through close location of businesses and/or people), private investment, product market competition or the generation and flow of ideas. Productivity effects will typically lead to higher wages, rather than higher employment. The benefits can be calculated from the different levels of total employment costs under different options.
>
> (HM Treasury 2020: 57)

The *Magenta Book* complements the *Green Book* by being more focused on the evaluation design. The revised version, issued in March 2020, is a broad guidance document aimed at both analysts and policy makers at all levels of government. It includes some technical instructions for evaluation which are of particular interest for policy and project analysts. It discusses in greater detail the key steps to follow when planning and undertaking an evaluation and how to answer evaluation research questions using different evaluation research designs. The evaluation steps recommended by the *Magenta Book* can be summarized as follows:

- Evaluation scoping: understanding the intervention (what should be evaluated), identifying the evaluation needs (for whom and by when), understanding the questions to be answered, For the understanding of the intervention, the guide suggest to produce a Theory of Change, which investigates how the intervention is expected to work (setting out all the steps expected to be involved in achieving the desired outcomes), the assumptions made, the quality and strength of the evidence supporting them, and wider contextual factors.
- Evaluation design: choosing the most appropriate evaluation approaches, both for analysis and data collection, that can answer the evaluation questions;
- Evaluation implementation: conducting the evaluation and, if needed, modifying design in response to learning and policy changes/stakeholder needs.
- Disseminate, use & learning: preparing final evaluation analysis and outputs.

9.1.2 France

France has the longest tradition in the evaluation of public policies. Public investment appraisal has historically been the most developed and sophisticated dimension of public policy evaluation, and it remains a key part of it (Prud'homme 2008).

Many engineers and economists contributed to the development of project evaluation and were in a position to practice or impose it. A well-known contribution was made by Arsène-Jules Dupuit (1804–1866), inspector general of Ponts et Chaussées, on the evaluation of the economic welfare of public works, in two papers dated 1844 and 1849, respectively, concerning the measure of utility of a bridge and the determination of the toll, the latter drawing on the concept of price discrimination. Dupuit developed the notion of the consumer's surplus, which is still at the heart of the standard economic analysis of transport projects. Among others, it is worth mentioning the Nobel Prize winner Maurice Allais, who made contributions on public investment in energy, and Marcel Boiteux (Chief Executive Officer at the Electricité de France), who developed the theory of optimal pricing for a monopoly with decreasing marginal costs and a budget equilibrium constraint, rediscovering the powerful insights of the Ramsey rule on optimal taxation, hence the notion of Ramsey–Boiteux pricing (Prud'homme 2008).

As confirmed by Quinet (2007: 164), since the early 1960s guidelines for road investment choices have been established in order to 'match the growing needs to the scarce financial resources. From that period, CBA has been gradually extended to other transportation modes and embedded in various procedures and public hearings'. A legislative act on transport of 1982, currently included in the 2010 Transport code, made the CBA mandatory for all major transport investment projects (Loi d'orientation des transports intérieurs, Art. 14 – Law 82-1153 of 30 December 1982).

The approach followed in France during the 1970s and 1980s distinguished itself from that adopted by the Anglo-Saxon countries by putting great emphasis on the need to integrate the various levels of project analysis: micro-economic, meso-economic and macro-economic. From the operational point of view, this led public departments in charge of development cooperation to work out a quite different method from that of Little and Mirrlees. This is the 'effects method' that proposes calculating the direct impact of the project (i.e. the added value created on users) and summing it with the 'first round indirect impact' (on suppliers), the 'second round indirect' (on sellers) and the 'secondary' impact (i.e. impacts generated by additional investments and consumption), in relation to the different social groups, firms, financial intermediaries, etc. The sum of these components makes up the total welfare change generated by the project. Conceptually, this partial equilibrium approach loosely draws on Keynesian Macroeconomics and implies the use of disaggregated input–output tables to estimate the effects of demand on the labour market, the balance of trade, etc.

From time to time, different commissions, hosted by the Commissariat Général du Plan[6] (CGP), were involved in the definition and revision of the parameters used for the evaluation of projects. For instance, according to Quinet (2007), in 1994 the GCP gave a new impulse to CBA and focused on the strict principles of economic theory and surplus analysis. In 2000, CGP's contribution was to define means to take into account external effects and fixed monetary values for those external effects. In 2005, greater attention was paid to the social discount rate and risk management.

The Act of 31 December 2012 about Public Finance Planning made it mandatory in France the requirement of CBA for all public civil investments exceeding EUR 20 million made by the State and its public institutions. Moreover, the Act establishes that an independent counter-expert assessment of the *ex-ante* CBA carried out by the project sponsor must be performed for projects that exceed EUR 100 million of public funding (see the Box below for more details).

Box 9.2 The use of counter-experts in France

For largest projects – for which funding by the State and its public institutions exceeds 100 million EUR – the Act no. 2012–1558 requires to carry out an independent counter-expert assessment of the *ex-ante* socioeconomic evaluation. This counter-expertise is paid for by the budget of the project. It is organized and conducted by the services of Commissioner General for Investment (CGI) reporting directly to the office of the Prime Minister. For each project, CGI gathers a team of several independent counter-experts. The number of counter-experts on a project depends on the complexity and skills required to assess the evaluation document and can range from 2 to 5 experts including at least a sector specialist and an economist (for projects in the health sector, the team is larger). Counter-experts are chosen for their competency, a selection made in the absence of any conflict of interest on the project under review. The counter-expert's approach is usually guided by the following questions:

i   Does the socio-economic assessment file comply with the specifications: the detailed description of the investment project; variants and alternatives to the investment project; the main data on its dimensioning and its provisional.

ii   Do socio-economic assessment methods selected for the project comply with methodological guides, especially those published by French Policy Planning Commission, or with other instructions from the ministry or the institution? In particular, are guardianship values well respected?

iii   How are the non-monetized but nevertheless critical, aspects taken into account for the evaluation of the project?

iv   Is the scope of the evaluation adequate or, on the contrary, has it been too circumscribed?

v   Are the choices (parameters, hypotheses) coherent and realistic, given the state of the art of evaluation and the availability of data?

Results of the independent assessment are summarized in the counter-expertise report.

Up to 2020, 85 projects, for a total value of EUR 81.2 billion, have been examined since the launch of this process in 2013.

Source: Authors based on Baumstark *et al.* (2021).

Accordingly, in 2013, the CBA guidelines were updated and deeply modified. The results of these revision works were firstly embedded in the 2013 Quinet report (Quinet 2013) and later on in the Guide to the socioeconomic evaluation of public investments, published in 2017 (France Stratégie and Trésor Direction Général 2017).[7] The guide outlines the guiding principles, concepts, and operational methods that can be used by project sponsors to assess a project. These two documents define the procedure currently in force and represents the main reference document for carrying out cost-benefit analysis of all types of infrastructure investments in France. They are complemented by a number of methodological documents[8] covering the following topics: (i) reference scenarios; (ii) official social value for non-market goods; (iii) market impacts, non-market direct impacts, externalities and their monetary values; (iv) the use of CO_2 value;

(v) decision rules with the criteria of socioeconomic NPV (net present value); (vi) residual value and projection time horizon; (vii) sensitivity analysis and financial analysis.

The key recommendations embedded in these reference documents can be summarized as follows:

- Calculation of several indicators, such as the Net Present Value, the Net Present Value per Euro spent, the Internal Rate of Return calculated on the basis of 50 years for transport sector and 30 years for other sectors, and the First Year Rate of Return which is equal to the surplus of the first year divided by the cost of the investment.
- Trying to assess the effects with respect to the different actors involved, such as users, taxpayers, neighbours of the infrastructure, operators.
- The social discount rate is fixed at 4 per cent and decreases (down to 3.5 per cent) after 30 years and then further decreases after 50 years (down to 3 per cent) to take into account the effects of growth rate volatility.
- The Quinet report specifically provides an update of values for the estimation of economic benefits, such as:

  i   The value of time on the basis of a survey of stated and revealed preference studies and traffic models outputs, mainly from French sources. These values are 10 per cent lower than the previous values (set in 1994 and updated in 2010). Values of time are differentiated for travel purposes as well as according to the comfort level in public transport, and to the reliability of travel time for both public transport and passenger cars.
  ii The value of statistical life and value of life year have been sharply increased, from around 1.9 to 3.0 million Euro (2010 values).
  iii Other specific values for noise and environment: approximate values are given per vehicle-km, differentiated according to local conditions (time of day, traffic and population densities). For CO_2 a sequence of values is defined, beginning in 2010 with 32€/t, reaching 100€/t in 2030, applying from then on a Hoteling-like rule, with a 4.5 per cent geometric annual increase.

- Taking into account spatial effects: the Quinet report specifically suggests to use land-use and transport interaction (LUTI) models in order to at least visualize the spatial consequences of major projects. It also gives qualitative indications on the effects of both urban and interurban investments on the spatial repartition of populations and employment. It recommends to estimate the agglomeration externalities and to add them to the welfare calculation. For this purpose, it gives precise rules (the elasticity of productivity vis-à-vis the density of employment is 2.4 per cent).
- Taking into account redistribution effects: an indicative index is proposed in order to take into account distributive effects on user's surplus.
- Sensitivity analysis is recommended and should take the form of estimation of the effects of alternative hypotheses for most sensitive variable (e.g. energy price, demand elasticity, etc.).
- The risk attached to project outcome should also be taken into account.[9]

Since 2017, a permanent committee of experts (including different ministries' experts and academics) has been established to specify the methodological rules for socioeconomic evaluation and define the studies and research necessary. In additional to the above reference documents, three additional sectoral reports have been approved by the Committee in 2019 on the following topics (i) socio-economic value to climate action (Quinet and Bueb 2019), (ii) socioeconomic evaluation of real estate projects in support of higher education and research activities (France Stratégie and Trésor Direction Général 2019), (iii) cost-benefit analyses for employment, health, and education policies (Fougere and Heim 2019).

9.1.3 United States of America

The US also has a long tradition of public investment appraisal. The Flood Control Act adopted during the Roosevelt Administration in 1936 was probably the first law to trigger the practical development of CBA. It required that the US Corps of Engineers carried out projects for the improvement of the waterway system only when the total benefits of a project to whomever they accrued exceeded the costs of that project. Thus, the Corps of Engineers created systematic methods for measuring such benefits and costs.

Guidelines for the evaluation of public investments and regulations at federal level are provided by the A-94 Circular Guidelines and discount rates for Benefit-Cost Analysis of Federal Programs, issued by the Office of Management and Budget (OMB 1992). The objective of this Circular is to promote efficient resource allocation through well-informed decision making by the Federal Government. The Circular provides general guidance for conducting cost-benefit and cost-effectiveness analyses as well as specific guidance on the discount rates to be used in evaluating Federal programmes whose benefits and costs are distributed over time. It is applied in all the federal agencies of the Executive Branch (with the exception of the District of Columbia and non-federal beneficiaries of loans, contracts or grants) and, more specifically, when they deal with decisions related to the initiative, its renewal, and the expansion of the programmes or projects (both public investment and regulatory) which would result in a series of measurable benefits or costs extending for at least three years. Specifically exempted from the scope of this Circular are decisions related to commercial activities, water resources and energy management, which are evaluated on the basis of sector-specific guidelines.

The most important aspects of the CBA approach, the A-94 Circular lays down, can be summarized as follows:

- The net present value should be based on incremental benefits and costs. Sunk costs and benefits realized in the past should be ignored and transfer payments excluded. Both indirect and international effects should be included.
- The market prices should be corrected in order to eliminate distortions caused by taxes, subsidies, externalities and monopolies. The general principle is, therefore, that of evaluating the resources according to their opportunity cost. The shadow prices calculated in this way are efficiency prices.
- Assumptions about future inflation should be avoided. When one is needed, the Circular recommends to use the rate of increase in the GDP deflator from the Administration's economic assumptions for the period of analysis.
- Public expenditure should be multiplied by a factor of 1.25 in order to take into account the excess burden (raising of taxes for financing the project). This rule applies to public investments, and exceptions are admitted if other analyses demonstrate that the fiscal burden is significantly different, such as for investments financed by

user charges (in this case, the excess burden would be zero) or projects that provide costs savings to the Federal Government and/or external social benefits.

- The discount rate can be real or nominal depending on whether the costs and benefits are measured in real or nominal terms. The nominal rate is supposed to be the market interest rate; the real one is calculated roughly by subtracting the expected rate of inflation from the nominal rate. For public investments and regulatory policies, one can choose between: (i) the basic case of a real rate of 7 per cent, which is supposed to approximate the pre-tax marginal rate of return of an average investment in the private sector in recent years; and (ii) inferring an appropriate shadow price of the capital, for which the approval of the Office of Management and Budget is required.[10]
- The risk analysis consists of a sensitivity analysis related to the costs and benefits on which the criterion of choice is most dependent; to the discount rate; to the rate of inflation; and to the assumptions about probability distribution of variables. The agencies are asked to provide indications of the minimum and maximum values of outcome indicators.
- The standard criterion for the investment decision is the NPV even though one is advised to quote the value of other criteria such as the IRR.
- For the analysis of the distributive effects, one is invited to group together the social group involved according to relevant criteria (e.g. the level of income, the geographical distribution); to clearly explain the adoption of compensatory measures; and to describe the distributive effects.
- The effects that are not quantifiable in monetary terms should be measured with alternative metrics or, if this is not possible, listed and described in qualitative terms.

More recently, sectoral CBA guidelines have been released for assessing investments in the transport (USDOT 2021) and defence (U.S. Army 2018) sectors.

Principal players in the evaluation of public investment projects are the following:

- The Office of Management and Budget (OMB);
- The Congressional Budget Office (CBO);
- The Government Accountability Office (GAO).

The OMB is the key department for the appraisal of public investment as well as the largest component of the Executive Office of the President. The OMB's core mission is to assist the President in overseeing the preparation of the Federal budget and to supervise its administration by the Executive Branch agencies (also known as federal agencies or federal departments). In helping to formulate the President's spending plans, the five OMBs' resource management offices assess the effectiveness of the agency programmes, policies, and procedures, weigh competing funding demands within and among agencies, and work with agencies to set funding priorities. Once the Budget is enacted, resource management offices are responsible for the execution of Federal budgetary policies and provide ongoing policy and management guidance to Federal agencies.[11]

The other two key offices for the evaluation of public investment projects are the CBO and the GAO, which are both within the US Congress. The CBO is an agency set up in 1974 to advise Congress on the approval of the budget. It provides long-term budget projections, prepares economic and financial analyses relative to the alternative levels of expenditure and income for the total budget, and evaluates the macroeconomic implications of the single expenditure programmes (e.g. the effects on Gross National Product of spending on infrastructures). It is an authoritative source of information for Congress and the other congressional agencies (including the GAO).

Finally, the GAO, often called the 'congressional watchdog', is in charge to assist Congress in overseeing the Federal Government, including agencies' stewardship of public funds. It provides support to Congress by:

- Auditing agency operations in order to assess whether Federal funds are being spent efficiently and effectively;
- Evaluating government programmes and policies in order to assess whether and how they are meeting their objectives;
- Performing policies analysis and outlining different options.

GAO widely uses cost-benefit analysis for its evaluation and mentions it in its Cost Assessment Guides as one of the best practices for estimating and managing programmes (GAO 2020).

Although the federal government's use of BCA is well documented, especially as a tool for regulatory decision-making (see Chapter 12), according to White and Van-Landingham (2015), little is known about the extent to which states use it, particularly outside of grant and rule-making. The authors identified cost-benefits reports produced by states (about 1,000) between 2008 and 2011 and assessed them in detail. They found that the states and the District of Columbia were increasingly mandating CBA to address a wide range of policy issues (health, technology, environment, etc.): the number of CBA reports they generated grew over time. Specifically, they found that CBAs were most frequently required for economic development initiatives, health care programs, procurement, and communications and information technology policies. Only 13 statutes required CBA for regulations. They found that most of the studies lacked at least some of the desired technical aspects of CBA, a notable proportion of studies had a reported impact on state policy and budget processes. Interviews across 50 states revealed three primary challenges that limited states' production and use of CBA, such as resource and data limitations, timing problems, and difficulty in gaining policymaker attention and confidence in the methodology and findings.

9.2 The use of cost-benefit analysis in the EC regional policy

The use of cost-benefit analysis for project's appraisal in the EU context has been increasingly demanded in the framework of the Cohesion Policy, which represents an important element of the EU budget.

In 1987, the Commission decided to start earmarking a five years budget for the Cohesion Policy, thus calling for a need to have common guidelines to evaluate and compare *ex-ante* different project applications of Member States.

In 1993 and 1994, the EC regulation governing Structural and Cohesion Fund[12] started to require a CBA, along with other types of information, for projects exceeding a certain financial threshold[13] and asking for EC co-financing. In the same year, the EC commissioned to a team of experts the first edition of its CBA Guide, which was a brief document of 28 pages, without any legal status, just intended to bring some discipline in the applications of Structural and Cohesion Fund interventions which were very heterogeneous. In this respect, a study conducted by Florio (1997) on a sample of major projects co-financed during the period 1988–1993 showed the severe dispersion in some key parameters of CBA, also highlighting the fact that key items of CBA were available only for few applications.

The second version of the Guide (84 pages) was issued in 1997 and presented minor methodological changes compared to the previous edition whilst the use of the Guide was also extended to the appraisal of Cohesion Fund applications. A revised edition of the Guide was released in 2002 and consisted of 135 pages. The legal bases of this new guide laid on a new set of updated regulations for Structural Funds, Cohesion Fund and ISPA applications, providing further and more specific indications on how to carry out the appraisal.

The turning point for the use of CBA took place in 2000s: the enlargement of EU to new countries (mainly from Eastern Europe) allowed to the necessity to have clearer guidance and common rules to select the best projects and facilitate learning mechanisms among players. To allow for timely preparation of projects, the Working Document n.4 – Guidance on the methodology for carrying out cost-benefit analysis was published in 2006 by the EC, leading toward higher levels of consistency and rigor in conducting CBA. It was followed by a new edition of the CBA Guide in 2008. Although it was still considered as a set of suggestions, for the first time the EC had to check whether different applications were coherent with these guidelines (e.g. in terms of working hypotheses and methods used for the calculation of performance indicators). Florio and Vignetti (2011) reported that the Guide – although not having a mandatory nature – has been used by more than 1,000 project teams, which have been involved in the preparation of applications to the EC for assistance under the Structural Funds.

The latest and current version of the Guide was released in 2014 (consisting of 358 pages, European Commission 2014). It offers comprehensive guidance for performing CBA and presents specific recommendations and case studies for five main sectors (transport, environment, energy, broadband, and Research & Development).

Florio *et al.* (2018) reports that CBA has been instrumental in creating a common evaluation framework among EU Member States, in spite of considerable variability of national socio-economic conditions, institutional capacity, administrative and legal specificities. The evolution of the role of CBA for major projects appraisal under the EU Structural Funds, from an initially timid approach to a mandatory framework shows, at the same time, its flexibility and success in increasing the homogeneity in evaluation mechanisms. In fact, the EC Guide has developed consistently over its five editions through an increasing number of case studies and technical refinements.

The *ex-post* evaluations of major transport and environmental projects supported by European Regional Development Fund and Cohesion Policy between 2000 and 2013, launched by DG Regio in 2018 and 2019 (European Commission 2018, 2019a) came out that an improvement in the quality of CBAs has occurred compared to the past programming periods .

The European Commission (2021) confirms that through the application of CBA to major projects over the years, Member States have gained a lot of experience in using the CBA as a tool supporting decision-making on EU-funded investments.

Building on such experience, a more flexible, yet rigorous, framework for project appraisal has been proposed for the programming period 2021–2027: there are no legal requirements for major projects with EU *ex-ante* approval, nor explicit mention of the need to perform CBA. This framework reflects the principle of delegation of approval to the National Authorities. Indeed, the common provision regulation calls for Managing Authorities to establish a methodology and related criteria for selection of operations (Art 73 of EU Regulation 2021/1060) with a major shift of responsibility from EU to Member States, in order to better take into account specific and national project contexts.

The 2014 CBA Guide (European Commission 2014) still remain the main reference document for carrying out the cost-benefit analysis in the cohesion policy framework or under different funds in the 2021–2027 financial perspective. Moreover, DG Regio has recently adopted the Economic Analysis Vademecum (EAV, European Commission 2021) to complement this Guide as follows:

- It introduces the principles of proportionality and flexibility to economic analysis, in particular for projects of a small scale or simple projects for which developing a fully-fledged CBA might be unnecessarily burdensome or costly.
- It facilitates the practical application of the economic analysis methodologies through the identification of established good practices.
- It covers additional sectors deemed to be relevant in the Multiannual Financial Framework 2021–2027.[14]

The box below provides an overview of the CBA approach currently envisaged in the EC framework.

Box 9.3　The CBA approach in the EC framework

The 2014 CBA Guide proposes a six-step approach to CBA, starting from the context analysis and project objectives. More specifically:

i　Step 1 consists in understanding the social, economic and institutional context in which the project will be implemented and in clearly defining the objectives of the project. The analysis of the objectives is meant to verify which of the specific objectives of the EU regional and cohesion policies can be achieved by the project and how the project, if successful, will influence the attainment of these objectives.

ii　Step 2 deals with the identification of the project. A project is clearly identified when: the object is a self-sufficient unit of analysis, thus meaning that no essential feature or component is left out of the scope of the appraisal;

　　indirect and network effects are taken into account adequately;
　　a proper perspective has been adopted in terms of defining the project's catchment area and the relevant stakeholders.

iii　Once the project has been identified, the next step (3) is about providing evidence that the project choice is the best among other feasible alternatives. For each project at least two alternatives could be considered:

- a 'do-minimum' alternative, usually involving minimal capital expenditure for the improvement of the existing infrastructure;
- a 'do-something' alternative (a greenfield investment or a best technology capacity improvement or upgrade).

The calculation of the financial and economic performance indicators must consider the difference between the alternatives and a counterfactual without the project scenario.

The core of the cost-benefit analysis is represented by the calculation of the project's financial and economic performance indicators, respectively with the financial (step 4) and economic analysis (step 5). These steps are in line with the methodology presented in Chapter 4.

In this regard, a simplified CBA approach has been introduced with the Economic Appraisal Vademecum (European Commission 2021) with regard the performance of economic analysis. It consists of the use of financial costs (based on market prices) instead of the economic costs (based on shadow prices). As the calculation of economic costs can be resource-intensive, conversion of market prices is not always necessary in a simplified CBA.

From the EU perspective, every project with an EIRR lower than the social discount rate or a negative ENPV is not worth financing since it uses too much of socially valuable resources to achieve too modest benefits for citizens.

iv   Once the economic performance of the base case project has been calculated, the last step (6), risk assessment, consists of studying the variability of the result as compared with the best estimate previously made. The procedure recommended by the CBA Guide for assessing risks is based on the steps described in Chapter 8, namely sensitivity, probability and risk analyses, followed by the assessment of acceptable levels of risk and the identification of risk mitigation measures and a risk management policy to prevent the project from the identified risks.

Source: Authors based on European Commission (2014, 2021).

Overall, CBA remains the recommended appraisal tool by European Commission (2021) although other tools – such as Least-Cost analysis, Cost-Effectiveness Analysis and Multi-Criteria Analysis – are also suggested in specific circumstances based on sector, project's type, and scale. CBA is considered also relevant also in other context beyond the Cohesion Policy (e.g. most projects applying to the Connecting Europe Facility, under all windows of the InvestEU Fund or in the framework of the preparatory phase of the European Strategy Forum on Research Infrastructures).

9.3 Multilateral development banks

9.3.1 The European Investment Bank

This section discusses how project evaluation is approached within the European Investment Bank, and in particular how the CBA tool is employed in day-to-day operations.

Evaluation at the EIB supports the decision-making process, as far as project investments are concerned, in two crucial and distinct phases of the project's life cycle: the project appraisal stage at the beginning of the cycle, and the *ex-post* evaluation stage at its closure. Although the same can be said for the European Commission and other institutions or governments, Carbonaro (2007) stresses that the EIB has been traditionally attentive to project appraisal, implementation and monitoring. A major issue lies in finding the best way to combine financial market instruments (provided by the EIB) with grants (provided by the EC). Determining the appropriate mix of grants, loans and cost recovery mechanisms requires therefore early involvement and joint cooperation between the institutions, as well as lengthy negotiations with the beneficiaries.

The financial and economic assessment of operations is carried out jointly by the EIB lending departments and the projects directorate, which is responsible for the economic appraisal of projects. Economists at the projects directorate have to perform appraisals in a relatively short period of time. Hence, they rely on standard models and readily available data from the project promoter. Exception is technical assistance operations where the economic appraisal assumes more of a planning role. In these cases, the project promoter is assisted by JASPERS experts (see Box 9.4).

In 2013, the EIB issued a manual presenting the economic appraisal methods that the Bank follows when assessing the economic viability (European Investment Bank 2013). The document is currently under review and a new version is forthcoming. This is, however, not intended as a prescriptive guide, but it gives a review of the methods and the analytical tools for economic appraisal used by the Bank across sectors.

The EIB project appraisal reports usually contain at least the following information:

- definition of the project's technical soundness, innovative technology, risks and mitigation measures;
- proposer's capability to implement the planned project and information on timing and employment generated during the project implementation;
- project proposer's capability to operate and maintain the project, information on production/service capacity, operating and maintenance costs, employment generated during its operational life;
- proof of compliance with applicable EU and national legislations and EIB guidelines on procurement;
- proof of compliance with applicable environmental legislation, as well as information on environmental impact assessment;
- analysis of the products/services demand over the project life, with reference to sector studies;
- information on project investment costs and its detailed components, along with comparison with the cost of similar projects;
- information on financial and economic profitability and related indicators: FNVP, FIRR, ENPV, EIRR, B/C ratio.

Evidence shows that corrections for employment benefits (e.g. through shadow wages) and, more generally, shadow prices are not applied systematically. Main corrections are instead those related to VAT or administrated prices. Whenever indirect effects, externalities and employment effects are considered relevant, they are described in qualitative terms to better qualify the under- (or over-) estimated economic rate of return. In some cases, especially in the transport sector, wider economic benefits generated in secondary markets are quantified and included in the economic analysis. Also, CBA is not carried out for all the projects (multi-sector operations are actually excluded), given the time and information constraints on the Bank services for this type of analysis. In fewer cases, when appropriate, cost-effectiveness (e.g. for Energy, Solid waste management and Water and wastewater) or multi-criteria analyses (e.g. for Education, Health and Urban and Regional Development) are carried out.

Project appraisal reports are submitted to the Board of Directors which eventually takes the financing decision on the basis of the technical feasibility, bankability and socioeconomic desirability of the project.

Beyond the EIB appraisal manual, JASPERS (see Box 9.4) occasionally publishes staff working papers on the application of CBA in specific sector or sub-sector levels. Some, non-exhaustive, examples are provided below for the energy and environment sectors.

The *JASPERS Staff Working Paper on the Calculation of GHG Emissions in Waste and Waste-to-Energy Projects* (Teichmann and Schempp 2013) which presents a methodology for the quantification of GHG emissions saved in projects developing individual facilities or groups of facilities for municipal waste management. It was developed with a view to produce the data basis for the quantification of economic benefits from GHG reductions as required for CBA of waste projects. It is supported a sample calculation model in Excel format that can be used by project developers or their consultants to calculate the GHG emissions of waste management projects.

The *JASPERS Staff Working Paper on Cost Benefit Analysis Framework for Broadband Connectivity Projects* (Mason 2013) which deals practical aspects of the cost-benefit analysis of broadband connectivity projects and includes two spreadsheets that are ready to be used for specific projects.

The *Jaspers Staff Working Paper on the Application of the Polluter Pays Principle in Waste-to-Energy* (Schempp 2011) providing general guidance to deal with the application of the Polluter Pays Principle in order to define an adequate level of the tariffs in waste and waste-to-energy projects as well as to ensure that these tariffs are compatible with affordability constraints.

The *JASPERS Staff Working Paper on the Economic Analysis of Gas Pipeline Projects* (Angelini 2011) deals with the practical aspects of the cost-benefit analysis of gas pipeline projects. The purpose is to present a methodology to evaluate the economic viability of investments in gas pipelines, while the objective is to provide the reader with practical, step-by-step guidance to prepare a cost-benefit analysis to assess the socio-economic and environmental impacts that the project would generate in the country where it is implemented. The document also includes a spreadsheet model which presents a worked example and serves as an indicative template for the economic appraisal of gas pipeline projects.

As far as *ex-post* evaluation is concerned, this is carried out by the Evaluation Unit, which evaluates both public and private sector projects, supported by all types of financial resources, as well as related policies and strategies. The objective of the evaluation is to assess EIB-funded projects with a view to identifying aspects which could improve their operational performance, accountability and transparency.

The criteria to carry out *ex-post* evaluations in EIB are consolidated. As a general rule, the Evaluation Unit designs and performs evaluations with a thematic focus, typically deriving evidence from a sample of single projects implemented in more than one country. Project *ex-post* performance is always assessed according to the criteria of relevance, efficacy, efficiency and sustainability, but typically only in qualitative terms.

9.3.2 The World Bank

The World Bank has been the most important international institution to promote the practice of project appraisal and *ex-post* evaluation over the past decades. An important attempt to conceptualize project appraisal dates back to the 1960s, when Albert

Box 9.4 JASPERS initiative

The Joint Assistance to Support Projects in European Regions (JASPERS) has been established in 2006 as a partnership between the European Commission and the European Investment Bank with the objective to support the project appraisal process in the EU Member States. In particular, JASPERS' roles include providing EU Member States with:

i   advisory support to project's promoter in design, preparation and implementation;
ii capacity-building support, such as strengthening capacity and transferring knowledge about project planning and preparation, climate and environmental proofing of investments, projects' compliance with EU legislation, and any related needs;
iii independent project appraisal support, such as carry out an independent quality review of projects on behalf of Member States, thus preparing the ground for the European Commission's decision.

JASPERS has provided support across two programming periods (2007–2013 and 2014–2020) and specifically supported 2,245 projects, with an estimated investment cost of €275.2 billion. Over this period, the European Commission approved 939 JASPERS-assisted major projects across all mandates, with a total investment cost of EUR 218.1 billion and a grant amount of EUR 117.9 billion.

In the 2021–2027 programming period, JASPERS will extend its role, specifically:

i   it will extend support to Member States through the DG REGIO mandate;
ii it will support pre-accession and Eastern Neighbourhood countries through mandates with the Directorate-General for Neighbourhood and Enlargement Negotiations;
iii it will scale up assistance to transport projects under the Connecting Europe Facility's mandate;
iv it will contribute to URBIS, a partnership between the European Commission and the EIB, which offers tailor-made technical and financial advice to urban authorities and both public and private entities to accelerate and unlock urban investment projects, programmes and platforms;
v   it will cooperate with national authorities to assist them in producing project proposals that meet EU requirements, and in identifying potential projects for assistance.

Overall, JASPERS' advisory function will continue to cover all aspects of project development, horizontal issues relevant to more than one project or country, and other project-related matters such as implementation support and capacity building.

In the 2021–2027 programming period, JASPERS' advisory budget will come from different funding streams: the Cohesion Fund, the European Regional Development Fund, the Just Transition Fund, the Connecting Europe Facility and the Instrument for Pre-Accession Assistance.

> The JASPERS Networking Platform is available since 2012 to complement JASPERS project advisory operations, by addressing specific project preparation issues of horizontal nature, enhancing knowledge sharing activities, dissemination of best practices and exchange of experiences among JASPERS Stakeholders, as well as implementing capacity building activities. Participation is open to JASPERS partners and relevant public authorities from EU member states and pre-accession countries.[15]
>
> Source: Authors based on European Investment Bank (2021).

Hirschman carried out the first in-depth evaluation of a series of World Bank-funded projects. Hirschman's study *Development projects observed* (1967) contributed to fixing project evaluation principles in the international development field. In particular, it shifted the attention from broad development theories to more empiric analysis of what happens at project level. Hirschman supported the idea of implementing a qualitative analysis of projects, taking into account issues such as governance, ownership, side effects etc., rather than ranking them on the basis of a quantitative calculation of economic index.[16]

Yet the Bank's officers considered Hirschman's methodological approach impractical (Alacevich 2012). On the contrary, the Bank's officers were particularly inclined to follow the evaluation practice adopted by the US government and were influenced by a series of studies on cost-benefit analysis published in the 1960s and 1970s. Among these, the Little–Mirrlees volume (issued in 1974), which focused on social cost-benefit analysis and on the use of shadow prices. In the mid-1970s, the World Bank standardized its cost-benefit analysis shadow pricing method on the approach proposed by Little and Mirrlees, restated for World Bank purposes in the book by Squire and van der Tak (1975 – eighth printing, 1995) and referred to hereinafter as the Trade Policy Approach. The appraisal of projects in developing countries at the World Bank has been relying on this approach until the 1990s. Although considerable budget and intellectual resources were spent between 1975 and 1980 on testing and demonstrating its potential for implementation, Trade Policy Social Approach proved impractical to use on every project. It became largely inappropriate for international development investment analyses by the 1990s. The Public Finance Approach proposed by Arnold Harberger – with its aggregate consumption numeraire and constrained optimization shadow pricing system – was then officially adopted.[17]

The textbook/guidelines version of the revised cost-benefit analysis approach is the *Handbook on economic analysis of investment operations*, published in 1998 (The World Bank 1998) updated in 2001 with a different ordering of author and co-authors. The Handbook provides guidelines for the economic analysis of investment operations. Its main recommendations can be summarized as follows:

- Each project design should be compared with other mutually exclusive alternatives and also the 'do-nothing' scenario should be considered. Costs and benefits generated by each alternative should be evaluated through an incremental approach, comparing the expected values with those of the 'do-nothing' scenario.
- For both financial and economic analysis, what matters is future costs and benefits. Therefore, sunk costs (costs incurred in the past in connection with the proposed

project) are ignored. All values should be stated in constant price terms, except where changes in relative real prices can be confidently forecasted.

- Flows should be considered at their opportunity cost values, and then shadow pricing applied. Externalities should be taken into account as far as possible. Discounting for the future is done on benefits, net of costs, usually at a conventional real rate ranging from 10 per cent to 12 per cent. A higher or lower discount rate could be used, as long as a sound justification is provided.
- To be acceptable, a project should have a positive expected net present value (NPV), which should be higher than or equal to the expected NPV of mutually exclusive project alternatives.
- The economic analysis should take into account the possible range in the values of the basic variables and assess the project's outcome with respect to changes in these values. For these reasons, the switching values of key variables and the sensitivity of the project's NPV to changes in the most important variables (considering, e.g. delays in implementation, cost overruns, overestimation of users or revenues and so on) should be assessed.

An overview of the Bank's approach to project appraisal and economic analysis of projects is provided in the Operational Manuals Statement (OMS) – first version dating back to the 1980s (OMS N° 2.20 and OMS N° 2.21) and latest version issued in 2015 (The World Bank 2015). The Operational Manual provides an outline of the project appraisal document (PAD, for investment project financing) or the Program Document (for development policy financing), along with other financial and legal documents, for submission to the Bank's Board of Executive Directors for consideration and approval.

Following the Bank's operational manual, a set of compulsory elements should be contained in the PAD: (i) a description of strategic context, (ii) a description of project's objectives; (iii) project descriptions (costs, financing, lessons learnt in project's design), (iv) implementation arrangements; (vi) analysis of risks and description of mitigation measures; (vi) appraisal summary including results of the economic and financial analysis.

Appraisal reports have been prepared for thousands of projects in all developing countries where the World Bank operates. Over the years they have been widely disseminated and have become a broadly accepted standard format for project evaluation. Similar reports are prepared by the Inter-American Development Bank, the Asian Development Bank, the African Development Bank and other multilateral development institutions.

As pointed by Payer (1982) in its study of the Bank's activity, the implementation of the CBA by the World Bank has deviated from the fundamentals of the theory (the Little–Mirrlees approach). The author states as follows:

> In practice [...] social cost—benefit analysis looks quite different than it does in academic circles. It turns out that the methodology is simply too complicated for use in the field, and 'shortcuts all around' is the rule. The choice of shadow prices, wages, and interest rates, for example, is largely arbitrary. The use of distributional weights is in practice extremely rare. And there is virtually no end to the calculations of externalities, and therefore an enormous range of choice of what to include in the calculations and what to ignore. With a system of shadow prices, anything can be justified.
>
> (Payer 1982: 80–81)

Little and Mirrlees (1990) remarked that in practice the CBA exercises implemented by the World Bank are not in line with the original Little–Mirrlees (1974) methodology. The authors carried out a review of a sample of projects financed during the 1970s and a set of interviews with public officials at the World Bank. On this basis, they drew the following conclusions:

- social prices, using distributional weights, were abandoned in practice;
- no distinction was made between public and private income, or between the use of income, either saved or invested;
- a set of sectorial conversion factors and shadow wage rates was estimated by staff members and consultants for nearly 20 countries, but they were applied in only a few cases;
- the values of non-traded goods were mostly converted to border values by a single standard conversion factor;
- the reorganization of the World Bank's system in the 1980s contributed to the decline of CBA, given that there was not a central project department in charge of promoting the implementation of a common methodology and ensure the quality of project appraisal.

In a report dating back to 2010 (The World Bank 2010a), the World Bank has admitted an inconsistent use of shadow prices or other technical adjustments to capture social benefits and costs. Also, the Bank underlined that cost-benefit analysis of completed projects is hampered by the failure to collect relevant data, particularly for low-performing projects. A general decline in the application of such analysis in all sectors is finally stressed: the percentage of Bank investment projects reporting estimates of the economic rates of return dropped from 70 per cent in the late 1970s to roughly 30 per cent in 2008. In this regard, the Independent Evaluation Group of the World Bank has concluded that more than half of the decline was due to the World Bank portfolio shift to sectors where cost-benefit analysis is more difficult or requires different evaluation methods (Ward 2019).

On this basis, the Bank claimed the need for reforms to project-appraisal procedures in order to ensure effective use of cost-benefit analysis in decision making. Also, it points out the need to revise its policy for cost-benefit analysis in a way that recognizes the legitimate difficulties in quantifying all the benefits deriving from projects, while preserving a high degree of rigour in justifying projects.

The Bank has discussed how to improve the economic analysis of its projects. It is recognized that the economic rate of return approach may still be applied for certain projects, particularly infrastructures, while it may not be particularly suited for evaluating the development impact of investment projects to build capacities and strengthen institutions. Measures to revive CBA in the World Bank have been envisaged, including appropriate staff incentives, standardization of CBA presentations and improved clarity among staff on the use of economic analysis tools for CBA, including EIRR (The World Bank 2010b).

In parallel to CBA, a qualitative assessment of project performance, aiming at complementing the quantitative CBA results, has been developed since the 1990s and formalized in 2002. Such assessment involves assigning a rate to all projects financed and completed[18] on the basis of their performance. This task is carried out by the Bank's operational staff. The rates are then reviewed and validated by the Independent Evaluation Group (IEG) of the World Bank.[19]

Overall, the rating system applied to the projects is effective since it is applied to all projects, thus allowing for comparability and aggregations of results deriving from the Bank's operations. However, a certain level of discretion is related to the project rating exercise and a mismatch usually occurs between the rates assigned by the Bank (self-evaluations) and those revised by the IEG of the World Bank, with the former being generally more optimistic than the latter. In this regard, the Annual Review of Development Effectiveness 2009 (The World Bank Independent Evaluation Group 2009) highlights that the actual rating system needs to become more meaningful (i.e. relying on more relevant indicators) and accurate.

As far as *ex-post* evaluation is concerned, the Bank puts a strong emphasis on evaluating the results achieved through its projects in terms of the impact generated on people and on their needs. A sort of *ex-post* CBA is implemented, basically consisting in re-estimating the economic rate of return of the project following the same methodology adopted *ex-ante*, but revising forecasted flows on the basis of recent information and data on costs and benefits that have already materialized. *Ex-post* analysis, including experience in the EC, is discussed in Chapter 10.

9.4 Further reading

For those readers who would go more in depth in the discussion of the available guidance, studies and reports adopted by international institutions and national governments, this section suggests a small list of references.

The Update of the *Handbook on estimation of external costs in the transport sector*, prepared by the European Commission's DG for Mobility and Transport (European Commission 2019b) presents the state of the art and best practice on external cost estimation. The most recent information for the following impact categories are provided: congestion; accidents, noise; air pollution; climate change; other environmental impacts (costs of up- and downstream processes); infrastructure wear and tear for road and rail. The updated Handbook provides for each cost category: (i) an overview of the latest methods for calculating external costs, their advantages and limitations; (ii) highlights on any differences in approach between the updated Handbook and the original 2008 Handbook; (iii) recommended approach for calculating external costs; (iv) updated recommendations for input values; and (v) updated recommended unit (marginal cost) values.

The *Stern Review on the Economics of Climate Change* is a report released for the British Government in 2006 by a team lead by Nicholas Stern, who discussed the effect of global warming on the world economy. The review (HM Treasury 2006) calculates the economic costs and benefits of actions aimed at reducing the emissions of greenhouse gases in three different ways: (i) considering the physical impacts of climate change on the economy, on human life and on the environment, and examining the resource costs of different technologies and strategies to reduce greenhouse gas emissions; (ii) using economic models that estimate the economic impacts of climate change; (iii) using comparisons of the current and future trajectories of the 'social cost of carbon'.

The *JASPERS Staff Working Paper on the Calculation of GHG Emissions in Waste and Waste-to-Energy Projects* (Teichmann and Schempp 2013) which presents a methodology for the quantification of GHG emissions saved in projects developing individual facilities or groups of facilities for municipal waste management.

Florio (2019) proposes using CBA to evaluate the socio-economic impact of public investment in large scientific projects. Florio's book develops a simple framework for accounting social welfare effects in the research infrastructure context and then offers a systematic analysis of the benefits in terms of the social agents involved. For an application of CBA to research infrastructures see Florio et al. (2016), Battistoni et al. (2016), and Castelnovo et al. (2018). In the same field, the *RIPATH Guidebook on Socio-economic Impact Assessment of Research Infrastructures* (Griniece *et al.* 2020) – funded by the Horizon 2020 programme – provides a model describing the socioeconomic impacts of research infrastructures as well as the pathways according to which they materialize and defines a set of indicators and appropriate methodologies (including cost-benefit analysis) to assess them.

The *Guide to Rapid Pre-appraisal of Urban Wastewater Projects*, developed by the Danube and Black Sea (DABLAS) Task Force in 2011, aims at providing a simple methodology to test the potential viability of urban wastewater projects in the Danube and Black Sea basin. It serves as a platform for cooperation for the protection of water and water-related ecosystems.

Within the energy sector, *ExternE – Externalities of Energy* (European Commission 2005b) is a study whose scope is to value the external costs generated by energy investments on economic activities, referred to both production and consumption. Its methodology provides a framework to transform external impacts that are expressed in different units into monetary values, such as environmental impacts, global warming impacts, accidents and energy security.

A milestone in application of cost-benefit analysis for electricity transmission projects is *Evaluation of an Expansion of the Electricity Transmission System in Mexico* by Glenn P. Jenkins, Henry B. F. Lim and Gangadhar P. Shukla (1999). This paper presents a practical method of integrated analysis in which the financial, economic, distributive and risk aspects of the project are first examined separately and then combined in the overall appraisal.

There are several national CBA guidelines (in addition to the ones mentioned above, such as the UK *Green Book* or the France Stratégie and Trésor Direction Général Guide 2017), for example, the ASEK recommendation for carrying out cost-benefit analysis in Sweden (ASEK 2020), the References and Economic Appraisal Parameters issued by the Irish Department of Public Expenditure and Reform (2019), the official Norwegian Report NOU 2012 *Cost Benefit Analysis* (NOU 2012: 16) and the *Guidance Manual for Cost Benefit Analysis (CBAs) Appraisal in Malta* (Parliamentary Secretariat for the EU Presidency 2017 and EU Funds of Malta 2013).

As far as results of CBA implementation across project samples are concerned, the '*Ex-post* evaluation of investment projects co-financed by the European Regional Development Fund and the Cohesion Fund in the period 2000-2013' (European Commission 2018, 2019a) analyzed the long-term contribution of selected projects in transport and environment sectors to economic development as well as the quality of life and well-being of society. This is discussed in Chapter 10.

Also, the *Cost-benefit Analysis in World Bank Projects*, developed by the World Bank IEG in 2010 (The World Bank 2010a), reviewed the characteristics of the appraisals of 100 projects, as compared with their *ex-post* performances, so as to draw reflections about the use and role of CBA in the World Bank's approach to project selection and financing.

9.5 Summary of Chapter 9

- Cost-benefit analysis is a central pillar of the evaluation systems adopted in the institutions and countries reviewed, although in some cases, for some sectors, it is progressively losing its role in the decision-making process.

- CBA is the main tool suggested for project appraisal in the UK. Shadow prices are not adopted since market prices are usually considered to be already reflecting the opportunity cost of goods.
- France has the longest tradition in evaluating public investments, and particularly infrastructures. The methodology embraces a partial equilibrium approach that sums up the project's direct impacts on users, suppliers and sellers along with indirect impacts generated in relation to different social groups, firms, financial intermediaries, etc. The sum of these components proxies the total welfare change generated by the project.
- In the US, the approach to CBA is founded on the concept of evaluating resources according to their opportunity cost so that market prices may be corrected in order to eliminate distortions caused by taxes, subsidies, externalities and monopolies.
- CBA has been – for years – at the heart of the EU multi-government co-financing mechanism for infrastructure investment. A common, harmonized, project appraisal methodology has been developed by DG Regio with a 'Guide to Cost-Benefit Analysis of EU Investment Projects' (the first version in 1994 and latest in 2014 complemented by the EAV issued in 2021). The core methodological underpinning of the Guide is that CBA requires an investigation of the project's net impact on economic welfare. This is done by converting observed prices or public tariffs into shadow prices, to better reflect the social opportunity cost of the good/service, and taking into account externalities to which a monetary value is given.
- CBA in the European Investment Bank is applied systematically, but with a relatively large degree of heterogeneity in the specific techniques used to evaluate non-market impacts and, in the parameters, adopted to run the model. No corrections for employment benefits are usually applied, nor are shadow prices applied systematically, corrections being mainly related to VAT or administrated prices. Wider effects and externalities, on the other hand, are usually quantified and valued.
- The World Bank has been the most important international institution to promote the practice of project appraisal. The Little and Mirrlees approach, centred on social cost-benefit analysis, was considered as the main reference for project appraisal in developing countries until the 1990s, especially for their use of shadow prices. A general decline in the application of cost-benefit analysis occurred in all sectors between 1980s and 1990s. Since 1990s, the Harberger's approach to cost-benefit analysis has been adopted since it was found more suitable to all sectors and even when markets are missing or incomplete.

End of chapter questions

- What are the main differences between the CBA approaches proposed by the *Green Book* and EC Guide?
- What is the practice of CBA in the USA and France?
- How has the role of CBA changed in the EU context?
- What are the peculiarities of CBA approach adopted by the EIB?
- How has the World Bank approach to CBA been changing over the years?

Notes

1 This chapter is co-authored with Gelsomina Catalano and Davide Sartori.
2 Including (i) Managing Public Money focused on the responsible use of public resources; (ii) Business Case Guidance for Strategic Portfolios focused on the development of strategic portfolios for the realization and management of policies through programmes and projects; (iii) the Business Case Guidance for Programmes focused on the development and approval of capital spending programmes; (iv) the Business Case Guidance for Projects focused on the development and approval of capital spending projects; (v) the Aqua Book setting standards for analytical modelling and assurance and (vi) the Magenta Book focused on evaluation methods.
3 A number of additional supplementary guidance are suggested by the Green Book 2020 Edition on the following topics: (i) assessing effects of subsidies; (ii) competition assessments in impact assessment; (iii) economic evaluation with stated preference techniques; (iv) intergenerational wealth transfer and social discounting; (v) environmental impacts in policy appraisal; (vi) optimism bias; (vii) policy appraisal and health; (viii) optimism bias in transport; (ix) regeneration, renewal and regional development; (x) the economic and social cost of crime; (xi) the orange book (risk); (xii) valuation of energy use and greenhouse emissions for appraisal; (xiii) value for money and the valuation of public sector assets; (xiv) valuing impacts on air quality; (xv) valuing infrastructure spend.
   Supporting documents are available here: https://www.gov.uk/government/collections/the-green-book-and-accompanying-guidance-and-documents.
4 SMART stands for Specific, Measurable, Achievable, Realistic, Time-limited.
5 The targets set out in Public Services Agreements provide a statement of what the government aims to achieve. They set out the government's objectives and priorities for improving public services and the specific results that the government is aiming to deliver.
6 The Commissariat Général du Plan was an inter-departmental administrative body which existed between 1946 and 2006 and was responsible for defining the economic planning of the country, particularly through five-year plans. The initial Plan Commission was appointed by General Charles de Gaulle in 1946. Following the suppression of the French system of five-year plans in 1993, the Plan Commission has been in charge of doing perspective studies and hosting public concertation teams and working groups. In 2006, it was suppressed and replaced by the Conseil d'Analyses Stratégiques. In 2013, it becomes Commissariat général à la Stratégie et la Prospective.
7 The Guide is available both in French and English.
   https://www.strategie.gouv.fr/sites/strategie.gouv.fr/files/atoms/files/fs-guide-evaluation-socioeconomique-des-investissements-publics-04122017_web.pdf.
   https://www.strategie.gouv.fr/english-articles/guide-socioeconomic-evaluation-public-investments-france.
8 Available here: https://www.strategie.gouv.fr/publications/guide-de-levaluation-socioeconomique-investissements-publics.
9 Two methods are suggested to carry out a systematic risk analysis One consists in valuing risk by correcting the value of each monetized component (e.g. time gains, safety, pollution, etc.) for their risk premiums, which will increase the project's value if the advantage component is negatively correlated to GDP, reduce it if the correlation is positive, and let it unchanged if there is no correlation. These corrected components remain discounted with a single "no risk" discount rate. The other method consists in keeping the mean value of each of the components as in usual CBA, but having it discounted with a rate adjusted accordingly to the project's risk characteristics. The discount rate will be increased if the investment's advantages are positively correlated with GDP or, otherwise, decreased.
10 A different discount rate is instead recommended for other types of appraisals, such as cost-effectiveness analysis. In particular, it is suggested to adopt a discount rate that is compatible with the market rate on Treasury bonds. Nominal Treasury borrowing rates should be taken from the economic assumptions for the budget. A table of discount rates based on these assumptions is presented in Appendix C of the Circular and is updated annually. The latest revision (valid for 2012 year) dates back to December 2011 (see http://www.whitehouse.gov/omb/circulars_a094/a94_appx-c/).

11 The Office of Information and Regulatory Affairs, within the OMB, is entrusted by the Clinton Executive Order to review the regulation proposed by the Federal agencies and ensure it has adequately defined the problem that it intends to address; considered alternatives; assessed available information, risks, costs, and benefits (both qualitative and quantitative). The aim is to ensure that the benefits of agency regulations justify the costs and that the chosen approach maximizes net benefits to society.
12 Art. 14, Reg. 2082/93 and Art. 10(5), Reg. 1164/94.
13 ECU 25 million for infrastructure investments or greater than ECU 15 million for productive investments. The financial threshold has been changed over the following programming periods, such as EUR 50 million during 2000–2006 programming period; EUR 25 million in the case of the environment and EUR 50 million in other fields during 2007–2013 programming period; 50 million or EUR 75 million, in the case of operations falling under Article 9(7) of Regulation (EU) No 1303/2013 during 2014–2020 programming period.
14 These include research and innovation infrastructure, renewable energy, energy efficiency, municipal waste management, transport, broadband, water and wastewater, healthcare, information and communication technologies, urban development.
15 For more details, see http://www.jaspersnetwork.org/display/HOME/Homepage.
16 Hirschman's approach can be synthesized as follows:

> How could it be expected that it is possible to rank development projects along a single scale by amalgamating all their varied dimensions into a single index when far simpler, everyday choices require the use of individual or collective judgment in the weighing of alternative objectives and in the trade-off between them?
>
> (Hirschman 1967: 179)

17 As reported by Ward (2019), while "the Public Finance Approach can be used in all sectors and even when markets are missing or incomplete, the Trade Policy Approach can be used only for projects involving private goods in policy-distorted markets and sometimes for quasi-private goods". While the Trade Policy Approach shadow prices are based on international/border prices, the Public Finance Approach shadow prices reflect constrained optimization values – that is, the marginal reduction in consumption values from taking a factor away from its alternative use on the cost side, and the marginal increase in consumption value from adding (avoiding loss of) a consumption unit on the benefit side.

For a more detailed comparison between these two approaches to Cost-Benefit Analysis, see Ward (2019).
18 The focus is on project performance five to eight years after the closure of loan disbursements.
19 The IEG is an independent unit within the World Bank Group in charge of carrying out independent and objective evaluation of the strategies, policies, programmes, projects, and corporate activities of the World Bank Group – which include the International Bank for Reconstruction and Development (IBRD), the International Development Association (IDA), the International Finance Corporation (IFC), and the Multilateral Investment Guarantee Agency (MIGA).

10 *Ex-post* project evaluation

Overview[1]

Cost-benefit analysis (CBA) is a standard methodology for project selection, but it can also be used after project implementation and closure to measure the actual net effects of the executed project. Depending on its timing and scope, it can serve multiple objectives, from accountability to policy learning. Examples of *ex-post* evaluation of large infrastructures carried out by academicians or professionals are available in the literature (among the most influential there is Flyvbjerg *et al.* 2003). Boardman *et al.* (1994) point to the importance of comparing *ex-ante* and *ex-post* CBA of the same project in order to learn from specific case histories. In addition to one-to-one comparisons, an informative exercise is also to compare large samples of project indicators. In this case, performance indicators are signals for decision making, and collecting and comparing performance indicators of different cohorts of projects (grouped by sectors, country, periods, and institutions) can reveal the causes of systematic *ex-ante/ex-post* deviations.

It is not surprising however that *ex-post* CBA is no common practice. First, retrospective evaluations come when all relevant decisions about the project have already been taken and, second, project promoters are not always particularly keen on assessing the actual effects of past projects. In addition, far from being as straightforward as it would appear to be, performing an *ex-post* CBA raises a number of interesting methodological issues.

This chapter explores the practice of *ex-post* CBA, first, by discussing how an *ex-post* CBA should be carried out from a methodological point of view, then, describing how its results can be used in the decision-making process and, finally, by illustrating the actual use and limitations in the international practice. The chapter is organized as follows: Section 10.1 reviews the typologies and purpose of CBA according to the timing of implementation in respect of the project life cycle; Section 10.2 provides an in-depth discussion of the adaptation that the *ex-post* perspective imposes on the standard CBA model; Section 10.3 illustrates international practices in the field of *ex-post* CBA; Section 10.4 presents a conceptual framework about how to interpret the *ex-ante ex-post* deviations of CBA results; 10.5 presents some empirical evidence of some of such comparisons carried out by national and international agencies; 10.6 discusses the value of comparing *ex-ante* and *ex-post* CBA results; and Section 10.7 discusses contractual arrangements and institutional settings that enable an *ex-post* evaluation to be framed within a performance-based mechanism. Some further reading is suggested in Section 10.8.

DOI: 10.4324/9781003191377-13

10.1 Timing and scope of CBA

As mentioned in Chapter 4, time horizon in CBA refers to the number of years for which the inflows and outflows are provided. CBA can be carried out at the beginning of the time period (*ex-ante* or perspective CBA), at the end (*ex-post* or retrospective CBA) or even during the lifetime of the project (*in medias res* CBA).[2] Re-appraisal, or post-decision analysis, carried out after the financing decision and during project implementation is more specific in scope and more immediately useful for decision making than retrospective CBA at the end of the project life. It may be carried out in two different points in time: at the end of the construction phase, or after some time of project operation. The former typology is more a monitoring activity aimed at reviewing the cost, time frame estimations and compliance with the technical requirements in the light of possible adjustments, and it is basically a reappraisal on the basis of updated information and data.[3] The latter is more a learning exercise aimed at measuring the actual effects brought about by the project.[4] This is a rather hybrid typology of CBA, sharing features of both *ex-ante* and *ex-post* CBA (see the next section).

The timing of CBA affects the purpose and nature of the analysis (Table 10.1), from increasing transparency and accountability by giving evidence to the effectiveness of the investments in relation to the stated objectives, to a learning opportunity for both analysts and decision makers. Retrospective analysis may feed into *ex-ante* CBA of future similar projects, for example by reducing optimism bias and providing a systematic collection of relevant project benchmarks. It can also trigger policy learning by verifying to what extent and under which conditions the funded project actually delivered the expected long-term net benefits.

In some specific cases, *in medias res* or *ex-post* CBA may rely on an existing and available *ex-ante* CBA of the same project. This fortunate event may provide additional insights in terms of assessment potentials. Comparing *ex-ante* and *ex-post* or *in medias res* CBA using the same CBA model (i.e. the same assumptions and working hypotheses) can provide a very specific type of analysis and can help identify past errors and the underlying reasons to avoid them in the future. It can also shed light on the efficiency and appropriateness of the decision-making process and the role played by CBA in it,

Table 10.1 Timing and purpose of CBA

Purpose	Ex-ante	After project completion	After some years of project operation	Ex-post	Comparison ex-ante/ex-post or ex-ante/in medias res
Resource allocation	+++	++	+		
Redirection		+	++		
Measure impacts			++	+++	
Policy learning			+	++	++
Accountability			+	++	+++
Feedback on future *ex-ante*			++	+	++

Symbols are used to indicate the more (+++) or less (+) relevant aim of each type of analysis.
Source: Adapted from Boardman *et al.* (2006).

by asking, for example, whether the information set upon which the decision-making process relied was sufficiently complete or whether the assumptions made for future estimates were reliable. Differently from an *ex-post* (or *in medias res*) analysis which aims at assessing the performance of an investment retrospectively, as described in the following section, this comparative analysis implies updating the *ex-ante* CBA model with actual values. This analysis has a clear accountability value and addresses the question 'was the financing decision worth taking?'. The value of this analysis stems not really from the assessment of the actual impact (which in some cases may require adjusting the *ex-ante* analytical framework and to some extent disregarding the circumstances leading to its financing, as specified in the next section), but mainly on the process, and introduces the possibility of challenging the assumptions and working hypotheses made *ex-ante*.

10.2 Performing *ex-post* CBA

This section discusses how performing an *ex-post* CBA[5] when it has the aim of measuring the effects generated by a given investment in a timeframe spanning, completely or for a major component, in the past.[6] In principle, an *ex-post* CBA should be carried out according to the same principles and methods of an *ex-ante* CBA but using historical rather than forecast data. It should also be undertaken from 'today's viewpoint'. The change in perspective ('the knowledge of what actually occurred rather than what is forecast to happen')[7] has many theoretical and empirical implications on how to perform the analysis. For example, it affects the choice of an appropriate reference scenario, the definition of the relevant project 'boundaries', as well as the choice of the key parameters such as the social discount rate or the conversion factors. Projects are not developed in isolation but are embedded in an evolving socioeconomic context, with moving project boundaries, objectives and time horizon. In addition, unless the entire project life has elapsed, the assessment of projects in the middle of their life cycles requires one to deal with the stock of knowledge accrued about the past performance of the project and the external environment as well as to assume likely future development.

   This twofold nature of the analysis implies a number of methodological considerations to fit the standard model into the *ex-post*. For example, the analysis comprises a set of historical data (from year zero until today), together with a set of forecasts of future demand, costs and revenues/benefits (from 'today' until the end of the time horizon), which calls for the adoption of two sets of discounting parameters to deal with a mix of past and future values.[8]

   This section illustrates some technical solutions to deal with this hybrid nature of *ex-post* CBA, drawing from the *ex-post* application of the CBA methodology to a number of *ex-post* evaluation studies carried out on behalf of the European Commission to assess samples of major infrastructure projects co-financed in the period 1994–2013.[9] The in-depth understanding of a number of case histories, in some cases related to flagship projects or projects determining a crucial turning point in the history of the local community benefiting from them, provides a unique evidence base to extract ideas for policy learning and especially for deriving recommendations regarding the causality chain leading to certain long-term effects of investments.

   The following sections provide practical recommendations on how to deal with all the key steps of an *ex-post* evaluation, from establishing the object of evaluation to identifying the reasons behind the success or failure of the intervention. In particular, considerations relate to:

- how to identify a unit of analysis;
- how to choose a counterfactual;
- how to deal with demand analysis;
- how to value the willingness-to-pay;
- how to calculate shadow prices;
- how to calculate the social discount rate.

10.2.1 Project border identification

Project border identification refers to the definition of the proper unit of analysis, i.e. the definition of the study area. The European Commission (2014) states that a self-sufficient unit of analysis is the starting point of the CBA.[10] In an *ex-post* perspective, the identification of the project boundaries (i.e. which infrastructures and operations are included in the project) may be complex and it affects the evaluation result. In selecting the relevant study unit for *ex-post* evaluation, the project should have been realized and should be mature enough to enable the assessment of the effects produced. The question of 'what needs to be compared with what' is a preliminary need that should be clearly stated. This implies also determining the research questions the analysis seeks to answer.

Although common sense would suggest sticking to the project identification made *ex-ante*, when looking at practical cases it is clear that this may not always be consistent. While in the project appraisal phase the object of the analysis is usually related to a financing decision (be it either public, private or a mix of both), after some time the initial investment may have undergone several modifications and expansions which have affected the initial project design for which the original financing decision was taken. Actually, project decisions and implementation are not isolated, but are part of a wider system of public interventions which may determine modifications to the original design, as well as highlighting the need to be physically integrated with other complementary infrastructures. This holds true especially for network infrastructures (typically transport and energy).

What to include and what to exclude from the *ex-post* CBA should be assessed by the analyst on a case-by-case basis. Two broad criteria can be used for the purpose: (i) sufficiency; (ii) pertinence.

The first criterion recalls the rationale that the object under scrutiny should be a stand-alone unit of analysis including all and only the necessary activities to deliver the service (neither a specific phase or component of a project, nor a strategy or a programme of interventions). It can differ from the one of the financing decision. This has two implications:

- If the *ex-ante* financing decision was addressed to a specific phase, or a sub-portion, of a given broader self-standing intervention, the latter should be considered as the subject of the CBA.
- In cases where the financing decision was related to a project that was part of a larger set of independent interventions (a programme) all aimed at achieving the same priority (but all of them being a self-sufficient unit of analysis), the former should be considered as the subject of the evaluation.

The second criterion concerns the pertinence of the investments and addresses the issue of deciding whether modifications, new components, development technologies, etc., introduced later during project implementation, have to be considered as part of the initial investment or not.

A key issue is to what extent limiting or broadening the scope of the initial investment is justified. Some considerations are the following:

- Investments incurred after the project's completion, but not occurring on the original infrastructure, should be excluded from the CBA, even if they affect its performance.
- Investments in the project incurred after its completion should be included in the analysis if pertaining to it and consistent with the original logic of intervention, e.g. for replacement of short lifetime equipment. This holds true also when such investments are undertaken by an institution other than the initial investor, for example, if different public agencies hold responsibilities in the operation of different segments of the same transport network. However, whenever these modifications or new components are of a scale that radically modifies the original project design so as to create a new project in themselves,[11] they have to be considered for all purposes a new project, outside the scope of analysis.
- Investments in the project incurred after its completion should not be included in the analysis if, although pertinent, they pursue objectives functionally disconnected to the original project's rationale.

10.2.2 Reference scenario

Costs and benefits need to be compared against a reference scenario in order to adopt an incremental approach. The with–without project comparison implies *ex-post* to identify a scenario defining – in principle – what would have happened in the absence of the project, i.e. a counterfactual scenario. Usually, as for the *ex-ante*, also for conservative reasons, a 'do–nothing' or 'do–minimum' option is preferred.[12]

The adoption of the 'business-as-usual' as an appropriate counterfactual is not problematic if the project is aimed at improving the delivery of an already existing service for which, in any case, the continuation of the position prior to the project is always plausible given the present circumstances and expectations about its future evolution. For example, in case of the construction of a new transport segment, the reference scenario may consist of continuing to serve the destination with the existing transport modes. In the case of an upgrading of an already existing infrastructure, the reference scenario may consist of maintaining the operations of the conventional service. Again, in a water supply project aimed at improving the reliability of supply, it may consist of keeping in operation the water distribution network as it is, with a minimum quality level of the water service.

However, in the case of projects that are motivated by the need to solve an urgent need which makes the *ex-ante* situation no longer sustainable for internal or external reasons (e.g. under-capacity of the existing system, need to comply with a new regulation), a 'do–minimum' option (i.e. the least-cost project that removes the endogenous or exogenous constraint) is considered more appropriate. As an extreme situation, the catastrophic 'business-as-usual' scenario (e.g. a circumstance implying a dramatic economic loss) is not an appropriate counterfactual since it would lower the threshold for acceptance of the proposed project.

In these cases, the 'do–minimum' (i.e. the technically minimum capital expenditure to ensure compliance) should be carefully defined, so that the counterfactual scenario is both feasible and realistic and does not cause undue expense with no real additional benefits. In practice, however, depending on sectors, the identification of an appropriate counterfactual may lend itself to an intricate debate. For instance, in the solid waste projects there are various technological options that range from a minimum to a maximum, in a scale of possible alternatives that can be adopted to reach the stated objective[13]; thus, a minimum capital expenditure to be used as basis for comparison of costs and benefits is generally identifiable.

In some cases, however, owing to technological constraints, it can be impossible to identify a technically viable minimum solution capable of reaching the stated objective, other than the project itself. In such cases, the 'business–as–usual' option should be considered an acceptable counterfactual, being the only technically feasible basis for comparison of costs and benefits of the project.

The above considerations apply to the *ex-ante* as well as to the *ex-post* CBA. However, some problems are typical of the *ex-post* situation. The choice of a proper reference scenario in the *ex-ante* phase is subject to a high degree of uncertainty about the future evolution of some of the key variables. In an *ex-post* perspective, the uncertainty is partly mitigated by the knowledge of how the circumstances have evolved, as well as how the project reacted to them. For instance, the observed trend in the demand evolution may restrict *ex-post* the possible ranges of reference scenarios potentially deemed feasible in an *ex-ante* perspective. There may be cases where the 'business–as–usual' scenario may have been considered unfeasible in an *ex-ante* phase in light of an expected demand increase, while *ex-post*, the same scenario may be considered acceptable on the observation of an actual decrease or steadiness in the demand trend.

At the same time, however, the choice of a proper counterfactual suffers from the well-known problems in historical reconstruction of the identification of realistic non–actual possible worlds. This relates not only to the choice of the initial situation but also to its evolution and the possible adaptation of the reference scenario to it. While *ex-ante* the future trends are based only on the forecasts of the key variables, *ex-post* possible external shocks should also be considered. Therefore, the point is to what extent the analyst should consider the *ex-post* knowledge about the development of prices and quantities in order, first, to set the counterfactual and, second, to estimate the possible evolution over time of key variables in the counterfactual scenario.

Although the choice of the counterfactual may reflect a so–called 'hindsight bias', which suggests that people cannot ignore a known outcome when assessing an event's likelihood (i.e. the analyst cannot ignore what the actual demand trend is), a realistic scenario is the one deemed feasible on the basis of the *ex-ante* knowledge. For example, the analyst should ignore the effect of an unpredictable exogenous event occurring after the project start when setting the counterfactual scenario. The same effect should however be considered, once the counterfactual is set, in estimating the financial and economic values.

10.2.3 Demand analysis

Demand analysis aims at measuring the need for a service or goods by assessing the current and future demand. CBA in the middle of the life cycle relies on observation of the past use of the given good or service and requires forecasting of expected outflows and inflows from today until the end of the time horizon (or adjusting forecasts made in the *ex-ante* CBA). The analysis deals with the expected demand of users, costs and revenues from today until the end of the time horizon. Future demand of passengers, freights, volumes of water supplied, volumes and composition of wastewater discharged, tonnage and composition of the waste treated, etc. – on which outflows and inflows depend – should be primarily determined on the basis of the indications provided by the service operators and other stakeholders in order to derive the most likely scenario ('base case').

Care should be taken to ensure that forecasts are consistent with available forecasts (on local/global trends, depending on the scope of the project) and the expected performance of providers of alternative services. When indications exist that a substantial deviation from previous performance is expected in the future years, forecasts should be based on new assumptions and models. For example, the opening of new transport axes can strongly affect the future demand of a transport project, for which a 'shock' in the existing demand model has to be considered.

To mitigate the risk error when forecasting the future, the main assumptions should always be tested in sensitivity, scenario and risk analyses, for all projects, so as to have a range of options and calculate the expected performance of the projects (see Chapter 8 on risk assessment methodologies).

10.2.4 Willingness-to-pay

As recalled in Chapter 4, Section 4.7, the total value of benefits and costs associated with a project are given by the maximum amount people would be willing to pay to enjoy the benefits or, alternatively, the maximum amounts that people would be willing to pay to avoid the costs. However, an *ex-post* evaluation offers the opportunity to observe already materialized effects. To provide an example, in a project of drinking water treatment, while *ex-ante* is more likely to use a willingness-to-pay estimate which reflects health benefits, *ex-post* the health benefits may have materialized as a consequence of the systematic provision of purified water and can be directly measured, for example, through saved costs for hospitalization. A similar approach could be adopted for a transport project aimed at reducing travel time for a given journey, by looking, *ex-post*, at the increased business volumes induced thanks to reduced travel times for freight.

The evaluation of materialized effects requires careful consideration of the attribution of the causality link. In fact, the observed welfare change may have been caused by a mix of factors not fully attributable to the project only. Again, in a drinking water treatment, the observed reduced morbidity may be the consequence of a mix of factors, including – but not exclusively – the project. Therefore, the analyst must single out the costs for hospitalization saved due only to reduced morbidity of a water quality-related disease. Similarly, a new road is likely to contribute to the creation of new businesses in its area of influence but other factors may be important too.

Generally, revealed preference approaches are more suitable in an *ex-post* situation than stated preference methods because they infer non-market benefits with data on observed behaviours. Instead, contingent evaluation is based on hypothetical questions on future behaviour, therefore it is more appropriate when assessing the desirability of a policy option rather than assessing the actual effects of it. An *ex-post* contingent valuation would imply gathering opinions based on actual knowledge and direct experience of the effects of an already taken decision rather than a hypothetical guess. However, ignoring a known outcome while recreating a decision is a difficult cognitive task. NOU (2012) points to the relevance of such an issue in the health sector when asking about the

WTP of a health treatment for a disease that the respondents have already contracted. The report stressed how the use of WTP in this *ex-post* situation is unreasonable. In such cases, the contingent valuation could rather address a willingness-to-accept for, say, giving up an already experienced benefit. Another way of accounting for past experience when valuing the economic benefit of a project is to rely on data of user satisfaction.

Comparisons of *ex-ante* with *ex-post* willingness-to-pay provides interesting results (see e.g. Whitehead and Cherry 2007). Experimental results in social psychology show the tendency for hypothetical willingness-to-pay to overestimate real willingness-to-pay. This is usually addressed with corrections in the survey design like, for example, reminding people of the budget constraints or trusting only the most certain respondents.

The *ex-post* knowledge influences the calculations of benefits and costs because perceptions and information evolving over time impact on the actual willingness-to-pay of users. In particular, *ex-post* valuation of non-market effects is based on better knowledge about the factors to which users attribute value. The underestimation *ex-ante* of the willingness-to-pay due to omitted factors (e.g. the inconvenience costs of travel flexibility in case of a fixed link with fixed-scheduled operations) is reported in Bråthen and Hervik (1997). The same was observed by Cho-Min-Naing *et al.* (2000) where the estimation of *ex-ante* and *ex-post* WPT for a Malaria Pf/Pv test kit in Myanmar led to higher post values, with determinants of WTP being the distance and traveling time between the residence of the respondents and the health centre. Similarly, an *ex-post* WTP higher than the *ex-ante* WTP was also found in Uzochukwu *et al.* (2010) for rapid diagnostic tests for the diagnosis and treatment of malaria in southeast Nigeria, with urban dwellers showing higher WTP than the rural dwellers.

As discussed in Heyne, Suessmuth, and Maennig, (2007), better knowledge about the attributes of the goods or services is crucial for 'experience goods', i.e. product or service whose characteristics can be ascertained in a clear way only upon consumption, for which a systematic increase in the *ex-post* WTP as compared to the *ex-ante* valuation is observed empirically.

Box 10.1 Illustrative case: *ex-post* WTP for a sporting event

For example, De Boer *et al.* (2019) measured the deviation of *ex-ante/e-post* contingent evaluation estimates of willingness to pay for a sporting event. Using panel data, the authors can distinguish between *ex-ante* and *ex-post* valuations within the research population as well as between visitors and non-visitors of the event. For the authors, a revealed preference method would not be ideal for sporting events since it would not capture the possible of intangible aspects including non-use values such as happiness or pride. So, they designed a contingent valuation survey addressing the hypothetical bias in the *ex-ante* estimation by incorporate in the questionnaire an extensive and realistic reasoning for contributing to the event (adjusted to the past for the post-event survey). They found an increase of 24.3 per cent of the average WTP before and after. However, while the WTP of people that *ex-ante* would not have paid anything increased significantly *ex-post*, the WTP of people with a positive *ex-ante* value decreased slightly. Moreover, they found that visiting the event and following the event in the media are important determinants of WTP.

Source: Authors.

Overall, empirical results show that the timing of the measurement of WTP affects their value, which is an interesting information for policy makers. More systematic evidence of *ex-ante/ex-post* deviations of WTP would provide a better understanding the determinants of WTP values and thus may shed light on how to improve the users and citizens acceptability of a planned public investment.

10.2.5 Shadow prices

As highlighted in Chapter 3, shadow prices are the solution of the maximization problem of the social planner under budgetary and side constraints. Practitioners usually apply proxy of shadow prices, estimated through different methodological short cuts and aimed at depurating costs and revenues from any element of distortion generated by taxes and subsidies (Chapter 4).

One of the main issues concerning shadow prices and specific to *ex-post* evaluation is that two sets of conversion factors can be developed for the two levels of analysis (past and future). Given the twofold nature of the analysis adopted, as for the social discount rate and other parameters, developing two different sets of conversion factors (one backward and one forward) would be appropriate. This is because the social opportunity cost of a good or service can change over time as a reflection of changes in fiscal requirements, levels of administered tariffs, composition of non-efficient markets, and so on.

For example, when choosing whether to calculate and apply different shadow wages and conversion factors for both the backward period and the forward one, following the analytical framework illustrated in Chapter 5, a general rule is to consider whether major changes in the labour market occurred in the past (in terms of level of unemployment, extent of the informal sector, degree of rurality, level of per capital income and migration flows), and whether it is reasonable to assume that changes are expected in the future. If the labour market is considered to be similar in the past and in the future the same conversion factors can be used for the two periods, otherwise both backward and forward conversion factors are recommended.

10.2.6 The social discount rates

In order to calculate the economic performance indicators from today's point of view, appropriate discount rates should be adopted in the analysis so as to capitalize the cash flows of the past and discount those of the future. The social discount rate is the rate that in *ex-ante* cost-benefit analysis is used to discount the economic flows.

According to the definition provided by the European Commission (2014), 'the social discount rate [...] reflects the social view on how future benefits and costs should be valued against present ones' and it is 'based on estimates of long-term growth potentials' of a given country. For this reason, it is reasonable to have a dual approach when performing a CBA in the middle of the life cycle. This is particularly evident when referring to the social rate of time preference, i.e. the rate at which society is willing to postpone a unit of current consumption in exchange for more future consumption. As illustrated in Chapter 6, one way to estimate the social rate of time preference is based on a formula obtained from the Ramsey growth model, in which the expected growth rate of per capita consumption or other welfare-related variable (e.g. income) enters into the calculation of the social discount rate. Recognizing that economic growth is not uniform between countries, different rates for different countries should be used and, within each country, two rates adopted for future and past values.

As the SDR reflects the opportunity cost of capital from an inter-temporal perspective for society as a whole, it is a variable depending upon the long-run growth opportunities of the country (see Chapter 6, the social time preference method). This is also true for several other shadow prices, which are instead usually treated as parameters in CBA. While treating shadow prices as parameters at any given point in the timeline is generally the most sensible approach, the SDR is too intimately related to growth prospects to ignore structural breaks in the country's growth prospects.

In the case of a significant global economic crisis, such as the one experienced as a result of the Covid-19 pandemic, the pragmatic baseline approach is to acknowledge this fact by using a backward and forward SDR, with the latter being in fact considerably lower than the former. In so doing, two subtle and interesting issues arise. First, it may be the case that the forward SDR is a more realistic estimate of the social opportunity cost of the capital for an economy, as the previous growth rate was unsustainable, for example, because it was inflated by an asset bubble or excessive debt. Hence, one should use a unique rate, the backward one being estimated by the forward one. At the same time, however, this may underestimate the potential of the economy, as the current growth prospects are hampered by structural imbalances which manifest themselves in a high unemployment rate and low utilized capacity. Using the two rates seems a realistic compromise between two possible errors in opposite directions. An alternative would be to use an average SDR. The impact of the different assumptions can be tested by an uncertainty analysis.

A second issue that arises when the SDR forward is lower than the backward is the following. The capitalized backward flows include most of the investment costs, and in initial years will typically be negative. The discounted future flows are made up of mostly operation flows, and are typically positive. A lower discount rate would necessarily increase the Net Present Value of the project. This may seem a paradox, as the crisis has a positive impact on the project performance. This counter-intuitive result is, however, consistent with the fact that the low utilization of real capital in the economy makes it less valuable, hence future flows need to be discounted less.

To sum up, since the SDR depends on economic growth potentials, the timing of an *ex-post* evaluation in terms of the economic cycle affects the value of the discount rates. In particular, worsening of the economic situation in some countries, by influencing the forecasts about the future economic growth rates, affects the results of the CBA through the estimation of a suitable SDR and may generate an increase in the economic viability of the projects. This can be accepted overall, but consideration should be given to the realism of the SDRs adopted, whose values should be always tested in an uncertainty analysis to verify that assumptions based on country macro-economic conditions are not distorting the results of the analysis.

Without entering into a complex debate about to what extent the economic growth reported in some countries is based on a solid economic trajectory rather than asset bubbles, it is worth highlighting here that:

- the choice of the two SDRs (backward and forward) affects the results of the CBA analysis;
- the adoption of country-specific reference values guarantees consistency across projects implemented in the same country;

- given the possible unrealism of the statistical indicators upon which SDRs are calculated, the latter should always be tested in an uncertainty analysis to verify the robustness of the model and, if the results show high sensitivity to the choice made, additional analysis should be carried out to identify the most appropriate values.

10.3 International practice of *ex-post* CBA

Ex-post project evaluation should focus on the comparison of the project's outputs and outcomes with the established objectives in the project design. For infrastructural investments, it is usually carried out two to three years or more after project construction, on a highly selective basis. Governments need, even in a basic way, to ensure that there is some learning and feedback from projects that will create a positive dynamic for improvement over time. Instead, sheer *ex-post* CBA of infrastructure projects, i.e. carried out 20 or 30 years after their financing, is not common practice within financing agencies.

Experience of *ex-post* CBA is a practice in use in some countries (e.g. the UK, France, Norway, and Chile) and institutions (e.g. the World Bank; see Chapter 9 for further details on international practices). From a sectoral point of view, transport is the field in which a more systematic use of *ex-post* practices and schemes have been reported (see Nicolaisen and Driscoll 2016 for an extensive review).

The World Bank (WB) has been the most important international institution to promote the practice of professional project appraisal and reappraisal for many decades (Jenkins 1997) and it required both *ex-ante* and *ex-post* evaluations of all projects in all sectors, mainly based on CBA. As put forward in a WB report, CBA 'helped establish the World Bank's reputation as a knowledge bank and served to demonstrate its commitment to measuring results and ensuring accountability to taxpayers' (World Bank 2010a). However, due to the encountered difficulty in quantifying all the projects' benefits, as well as a shift in the project portfolio to sectors where CBA is less used, during the 1990s the use of CBA in the Bank declined both *ex-ante* and *ex-post*[14] and the practice of evaluation moved away to a more qualitative assessment that complemented CBA results.[15]

At national level, a country with longstanding practice of CBA is the UK. An interesting example of ongoing evaluation of infrastructure investments is the POPE (Post Operations Project Evaluation) system introduced in 2001 by the Highways Agency, now Highway England.[16] It is an ongoing programme of evaluation for road schemes which compares the costs and benefits estimated in the pre-construction phase with the 'outturn' effects recorded after completion. Benefits and costs are identified for a number of overarching objectives, i.e. environment, safety, economy, accessibility and integration. Under this system all roads within the Major Scheme (individually valued over GBP 10 million) are subject to a reassessment one year and five years after completion. For small-scale improvement programmes POPE is done on a sample basis. Every two years the agency carries out an independent review (the so-called 'meta-report') of the whole programme to assess emerging trends. To stress the transparency purpose of this exercise, all the POPE reports and the 'meta-report' are published on the agency website or are available upon request.[17]

In France, *ex-post* assessment is compulsory for transport project since the early 80s[18] and should be carried out at the latest five years of operation, in particular for the largest-scale projects, i.e. exceeding 83 million euros of total costs. For other sectors, feedback practice comparing results to objectives is recommended and in principle facilitated by the existence of specific guidelines. Such guidelines, for example, specify that *ex-post* should use observed historical data rather than forecasts and compare them with target outcome. This has to be done comparing the observed results with those in the absence of investment ('*ex-post* baseline option') and with one or more other possibilities considered *ex-ante*. Not only it should estimate whether the investment has achieved its objectives but also try to establish the reasons for the possible non-achievement. Moreover, *ex-post* assessment should try to identify those impacts that were not or wrongly identified or assessed during the *ex-ante* phase.

Provisions for *ex-post* evaluation are part of the Chilean National Public Investment System (SNI), one of the most advanced and consolidated investment appraisal systems (see Gómez-Lobo 2012). The Planning Ministry (Mideplan) is the central agency in charge of *ex-ante* and *ex-post* evaluation of investment initiatives. *Ex-post* evaluations are carried out in a simplified form on a sample of projects when the construction phase is concluded, to check for the costs and time frame forecasts. In addition, but less common, there are more in-depth *ex-post* evaluations undertaken after some years of project operation, to check the attainments of benefits and costs.

A longstanding tradition of *ex-post* evaluation has also been developed by the Norwegian Public Roads Administration. Since 2006 the Norwegian Department of Public Roads has been keeping records and continuously verifying the actual effects of road projects after construction, according to the principles set out in a dedicated guide. Every year, from three to five projects open for traffic in at least five years are *ex-post* evaluated. The baseline for ex-post assessments are the assessments that backed the decision making process when the funding decision was made (the go-ahead decision). Different *ex-ante* estimates (evolving during the project planning phase) are compared to the actual costs and the focus is on monetized impacts only. The dataset used *ex-ante* is the starting point of the analysis where, using the same software used *ex-ante*, outturn data for costs, traffic, accident and average speed are substituted. A number of studies (see Odeck 2013, 2014; Odeck and Welde 2017; Odeck, and Kjerkreit 2019) about the source of discrepancies in *ex-ante/ex-post* measurements were fuelled by the data collected by the agency, and the forecasting system improved accordingly.

Within the European Commission, attempts to perform *ex-post* CBA of major project investments were made since the years 2000s. A first exercise was carried out on a sample of infrastructure projects co-financed by the Cohesion Fund in the period 1993–2002 (European Commission 2005a) which implemented an in-depth project review to evaluate the efficiency, effectiveness management and impact of 60 selected projects in the transport and environment sectors. Despite problems with data availability and consistency, for the majority of the projects the economic rates of return have been re-computed in order to show the actual socio-economic impact of projects analysed and their deviation from the *ex-ante* forecasts. Later, a sample of projects financed by the Cohesion Fund in the 2000–2006 programming period in EU and former ISPA countries was the subject of an *ex-post* evaluation in order to check, among other matters, the suitability of the CBA methodology and its actual use in decision making.[19] *Ex-post* CBA of ten selected transport (rail and road) and environmental projects (water, waste water and waste management) have been carried out following the methodology illustrated in Section 10.2. Following the same approach, ten transport and ten environmental infrastructures funded in the period 2000–2013 were assessed with an *ex-post* CBA, to draw lessons on how to improve the selection and management of major infrastructure projects.[20]

10.4 CBA and the decision-making process

There is no reason to think that the outcome of a development project will be exactly what was predicted in advance. There are a number of reasons explaining *ex-ante/ex-post* deviations, but the key consideration is whether they are of an endogenous (e.g. errors or inaccuracies incurred *ex-ante* or during project implementation[21]) or an exogenous nature (e.g. change to the external environment caused by the materialization of unpredictable events). Project evaluation cannot do much in relation to external shocks, since they are hardly predictable and outside the control of the project management. However, there is a large scope for reducing endogenous sources of risks that influence project performance. The main idea here is that endogenous forecasting error is a matter of cost, effort or incentive of the *ex-ante* evaluation. Following Flyvbjerg (2007), there are three broad categories of explanations for forecasting errors:

*   technical explanations: errors and pitfalls in forecasting techniques;
*   psychological explanations: planning fallacy and optimism bias;
*   political–economic explanations: planners and promoters may deliberately and strategically overestimate benefits and underestimate costs when forecasting the outcomes of projects.

While standard CBA theory virtually offers a solid framework for project planning and evaluation, the information and incentive structure surrounding these activities is often such that it undermines the credibility of CBA itself.

When assessing the complexity of the stakeholders' maps there could be a recognition of possible conflicting objectives during the decision-making process. The functioning and interests of the different levels of public administration and other stakeholders can make the decision-making processes slow and open to mismanagement, therefore causing delays that influence the project costs negatively.[22] When opportunistic or myopic behaviours are at play, the decision-making process will necessarily depart from the rationale of social welfare maximization. Not only are there different 'bureaucratic lenses', as put by Boardman *et al.* (2018), to watch at the CBA due to organization and political pressures (e.g. competition for scarce funds), but there are often hidden agendas and clear economic or political interests in disregarding and even manipulating the CBA results. For example: central funding agencies may follow an expenditure-driven approach to raise political consensus and have different constituencies from line departments or local administrators; line agencies compete for scarce funds; private companies tend to adopt the cheapest technology to maximize their profit; project analysts may be willing to praise the client rather than critically scrutinize the projects in order to get additional assignments in the future, or not invest in sophisticated and reliable but costly forecasting techniques.

The problems described above may be mitigated or exacerbated by specific features of the institutional setting or the funding mechanism. For example, Florio and Vignetti (2005) and Florio (2007) show the incentives at play in strategic misrepresentation in the EU Cohesion Policy framework, characterized by a multi-level governance setting with information asymmetries and potentially unaligned strategic objectives of the different institutional layers, as well as a funding mechanism designed to co-fund the financial gap in investment costs rather than reward the best performing projects in terms of expected development effects. In this setting, there may be incentives for national and regional authorities to maximize the absorption of funds and promote ready-to-implement, low-risk and consensus-driven investment projects. In addition, since CBA results are used to decide on co-financing and determine the grant amount, there is an incentive to overestimate both investment costs and social benefits.

In the same vein, Gómez-Lobo (2012) illustrates how a consistent framework for identifying, coordinating, evaluating and implementing public investment projects is embedded in Chile's National Public Investment System (SNI), including, among others, (i) a legal requirement to evaluate all investment initiatives; (ii) a system of 'checks and balances' which separates the institution that reviews and approves the appraisal of projects from the institutions promoting projects; (iii) multistage evaluations with various filters and supervisory and quality control mechanisms; (iv) a system of norms, procedures and methodological support, including the centralized definition of social prices; and (v) *ex-post* evaluation.

10.5 Interpretation of variability of *ex-ante* vs *ex-post* or re-estimated internal rates of return

Data accessibility is often quite limited for projects funded by public agencies. Most projects that are eligible for public or government-sponsored funds will be approved only if they pass some kind of test (legal, administrative, financial, socio-economic, political) and the information concerning this process will be recorded by the financing institution. However, the incentives to standardize data, collect them regularly and make them available to the public are apparently weaker in most governmental bodies. In this way, a wealth of potentially useful knowledge is substantially unavailable to researchers and practitioners.

In order to extract the maximum informational content from the rates of return of past projects, the values of financial and economic rates of return, both *ex-ante* and *ex-post* (thus four sets of data, as shown in Figure 10.1) are needed for each project, along with a sector and country breakdown, years of approval and completion of the project, scale indicators (total investment and labour costs and the level of employment)[23] and information on the co-financing rate, if any.[24]

The systematic comparison of *ex-ante* with *ex-post* rates of return on large project portfolios can highlight differences and similarities across projects, investment sectors, countries, and financing institutions. But how to interpret the variability of *ex-ante*

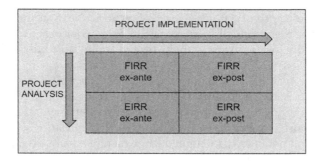

Figure 10.1 The four project rates of return.
Source: Authors.

internal rates of return (either financial or economic) and *ex-post* or re-estimated internal rates of return?

The observed average values of the rates of return of projects approved by an institution are the result of a long chain of selection processes. Starting from thousands of potential candidates, only a selection of received projects will be considered, a part of which will be approved, and for just a fraction of these will the rates of return be recorded. Thus, when using statistics on projects' rates of return, the nature of the sampling process that created the observations must be considered and understood.[25] Whatever the reasons for different sample average values, one has to check whether the averages reflect different populations of approved projects, for example, across countries or sectors.

The conceptual relationship between rates of return and the more general, but vaguer, issue of performance in a formal setting is presented (on this issue, see also Isham and Kaufmann 1999).

The basic idea behind such an analysis is to consider projects' rates of return as signals for decision making, determined by unknown variables, including true structural parameters and measurement error. Thus, data on rates of return may be considered as the result of experiments, and should be treated accordingly. One key issue is how to distinguish between variations in rates of return determined by project-specific factors (including forecasting or data collection and elaboration errors) and sector-specific or source-specific factors, related to the financing institution. Further analysis may then distinguish between structural economic factors and systematic bias at the appraisal or evaluation level within each organization. The variability of rates of return is the starting point for a more in-depth review of the appraisal process as advocated by Gramlich (1994).

The four internal rates of return for any project are thus estimated (*ex-ante*) and observed (*ex-post*) financial rate of return and estimated and observed economic rate of return. Some simple conceptual relationships among these project performance indicators can be highlighted.

A preliminary remark is that the observed internal rates of return are indeed project-specific. However, they depend upon parameters, namely prices (the observable prices in financial analysis and shadow prices in economic analysis)[26] and quantities. These parameters, in turn, are related to the project's environment and the project technology. In fact, prices and the technologies available to the investor change with industries, countries and other economic and structural factors.

Moving to the relationship among the different project performance indicators in this framework, one may expect the following observations to be true.

First, for the project population or for a large unbiased sample of optimally selected projects by a single development agency, *ex-ante* and *ex-post* internal rates of return, either economic or financial, should be correlated. On average, positive and negative deviations from the *ex-ante* return compensate each other (to a certain extent), and the *ex-ante* return is a predictor of the *ex-post* return, *ceteris paribus*, i.e. after controlling for the environment, sector and other project characteristics.

Second, under a systematic optimism bias, *ex-post* economic internal rate of return should be lower than *ex-ante* economic internal rate of return. Hence, appropriate *ex-ante/ex-post* comparisons allow one to measure the extent of this optimism bias and assess, for example, whether forecasting errors are evenly dispersed across the project portfolio or whether they occur more frequently in some countries and sectors.

Third, a portfolio of approved projects (unconstrained by capital rationing) comprises all the projects with an *ex-ante* rate of return that is higher than a required rate of return. An organization may, however, assign different weights to country/sector-specific factors or have sector preferences. While in principle the planner or the development agency should have no preference over countries or regions (e.g. because the shadow prices in economic analysis include the distributional characteristics of goods) or industries (e.g. because all externality impacts are included in project returns through the shadow prices vector), a systematic bias often reveals implicit institutional preferences.

Fourth, in general the variability of *ex-ante* economic rates of return should not be greater than the variability of financial rates of return. When their standard deviation is considered and this information is compared, it should not be expected that systematically economic analysis increases variability of returns as compared with financial analysis. In fact, the transition from observable (distorted) prices to economic prices may be neutral or even decrease this variability, for example, because price discrimination, monopoly prices, different duties on imported goods are wiped out by the standard rules for shadow pricing. If an increase of standard deviation of returns from financial to economic analysis is observed, this may be the starting point for understanding whether cost-benefit analysis at project level has mixed up the results (for instance with inconsistent shadow pricing, as often happens in practice).

10.6 Comparison between *ex-ante* and *ex-post* economic rates of return

Though no common practice, systematic assessments of project portfolios are available. Meta-reports are prepared every two years within the POPE scheme described in Section 10.3. Summary tables are also available, reporting the values of expected and actual impacts by categories (carbon emissions, safety, traffic), and the first year rate of return is provided. Although the scheme is about calculating the impact of the project results, meta-reports are actually used at the strategic level to improve the robustness of the decision-making process.

The same kind of reviews is available for the Norwegian Public Road Administration. On the basis of a survey of *ex-ante/ex-post* comparison, Kjerkreit and Odeck (2009) and Odeck and Kjerkreit (2019) found that the accuracy of *ex-ante* analysis in Norway had increased since transport models were improved. Contrary to the expectations of optimism bias, the most recent study comparing *ex-ante* and *ex-post* CBA for 27 Norwegian projects reveals that *ex-ante* NPVs are lower than *ex-post* ones by 50 per cent on average and that the traffic level and traffic growth rates are also often underestimated *ex-ante*, by a higher percentage of the underestimation of construction costs, which ultimately lead to an underestimation of net benefits.

On the incentives for increased accuracy, Welde and Odeck (2011) argue that as long as the road financing shifted from a toll-free to a tolled system, opening the door to potential investors holding financial interests, an increased scrutiny on the accuracy of financial forecasts by credit rating agencies provided an incentive to perform systematic *ex-ante/ex-post* comparisons to improve the reliability of *ex-ante* forecasts. Interestingly, this is confirmed also by Bain (2009), arguing that toll road forecasts are subjected to more rigorous, multi-party scrutiny than traditional public sector (toll-free) road forecasts.

Re-estimated economic rates of return (REIRR) are available for the WB. They are based on a new appraisal of the project's cost and benefit estimates some years after the approval of the project. In spite of these limitations, the comparison of WB EIRR–REIRR data may still be of general interest. By analysing the standardized wedge [(REIRR − EIRR)/EIRR] as a relative measure of the initial forecasting error by the project appraisers, in a sample of projects approved in 1988–1997, Del Bo and Florio (2010) found no statistically significant differences between EIRRs *ex-ante* and *ex-post*, while for the same do not apply to other groups of projects.[27] When looking at *ex-post* returns at sector level, the highest error is with industry, the lowest with roads. The latter might be influenced by the fact that projects in the roads sector are more standardized and inherently less risky. However, the distribution of forecasting error across sectors shows in general large differences that may need specific inquiry. Finally, when looking at *ex-post* returns against the industry EIRR benchmark, a clear and consistent ranking across sectors appears: the most socially profitable projects in the WB portfolio are roads and highways (twice the return of industry), ports and airports, energy distribution and telecommunication infrastructures: all these sectors show higher returns than industry projects. Railways show returns close to those of industry, energy production shows returns decreasing over time, while water is confirmed to be, it seems, a low-return sector. Again, these results may be signalling that either the portfolio is sub-optimal in terms of the maximum rate of return, or, and more probably, that EIRR calculation fails in some cases to capture important externalities, or is based on *ad hoc* sectoral assumptions.

The average difference between the EIRR and the REIRR at the WB in more recent years is diminishing, so much that in the most recent (and smallest) sample there is virtually no statistical difference between the two values. This finding is corroborated by a more recent review of WB use of CBA (World Bank 2010b), highlighting an increase in the average *ex-ante* calculated ERR and a diminishing wedge with the recalculated ERR. Among the possible explanation there are a recalculation bias (projects with low ratings by the Independent Evaluation Group of the World Bank are less likely to have their ERRs recalculated) which points to a lack of a proper incentive to carry out and use the results of *ex-post* CBA, as indicated at the beginning of the chapter. As indicated in World Bank (2010b), the decision-making structure and related incentives, influences the quality and accuracy of cost-benefit analysis. In the case of the WB, it was noted that there are few positive incentives are in place to invest time and energy to carry out accurate cost-benefit analysis when there is high pressure to use CBA results to confirm a decision already taken.

This finding is in line with those of the recent *ex-post* evaluations of major projects funded by the European Regional Development Fund and the Cohesion Fund of the European Commission (2018, 2019a). The findings point to a strong case for carrying out CBA for designing and selecting the most promising projects on the basis of the assessment of their expected net social benefits, but only if it is properly carried out. In fact, the practice in use in the period under assessment was often to select and implement the projects according to political considerations and use the CBA as a sort of 'ex-post rationalization' of a decision already taken. The fact that the CBA was a mandatory requirement when applying for co-financing and that the CBA results are used for calculating the EU grant, emphasizes a 'tick the box' approach and provides an incentive for strategic misrepresentation in the CBA results. This issue is well known in the literature (see e.g. Flyvbjerg 2007; Boardman *et al.* 2018). The next section explores it further and discusses its implications for the decision-making process.

10.7 CBA and incentives

When *ex-post* evaluation is part of the project cycle and the decision-making process, it can improve the *ex-ante* appraisal and project management by speeding up the process and taking corrective actions, thus enhancing a result-oriented behaviour. Besides helping to make more realistic estimates in the future, *ex-post* evaluation can be even more useful as a means to take corrective action and to build confidence in the appraisal process by introducing the concept of linking the access to funds to the conditionality of achieving the targets initially set. This is achieved by formalizing the process of deciding on the allocation of funds in such a way that availability of the funds is conditional on the achievement of results, as described by a set of performance indicators.

Ex-post CBA is more effective if incentives at different points of the decision-making process are introduced to promote rationality in the *ex-ante* analysis of the project's future performance, strengthening budget constraints and financial responsibilities. The incentive mechanism should be designed in such a way that a bond between whoever takes the decision and whoever will be responsible for it in the long term is ensured.

The concept of conditionality on results, in a situation of asymmetric information, stems from incentive theory following Laffont and Tirole (1993) and several other contributions including Laffont (2005). *Ex-ante* project returns are generated by a process whereby there is some uncertainty and asymmetric information between the funding agency and the project proponent. This theory deals with the study of the mechanisms that push to act in a certain direction which would not be undertaken in the absence of some incentives.

The incentive systems are tools for monitoring efficiency and reducing the risk of moral hazard. Within this analytical framework, Cella and Florio (2007) propose an investment game with *ex-ante* and *ex-post* evaluation, with a simple principal-supervisor-agent game model between a supranational player (the principal), such as the European Commission (EC), a regional government (the supervisor) and a private firm (the executing agency). They show that the role of providers of additional information, both *ex-ante* and *ex-post*, is crucial to avoid the appropriation of undue private rents in grant calculation and to counteract the inefficiencies caused by asymmetric information. To do so, however, the contract between the EC should establish a formal mechanism of rewards and punishments. See also Florio (2007) and Florio and Sartori (2010).

Providing the right incentive and promoting a systematic use of *ex-post* data are among the four steps of reforms advocated also in Flyvbjerg and Bester (2021) to address the CBA fallacy, i.e. the situation where individuals behave as if cost-benefit estimates are accurate when in fact they are largely biased. In order to fix the situation, the authors suggest (i) systematic use of de-biasing methods, i.e. adjustments made on *ex-ante* forecasts on the basis of information about actual estimation errors in previous investments based on *ex-post* studies; (ii) better incentives for accurate *ex-ante* CBA; (iii) independent audits separated from political motivations; (iv) adaptation to the current (democratic, non-technocratic and non-expert) decision-making process.

10.8 Further reading

On the comparison *ex-ante* and *ex-post* of WTP, Heyne *et al.* (2007) carried out an analysis of *ex-ante/ex-post* comparison of WTP of the 2006 Football World Cup in Germany, while other studies on *ex-post* WTP for sporting events were not carried out by the same authors and using the same methodology, so they may be poorly comparable (see for example the Atkinson *et al.* 2008; Walton *et al.* 2008; British Broadcasting Corporation 2013 for the 2012 London Olympic game). On the determinants of WTP, López-Mosquera and Sánchez (2014) explores the cognitive and affective determinants of WTP and in particular show how positive cognitive and emotional past experiences can raise the economic valuation of the conservation of a natural area.

There is an increasing interest in *ex-post* evaluation of projects and a growing literature on empirical evidence of specific projects. In the transport and environment sectors, it is recommended to look at the ten intermediate case-study reports developed in the framework of European Commission (2018, 2019a).

The results of *ex-ante* and *ex-post* analyses may differ and identifying the drivers of this wedge is an important task, as suggested in the chapter. Percoco (2012) suggests a different way, with respect to the methodology presented here, of approaching this issue. The author evaluates the accuracy of estimates on which project appraisals are based by testing their rationality. Rationality is defined as an alignment of *ex-ante* and *ex-post* economic rates of return. The empirical methodology is developed and tested by considering 802 World Bank projects in emerging countries. This exercise is based on the definition of a loss function that minimizes the difference between the *ex-ante* and *ex-post* economic rates of return. According to the author, the empirical results suggest, given the information on EIRR, REIRR and the information available at the time of the *ex-ante* appraisal, that rationality is indeed a feature of World Bank project appraisals, as *ex-ante* rates do not differ much from *ex-post* rates.

The paper by Boardman *et al.* (1994) provides an interesting discussion on the significance of comparing *ex-ante* with *ex-post* CBA, arguing that the informative value of such an exercise is different from simply performing an *ex-post* CBA. In fact, only through this comparison is it possible to assess the value of CBA in terms of a decision-making tool. In addition, it categorizes four types of errors in CBA studies. For a systematic discussion of the reasons for deviation of *ex-ante/ex-post* performance in the transport sector, essential contributions are by Cantarelli *et al.* (2010), Flyvbjerg *et al.* (2003) and Mackie and Preston (1998).

Regarding international experience in the field of *ex-post* CBA, the reader can refer to the websites of the POPE initiative (http://www.highways.gov.uk/our-road-network/post-opening-project-evaluation-pope/) where the *ex-post* evaluation of individual schemes as well as meta-evaluations of a sample of projects are available. In addition, on the lessons learned from the Norwegian experience we recommend Odeck (2013, 2014), Kjerkreit and Odeck (2009), Odeck and Kjerkreit (2019).

If there is an interest in deepening the understanding of the role of evaluation in the decision-making process, an interesting illustration is presented in the World Bank paper by Rajaram *et al.* (2010), who propose a framework of analysis to identify the specific weaknesses in project management systems that contribute to poor outcomes and suggest appropriate institutional and technical remedies that could correct such failures. Thus, a number of key 'must-have' features of a well-functioning public investment system are formulated.

10.9 Summary of Chapter 10

*   CBA can be performed at different points in time of the project time horizon. Accordingly, it can have a different nature in scope and rationale, ranging from resource allocation to project restructuring and to policy learning and provision of feedback to the *ex-ante* stage.

- *Ex-post* or mid-term CBA implies having a backward-looking perspective. While in principle this means using actual instead of forecast values on the same methodological approach of the *ex-ante* stage, in practice there are a number of considerations that are typical of the *ex-post* perspective.
- The definition of the unit of analysis requires isolating the original project investment and including in the analysis the subsequent investment strands aimed at expansion and upgrading only if pertinent to the original project and not constituting an independent, additional project.
- The reference scenario implies choosing an appropriate counterfactual and providing a hypothesis on its hypothetical evolution over the years, including the reactions to possible endogenous shock that have actually materialized during project implementation.
- Demand analysis stems from the observed past trend and requires one to assume whether the future trend would evolve inertially or with a significant deviation from the past trend.
- Considerations should be given to the most appropriate method to estimate the willingness-to-pay of users in an *ex-post* perspective. In addition, reasons for deviations of *ex-post* willingness to pay to *ex-ante* values should be duly acknowledged.
- In the economic analysis key parameters can change over time as a reflection of changes in fiscal requirements, level of administered tariffs, composition of non-efficient markets and so on.
- Given the twofold nature of the analysis (past and future), developing two sets of parameters (backward and forward) is appropriate. However, while it is justified for social discount rate, such an approach for conversion factor of goods and services in a context of the EU-15, where markets can be considered relatively stable, would produce negligible results.
- Evidence from international practice shows that *ex-post* CBA is not as widespread as its potential role in terms of policy learning would recommend. The WB is a leading institution in this respect; other relevant experiences are the POPE scheme for road projects in the UK and the Norwegian Authority for Roads, which has introduced compulsory *ex-post* CBA since 2005 on all the road schemes.
- Projects' financial and economic rates of return, both *ex-ante* and *ex-post*, contain useful information for understanding how the CBA results may vary depending on a number of factors, such as investment sectors, financing institutions and the time of project's approval.
- The informational content of projects' rates of return is valuable and is needed for cost-benefit analyses. Sectors, countries and funding institutions explain much of the variability of these rates. Therefore, the collection of standardized and comparable *ex-ante* and *ex-post* data must be advocated and promoted.
- Evidence from *ex-post* evaluation and comparison of *ex-ante/ex-post* results, either for one-to-one or for an entire project portfolio, is a very informative exercise that can shed light on possible biases in the *ex-ante* and improve therefore their quality in the long-term.
- Mechanisms to generate better evaluation and planning revolve around the proposal that information on *ex-ante* and *ex-post* project returns be accumulated within the institutions and be used to establish benchmarks and incentives for best performers.

End of chapter questions

- Which are the main reasons of observed *ex-ante/ex-post* deviations of CBA results? Discuss the possible measures suggested by the literature to mitigate potential forecasting biases and improve CBA accuracy.
- If a complex infrastructural project has been implemented in three different phases with three different financing decisions, would you carry out three different *ex-post* CBA for each of the phases or one single CBA for the individual project? If, after the implementation of the third phase, a further expansion of the infrastructure has been necessary to accommodate the excess demand, would you consider the additional capacity in your *ex-post* CBA? Would it be justifiable to carry out a post–approval CBA of the first phase, after five years of construction, if the last phase is still not complete?
- An investment aimed at introducing an augmented reality solution to improve the experience of a museum visit is *ex-post* evaluated using a CBA. A contingent valuation survey is carried out to museum visitors to measure the willingness to pay for this cultural experience and the results are compared to those of a similar survey carried out *ex-ante*. How would you expect the *ex-post* willingness to pay to be as compared to the *ex-ante* estimation? Which aspects are likely to influence the results of such a survey?
- An airport expansion is implemented during a period of positive global economic prospects and expected increase in the demand of air traffic, and *ex-post* evaluated just after the Covid-19 pandemic. How would you expect the value of the SDR adopted for the *ex-post* CBA, both backward and forward, to be in respect of the one adopted in the *ex-ante* CBA, the rest being equal? How would you mitigate the possible bias in the *ex-post* CBA related to its timing in the economic cycle?
- If a project with a high *ex-ante* ERR experiences slight cost overruns due to implementation delays but a rapid take up of the service after the construction, at a level which is well beyond the forecasted demand, how would you expect the *ex-post* ERR, ceteris paribus? And what if, to accommodate the increased demand, additional unforeseen capital investments are necessary on top of those originally planned?

Notes

1 This chapter is co-authored with Silvia Vignetti.
2 See Boardman *et al.* (2018).
3 An argument against using the first year of operation as the basis for *ex-ante/ex-post* comparison is the concept of demand ramp–up (demand depends on variables that might take years to spread through the system).
4 As HM Treasury (2020a) puts it, evaluation can be 'informative' during implementation allowing improved management and adaptation of implementation, or 'summative' after implementation providing an assessment of the outcome of the intervention.
5 For the sake of conciseness, the section refers only to *ex-post* CBA but it holds for *in medias res* CBA as well.
6 This section does not apply to comparative types of CBA that compares an *ex-ante* CBA with *ex-post* CBA or in medias res CBA of the same project. In this case, the *ex-post* CBA should be performed exactly as an *ex-ante* CBA but using historical rather than forecast data.
7 HM Treasury (2003).
8 The mix of historical and forecast data also affects the choice of the prices to be used, i.e. whether to use nominal (current) or real (constant) prices. A standard approach to be adopted

is to use constant prices. This requires the following adjustments: (i) data from today onwards should be estimated in real terms (today's prices, no inflation); (ii) data up to and including the last reference year are historical and therefore expressed in nominal terms. In order to align the two levels of analysis, and to have only one price basis, the historical prices should be reflated so as to turn them into prices at today's *numéraire*.

9 See in particular the '*Ex-post* evaluation of investment projects co-financed by the European Fund for Regional Development (ERDF) and Cohesion Fund (CF) in the period 1994–1999', carried out by CSIL – Centre of Industrial Studies (Milan), in partnership with DKM, Economic Consultants (Dublin), on behalf of the European Commission, Directorate General Regional Policy; the 'Ex post evaluation of major projects supported by the European Regional Development Fund (ERDF) and Cohesion Fund between 2000 and 2013' Lot 1-Transport, carried out by CSIL, Centre for Industrial Studies (Italy) – in partnership with Ramboll Management Consulting A/S (Denmark), Significance BV (The Netherlands), and TPLAN Consulting (Italy) and Lot 2 – Environment, carried out by CSIL, Centre for Industrial Studies (Italy) – in partnership with Ramboll Management Consulting A/S (Denmark). Cost-benefit analysis was the key evaluation tool, but it was complemented by other more qualitative instruments, and the final assessment relied on a wide array of evidence combining primary data collection (face-to-face interviews with stakeholders and policy makers) as well as secondary sources such as official documents related to the financing decision, scientific publication and reports, press and other media.

10 As the European Commission (2014) puts it, a project is defined as a 'series of works, activities or services intended to accomplish an indivisible task of a precise economic or technical nature'.

11 For example, a new capital expenditure for a port extension of a scale that doubles the existing port capacity.

12 The 'do-nothing' consists of a continuation of the position prior to the project. In the case of an upgrade of an already existing infrastructure, this means keeping in operation the system as it was before the project's realization, including incurring appropriate operations and maintenance costs. For this reason, it is also called 'business-as-usual'. The 'do-minimum' consists of the least-cost solution involving a minimum capital expenditure to address – at least partially – the stated objectives.

13 For example, EU Directive 2008/98/EC (known as the Waste Framework Directive) introduces a five-step waste management hierarchy in which prevention, i.e. reduction of waste generation, is to be considered as the favoured option, followed by re-use, recycling and other forms of recovery, including energy recovery through incineration and composting, with disposal to landfill as the last resort management system.

14 The percentage of projects with an *ex-ante* CBA dropped from 70 per cent to 25 per cent between the early 1970s and the early 2000s, and the decline is even sharper for *ex-post* CBA (World Bank 2010b).

15 Performance ratings are provided by the Bank's operational staff and validated by the Independent Evaluation Group to assess (i) how the achieved outcomes of a project compare against those set *ex-ante*, (ii) sustainability of results, and (iii) the impact of institutional development. Project ratings range from highly satisfactory to highly unsatisfactory.

16 See https://www.gov.uk/government/collections/post-opening-project-evaluation-pope-of-major-schemes (visited 08 October 2021).

17 For example, the most recent meta-report can be found here (last visited on 19th October 2021): https://assets.publishing.service.gov.uk/government/uploads/system/uploads/attachment_data/file/497241/POPE___Meta_2015_Final_210116_-_FINAL.pdf.

18 In line with Act no. 82-1153 of 30 December 1982 bearing on transport guidelines.

19 See European Commission (2012).

20 See European Commission (2018, 2019a).

21 Flyvbjerg (2007) calls it the 'survival of the unfittest', that is to say, it is not the best projects that are built, but the most misrepresented ones.

22 There are 'guardians' (i.e. central budgetary agencies which tend to have a bottom-line budgetary orientation, with controllership or accounting functions within line agencies) and 'spenders' (i.e. line departments managing expenditure programmes, with a tendency to regard expenditures on constituencies as benefits rather than costs) as opposed to analysts.

23 Although the rates of return used in this chapter are scale invariant.
24 For example, Florio *et al.* (2018) uses a dataset of *ex-ante* rates of return of around 1,000 major project applications, submitted during the period 2007–2013 by 22 European countries.
25 For example, the World Bank invests in Africa, while the EU and the EBRD do not. Africa may be a difficult region for project implementation, for a number of reasons. Thus expectations and risks of the World Bank portfolio will be influenced by its country composition.
26 Only very large projects are non-parametric in prices. This case is here ignored since it has less practical relevance.
27 This is a rather interesting result that may need some interpretation. The 1988–1997 sample is more recent and smaller than the other ones. Is there a trend towards better predictability of project returns, e.g. because of greater macroeconomic stability? A larger sample may be necessary to discuss the conjecture.

11 The use of cost-benefit analysis in regulatory policy

Overview[1]

Globally, the adoption of cost-benefit analysis (CBA) to assess the impacts of regulation has become a subject of increasing interest over the last decades and is commonly recognized as a key practice for good governance. Regulations are among the core fields of application in present-day uses of CBA.

Even though theory and practice for project appraisal have a longer and more robust tradition, CBA today represents a pillar of regulatory impact assessments (RIAs) as well. Despite a similar purpose and theoretical justification, however, the assessment of costs and benefits of regulation differs from project appraisal. This chapter offers an overview of the use of CBA in regulatory policy, presenting its principal historical developments and methodological tenets, and sheds light on the practices that have taken shape over time in different institutional contexts.

After a presentation of the main characteristics of CBA for RIA (11.1), a review of international practices is presented (11.2), focusing on three experiences – the United States, the United Kingdom, and the European Union – that can safely be considered among the most established ones on the international landscape, despite their differences. Other national examples, less frequently analyzed in the literature but no less interesting, are presented as well. The final section investigates general methodological limitations and practical challenges, explores recent trends, and concludes by framing the use of CBA for RIAs in the wider perspective of good governance (11.3).

11.1 Adopting CBA for regulatory impact assessment: rationale and main elements

The RIA is an analytical approach for evaluating the effects of policy measures and regulations. Its purpose lies in supporting decision-making processes by offering evidence about the need for regulatory or policy intervention, and about the socio-economic impacts expected to be generated by the available policy options on different categories of stakeholders. At a minimum, an RIA typically offers a detailed description of the policy problem to be addressed, the objectives of the proposed intervention, the practical options to achieve those objectives, and an evaluation of costs and benefits which contributes to identifying the policy option that maximizes social welfare. Usually, the RIA gathers inputs from relevant stakeholders and experts through ad-hoc consultation activities. In addition to its usage in support of the early legislative process, an RIA can also be performed at a later stage of the policy cycle to evaluate, *in medias res* or *ex-post*, the effects of policy measures or regulations already in place (see Box 11.1).

DOI: 10.4324/9781003191377-14

Box 11.1 Retrospective cost analyses of regulations

Ex-post regulatory impact assessment or similar mechanisms, called post-implementation policy evaluations, may serve a variety of goals. As suggested by Bennear and Wiener (2021), it is possible to distinguish at least three broad goals. First, the *rule relevance* goal, i.e., identifying rules that are outdated, redundant, or obsolete – no longer applicable, or lacking statutory authority – and removing them. Second, the *rule improvement* goal, i.e., improving the outcomes of regulation – in particular, revising each rule, taken one at a time, to improve its performance. In practice, this has often meant identifying specific past rules that have turned out to incur high costs and seeking to reduce those costs through revisions. According to the authors, most retrospective reviews to date have focused on the rule relevance goal and, to some extent, on the rule improvement goal, but with a narrow focus on costs. Third, a *regulatory learning* goal, i.e., learning from multiple past rules and analyses, in order to improve future rules and analyses. Retrospective review can contribute to broader learning about regulation in several ways. For example, it can improve the understanding of the performance of alternative policy designs or instruments, to evaluate how well they work in practice, compared to predictions in theory. It can also improve the accuracy of methods used to conduct *ex-ante* RIAs, as exemplified by *ex-post* assessments carried out by the US Environmental Protection Agency (see Kopits *et al.* 2014). In addition, it can improve understanding of the interaction effects of multiple regulations. For example, retrospective review could assess the cumulative impacts of multiple rules on an industry.

Source: Authors, based on Bennear and Wiener (2021).

Different types of regulatory measures can be covered by the RIA. In principle, every policy action requiring some form of regulatory initiative can be subjected, at any stage of the policy cycle, to an impact assessment, if it is expected to generate certain economic, social, environmental or strategic impacts on society. Around the world, RIAs have been performed on both primary legislation (the form of law issued by the legislative power) and secondary or delegated legislation (which is issued by the executive, under the authority of a primary law). They have also been performed on policy initiatives such as expenditure programs, negotiating guidelines to finalize agreements, and documents proposing actions in specific fields.

In light of the high variability in the nature, size, and relevance of regulatory measures potentially at hand, and of the potential costs and benefits, international guidance on RIAs underlines the need for a proportionate and flexible approach. According to the principle of proportionality, depending on the regulation's features and the possibility of collecting quality data, as well as the available resources for conducting the analysis, an RIA's depth can vary, and different methodological tools can be adopted within its framework.

Impacts of regulation can in fact be assessed through various approaches. One preliminary choice concerns the adoption of partial versus general equilibrium analysis. For measures that have considerable indirect impacts dispersed across different economic sectors, general equilibrium analysis better captures the breadth of causal chains and cumulative impacts. However, the necessary modelling for this methodology requires significant resources and skills and is time-consuming. For this reason, experience shows that partial equilibrium analysis is most frequently chosen (OECD 2020b). When performing partial equilibrium analysis, CBA is recognized as a best practice (OECD 2008). However, alternatives such as least-cost analysis, cost-effectiveness analysis, and multi-criteria analysis may be applied in specific cases (see Box 11.2).

As a general rule, irrespective of the methodology adopted, RIAs should aim to identify and detail all the main impacts generated by the options proposed (including potential non-regulatory solutions to the identified problem) and to provide a form of assessment on their expected effects. CBA is commonly considered the most suitable tool for performing in-depth RIAs, due to its ability to evaluate options with a number of different attributes through a single measure – monetary units – and due to this method's solid academic and practical tradition (OECD 2008). By offering a quantified and monetized estimate of socio-economic effects and complementing it with a qualitative description of non-quantifiable effects, CBA makes a strong case as to which policy alternative maximizes social welfare, thus providing a sound justification contributing to the choice of a policy alternative.

Within RIAs, the assessment of costs and benefits occurs after the description of the problem at hand, the definition of the objectives to pursue, and the specification of policy alternatives. Among the alternatives, a "do nothing" option must be included corresponding to the situation in case no action is taken. This scenario is typically adopted as the baseline against which the costs and benefits of the other options are incrementally assessed. The CBA (if this is the analytical tool chosen to perform the assessment of costs and benefits within the RIA) is then composed of two core-building blocks: identifying impacts and estimating their values.

Regarding identification, international guidance postulates the need to consider the full set of impacts generated directly and indirectly by the measure evaluated. Costs and benefits should be identified for different stakeholder types, usually corresponding to businesses, users, public administration, society as a whole, and other countries (in

---

Box 11.2 Alternatives to CBA in RIAs

Least-cost analysis, which only assesses costs and aims at identifying the least costly policy option, is adopted in cases where benefits do not vary based on the alternative chosen. Cost-effectiveness analysis, which quantifies socio-economic impacts but does not attach a financial value to them, can be a suitable tool especially when the primary impacts cannot be monetized; it is used chiefly in the areas of health, education, and security. Generally, it facilitates singling out the most the most cost-effective option, but it does not indicate whether that option is *per se* worthwhile; that can be done by comparing the results of the analysis with appropriate benchmarks. In turn, multi-criteria analysis assesses impacts not based on a single dimension (e.g., finances), but along several criteria, frequently of a qualitative nature (e.g., level of protection of consumer rights), and ranks options using weighted criteria. Thanks to these features, it can be of particular help in cases where various policy goals need to be considered. It can also be performed as a complement to CBA.

Source: Adapted from OECD (2020b) and European Commission (2021).

cases where the regulation has cross-border or worldwide impacts). While individual guidelines across the world suggest different taxonomies of impacts for structuring the analysis, common features are recognizable and give shape to a general map of costs and benefits (CEPS 2013).

Among direct costs, the main categories include: direct compliance costs (regulatory charges, substantive compliance costs, and administrative burdens) and hassle costs (associated with waiting time, delays, and redundancies or gaps in legal provisions). Indirect costs are generated outside the precise scope of the evaluated regulatory measure, for instance, through changes in price structure, availability, and the nature of goods of services regulated. They may consist in increased costs experienced in related markets or borne, as an ultimate outcome of the regulatory measure, by users, public administrations, or other stakeholders not specifically addressed by the regulation (substitution effects, transaction costs, reductions in efficiency, competition, innovation, and market access). In addition to direct and indirect costs, enforcement costs must be carefully assessed within RIAs. They are the costs of the activities necessary to implement the regulatory measure (including for instance management, monitoring, and litigation costs).

On the side of benefits, direct impacts to be considered cover improved wellbeing (which may point to health, environmental, or safety aspects, depending on the sector at hand) and market efficiency improvements (cost savings, improved availability of information, or better quality of goods and services for end users). Finally, indirect benefits consist in: spill-over effects; macroeconomic benefits (growth in indicators such as GDP, productivity, employment)[2]; other strategic benefits (related, for instance, to upholding human rights, territorial cohesion, or national or international stability).

Once the applicable impacts have been identified, quantification and monetization can be undertaken as part of the CBA. As in the appraisal of infrastructure projects, the methods used to calculate estimates vary based on the individual impact, data availability and quality, and available resources.

Direct compliance costs are typically estimated by multiplying the population bearing the cost at hand (for instance, that of a license) by the unit cost and its frequency. As the unit cost is already expressed in monetary terms, the assessment of this impact is relatively straightforward. Administrative burdens can be more challenging. A shortcut for assessing them can be found in the standard cost model originally adopted in the Netherlands (OECD 2004). To calculate the cost of an administrative activity, its price (or unit cost) is multiplied by its quantity. The price is calculated by multiplying the number of staff hours necessary for the activity by the relevant hourly salary rates. In turn, the quantity corresponds to the frequency of the administrative activity multiplied by the relevant population, i.e., the number of organizations having to perform it. In some cases, data collection for this estimation can be resource-consuming, as the price of the activity may vary between different organizations and exhibit geographical differences. Ensuring that the data collected to this end are representative of the whole affected population is therefore key for ensuring the quality of the results. The assessment of hassle or irritation costs, if performed in a quantitative way, can also be data-demanding. In principle, however, these costs can be assessed by identifying foregone profits, additional direct costs of staff, or the opportunity cost of time lost. To assess enforcement costs, incremental staff costs are considered, but also capital costs, if applicable; the impact of the different policy options on the level of litigation should also be assessed.

While the costs of regulation tend to be generated up front, the extent of the expected benefits is often more ambiguous. Their assessment is complicated by the fact that they are not subject to monetary transactions and generally require a longer and less certain timeframe to manifest. Overall, the main methodological approaches applied are the following three: revealed preference models, stated preference models, and the benefit transfer approach (see Chapter 4). Other methods include the life satisfaction approach (which relies on evidence from surveys to assess individual preferences related to non-market goods), econometric models that investigate the relationship between independent and dependent variables (for instance, holding all parameters constant in the model except for one affected by the policy measure), and perception surveys to gauge the extent of changes in regulatory burden (CEPS 2013).

In a regulatory CBA, cost savings are likely to be an element of great interest to decision makers, especially when the regulation pursues the goals of simplification and burden reduction. This type of benefit can be identified whenever, under the assessment of costs, the results point to a cost reduction compared to the baseline (usually in terms of compliance cost, administrative burden, or enforcement cost).

All monetized costs and benefits, assessed for a timeframe sufficient to cover all expected impacts, are subject to discounting, using rates normally set out in national or supranational guidance (see Chapter 6). Then, the difference between the discounted total benefits and costs, i.e., the net benefits (or the net present value), represents the indicator that — if complemented with qualitative considerations on non-quantified impacts — supports the identification of the policy alternative that maximizes social welfare. An *ad hoc* analysis of distributional impacts can complement the CBA as well (see Chapter 7).

Once the CBA is completed, its results feed into the RIA's final assessment, identifying the preferred policy solution. This overview of the use of CBA to assess regulatory impacts within RIAs, however, is only archetypical: In different contexts, the actual performance of CBAs and their roles in policy-making have varied, as is explained next.

11.2 International practices

In the history of CBA, its adoption in regulatory policy is a relatively recent development. This section investigates how this use originated and evolved over time in different jurisdictions. Adopting a comparative and historical perspective, it sheds light on the varying role a regulatory CBA can assume in the policy making process, its relationship with different institutional settings and political currents, and the reasons behind differences in methodologies adopted. In addition, an analysis of CBA use within RIAs in some of the most solid settings worldwide for this practice is instrumental to set the background against which the Section 11.3 develops considerations on methodological limits and implementation challenges, trends, and critical aspects.

11.2.1 United States

The application of CBA in regulatory policy has a date and place of birth: 1981, United States of America. In a country that had witnessed an increase in the number of federal agencies and regulations, newly elected president Ronald Reagan, who had run on a platform promising to reduce the burden of federal regulation on the economy, issued Executive Order 12291, effectively marking the start of a new era in regulatory policy.

While his predecessors had already engaged in efforts to limit the perceived intrusiveness of regulatory requirements and to deregulate, Reagan's innovation required agencies to calculate costs and benefits of all regulatory options for major rules; to undertake regulatory action only if potential benefits to society outweigh potential costs; to choose regulatory objectives that maximize the net benefits to society; to choose the option involving the lowest net cost to society. The order's scope was relatively broad, as the definition of 'major rule' included any federal regulation (i.e., secondary legislation, promulgated by an executive branch agency) likely to have at least one of the following three consequences: an annual effect on the economy of at least USD 100 million; a major increase in costs or prices for consumers, individual industries, geographic regions, or government agencies (at the federal, state, or local level); significant adverse effects on competition, employment, investment, productivity, innovation, or the ability of US-based enterprises to compete with foreign-based enterprises.

For every proposed regulation, the order mandated the proposing agency to submit an RIA to the Office of Information and Regulatory Affairs (OIRA), within the Office of Management and Budget (OMB, which is part of the Executive Office of the President). The RIA was meant to do each of the following: describe potential costs and benefits of the rule, including those not quantifiable; identify which actors the effects were likely to impact on; describe alternative approaches that could achieve the same regulatory objective at lower cost; explain why those approaches could not be adopted. This formal mechanism introduced a centralized review of draft regulations and put CBA at the core of the regulatory state.

In 1993, President Clinton's Executive Order 12866 confirmed the previous approach, thereby inaugurating an extended period of bipartisan consensus over CBA in regulatory policy (Dudley 2020). Further consolidation took place under President G. W. Bush, when methodological guidance was issued, under the name of Circular A-4 (see OMB 2003), that pursued the goal of analytical consistency in the evaluation of costs and benefits across regulations and agencies; this document still guides the performance of CBA by federal agencies.[3] Circular A-4 requires costs and benefits to be assessed against a baseline, usually consisting of a "no action" or "next best alternative" scenario, and provides a detailed illustration of CBA's core concepts (opportunity cost, willingness-to-accept, willingness-to-pay, and discounting) and methods for estimating costs and benefits (revealed preference and stated preference methods, benefit transfer, and methods for treating non-monetized benefits and costs). The Obama administration reaffirmed the principles enshrined in Executive Order 12866 and strengthened the requirements for retrospective analysis of regulation (Executive Order 13563).[4]

More recently, the increasing prominence of CBA has suffered some setbacks. Even though the regulatory principles and methodological guidance remain in place, three main factors contributed to weakening CBA practices. As part of a deregulation approach, the Trump administration required, firstly, that new regulations have a net cost of zero and, secondly, that for every regulation adopted, two should be repealed. *De facto*, these two requirements acted as severe limits to the role of CBA as a decisive tool contributing to policy-making (Sunstein 2018) and suggested a lack of consideration for benefits (Katzen 2020). The literature highlights a third factor: the decreased quality of CBAs. As a result, when regulations were challenged in court, the administration lost cases more frequently than in the past (Livermore and Revesz 2020).

The role of courts in relation to CBA, in fact, is in itself a peculiar development of the US system. Throughout the 2010s, when confronted with legal cases about federal regulations, courts across the country have become increasingly favourable toward including in their reasoning an assessment of the quality of the supporting CBA, partly due to the activity of think tanks advocating for such reviews. The proactive role of courts, which have become one of the conflicting forces shaping the role of CBA in the present day, represents a development that needs to be considered from different perspectives. On one hand, judicial review further cements CBA as part of the legitimation of a regulation; on the other hand, depending on the focus and the depth of the review (for instance, whether the court confines itself to logical fallacies or, rather, questions the economic aspects of the analysis), concerns may arise about whether courts are adequately equipped to assess the quality of a CBA (Sunstein 2018).

In 2021, a memorandum issued on the first day of the new Biden administration reaffirmed the reliance on CBA. At the same time, it announced a revision of Circular A-4, emphasizing the need to better account for benefits that are difficult to quantify, thereby downplaying the focus on regulatory costs that had characterized the previous years. In addition, the memorandum stressed the importance of including an analysis of distributional equity. In fact, distributional analysis was already required by Circular A-4, though without punctual guidelines on methods or the identification of the units of analysis, and without systematic inclusion in the actual performance of CBAs (Robinson *et al.* 2016), as a consequence of both methodological challenges and a lack of political impetus. Ultimately, the memorandum is placed in continuity with the preceding forty-year tradition, but simultaneously promises to open a new page for the use of CBA in regulatory policy in the country that pioneered it.

11.2.2 United Kingdom

The UK government took its first steps towards assessing the impacts of regulation during the premiership of Margaret Thatcher in the 1980s, in the context of public sector reform aimed at promoting performance orientation and efficiency, and more widely as part of vigorous deregulation. In 1985, in particular, it introduced compliance cost assessment (CCA), which required government departments proposing new rules through statutory instruments (the main form of secondary legislation in the UK) to first assess the potential costs for firms, under the coordination of a dedicated task force pushing for the reduction of administrative burdens. Later, in the 1990s, the government continued the deregulation effort and established sector-specific task forces overseeing the assessment of regulation impacts. In addition, it promoted the "Think Small First" principle (which required an early focus on the effects of regulation on small businesses), expanded the CCA's scope to include parliamentary bills and the transposition of EC directives, and added the requirement to assess benefits.

In 1998, CCAs were replaced by RIA procedures, foreseeing the analysis of costs and benefits of different regulatory options, including the so-called "zero option," and regulatory impact units were established in individual departments. Moreover, a new Better Regulation Task Force was put in charge of methodological guidelines and advising departments on impact assessments. Guides to RIA were developed in the early 2000s, detailing CBA methodologies to be employed in RIAs. During the first decade of the new century, different organizational changes were introduced in the area of Better Regulation, but the use of RIAs within the policy-making process remained unsatisfactory, according to the National Audit Office; the assessment of costs and benefits represented one of the system's main weaknesses, due to deficiencies in the evidence base used and the limited used of robust economic methodologies (National Audit Office 2007).

In the early 2010s, the government established quantified targets for deregulation (for instance, GBP 10 billion cuts in administrative burdens for businesses planned for 2015–2020) and increasingly incisive rules on deregulation (from a "one-in-one-out" rule in 2010 – whereby the introduction of each new rule imposing a net cost on businesses had to be accompanied by a regulatory burden cut of the same amount – to a "one-in-three-out" rule in 2015). Over the same years, public discourse emphasized regulatory costs in general, and those deriving from EU regulations in particular. This context led to RIAs being especially focused on costs for businesses, and the Regulatory Policy Committee (RPC, an independent body tasked with evaluating the quality of each impact assessment) publicly expressed concerns over the insufficient analyses of impacts on society as a whole. In more recent years, as the UK went through major political changes associated with the decision to exit the European Union, no landmark innovation was introduced in regulatory policy. At the end of 2020, however, in a context of regulatory challenges brought about by the end of the Brexit transition period, among other factors, the government set its deregulation target at zero for the parliament term scheduled to last until 2024. This simultaneously announcing a review and a subsequent revision of the methodologies used to assess regulatory impacts.

Under the Better Regulation Framework (Department for Business, Energy and Industrial Strategy 2018) published in 2018 (updated in 2020) and updating previous guidance documents, an RIA with a detailed CBA is carried out on each proposal with an equivalent annual net direct cost to businesses (EANDCB) which, according to a preliminary assessment, exceeds GBP 5 million. Below this threshold, a simplified CBA is performed. Key bodies in the current framework are the Better Regulation Executive responsible for issuing guidance and providing advice across government, the Better Regulation Units established in each government department and ensuring compliance with the country's regulatory policy, and the above-mentioned RPC scrutinizing the evidence presented in support of regulatory innovations that impact businesses and civil society organizations in RIAs.

The government produced a standardized RIA template, accompanied by a user manual aiding departments in completing the document. Together with qualitative information, the RIA template foresees the inclusion of quantitative data derived from a CBA ("full economic assessment"). For the performance of the CBA itself, a spreadsheet template is made available as well, with a related short user guide. This standard spreadsheet, called the Impact Assessment Calculator, facilitates automatic calculation of the indicators required by the RIA, i.e., a total Net Present Social Value (representing the net benefit for society as a whole), the Net Present Value for business, and the EANDCB of each option.

CBA principles and methods set out in the *Green Book*, the government's guide on appraisal and evaluation (see Chapter 9), apply to RIAs as well. A general categorization of costs to be appraised is as follows: direct and indirect public costs; wider costs to UK society; costs of mitigating and managing risks. Benefits include direct and indirect public sector benefits and wider benefits to UK society. The *Green Book* also contains key methodological recommendations concerning, among other things, inflation adjustments, time horizons, the discount rate, optimism biases, and the valuation approaches for different costs and benefits that feed into the actual CBA performance in the RIA framework. Moreover, the *Green Book* recommends complementing CBA with a sensitivity analysis. Although not included in the spreadsheet, the sensitivity analysis is in fact another part of the RIA template.

11.2.3 European Union

The evolution of regulatory impact assessment in the European Union has gone through three phases. While the regulatory policy of the EU is today recognized among the international best practices by experts, the EU's initial attempts at introducing practices of regulatory impact assessment, starting in the mid-1980s, were ultimately ineffective, until reform initiatives taken in the early 2000s opened a new chapter, establishing a framework for the whole regulatory cycle. In the mid-2010s, another defining moment came about, as a wide-ranging regulatory strategy renewed the architecture and the methodological guidance.

In 1986, during the UK Presidency of the Council, a procedure called the Business Impact Assessment (BIA) was introduced for the first time, following the model of the CCA introduced by the Thatcher government (see Section 11.2.2). Hence, when the European Commission (which is both the executive branch and the institution with the right of legislative initiative) proposed a new legislation likely to have substantial impact on businesses in terms of compliance costs, a BIA was conducted on it. Like CCA, the BIA was focused on costs falling on businesses, not on society as a whole. Concretely, a standard template required the Commission Directorate-General proposing the legislation to list the new requirements imposed on businesses and to estimate the cost of each, specifying, in particular, taxes, costs related to monitoring and reporting, and other compliance costs. In addition, the expected macroeconomic effects were assessed, focusing on employment, investments, and competitiveness of the affected businesses. Soon, the BIA procedure showed limits related to its narrow focus on firms, its lack of identification of alternative policy options, and methodological weaknesses (Renda 2006). Over time, the BIA was complemented with a series of separate initiatives, including sustainability impact assessments, impact notes, tools focused on simplification and *ex-post* assessment, and permanent consultation mechanisms for businesses affected by regulation.

Dissatisfaction with the results of this fragmented approach to regulatory policy, combined with the urgency to address recurrent calls to reduce a perceived excess of EU regulation, led the European Commission to take bold steps towards a new model. In 2002, the Commission issued a communication on better law-making and a related action plan, as well as impact assessment guidelines, thus marking the beginning of a second phase. All types of *ex-ante* assessment were unified in an integrated impact assessment (IIA), in place since 2003 and covering economic, social, and environmental effects of regulation. Under the IIA framework, a two-step approach was introduced, consisting in a preliminary assessment followed by an extended one, and applied not only on proposed regulations and directives, but also on other policy proposals such as white papers,[5] expenditure programs, and guidelines for the negotiation of international agreements expected to bring about economic, social, and environmental effects. The IIA was considerably more ambitious than the BIA. While a CBA of the different shortlisted options was supposed to be at the core of the extended assessment, methodological problems soon became apparent, including inadequate consideration of social and environmental effects, inconsistent approaches to discounting rates, frequently missing quantification of costs and benefits, and excessive concentration on a single policy option. In 2005, the EU strategy was revised, increasing the emphasis of impact assessments on administrative costs and compliance costs, and reaffirming CBA's role. Impact assessment guidelines were updated in 2005, and again in 2009.

The third phase of this evolution opened in 2015, with the Commission's Communication on Better Regulation for Better Results. To strengthen the institutional framework around RIAs, the EU produced new Better Regulation Guidelines and a "toolbox" (a document of over 500 pages) providing, among other things, detailed guidance on the principles and the steps of an impact assessment, the methods for identifying and quantifying impacts, and the performance of stakeholder consultation. Change, however, was not limited to methodological updates. As part of an extensive effort to establish a solid institutional and methodological framework, a new independent oversight body was established, called the Regulatory Scrutiny Board (RSB), and was tasked with checking the quality of major impact assessments and evaluations at the early stages of the legislative process.

Despite its ambitious and comprehensive approach, however, a well-established practice of regulatory impact assessments of consistently high quality still has to come about, especially as regards the quantification of costs and benefits. In its annual reports, the RSB has underlined the persistence of weaknesses in problem definition, incomplete sets of options assessed, and insufficient justification for the preferred option (Regulatory Scrutiny Board 2021).

Based on the Better Regulation Guidelines, the choice of CBA as the tool for assessing regulatory impacts is not mandatory. Most Commission impact assessments and evaluations attempt to quantify costs and benefits to the extent possible, but some specificities of the EU context pose hurdles that are difficult to overcome. According to CEPS (2013), there are three main specificities of the EU IA system. First, impact assessments in the EU do not concern only narrow, technical policy measures (as is the case in the US, where RIA is mandatory only for secondary legislation, mostly of a technical nature), but also cross-cutting policy initiatives with very far-reaching and heterogeneous impacts. Second, the breadth of the assessment both in terms of ambitions (as an integrated assessment of economic, social, and environmental impacts is required) and geographical coverage (as data have to be collected from all member states) makes the assessment of impacts particularly challenging. Third, the multi-level nature of EU policymaking makes it very difficult to predict enforcement patterns and the related costs for public administrations at the national level at the *ex-ante* stage. Therefore, the use of CBA in the EU RIA context is more challenging compared to other contexts in terms of data availability, quantification and monetization of certain categories of costs and benefits, uncertainty surrounding implementation choices, and enforcement falling under member state responsibility (CEPS 2013). As a result, quantification of costs and benefits is ultimately a weak point in the EU system, which does not lend itself well to standard CBA (Goldberg 2018).

In 2021, the Commission issued a new communication aimed at further improving the existing regulatory policy. It announced a simplification of public consultation procedures and the introduction of a "one-in-one-out" approach to regulatory burdens, but also the integration of sustainability, digital transformation, and strategic foresight into better regulation – an improvement to be reflected in a forthcoming revision of the Better Regulation toolbox.

11.2.4 Other experiences

The use of CBA in regulatory policy has expanded internationally beyond the three experiences analyzed so far in this chapter. Today, all OECD countries have some form of RIA. Australia, for instance, has an especially developed framework in place. The Australian impact assessment process is structured in well-defined steps: a preliminary assessment determining whether a Regulatory Impact Statement (RIS) is required; an early and a final submission of the RIS to be reviewed by a central body placed within the Department of the Prime Minister and Cabinet, namely, the Office of Best Practice Regulation (OBPR); the publication of the RIS; a post-implementation review. The whole process is supported by user-friendly guidance documents, templates, examples, and also a publicly available online course covering the overall approach to impact analysis and CBA, in particular, based on methodological advice developed by the OBPR. Available guidance documents cover the CBA itself (expressly recognizing that in CBAs applied to regulatory proposals, impacts are more difficult to quantify than in the case of infrastructure projects), individual impact types (for instance, impacts on competition, trade, and environment), the specificities of assessing impacts for different stakeholder types (individuals, community organizations, and small businesses), and single CBA sections (distributional analysis and risk analysis).

Importantly, RIA is not a feature of regulatory systems only in the most advanced economies. Among other countries where RIA is conducted, Mexico is one of the most interesting examples (Querbach and Arndt 2017). Its experience in the field started in 1992, when the adoption of CBA was introduced as a requirement for the development of technical regulations. The establishment of RIA requirements followed in 1996, covering draft regulations with a potential impact on business activities and constituting a centralized quality assurance mechanism. In 2010, in response to OECD recommendations, a distinction was drawn between regulations expected to have moderate impacts and those expected to have high impacts and was operationalized through an online tool called the Regulatory Impact Calculator. High-impact regulations were required to undergo a detailed and data-driven assessment, with CBA being conducted on all policy options identified (OECD 2014; OECD 2020a). In 2018, Mexico further strengthened the mandatory use of RIA and the performance of stakeholder engagement and established new provisions to conduct *ex-post* evaluations of regulations generating compliance costs (OECD 2021b).

International organizations have had an important role in elevating the use of CBA in regulatory policy to the status of standard practice. OECD, in particular, has been very active on the subject of RIA over the last decades, providing regular outlooks on regulatory policy and country profiles, but also methodological guidance for the performance of RIA's steps – including CBA – and for RIA's integration in the policy-making process.

The World Bank, in turn, maintains an open database gathering guidance documents related to RIA published by national governments worldwide as well as studies on national applications. Moreover, as part of its work on regulatory governance, the World Bank issues reports on global practices of RIA (Lemoine 2019) and supports the development of RIA reforms in developing countries (Ladegaard *et al.* 2018).

11.3 A key tool for good governance? Some critical considerations

The history of impact assessment in regulatory policy is one of an expanding scope. The institutional frameworks in which the performance of RIAs is embedded have evolved, and practical guidance for analysts has increasingly been made available. Over time, international practice has moved away from an approach focused on the minimization of regulatory costs for businesses towards a wider one, ideally encompassing all generated effects. In this transition, there is a recognizable movement towards a gradual endorsement of the use of CBA (Renda 2018). However, CBA in RIA generally serves as a protocol for assessing efficiency, and (unlike infrastructure project appraisals) it is embedded within a multi-goal analysis in which efficiency is one of the criteria (Vining and Boardman 2006; Vining and Weimer 2015).

Despite its crucial role, the use of CBA in regulatory policy is confronted with limitations of a different nature. For analytical purposes, they can be divided into three kinds of challenges: context-related, methodological, and practical. Taken together, they point to the permanence of a certain fragmentation and, conversely, to the need for appropriate guidance and capacity building.

Firstly, institutional context-related challenges are linked to the incentive system, the variety of types of regulation, and the administrative culture. To begin with, (much like infrastructure project appraisal) CBA in the context of RIA risks becoming a compliance-driven or politically-driven exercise, performed in response to legal requirements but not actually contributing to decision making. This occurs, for instance, when it is used to justify a policy choice already made for other reasons (Keohane 2009; Dudley 2011; Carrigan and Shapiro 2016) instead of examining different alternatives in depth. Indeed, there is a natural tension between the political decision-making process and the RIA principles. In the words of Baldwin *et al.* (2011),

> within the impact assessment procedure, policymakers are supposed to consider and compare the array of regulatory routes to a policy objective but, in the real world, a proposal may be the product of a process of political negotiation.
>
> (Baldwin *et al.* 2011)

To overcome such tension, an RIA should be embedded in an appropriate incentive system. OECD (2020b) provides an overview of best practice principles for designing such a system. Among other things, establishing guidelines that enjoy a wide consensus and are stable in time and ensuring their respect through an appropriate oversight system are key to promoting a fair assessment and minimizing the risk of bias or manipulation (the latter is one of the challenges devised by Baldwin *et al.* 2011).

Second, given the potentially wide spectrum of regulatory measures that can be subjected to RIAs (due to the number of domains that can be regulated, but also in light of the different forms of regulations) and the wide scope of the assessment (e.g., in the EU, the IA should also include impacts on fundamental rights), CBA is often criticized for being unable to offer a sufficiently comprehensive assessment (Renda 2006, 2018). In this respect, sector-specific models and guidance have the potential to improve the accuracy of CBA in the context of RIA and minimize methodological variations that generate difficulties in interpreting CBA results.

Still with reference to context-related issues, Baldwin *et al.* (2011) notice that one of the most serious impediments to the effective use of CBA within RIA is the bureaucratic resistance encountered by officials. Indeed, proper application of the CBA requires appropriate knowledge and educational background going beyond legal aspects. Especially in jurisdictions where the legislative and administrative culture is permeated by a legalistic approach (e.g., policy officials mainly have a legal background in continental European administrations), ensuring good levels of administrative capacity in this field is not merely a matter of skills but is also related to the promotion of a cultural change within administrations and policy makers (Jacob *et al.* 2012).

Moreover, some methodological issues still appear to lack solutions. The first challenge has to do with the definition and the modelling of the baseline, which is crucial for CBA.[6] For regulatory policy, a "no action" baseline (i.e., assuming no change in the regulatory regime) is a common choice but, in many cases, this may not be an accurate representation of the state of the word in the absence of the proposed regulation. Indeed, there may be changes in the regulatory regime even in the absence of the proposed regulation. For instance, the world absent the regulation may be affected by the expiration or changes of existing regulations. Modelling the word without a policy requires consideration of a wide range of factors. According to OMB (2003), they include: the evolution of the market; changes in external factors; changes due to other promulgated regulations; the degree of compliance with these promulgated regulations. If all these factors are not properly accounted for when modelling the baseline, there is a risk of an inaccurate, if not misleading, estimation of the incremental costs and benefits of the proposed regulation. However, phenomena, such as artificial intelligence and the Internet of Things, evolve so rapidly as to render predictions about the world both with and without the proposed regulation very challenging. This calls for continuous, adaptive impact assessment and constant, ongoing market monitoring.

The second methodological challenge concerns predicting the consequences, especially in terms of consumer behaviour and technological change brought about by the proposed regulation. Some regulations, especially environmental ones, are specifically designed to affect consumers' behaviour and technological choice. Therefore, disregarding adaptive responses would be a mistake. The problem is exacerbated when regulations involve "hidden" costs, such as reductions in productivity, a dulling of incentives, and distortions on investment and production, which further complicate the prediction and quantification problem (Baldwin *et al.* 2011). At the same time, adaptive responses and the costs and benefits associated with a regulation also depend on how it is enforced and the pattern of compliance (Baldwin *et al.* 2011). All this calls for the use of different scenarios.

Linked to the second challenge, there is the problem that regulations' targets often have multiple interacting causes, making it difficult to cleanly determine the effect of the regulation in isolation (Dudley *et al.* 2017).

Clearly, the methodological challenges are exacerbated when CBA applies to primary legislation, because this merely establishes a broad framework whose impacts are even more difficult to predict. The real regulatory substance is spelt out in secondary legislation. That is why CBA is, in many instances, used only for assessing secondary legislation.

Thirdly, experience has shed light on practical challenges. Both the literature and oversight bodies have in fact criticized the actual performance of CBAs in regulatory policy for a variety of shortcomings, including weakness in the data collected, a lack of discounting, failures in quantification of relevant impacts, excessive concentration on a particular policy option, insufficient justification for the selected alternative (Renda

2006; National Audit Office 2007; Regulatory Scrutiny Board 2021). Frequently, such problems boil down to a lack of quality data. This makes it difficult to apply the CBA principles, such as the monetization of all effects for a long period and the discounting of future costs and benefits and, in turn, poses a threat to the quality of CBA. The lack of quality data is often exacerbated by the time or resources constraints faced by the regulatory authorities and hired external consultants (Baldwin *et al.* 2011).

Stakeholder consultation, while crucial, is not necessarily a guarantee of comprehensive and unbiased datasets. In this regard, a push for mainstreaming monitoring systems across policy implementation as well as the introduction of technological innovations in regulatory systems can help. The use of new technologies and artificial intelligence applications enables continuous data collection and transforms regulatory delivery; examples across the globe include the use of satellite imagery to monitor environmental policy compliance in Chile, the use of social media data to target inspections in the US, and cooperation between German food authorities and online marketplaces to control online trade (Mangalam and Vranic 2020; OECD 2021b).

In addition to challenges of a different nature, the future of CBA in regulatory policy is influenced by some trends that can be singled out. To begin with, in terms of types of impacts considered, recent evolutions include an increased interest in the environmental dimension, in line with the growing political focus on the prevention and mitigation of climate change, and the associated distributional aspects. The latter often translates into an analysis of the different effects that a regulatory measure generates on separate sets of stakeholders (disaggregated, for instance, by age, gender, location, type of stakeholder, or organization size), but also into an examination of the likely extents to which compliance costs are passed from businesses to end users. A lack of widespread experience in this type of analysis, however, leads to a need for further methodological consolidation on how to perform it, and on questions regarding the relationship such an analysis needs to have with CBA – a topic on which the debate is still ongoing (Williams and Broughel 2015; Robinson *et al.* 2016).

Furthermore, in parallel with landmark developments of economic studies in the last decades, behavioural insights are also gaining traction in RIAs, in an attempt to account for behavioural responses to regulatory changes by different stakeholders. Insights from psychology, cognitive science, and social science are increasingly used to anticipate the behavioural consequences of regulations and policies by using behaviourally-informed strategies to guide decision making (OECD 2019).

Increasingly, some aspects are being recognized as not quantifiable under a standard CBA. Such a conclusion emerges not only in relation to intangible values, such as human rights or social cohesion, but also concerning economic concepts, such as competitiveness (OECD 2021a). While the aim of RIAs, over the last decades, has increasingly been linked to quantification of costs and benefits, the ever-growing experience with actual CBAs in regulatory policy suggests that CBA cannot be a one-size-fits-all solution; other analytical tools may be more adequate, under some conditions, in the context of RIAs.

To conclude, the post-implementation reviews (OECD 2015) reveal a growing role for the RIA as a central tool at different steps of the policy cycle. In this sense, while the importance of RIAs can be expected to be more and more recognized globally in the near future, the role of CBA in RIAs could narrow down to applications where its usefulness is maximized, e.g., for technical regulations. Despite CBA's existing limitations in the context of RIA, its use today represents an indispensable tool of good governance.

11.4 Further reading

For an introduction to the topic of RIAs, guidance material issued by the OECD is a good starting point. OECD (2020b), in particular, offers a synthesis of best practices in the design of RIA systems and the performance of the analysis. OECD's Regulatory Policy Outlooks illustrate RIA's most recent trends and challenges, building on punctual examples from individual countries. They also present the main conclusions from OECD research on specific aspects, such as the proportionality principle in RIA (OECD 2020a) or the assessment of regulatory impacts on competitiveness (OECD 2021a).

As regards the use of CBA within RIAs, CEPS (2013) maps the costs and benefits of regulation as well as the methods used at the global level to assess them, and illustrates the practical steps to be followed to perform CBA. Chapter 15 of Baldwin *et al.* (2011) offers a critical analysis of the relationship between CBA and RIA.

Dudley *et al.* (2017) offers non-specialist policy makers and other interested stakeholders of RIAs 10 tips for asking informed questions when reviewing and interpreting them. More specifically, this guide explains why RIAs are valuable, reviews their key elements, describes best practices, points out the ways in which RIAs might fall short of achieving these best practices, helps readers to better judge the quality of information provided in RIAs and make discerning assessments about the methods employed, and improves readers' capacity to critically evaluate the justification offered to support regulatory actions.

As for different international practices, a useful summary is available in Lemoine (2019). For a detailed overview of impact assessment models – including the use of CBA – in the US, the UK, and the EU, see Renda (2006). More recent studies on these three jurisdictions allow for a reconstruction of the latest developments and help identify critical trends. Cass Sunstein, former OIRA administrator and renowned scholar, has written extensively on CBA principles and usage in the US. His 2018 book *The Cost-Benefit Revolution* offers an excellent presentation of CBA and its relationship with the US political and institutional system, celebrating its contribution to policy making and carefully examining problems as well as new frontiers. For the UK, a paper by the independent body in charge of RIA oversight investigates the overall quality of RIAs and puts forward some suggestions for the system's improvement (Regulatory Policy Committee 2020). Similarly, the latest annual report of the EU Regulatory Scrutiny Board sets out trends and challenges in a concise form (Regulatory Scrutiny Board 2021). For the Australian case, the website of the Office of Best Practice Regulation (https://obpr.pmc.gov.au/) is an excellent source for accessing materials, guidance, and templates and for gaining a good understanding of the national approach.

11.5 Summary of Chapter 11

- Originally a tool to ensure burden minimization for economic actors affected by new policy measures, the RIA has evolved into a wide-ranging exercise, supporting an evidence-based, transparent policy-making process and fostering technocratic legitimation of regulation.
- At a minimum, RIAs typically present the policy problem to be addressed, the objectives to be achieved, the available policy alternatives, and an evaluation of costs and benefits of the different options.

- Within RIAs, CBA can be adopted to assess costs and benefits of the regulatory measure at hand. It is, however, not the only analytical tool that can be chosen for this purpose.
- While RIAs have, over the last decades, increasingly aimed to align with CBAs for the quantification of impacts, CBA is not necessarily the most adequate tool for all types of regulation. In particular, in the case of primary regulations of wide scope and with large indirect impacts, CBA may not be feasible, or its results may be less reliable than for more technical regulations.
- Despite persistent limitations and challenges, RIA is globally recognized as crucial for good governance, and its role in policy-making is increasing.

End of chapter questions

- What are the purposes and the key components of an RIA?
- Which are the typical costs and benefits assessed in an RIA?
- What are the key differences of the RIA's evolution and practices in the US, the UK, and Europe?
- What are the conditions for the use of CBA in RIAs? What are the limitations?

Notes

1 This chapter is co-authored with Matteo Pedralli.
2 Macroeconomic benefits are quantified only in cases where a general equilibrium analysis is adopted. CBA, which follows a microeconomic approach, does not capture macroeconomic effects.
3 Agencies have also developed detailed guidance specific to their regulatory mandates (for example, US Environmental Protection Agency 2010).
4 During the Obama administration, the Office of Management and Budget provided an RIA Checklist (2010), FAQs (2011a), and Primer (2011b). According to the latter, the three basic elements that each RIA should include are (1) "a statement of the need for the regulatory action," (2) "a clear identification of a range of regulatory approaches," and (3) "an estimate of the benefits and costs – both quantitative and qualitative – of the proposed regulatory action and its alternatives." Thus, RIAs often involve considerations and analyses that go beyond CBA. Nevertheless, the latter is an important component of the RIA framework (Dudley *et al.* 2017).
5 European Commission white papers are documents containing proposals for EU action in a certain areas. The goal of a white paper is to launch a discussion with the public, stakeholders, the European Parliament, and the Council in order to reach a political consensus.
6 Perhaps the most complete discussion of baseline issues in CBA is provided in US Environmental Protection Agency (2010).

Bibliography

Abdulai, A. and Regmi, P. (2000) 'Estimating labour supply of farm households under non separability: empirical evidence from Nepal', Agricultural Economics, 22(3): 309–320.

Abelson, P. (2020) 'A partial review of seven official guidelines for cost-benefit analysis', Journal of Benefit-Cost Analysis, 11(2): 272–293.

Acocella, N. (2005) Economic Policy in the Age of Globalisation, Cambridge: Cambridge University Press.

Adler, M.D. (2016) 'Benefit–cost analysis and distributional weights: an overview', Review of Environmental Economics and Policy, 10: 264–285.

Adler, M.D. and Posner, E.A. (2006) New Foundations of Cost-Benefit Analysis, Cambridge, MA: Harvard University Press.

Ahmad, E., Coady, D. and Stern, N. (1988) 'A complete set of shadow prices for Pakistan: illustrations for 1975–76', The Pakistan Development Review, 27(1): 7–43.

Ahmad, E. and Stern, N.H. (1984) 'The theory of reform and Indian indirect taxes', Journal of Public Economics, 15(3): 259–298.

Ahmad, E. and Stern, N.H. (1986) 'Tax reform for Pakistan: overview and effective taxes for 1975/76', The Pakistan Development Review, 25(1): 43–72.

Ahmad, E. and Stern, N.H. (1990) 'Tax reform and shadow prices for Pakistan', Oxford Economic Papers, 42(1): 135–159.

Ainslie, G. and Haendel, V. (1983) 'The motives of the will', in Gottheil, E., Druley, K.A., Skoloda, T.E. and Waxman, H. (eds) Etiologic Aspects of Alcohol and Drug Abuse, Springfield, IL: Charles C. Thomas.

Alacevich, M. (2012) 'Visualizing uncertainties, or how Albert Hirschman and The World Bank disagreed on project appraisal and development approaches', Policy Research Working Paper 6260. Online. http://elibrary.worldbank.org/docserver/download/6260.pdf?expires=1373619452&id=id&a ccname=guest&checksum=9D208CEEE016F22D670A9630961B8069.

Albert, M. and Hahnel, R. (2017) Quiet Revolution in Welfare Economics, Princeton, NJ: Princeton University Press.

Alegre, H., Melo Baptista, J., Cabrera, E. Jr, Cubillo, F., Duarte, P., Hirner, W. and Parena, R. (2006) Performance Indicators for Water Supply Services, 2nd edn, London: IWA Publishing.

Alfred, A.M. and Evans, J.B. (1971) Appraisal of Investment Projects by Discounted Cash Flows, London: Chapman & Hall.

Almansa, C. and Martinez-Paz, J.M. (2011) 'What weight should be assigned to future environmental impacts? A probabilistic cost-benefit analysis using recent advances on discounting', Science of the Total Environment, 409: 1305–1314.

Amiel, Y., Creedy, J. and Hurn, S. (1999) 'Measuring attitudes towards inequality', Scandinavian Journal of Economics, 101: 83–96.

Anand, P.B. (2012) 'Environmental valuation', in Weiss, J. and Potts, D. (eds) Current Issues in Project Analysis for Development, Cheltenham and Northampton, MA: Edward Elgar Publishing.

Anderson, J.R. (1989) *Forecasting, Uncertainty and Public Project Appraisal*, Washington, DC: World Bank.

Andersson, H. (2018) 'Application of BCA in Europe–experiences and challenges', *Journal of Benefit-Cost Analysis*, 9(1): 84–96.

Angelini, F. (2011) '*Economic analysis of gas pipeline projects*', JASPERS Knowledge Economy, Energy and Waste Division Staff Working Paper. Online. http://www.jaspersnetwork.org/jaspersnetwork/download/attachments/4948004/Economic_Analysis_of_Gas_Pipeline_Projects_Final.pdf?version=1&modificationDate=1366387572000.

Antoniou, C. and Matsoukis, E. (2007) 'A methodology for the estimation of value-of-time using state-of-the-art econometric models', *Journal of Public Transportation*, 10(3): 1–19.

ASEK – Arbetsgruppen för SamhällsEkonomiska Kalkyler (2020) *Kapitel 20 English Summary of ASEK Recommendations, Guidelines*.

Arrow, K. (1995) '*Intergenerational equity and the rate of discount in long-term social investment*', paper presented at the IEA World Congress, Tunis, Tunisia.

Arrow, K.J., Cline, W.R., Mäler, K.H., Munasinghe, M., Squitieri, R. and Stiglitz, J.E. (1996) 'Intertemporal equity, discounting, and economic efficiency', in Bruce, J.P., Lee, H. and Haites, E.F. (eds) *Climate Change 1005: Economic and Social Dimensions – Contribution of Working Group III to the Second Assessment Report of the Intergovernmental Panel on Climate Change*, Cambridge: Cambridge University Press.

Arrow, K., Dasgupta, P. and Mäler, K.-G. (2004) 'Evaluating projects and assessing sustainable development in imperfect economies', *The Economics of Non-Convex Ecosystems*, 4: 149–187.

Arrow, K. and Debreu, G. (1954) 'Existence of an equilibrium for a competitive economy', *Econometrica: Journal of the Econometric Society*, 265–290.

Arrow, K. and Hahn, F.H. (1971) *General Competitive Analysis*, Amsterdam: North-Holland.

Arrow, K. and Lind, R. (1970) 'Uncertainty and the evaluation of public investment decisions', *American Economic Review*, 60(3): 364–378.

Arbetsgruppen för SamhällsEkonomiska Kalkyler (ASEK) (2020) *Kapitel 20 English Summary of ASEK Recommendations, Guidelines*.

Asian Development Bank (2002) *Handbook for Integrating Risk Analysis in the Economic Analysis of Projects*, Asian Development Bank. Online. http://www.adb.org/sites/default/files/integrating-risk-analysis.pdf.

Atkinson, G., Mourato, S., Szymanski, S. and Ozdemiroglu, E. (2008) 'Are we willing to pay enough to back the bid? Valuing the intangible impacts of London's bid to host the 2012 summer Olympic games', *Urban Studies*, 45: 419–444.

Atkinson, A.B. and Stern, N.H. (1974) 'Pigou taxation, and public goods', *Review of Economic Studies*, 41(1): 117–127.

Atkinson, A.B. and Stiglitz, J.E. (1980) *Lectures on Public Economics*, New York: McGraw Hill.

Australian Government (March 2020) *Cost–Benefit Analysis: Guidance Note*, https://www.pmc.gov.au/sites/default/files/publications/cost-benefit-analysis_0.pdf.

Aven, T., Nilsen, E.F. and Nilsen, T. (2004) 'Expressing economic risk: review and presentation of a unifying approach', *Risk Analysis*, 24(4): 989–1005.

Back, E.B., Boles, W.W. and Fry, J.T. (2000) 'Defining triangular probability distributions from historical cost data', *Journal of Construction Engineering and Management*, 126(1): 29–37.

Backhouse, R., Baujard, A. and Nishizawa, T. (2021) *Welfare Theory, Public Action, and Ethical Values: Revisiting the History of Welfare Economics*, Cambridge: Cambridge University Press.

Backhouse, R. and Boianovsky, M. (2013) *Transforming Modern Macroeconomics. Exploring Disequilibrium Microfoundations, 1956–2003*, Cambridge: Cambridge University Press.

Bain, R. (2009) 'Error and optimism bias in toll road traffic forecasts', *Transportation*, 36(5): 469–482.

Balcombe, K.G. and Smith, L.E.D. (1999) 'Refining the use of Monte Carlo techniques for risk analysis in project planning', *Journal of Development Studies*, 36(2): 113–135.

Baldwin, R., Cave, M. and Lodge, M. (2011) *Understanding Regulation: Theory, Strategy, and Practice*, Oxford: Oxford University Press.

Barone, E. (1935) 'The ministry of production in the collectivist state', in Hayek, F.A. (ed.) *Collectivist Economic Planning*, London: Routledge.

Barrett, S., Dasgupta, P. and Maler, K. (1999) 'Intergenerational equity, social discount rates, and global warming', in Portney, P. and Weyant, J. (eds) *Discounting and Intergenerational Equity*, Washington, DC: Resources for the Future.

Barrett, C.B., Sherlund, S.M. and Adesina, A.A. (2008) 'Shadow wages, allocative inefficiency, and labor supply in smallholder agriculture', *Agricultural Economics*, 38(1): 21–34.

Barrios, S., Pycroft, J. and Saveyn, B. (2013) 'The marginal cost of public funds in the EU: the case of labour versus green taxes', *Fiscal Policy and Growth*: 403–431.

Barsky, R., Kimball, M., Juster, T. and Shapiro, M. (1995) '*Preference parameters and behavioural heterogeneity: an experimental approach in the health and retirement survey*', NBER Working Paper No. 5213, Cambridge: National Bureau of Economic Research.

Bartik, T.J. (2012) 'Including jobs in benefit-cost analysis', *Annual Review of Resource Economics*, 4(1): 55–73.

Barzel, Y. (2002) *A Theory of the State: Economic Rights, Legal Rights, and the Scope of the State*, Cambridge: Cambridge University Press.

Basu, K. (1980) *Revealed Preference of Government*, Cambridge: Cambridge University Press.

Bator, F. (1958) 'The anatomy of market failures', *Quarterly Journal of Economics*, 72(3): 351–379.

Battaile, W. and Candler, W. (1997) '*The ERR and the Hawthorne Effect in Development Operations*', unpublished draft, Washington, DC: OED.

Battistoni, G., Genco, M., Marsilio, M., Pancotti, C., Rossi, S., Vignetti, S. (2016) 'Cost–benefit analysis of applied research infrastructure. Evidence from health care', *Technological Forecasting and Social Change*, 112: 79–91.

Baumol, W.J. and Quandt, R.E. (1965) 'Investment and discount rate under capital rationing: a programming approach', *Economic Journal*, 75: 317–329.

Baumstark, L., Guesnerie, R., Ni, J. and Ourliac, J.P. (2021) 'Cost–benefit assessment of public investments in France: the use of counter-experts', *Journal of Benefit-Cost Analysis*, 12(1): 152–169.

Bell, C. and Devarajan, S. (1983) 'Shadow prices for project evaluation under alternative macro-economic specifications', *Quarterly Journal of Economics*, 97: 454–477.

Belova, A., Fann, N., Haskell, J., Hubbell, B. and Narayan, T. (2020) 'Estimating lifetime cost of illness. An application to asthma', *Annals of the American Thoracic Society*, 17(12):1558–1569.

Benassy, J.P. (1990) 'Non-Walrasian equilibria, money and macroeconomics', in Friedman, B. and Hahn, F.H. (eds) *Handbook of Monetary Economics*, Amsterdam: North-Holland.

Benassy, J.P. (1993) 'Non clearing markets: microeconomic concepts and macroeconomic applications', *Journal of Economic Literature*, 31(2): 732–761.

Benassy, J.P. (2006) '*Non clearing markets in general equilibrium*', Working Paper 2006–2025, Paris-Jourdan. Sciences Economiques.

Bennear, L. and Wiener, J. (2021) 'Institutional roles and goals for retrospective regulatory analysis', *Journal of Benefit-Cost Analysis*, 12(3): 466–493.

Bentham, J. (1789) *An Introduction to the Principles of Morals and Legislation*, 1st edn, Oxford: Clarendon Press.

Berechman, J. and Chen, L. (2011) 'Incorporating risk of cost overruns into transportation capital projects decision-making', *Journal of Transport Economics and Policy*, 45(1): 83–104.

Bergson, A. (Burk) (1938) 'A reformulation of certain aspects of welfare economics', *The Quarterly Journal of Economics*, 52(2): 310–334.

Bergson, A. (1983) 'Pareto on social welfare', *Journal of Economic Literature*, 21(1): 40–46.

Beria, P., Giove, M. and Miele, M. (2012) 'A comparative analysis of assessment approaches. six cases from Europe', *International Journal of Transport Economics*, 39(2): 185–217.

Binkowitz, B.S. and Wartenberg, D. (2001) 'Disparity in quantitative risk assessment: a review in input distributions', *Risk Analysis*, 21(1): 75–90.

Blaug, M. (2007) 'The fundamental theorems of welfare economics', *History of Political Economy*, 39(2): 185–207.

Blundell, R., Browning, M. and Meghir, C. (1994) 'Consumer demand and the life-cycle allocation of household expenditures', *Review of Economic Studies*, *61*: 57–80.

Boadway, R. (1976) 'Integrating equity and efficiency in applied welfare economics', *Quarterly Journal of Economics*, *90(4)*: 541–556.

Boadway, R. (2016) 'Cost-benefit analysis', in Adler, M.D. and Fleurbaey, M. (eds) *The Oxford Handbook of Well-Being and Public Policy*, 47–81. New York: Oxford University Press.

Boadway, R. and Bruce, M. (1984) *Welfare Economics*, Oxford: Basil Blackwell.

Boadway, R. and Flatters, F. (1981) 'The efficiency basis for regional employment policy', *Canadian Journal of Economics*, *14(1)*: 58–77.

Boardman, A., Greenberg, D., Vining, A. and Weimer, D. (2020) 'Efficiency without apology: consideration of the marginal excess tax burden and distributional impacts in benefit–cost analysis', *Journal of Benefit-Cost Analysis*, *11(3)*: 457–478.

Boardman, A.E., Greenberg, D.H., Vining, A.R. and Weimer, D.L. (2018) *Cost-Benefit Analysis: Concepts and Practice*, 5th edn, Cambridge: Cambridge University Press.

Boardman, A.E., Laurin, C., Moore, M.A. and Vining, A.R. (2013) 'Efficiency, profitability and welfare gains from the Canadian National Railway privatization', *Research in Transportation Business & Management*, *6*: 19–30.

Boardman, A.E., Mallery, W.L. and Vining, A.R. (1994) 'Learning from *ex ante/ex post* cost-benefit comparisons: the Coquihalla highway example', *Socio-Economic Planning Sciences*, *28(2)*: 69–84.

Boardman, A.E., Greenberg, D.H., Vining, A.R. and Weimer, D.L. (2006) Cost-Benefit Analysis: Concepts and Practice, 3rd edn, Upper Saddle River, NJ: Pearson Prentice Hall.

Boardman, A.E., Moore, M.A. and Vining, A.R. (2010) 'The social discount rate for Canada based on future growth in consumption', *Canada Public Policy*, *36(3)*: 325–343.

Bock, K. and Trück, S. (2011) 'Assessing uncertainty and risk in public sector investments projects', *Technology and Investments*, *2(2)*: 105–123.

Bos, F., van der Pol, T. and Romijn, G. (2019) 'Should benefit-cost analysis include a correction for the marginal excess burden of taxation?', *Journal of Benefit-Cost Analysis*, *10(3)*: 379–403.

Bostani, M. and Malekpoor, A. (2012) 'Critical analysis of Kaldor-Hicks efficiency criterion, with respect to moral values, social policy making and incoherence', *Advances in Environmental Biology*, *6(7)*: 2032–2038.

Bowles, S. (2004) *Microeconomics: Behavior, Institutions, and Evolution*, Princeton, NJ and Oxford: Princeton University Press.

Bradford, D.F. (1975) 'Constraints on government investment opportunities and the choice of discount rate', *American Economic Review*, *65(5)*: 887–899.

Bråthen, S. and Hervik, A. (1997) 'Strait crossings and economic development: developing economic impact assessment by means of ex post analyses', *Transport Policy*, *4(4)*: 193–200.

Brau, R. and Florio, M. (2004) 'Privatisations as price reforms: evaluating consumers' welfare changes in the UK', *Annales d'Economie et de Statistique*, *75–76*: 109–133.

Bray, J.H. and Maxwell, E.M. (1985) 'Multivariate analysis of variance', *SAGE Publications Incorporated*, 7–10.

Brekke, K.A. (1997) 'The numéraire matters in cost-benefit analysis', *Journal of Public Economics*, *64*: 117–123.

Brent, R.J. (1984) 'Use of distributional weights in cost-benefit analysis: a survey of schools', *Public Finance Quarterly*, *12*: 213–230.

Brent, R.J. (1991a) 'On the estimation technique to reveal government distributional weights', *Applied Economics*, *23*: 985–992.

Brent, R.J. (1991b) 'The shadow wage rate and the numbers effect', *Public Finance*, *46(2)*: 186–197.

Brent, R.J. (1998) *Cost-Benefit Analysis for Developing Countries*, Cheltenham: Edward Elgar.

Brent, R.J. (2006) *Applied Cost-Benefit Analysis*, 2nd edn, Cheltenham: Edward Elgar.

Briggs, A. and Schulper, M. (1995) 'Sensitivity analysis in economic evaluation: a review of published studies', *Health Economics*, *4(5)*: 355–371.

British Broadcasting Corporation (2013) London 2012: Olympics and Paralympics £528m under Budget. Retrieved from http://www.bbc.com/sport/0/olympics/20041426.

Broome, J. (1992) *Counting the Cost of Global Warming*, Cambridge: The White Horse Press.

Buchanan, J.M. and Musgrave, R.A. (1999) *Public Finance and Public Choice: Two Contrasting Visions of the State*, Cambridge: MIT Press.

Burg, Van Der T. (1996) *Project Appraisal and Macroeconomic Policy*, Dordrecht: Kluwer Academic Publishers.

Burgess, D. (1989) 'The social opportunity cost of capital in the presence of labour market distortions', *Canadian Journal of Economics*, 26(2): 366–379.

Burton, R. and Damon, W.W. (1974) 'On the existence of a cost of capital under pure capital rationing', *The Journal of Finance*, 29(4): 1165–1173.

Cahill, N. and Dr O'Connell, L. (2018) '*Cost-benefit analysis, environment and climate change*', NESC Secretariat Papers Paper No. 15.

Cantarelli, C.C., Flyvbjerg, B., Molin, E.J.E. and van Wee, B. (2010). Cost overruns in large-scale transport infrastructure projects: explanations and their theoretical embeddedness. *The European Journal of Transport and Infrastructure Research*, 10(1): 5–11.

Campos, J., Serebrisky, T. and Suárez-Alemán, A. (2015) *Time Goes By: Recent Developments on the Theory and Practice of the Discount Rate*. Washington, DC: Inter-American Development Bank.

Caplin, A. and Leahy, J. (2004) 'The social discount rate', *Journal of Political Economy*, 112(6): 1257–1268.

Carbajo, J. (2007) 'Assessing the contribution of investment projects to building a market economy: beyond cost-benefit analysis?', in Florio, M. (ed) *Cost Benefit Analysis and Incentives in Evaluation: The Structural Funds of the European Union*, Cheltenham: Edward Elgar.

Carbonaro, G. (2007) 'Assessing projects and programmes for cohesion policy at the EIB', in Florio, M. (ed.) *Cost Benefit Analysis and Incentives in Evaluation: The Structural Funds of the European Union*, Cheltenham: Edward Elgar.

Carrigan, C. and Shapiro, S. (2016) 'What's wrong with the back of the envelope? A call for simple (and timely) benefit-cost analysis', *Regulation & Governance*, 11(2): 203–212.

Carson, R.T. (2011) *Contingent Valuation: A Comprehensive Bibliography and History*, Chaltenham: Edward Elgar.

Carson, R.T. and Groves, T. (2007) 'Incentive and informational properties of preference questions', *Environmental and Resource Economics*, 37(1): 181–210.

Castelnovo, P., Florio, M., Forte, S., Rossi, L. and Sirtori, E. (2018) 'The economic impact of technological procurement for large-scale research infrastructures: Evidence from the Large Hadron Collider at CERN', *Research Policy*, 47(9): 1853–1867.

Catalano, G. and Pancotti, C. (2022) '*Estimations of SDR in selected countries*', Working Paper CSIL, forthcoming.

Cella, M. and Florio, M. (2007) '*Hierarchical contracting in grant decisions: ex-ante and ex-post evaluation in the context of the EU structural funds*', Working Paper 22, University of Milan, Research Papers in Economics, Business, and Statistics.

CEPS (2013) *Assessing the Costs and Benefits of Regulation*, a study prepared for the European Commission's Secretariat General, Brussels: CEPS. https://ec.europa.eu/smart-regulation/impact/commission_guidelines/docs/131210_cba_study_sg_final.pdf

CERRE (2015) *Affordability of Utilities' Services: Extent, Practice, Policy*, Brussels: CERRE. https://cerre.eu/wp-content/uploads/2020/07/151022_CERRE_AffordabilityUtilitiesSer-vices_ResearchPaper_5.pdf

Chau, K.W., Wong, S.K., Chan, A.T. and Lam, K. (2006) 'How do people price air quality: empirical evidence from Hong Kong', paper presented at the *12th Annual Conference of the Pacific Rim Real Estate Society*, University of Auckland Business School, Auckland, New Zealand.

Cho-Min-Naing, Lertmaharit, S., Kamol-Ratanakul, P., Saul, A.J. (2000) 'Ex post and ex ante willingness to pay (WTP) for the ICT Malaria Pf/Pv test kit in Myanmar', *The Southeast Asian Journal of Tropical Medicine and Public Health*, 31(1): 104–11. PMID: 11023075.

Clemen, R.T. and Reilly, T. (1999) 'Correlations and copulas for decision and risk analysis', *Management Science*, *45(2)*: 208–224.

Clower, R.W. (1995) 'Axiomatics in economics', *Southern Economic Journal*, *62(2)*: 307–319.

Coady, D. (2006) 'Indirect tax and public pricing reforms', Chapter 5 in Coudoule, A. and Paternostro, S. (eds) *Analyzing the Distributional Impacts of Reforms*, Washington, DC: The World Bank Group.

Coady, D. and Drèze, J. (2002) 'Commodity taxation and social welfare: the generalized Ramsey rule', *International Tax and Public Finance*, *9(3)*: 295–316.

Coady, D.P. and Harris, R.L. (2004) 'Evaluating transfer programmes within a general equilibrium framework', *The Economic Journal*, *114(498)*: 778–799.

Coco, G. and Fedeli, S. (2014) 'Marxian public economics', in Forte, F. and Navarra, P. (eds) *A Handbook of Alternative Theories of Public Economics*, Cheltenham: Edward Elgar, forthcoming.

Colell, M.A., Whinston, M.D. and Green, J.R. (1995) *Microeconomic Theory*, Oxford: Oxford University Press.

Commonwealth of Australia (2006) *Australian Handbook of Cost-Benefit Analysis*, Financial Management Reference Material N.6, Department of Finance Administration. http://www.finance.gov.au/publications/finance-circulars/2006/docs/Handbook_of_CB_analysis.pdf.

Corlett, W.J. and Hague, D.C. (1953) 'Complementarity and the excess burden of taxation', *The Review of Economic Studies*, *21(1)*: 21–30.

Cornwall, R.R. (1984) *Introduction to the Use of General Equilibrium Analysis*, Amsterdam: North-Holland.

Cowell, F.A. and Gardiner, K. (1999) '*Welfare weights*', STICERD, London School of Economics, Economics Research Paper No. 20.

Cowell, F. and Mercader-Prats, M. (1999) 'Equivalence scales and inequality', Distributional Analysis Research Programme, DARP 27, STICERD, London: London School of Economics and Political Science.

CPB Netherlands Bureau for Economic Policy Analysis and PBL Netherlands Environmental Assessment Agency (2013) *General Guidance for Cost Benefit Analysis*, The Hague.

Curry, S. and Weiss, J. (2000) *Project Analysis in Developing Countries*, London: Macmillan.

Dabla-Norris, E., Brumby, J., Kyobe, A., Mills, Z. and Papageorgiou, C. (2012) 'Investing in public investment: an index of public investment efficiency', *Journal of Economic Growth*, *17(3)*: 235–266.

Dahlby, B. (2008) *The Marginal Cost of Public Funds: Theory and Applications*, Cambridge: MIT Press.

Daily, G.C. (1997) *Nature's Services: Societal Dependence on Natural Ecosystems*, Washignton, DC: Island Press.

Dasgupta, P. (2007) 'Commentary: the Stern review's economics of climate change', *National Institute Economic Review*, *199(4)*: 4–7.

Dasgupta, P. (2008) 'Discounting climate change', *Journal of Risk and Uncertainty*, *37(2)*: 141–169.

Dasgupta, P. (2021) *The Economics of Biodiversity: The Dasgupta Review*, London: HM Treasury.

Dasgupta, P., Marglin, S. and Sen, A.K. (1972) *Guidelines for Project Evaluation*, New York: UNIDO.

Davis, R.K. (1964) 'The value of big game hunting in a private forest', in *Transactions of the Twenty-Ninth North American Wildlife Conference*, Washington, DC: Wildlife Management Institute.

Day, B. (2001) *The Valuation of Non-Market Goods 2*, London: Imperial College, unpublished.

De Boer, W.I.J., Koning, R.H. and Mierau, J.O. (2019) 'Ex ante and ex post willingness to pay for hosting a large international sport event', *Journal of Sports Economics*, *20(2)*: 159–176.

De Borger, B. (1993) 'The economic environment and the public enterprise behaviour: Belgian railroads, 1950–1986', *Economica*, New Series, *60(240)*: 443–463.

De Rus, G. (2010) *Introduction to Cost Benefit Analysis: Looking for Reasonable Shortcuts*, Cheltenham: Edward Elgar.

Debreu, G. (1959) *Theory of Value: An Axiomatic Analysis of Economic Equilibrium*, New Haven, CT and London: Yale University Press.

Del Bo, C. and Florio, M. (2010) 'Cost-benefit analysis and rates of return of infrastructure projects: evidence from international organizations', *Transition Studies Review*, 17(3): 587–610.

Del Bo, C. and Florio, M. (2012) 'Public enterprises, policy adoption and planning: three welfare propositions', *Journal of Economic Policy Reform*, 15(4): 263–279.

Del Bo, C., Fiorio, C. and Florio, M. (2011) 'Shadow wages for the EU regions', *Fiscal Studies*, 32(1): 109–143.

Department for Business, Energy and Industrial Strategy (2018) *Better Regulation Framework. Interim Guidance*.

Department of Public Expenditure and Reform (2019) Public Spending Code. Central Technical References and Economic Appraisal Parameters, https://assets.gov.ie/20001/35c13bb-d055a4a09961a4ec59c93c798.pdf (accessed on May 18th 2021).

Devroye, L. (2003) *Non-Uniform Random Variate Generation*, Springer. http://luc.devroye.org/rnbookindex.html.

Diamond, J. and Mirrlees, A. (1971) 'Optimal taxation and public production, I: production efficiency, II: tax rules', *American Economic Review*, 61(1): 8–27 and 61(3): 261–278.

Dinwiddy, C. and Teal, F. (1996) *Principles of Cost Benefit Analysis for Developing Countries*, Cambridge and New York: Cambridge University Press.

Diwekar, U.M. and Kalagnanam, J.R. (1997) 'Efficient sampling technique for optimization under uncertainty', *American Institute of Chemical Engineers Journal*, 43(2): 440–447.

Dixon, J., Fallon Scura, L., Carpenter, R. and Sherman, P. (1994) *Economic Analysis of Environmental Impacts*, London: Earthscan.

Dobb, M. (1955) *On Economic Theory and Socialism*, New York: International Publishers.

Donzelli, F. (1997) 'Pareto's mechanical dream', *History of Economic Ideas*, 5(3): 125–178.

Donzelli, F. (2007) 'Equilibrium and Tâtonnement in Walras's Eléments', *History of Economic Ideas*, 15(3): 155–177.

Donzelli, F. (2008) 'Marshall vs. Walras on equilibrium and disequilibrium', *History of Economics Review*, 48(2): 1–38.

Drèze, J. (1998) 'Distribution matters in cost-benefit analysis: comment on K.A. Brekke', *Journal of Public Economics*, 70(3): 485–488.

Drèze, J.H. (1995) 'Forty years of public economics: a personal perspective', *The Journal of Economic Perspectives*, 9(2): 111–130.

Drèze, J. and Stern, N. (1987) 'The theory of cost-benefit analysis', Chapter 14 in Auerbach, A.J. and Feldstein, M. (eds) *Handbook of Public Economics*, Amsterdam: North-Holland and Elsevier Science Publishers.

Drèze, J. and Stern, N. (1990) 'Policy reform, shadow prices and market prices', *Journal of Public Economics*, 42(1): 1–45.

Drupp, M., Freeman, M., Groom, B. and Nesje, F. (2015) '*Discounting disentangled: an expert survey on the determinants of the long-term social discount rate*', Centre for Climate Change Economics and Policy Working Paper, 195.

Drupp, M.A., Freeman, M.C., Groom, B. and Nesje, F. (2018) 'Discounting disentangled', *American Economic Journal: Economic Policy*, 10(4): 109–134.

DtF – Department for Transport (2016) *Understanding and Valuing Impacts of Transport Investment. Updating Wider Economic Impacts Guidance*, London: OGL.

Dublin, L.I. and Lotka, A.J. (1946) *The Money Value of a Man*, 2nd edn, New York: Ronald Press Company.

Duesenberry, J.S. (1949) *Income, Saving, and the Theory of Consumer Behavior*, Cambridge, MA: Harvard University Press.

Dudley, S. (2020) 'Regulatory oversight and benefit-cost analysis: a historical perspective', *Journal of Benefit-Cost Analysis*, 11(1): 62–70.

Dudley, S. (2011) 'Observations on OIRA's thirtieth anniversary', *Administrative Law Review*, 63: 113–130.

Dudley, S. Belzer, R., Blomquist, G., Brennan, T.J., Carrigan, C., Cordes, J., Cox, L., Fraas, A., Graham, J., Gray, G., Hammitt, J.K., Krutilla, K., Linquiti, P., Lutter, R., Mannix, B., Shapiro, S.,

Smith, A., Viscusi, W.K., and Zerbe, R. (2017) 'Consumer's guide to regulatory impact analysis: ten tips for being an informed policymaker', *Journal of Benefit-Cost Analysis*, 8(2): 187–204.

Durante, F. and Sempi, C. (2010) 'Copula theory: an introduction', in Jaworski, P., Durante, F., Hardle, W. and Rychlik, T. (eds) *Copula Theory and Its Applications*. Lecture Notes in Statistics – Proceedings, Springer, pp. 3–31.

Duvigneau, J.C. and Prasad, R.N. (1984) '*Guidelines for calculating the financial and economic rates of returns for DFC project*', World Bank Technical Paper No. 33, Industry and Finance Series, 9, Washington, DC: The World Bank.

Eckhardt, R. (1987) 'Stan Ulam, John von Neumann, and the Monte Carlo method', *Los Alamos Science*, Special Issue Dedicated to Stanislaw Ulam: 15:131–136.

Eckstein, O. (1958) *Water Resource Development: The Economics of Project Evaluation*, Cambridge, MA: Harvard University Press.

Elton, E.J. (1970) 'Capital rationing and external discount rates', *The Journal of Finance*, 25(3): 573–584.

Englin, J. and Shonkwiler, J.S. (1995) 'Estimating social welfare using count data models: an application to long-run recreation demand under conditions of endogenous stratification and truncation', *Review of Economics and Statistics*, 77(1): 104–112.

Eskeland, G.S. and Kong, C. (1998) '*Protecting the environment and the poor: a public goods framework, and an application to Indonesia*', Development Research Group Paper, The World Bank.

European Commission (2005a) *Ex Post Evaluation of a Sample of Projects Co-financed by the Cohesion Fund (1993–2002)*, Brussels: DG Regional Policy.

European Commission (2005b) *ExternE – Externalities of Energy – Methodology 2005 Update*, Luxembourg: Office for Official Publications of the European Communities. Online. http://ec.europa.eu/research/energy/pdf/kina_en.pdf.

European Commission (2012) *Ex Post Evaluation of Investment Projects Co-financed by the European Fund for Regional Development (ERDF) and Cohesion Fund (CF) in the Period 1994–1999*, Brussels: DG Regional Policy.

European Commission (2014) *Guide to Cost-Benefit Analysis of Investment Projects. Economic Appraisal Tool for Cohesion Policy, 2014–2020*, Directorate for Regional Policy, authored by Sartori, D., Catalano, G., Genco, M., Pancotti, C., Sirtori, E., Vignetti, S. and Del Bo, C.

European Commission (2018) *Ex Post Evaluation of Major Projects Supported by the European Regional Development Fund (ERDF) and Cohesion Fund between 2000 and 2013-Transport*, Brussels: DG Regional Policy.

European Commission (2019a) *Ex Post Evaluation of Major Projects Supported by the European Regional Development Fund (ERDF) and Cohesion Fund between 2000 and 2013-Environment*, Brussels: DG Regional Policy.

European Commission (2019b) *Handbook on the External Costs of Transport*, Brussels: V.1.1 Directorate-General for Mobility and Transport.

European Commission (2021) *Economic Appraisal Vademecum*, report prepared by DG Regio with the support of JASPERS experts involved in project economic appraisal.

European Communities, International Monetary Fund, Organization for Economic Cooperation and Development, United Nations and World Bank (2009) *System of National Accounts 2008*, New York: United Nations.

European Investment Bank (2013) *The Economic Appraisal of Investment Projects at the EIB Version March 2013 – Under Review*, https://www.eib.org/en/publications/economic-appraisal-of-investment-projects (accessed on May 18th 2021).

European Investment Bank (2021) 'Jaspers: helping to improve people's lives', https://doi.org/10.2867/756435

European Parliament and Council (2012) *Regulation (EU, Euratom) No 966/2012 of 25 October 2012 on the Financial Rules Applicable to the General Budget of the Union and Repealing Council Regulation (EC, Euratom) No 1605/2002*, Brussels.

EVA-TREN (2007) 'Deliverable 1: evaluating the state-of-the-art in investment for transport and energy networks, policy-oriented research in the framework of the Sixth Framework

Programme 2002–06', in *Improved Decision-Aid Methods and Tools to Support Evaluation of Investment for Transport and Energy Networks in Europe*. Online. http://www.transport-research. info/Upload/Documents/201212/20121215_150641_58200_Deliverable_1.pdf (accessed on July 3rd 2013).

Evans, D. (2004a) 'The elevated status of the elasticity of marginal utility of consumption', *Applied Economics Letters*, *11*: 443–447.

Evans, D. (2004b) 'A social discount rate for France', *Applied Economics Letters*, *11*: 803–808.

Evans, D. (2005) 'The elasticity of marginal utility of consumption; estimates for 20 OECD countries', *Fiscal Studies*, *26*: 197–224.

Evans, D. (2007) 'Social discount rates for the European Union', in Florio, M. (ed.) *Cost-Benefit Analysis and Incentives in Evaluation: The Structural Funds of the European Union*, Cheltenham: Edward Elgar.

Evans, D., Kula, E. and Sezer, H. (2005) 'Regional welfare weights in the UK: England, Scotland, Wales and Northern Ireland', *Regional Studies*, *39*: 923–937.

Evans, D. and Sezer, H. (2002) 'A time preference measure of the social discount rate for the UK', *Applied Economics*, *34*: 1925–1934.

Evans, D. and Sezer, H. (2004) 'Social discount rates for six major countries', *Applied Economics Letters*, *11*: 557–560.

Evans, D. and Sezer, H. (2005) 'Social discount rates for member countries of the European Union', *Journal of Economic Studies*, *32*: 47–59.

Fankhauser, S. and Tepic, S. (2007) 'Can poor consumers pay for energy and water? An affordability analysis for transition countries', *Energy Policy*, *35*: 1038–1049.

Feldman, A.M. (1987) 'Welfare economics', *4*: 889–895 in Eatwell, J., Newman, P. and Milgate, M. (eds) *The New Palgrave: A Dictionary of Economics*, Four volumes, London: Macmillan.

Feldman, F. (2004) *Pleasure and the Good Life: Concerning the Nature, Varieties, and Plausibility of Hedonism*, Oxford: Clarendon Press.

Feldstein, M. (1964) 'The social time preference rate in cost benefit analysis', *Economic Journal*, *74*: 360–379.

Feldstein, M. (1965) 'The derivation of social time preference rates', *Kyklos*, *18(2)*: 277–287.

Feldstein, M. (1972) 'Distributional equity and the optimal structure of public prices', *The American Economic Review*, *62(1/2)*: 32–36.

Feller, W. (1948) 'On the Kolmogorov-Smirnov limit theorems for empirical distributions', *Annals of Mathematical Statistics*, *19(2)*: 177–189.

Fellner, W. (1967) 'Operational utility: the theoretical background and a measurement', in Fellner, W. (ed.) *Ten Economic Studies in the Tradition of Irving Fisher*, New York: John Wiley and Sons.

Fisher, I. (1927) 'A statistical method for measuring marginal utility and justice of a progressive Income Tax', in Fellner, W. (ed.) *Ten Economic Essays Contributed in Honour of J. Bates Clark*, London: Macmillan.

Fitzgerald, E.V.K. (1976) 'The urban service sector, the supply of wagegoods and the shadow wage rate', *Oxford Economic Papers*, New Series, *28(2)*: 228–239.

Fleurbaey, M. (2009) 'Beyond GDP: the quest for a measure of social welfare', *Journal of Economic Literature*, *47(49)*: 1029–1075.

Fleurbaey, M. and Rafeh, R.A. (2016) 'The use of distributional weights in benefit-cost and distributional weights analysis: insights from welfare economics', *Review of Environmental Economics and Policy*, *10(2)*: 286–307.

Florio, M. (1988) 'Vilfredo Pareto fra scienza delle finanze e welfare economics: alle origini del dibattito sui criteri del benessere sociale', in *Rivista di Diritto Finanziario e Scienza delle Finanze*, *4* (Dicembre).

Florio, M. (1990) 'Cost-benefit analysis and the control of public expenditure: an assessment of British experience in the 1980s', *Journal of Public Policy*, *10(2)*: 103–131.

Florio, M. (1997) 'The economic rate of return of infrastructures and regional policy in the European Union', *Annals of Public and Cooperative Economics*, *68(1)*: 39– 64.

Florio, M. (1999) '*An international comparison of the financial and economic rate of return of development projects*', Working Paper No. 99.06, Department of Political and Business Economics, University of Milan. Online. http://ssrn.com/abstract=455700.

Florio, M. (2001) 'On cross-country comparability of government statistics: public expenditures trends in OECD national accounts', *International Review of Applied Economics*, 15(2): 181–198.

Florio, M. (2003) *La Valutazione degli Investimenti Pubblici. I progetti di sviluppo nell'Unione Europea e nell'esperienza internazionale*, Vol. I, 2nd edn, Milan: Franco Angeli.

Florio, M. (2006) 'Cost-benefit analysis and the European Union cohesion fund: on the social cost of capital and labour', *Regional Studies*, 40(2): 211–224.

Florio, M. (2007) 'Introduction: multi-government cost-benefit analysis, shadow prices and incentives', in Florio, M. (ed.) *Cost-Benefit Analysis and Incentives in Evaluation, the Structural Funds of the European Union*, Cheltenham: Edward Elgar Publishing.

Florio, M. (2013) *Network Industries and Social Welfare: The Experiment that Reshuffled European Utilities*, Oxford: Oxford University Press.

Florio, M. (2014) 'On Marx and public economics: a comment', comment to the article by Coco and Fedeli included in F. Forte and P. Navarra (eds) *Handbook of Alternative Theories of Public Economics*, Cheltenham: Edward Elgar Publishing, forthcoming.

Florio, M. (2019) *Investing in Science. Social Cost-Benefit Analysis of Research Infrastructures*, Cambridge: MIT Press.

Florio M. and Giffoni F. (2020) 'A contingent valuation experiment about future particle accelerators at CERN', *PLoS ONE* 15(3): e0229885.

Florio, M., Forte, S. and Sirtori, E. (2016) 'Forecasting the socio-economic impact of the Large Hadron Collider: A cost–benefit analysis to 2025 and beyond', *Technological Forecasting and Social Change*, 112: 38–53.

Florio, M., Morretta, V. and Willak, W. (2018) 'Cost-benefit analysis and European Union cohesion policy: economic versus financial returns in investment project appraisal', *Journal of Benefit-Cost Analysis*, 9(1): 147–180.

Florio, M. and Sartori, D. (2010) '*Getting incentives right: do we need ex post CBA?*', CSIL Working Paper Series N.01/2010.

Florio, M. and Sirtori, E. (2013) '*The social cost of capital: recent estimates for the EU countries*', CSIL Working Paper Series N. 03/2013.

Florio, M. and Vignetti, S. (2005) 'Cost-benefit analysis of infrastructure projects in an enlarged European Union: return and incentives', *Economic Change and Restructuring*, 38: 179–210.

Florio, M. and Vignetti, S. (2011) 'Intellectual bridges across project evaluation traditions: the contribution of EU Regional Policy', *Cuadernos Economicos de ICE*, 80: 29–48.

Flyvbjerg, B. (2007) 'Policy and planning for large-infrastructure projects: problems, causes, cures', *Environment and Planning B: Planning and Design*, 34(4): 578–597.

Flyvbjerg, B. (2011) 'Over budget, over time, over and over again: managing major projects', in Morris, P.W.G., Pinto, J.K. and Söderlund, J. (eds) *The Oxford Handbook of Project Management*, 321–344, Oxford: Oxford University Press.

Flyvbjerg, B. (2014) 'What you should know about megaprojects and why: an overview', *Project Management Journal*, 45(2), April–May: 6–19.

Flyvbjerg, B. and Bester, D.W. (2021) "The cost-benefit fallacy: why cost-benefit analysis is broken and how to fix it", *Journal of Benefit-Cost Analysis*, 12(3): 395–419.

Flyvbjerg, B., Bruzelius, N. and Rothengatter, W. (2003) *Megaprojects and Risk: An Anatomy of Ambition*, Cambridge: Cambridge University Press.

Forte, F. (2010) *Principles of Public Economics: A Public Choice Approach*, Aldershot: Edward Elgar.

Fougere, D. and Heim, A. (2019) *L'évaluation socioéconomique de l'investissement social: Comment mettre en oeuvre des analyses coûts-bénéfices pour les politiques d'emploi, de santé et d'éducation*. https://www.strategie.gouv.fr/publications/levaluation-socioeconomique-de-linvestissement-social.

France Stratégie and Trésor Direction Général (2017) *Guide de l'évaluation socioéconomique des investissements publics*. https://www.strategie.gouv.fr/sites/strategie.gouv.fr/files/atoms/files/fs-guide-evaluation-socioeconomique-des-investissements-publics-04122017_web.pdf.

France Stratégie and Trésor Direction Général (2019) *L'évaluation socioéconomique des projets immobiliers de l'enseignement supérieur et de la recherché.* https://www.strategie.gouv.fr/sites/strategie.gouv.fr/files/atoms/files/fs-2019-rapport-eseesr-12022019-final.pdf.

Frederick, S., Loewenstein, G. and O'Donoghue, T. (2002) 'Time discounting and time preference: a critical review', *Journal of Economic Literature*, 40(2): 351–401.

Freeman, A.M. (2003) *The Measurement of Environmental and Resource Values: Theory and Methods*, Washington, DC: Resources for the Future.

Freeman, M., Groom, B. and Spackman, M. (2018) Social discount rates for cost–benefit analysis: a report for HM treasury, published on the HMT Green Book web page.

Frees, E.W. and Valdez, E.A. (1998) 'Understanding relationships using copulas', *North American Actuarial Journal*, 2(1): 1–25 and 137–141 (discussion by Wang, S.S.).

French Ministry of Transport (1995) 'Instruction cadre relative aux méthodes d'évaluation économique des grands projets d'infrastructures de transport', Directive dated 3 October.

French Ministry of Transport (2004) 'Harmonisation des méthodes d'évaluation des grands projets d'infrastructures de transport', Directive dated 25 March.

French Ministry of Transport (2005) 'Harmonisation des méthodes d'évaluation des grands projets d'infrastructures de transport. Mise à jour de l'instruction cadre du 25 Mars 2004', Directive dated 27 May.

Frey, B.S. and Stutzer, A. (2018) *Happiness and Economics*, New York: Springer International Publishing.

Frisch, R. (1932) *New Methods of Measuring Marginal Utility*, Tubingen: J.C.B. Mohr.

GAO (2020) *Cost Estimating and Assessment Guide: Best Practice for Developing and Managing Program Costs*, https://apps.dtic.mil/sti/pdfs/AD1098874.pdf.

Geanakoplos, J. (1987) 'Arrow-Debreu model of general equilibrium', 1: 116–124 in Eatwell, J., Newman, P.P. and Milgate, M. (eds) *The New Palgrave: A Dictionary of Economics*, Four volumes, London: Macmillan.

German Federal Environment Agency (UBA) (2012) *Economic Valuation of Environmental Damage—Methodological Convention 2.0 for Estimates of Environmental Costs*, report prepared by Schwermer, S. Berlin, Germany.

Godelier, M. (1971) 'Salt currency and the circulation of commodities among the Baruya of New Guinea', in Dalton, G. (ed.) *Studies in Economic Anthropology*, Washington, DC: Anthropological Studies, American Anthropological Association.

Goldberg, E. (2018) *'Better regulation: European Union style'*, M-RCBG Associate Working Paper Series: No. 98. Mossavar-Rahmani Center for Business & Government – Harvard Kennedy School.

Goldfarb, R.S. and Woglom, G. (1974) 'Government investment decisions and institutional constraints on income redistribution', *Journal of Public Economics*, 3(2): 171–180.

Gollier, C. (2002a) 'Discounting an uncertain future', *Journal of Public Economics*, 85(2): 149–166.

Gollier, C. (2002b) 'Time horizon and the discount rate', *Journal of Economic Theory*, 107(2): 463–473.

Gollier, C. (2010) 'Ecological discounting', *Journal of Economic Theory*, 145(2): 812–829.

Gollier, C. (2006) *'An evaluation of Stern's report on the economics of climate change'*, IDEI Working Paper, no. 464.

Gollier, C., Koundouri, P. and Pantelidis, T. (2008) 'Declining discount rates: economic justifications for implications for long-run policy', *Economic Policy*, 23(56): 757–795.

Gómez-Lobo, A. (2012) 'Institutional safeguards for cost benefit analysis: lessons from the Chilean National Investment System', *Journal of Benefit-Cost Analysis*, 3(1): Article 1.

Gosling, J.P., Hart, A., Mouat, D.C., Sabirovic, M., Scanlan, S. and Simmons, A. (2012) 'Quantifying experts' uncertainty about the future cost of exotic diseases', *Risk Analysis*, 32(5): 881–893.

Gramlich, E.M. (1994) Infrastructure investment: a review essay, *Journal of Economic Literature*, 32: 1176–1196.

Greenwald, B. and Stiglitz, J.E. (1988) 'Pareto inefficiency of market economies: search and efficiency wage models', *American Economic Association Papers and Proceedings*, 78: 351–355.

Greenwald, B.C. and Stiglitz, J.E. (1986) 'Externalities in economies with imperfect informa-tion and incomplete markets', *Quarterly Journal of Economics, 101*(2): 229–264.

Griniece, E., Angelis, J., Reid A, Vignetti, S., Catalano, J., Helman, A., Barberis Rami, M. (2020) *Guidebook for Socio-Economic Impact Assessment of Research Infrastructures.* https://ri-paths.eu/wp-content/uploads/2018/03/D5.4_RI-PATHS_Guidebook.pdf.

Grogger, J. and Carson, R. (1991) 'Models for truncated counts', *Journal of Applied Econometrics, 6*(3): 225–238.

Groom, B. and Maddison, Pr., D. (2019) 'New estimates of the elasticity of marginal utility for the UK', *Environmental & Resource Economics, 72*(4): 1155–1182.

Guesnerie, R. (1980) *Modèles de l'économie publique*, Paris: Editions du CNRS.

Guesnerie, R. (1995) 'The genealogy of modern theoretical public economics: from first best to second best', *European Economic Review, 39*(3–4): 353–381.

Gupta, M.R. (1986) 'Shadow wage rate in a dynamic Harris-Todaro model', *Oxford Economic Papers*, New Series, *38*(1): 131–140.

Haab, T.C. and McConnell, K.E. (2002) *Valuing Environmental and Natural Resources: The Econometrics of Non-Market Valuation.* Cheltenham: Edward Elgar Publishing.

Haas, C.N. (1999) 'On modeling random variables in risk assessment', *Risk Analysis, 19*(6): 1205–1214.

Hall, J.H. (2000) 'Investigating aspects of the capital budgeting process used in the evaluation of investment projects', *South African Journal of Economic and Management Sciences, 3*(3): 353–368.

Hammitt, J.K. (2021) 'Accounting for the distribution of benefits and costs in benefit–cost analysis', *Journal of Benefit Cost Analysis, 12*(1): 64–84.

Hanley, N. and Spash, C. (1993) *Cost-Benefit Analysis and the Environment*, Cheltenham: Edward Elgar.

Harberger, A.C. (1969) 'On measuring the social opportunity cost of public funds', *Proceedings of the Committee on the Economics of Water Resources Development of the West: The Discount Rate in Public Investment Evaluation*, Western Agricultural Economics Research Council, Denver, CO.

Harberger, A.C. (1971a) 'On measuring the social opportunity cost of labour', *International Labour Review, 103*: 559–579.

Harberger, A.C. (1971b) 'Three basic postulates for applied welfare economics: an interpretive essay', *Journal of Economic Literature, 9*: 785–797.

Harberger, A.C. (1972) *Project Evaluation: Collected Papers*, London: Macmillan.

Harberger, A.C. (1978) 'On the use of distributional weights in social cost-benefitanalysis', *Journal of Political Economy, 86*: S87–S120.

Harberger, A.C. (1984) 'Basic needs versus distributional weights in social cost-benefit analysis', *Economic Development and Cultural Change, 32*(3): 455–474.

Harberger, A.C. and Jenkins, A.C. (eds) (2002) *Cost-Benefit Analysis*, Cheltenham: Edward Elgar.

Harris, J.R. and Todaro, M.P. (1970) 'Migration, unemployment and development: a two sector analysis', *American Economic Review, 60*: 126–142.

Harrison, M. (2010) '*Valuing the future: the social discount rate in cost-benefit analysis*', Visiting Researcher Paper, Productivity Commission, Canberra. Online. http://pc.gov.au/__data/as-sets/pdf_file/0012/96699/cost-benefit-discount.pdf.

Harsanyi, J.C. (1955) 'Cardinal welfare, individualistic ethics and interpersonal comparisons of utility', *Journal of Political Economy, 63*(4): 309–321.

Haveman, R.H. and Farrow, S. (2011) 'Labor expenditure and benefit-cost accounting in times of unemployment', *Journal of Benefit-Cost Analysis, 2*(2): Article 7.

Haveman, R.H. and Weimer, D.L. (2015) 'Public policy induced changes in employment: valu-ation issues for benefit-cost analysis', *Journal of Benefit–Cost Analysis, 6*: 112–115.

Heal, G.M. (1973) *The Theory of Economic Planning*, Amsterdam: North-Holland.

Helton, J.C. and Davis, F.J. (2003) 'Latin hypercube sampling and the propagation of uncer-tainty in analyses of complex systems', *Reliability Engineering and Systems Safety, 81*: 23–69.

Hepburn, C. (2003) '*Hyperbolic discounting and resource collapse*', Economic Series Working Paper No. 159, University of Oxford, Department of Economics.

Heyne, M., Maennig, W. and Suessmuth, B. (2007) 'Mega-sporting events as experience goods', *Hamburg Contemporary Economic Discussions*, 5: 203–220.

Hicks, J. (1939) 'The foundations of welfare economics', *The Economic Journal*, 49(196): 696–712.

Hildebrand, W. and Kirman, P. (1988) *Equilibrium Analysis: Variations on Themes by Edgeworth and Walras*, Amsterdam: North-Holland.

Hindriks, J. and Myles, G.D. (2006) *Intermediate Public Economics*, Cambridge: MIT Press.

Hirschman, A.O. (1967) *Development Projects Observed*, Washington, DC: The Brookings Institution.

HM Treasury (2003) *The Green Book – Appraisal and Evaluation in Central Government*, Treasury Guidance, London: TSO.

HM Treasury (2020a) *The Green Book: Central Government Guidance on Appraisal and Evaluation*, Treasury Guidance, London.

HM Treasury (2020b) *The Magenta Book: Guidance for Evaluation*, Treasury Guidance, London.

Hoff, K. (1994) 'The second theorem of the second best', *Journal of Public Economics*, 54(2): 223–242.

Honohan, P. (1998) 'Key issues of cost-benefit methodology for Irish industrial policy', General Research Series 172, Dublin: Economic and Social Research Institute.

Horbulyk, T.M. (2001) 'The social cost of labor in rural development: job creation benefits re-examined', *Agricultural Economics*, 24(2): 199–208.

Hughes, G. (1987) 'The incidence of fuel taxes: a comparative study of three countries', Chapter 20 in Newbery, D. and Stern, N. (eds) *The Theory of Taxation for Developing Countries*, Oxford and New York: Oxford University Press.

Irvin, G. (1978) *Modern Cost-Benefit Methods: An Introduction to Financial, Economic and Social Appraisal of Development Projects*, London: Macmillan Publishers Ltd.

Isham, J. and Kaufmann, D. (1999) 'The forgotten rationale for policy re-form: the productivity of investment projects', *Quarterly Journal of Economics*, 114(1): 149–184.

Italian Ministry of Infrastructure and Transport (2006) 'Note sulla determinazione dei fattori di conversione utilizzati nell'analisi costi-benefici dei grandi progetti', Rome.

Invitalia (2014) *Guida all'analisi costi-benefici dei progetti d' investimento: Strumento di valutazione economica per la politica di coesione 2014–2020*, https://people.unica.it/elisabettastrazzera/files/2017/10/LineeGuidaACB.pdf.

ITF (2015) *Adapting Transport Policy to Climate Change: Carbon Valuation, Risk and Uncertainty*, ITF Research Reports, OECD Publishing, Paris, https://doi.org/10.1787/9789282107928-en.

Jacob, K., Ferretti, J. and Guske, A. (2012) *Sustainability in Impact Assessments: A Review of Impact Assessment Systems in Selected OECD Countries and the European Commission*, Paris: OECD Publishing.

Jacoby, H.G. (1993) 'Shadow wages and peasant family labour supply: an econometric application to the Peruvian Sierra', *Review of Economic Studies*, 60: 903–921.

Jenkins, G. (1997) 'Project analysis and the World Bank', *The American Economic Review*, 87(2): 38–42.

Jenkins, G. and Harberger, A. (1994) *Manual – Cost Benefit Analysis of Investment Decisions*, Cambridge, MA: Harvard Institute for International Development.

Jenkins, G., Lim, H.B.F. and Shukla, G.P. (1999) 'Evaluation of an expansion of the electricity transmission system in Mexico', HIID Development Discussion Paper No. 688.

Jha, R. (1998) *Modern Public Economics*, London: Routledge.

Johansson, P.O. (1982) 'Cost benefit rules in general disequilibrium', *Journal of Public Economics*, 18: 121–137.

Johansson, P.O. (1984) 'Disequilibrium cost-benefit rules for natural resources', *Resources and Energy*, 6(4): 355–372.

Johansson, P.O. (1991) *An Introduction to Modern Welfare Economics*, Cambridge: Cambridge University Press.

Johansson, P.O (1993) *Cost-Benefit Analysis of Environmental Change*, Cambridge: Cambridge University Press.

Johansson, P.O. (1998) 'Does the numéraire matter in cost-benefit analysis?', *Journal of Public Economics*, 70: 489–493.

Johansson, P.O. (2010) 'On the treatment of taxes in cost-benefit analysis', *Cuadernos económicos de ICE*, no. 80.

Johansson, P.O. and Kriström, B. (2018) 'Partial equilibrium versus general equilibrium evaluations or small versus large projects', in Farrow S. (ed.) *Teaching Benefit-Cost Analysis*, Cheltenham: Edward Elgar Publishing.

Johansson, P.O. and Kriström, B. (2020) 'On the social opportunity cost of unemployment', *Journal of Economic Policy Reform*, 1–11.

Johansson-Stenman, O. and Sterner, T. (2011) '*Discounting and relative consumption*', Resources for the Future Discussion Paper 11–38, Washington, DC. Online. http://www.rff.org/documents/RFF-DP-11-38.pdf.

Jones, C.M. (2005) *Applied Welfare Economics*, Oxford: Oxford University Press.

Just, R.E., Hueth, D.L. and Schmitz, A. (2004) *The Welfare Economics of Public Policy. A Practical Approach to Project and Policy Evaluation*, Cheltenham and Northampton: Edward Elgar.

Kahn, A. (1988) *The Economics of Regulation: Principles and Institutions*, Cambridge: MIT Press.

Kahneman, D. and Tversky, A. (eds) (2000) *Choices, Values, and Frames*, New York: Cambridge University Press.

Kaldor, N. (1939) 'Welfare propositions in economics and interpersonal comparisons of utility', *The Economic Journal*, 49(*195*): 549–552.

Källström, M.N. (2010) *Testing Different Approaches to Benefit Transfers between Two Sites in the Same Country, Valuing the Improvement of Water Quality*, Aarhus: Aarhus University.

Kaplow, L. (1996) 'The optimal supply of public goods and the distortionary cost of taxation', *National Tax Journal*, 49(*4*): 513–533.

Kaplow, L. (2010) *The Theory of Taxation and Public Economics*, Princeton, NJ: Princeton University Press.

Katzen, S. (2020) 'Cost-benefit analysis without the B: how rewriting OIRA's past threatens its future', *Journal of Benefit-Cost Analysis*, 11(*1*): 49–54.

Kaufman, L. and Rousseeuw, P.J. (1990) *Finding Groups in Data: An Introduction to Cluster Analysis*, New York: Wiley.

Kayaloff, I. (1988) *Export and Project Finance: A Creative Approach to Financial Engineering*, London: Euromoney Publications.

Kazlauskienė, V. (2015) 'Application of social discount rate for assessment of public investment projects', *Procedia-Social and Behavioral Sciences*, 213: 461–467.

Kelly, C., Laird, J., Costantini, S., Richards, P., Carbajo, J. and Nellthorp, J. (2015) 'Ex post appraisal: what lessons can be learnt from EU cohesion funded transport projects?', *Transport Policy*, 37: 83–91.

Keohane, N.O. (2009) 'The technocratic and democratic functions of the CAIR regulatory analysis', in Harrington et al. (ed.) *Reforming Regulatory Impact Analysis*, 33–55, Washington, DC: Resources for the Future Press.

Keynes, J.M. (1936) *The General Theory of Employment, Interest and Money*, London: Macmillan.

Kirkpatrick, C. (1994) 'New developments in project appraisal in developing countries: editor's introduction', *Journal of International Development*, 6(*1*): 1.

Kjerkreit, A. and Odeck, J. (2009) '*The accuracy of ex-ante benefit cost analysis – a post opening evaluation in the case of Norwegian road projects*', article presented at International Transport Economics Conference (ITrEC), University of Minnesota, Minneapolis, MN.

Knight, F. (1921, 2nd edn 1964) *Risk, Uncertainty and Profit*, New York: Sentry Press.

Kopits, E., McGartland, A., Morgan, C., Pasurka, C, Shadbegian, R., Simon, N., Simpson, D. and Wolverton, A. (2014) 'Retrospective cost analyses of EPA regulations: a case study approach', *Journal of Benefit-Cost Analysis*, 5(*2*): 173–193.

Kornai, J. (1971) *Anti-Equilibrium*, Amsterdam: North-Holland.

Koutsougeras, L.C. and Ziros N. (2015) 'The second welfare theorem in economies with non-Walrasian markets', *Journal of Public Economic Theory*, 17(*3*): 415–432.

Kroese, D.P., Taimre, T. and Botev, Z.I. (2011) *Handbook of Monte Carlo Methods*, Hoboken, NJ: John Wiley & Sons.

Kula, E. (1984) 'Derivation of social time preference rates for the United States and Canada', *The Quarterly Journal of Economics*, November: *99*(4): 873–882.

Kula, E. (2002) 'Regional welfare weights in investment appraisal – the case of India', *Journal of Regional Analysis and Policy*, *32*(1): 99–114.

Kula, E. (2007) 'Regional welfare weights', in Florio, M. (ed.) *Cost-Benefit Analysis and Incentives in Evaluation*, Cheltenham: Edward Elgar.

Kula, E. (2012) 'Discounting: does it ensure intergenerational equity?', in Weiss, J. and Potts, D. (eds) *Current Issues in Project Analysis for Development*, Cheltenham: Edward Elgar.

Ladegaard, P., Lundkvist, P. and Kamkhaji, J. (2018) *Giving Sisyphus a Helping Hand. Pathways for Sustainable RIA Systems in Developing Countries*, Washington, DC: World Bank Group.

Laffont, J.J. (1988) *Fundamentals of Public Economics*, Cambridge: MIT Press.

Laffont, J.J. (2005) *Regulation and Development*, Cambridge: Cambridge University Press.

Laffont, J.J. and Tirole, J. (1993) *A Theory of Incentives in Regulation and Procurement*, Cambridge: MIT Press.

Laffont, J.J. and Tirole, J. (2000) *Competition in Telecommunications*, Cambridge: MIT Press.

Laibson, D. (1997) 'Golden eggs and hyperbolic discounting', *Quarterly Journal of Economics*, *112*(2): 443–477.

Lal, D. (1973) 'Disutility of effort, migration and the shadow wage rate', *Oxford Economic Papers*, *25*: 112–126.

Lang, H. and Riess, A.-D. (2019) '*Shadow wages in cost-benefit rules for project and policy analyses: estimates for OECD countries*', DEM Discussion Paper Series 19-05, Department of Economics at the University of Luxembourg.

Lange, O. and Taylor, F. (eds) (1948) *On the Economic Theory of Socialism*, Minneapolis: University of Minnesota Press.

Layard, R. (2005) *Happiness: Lessons from a New Science*, London: Penguin Books.

Layard, R. and Glaister, S. (eds) (1994) *Cost-Benefit Analysis*, 2nd edn, Cambridge: Cambridge University Press.

Layard, R., Mayraz, G., Nickellc, S. (2008) 'The marginal utility of income', *Journal of Public Economics*, *92*(8–9): 1846–1857.

Leach, J.A. (2003) *A Course in Public Economics*, Cambridge: Cambridge University Press.

Le Grand, J. and New, B. (2015) *Government Paternalism: Nanny State or Helpful Friend?*, Princeton, NJ: Princeton University Press.

Lemoine, J. (2019) *Global Indicators of Regulatory Governance: Worldwide Practices of Regulatory Impact Assessments*, Washington, DC: World Bank Group.

Lerner, A.P. (1946) *The Economics of Control: Principles of Welfare Economics*, New York: Macmillan.

Lewis, W.A. (1954) 'Economic development with unlimited supplies of labour', *The Manchester School*, *22*: 139–191.

Ley, E. (2007) *On the Improper Use of the Internal Rate of Return in Cost-Benefit Analysis*, Washington, DC: World Bank Institute.

Lind, R.C. (1990) 'Reassessing the government's discount rate policy in light of new theory and data in a world economy with high degree of capital mobility', *Journal of Environmental Economics and Management*, *18*: S8–S28.

Lindahl, E. (1919) 'Just taxation – a positive solution', in R. Musgrave and A. Peacock (eds) *Classics in the Theory of Public Finance*, New York: St Martins Press.

Lipsey, R. and Lancaster, K. (1956) 'The general theory of second best', *Review of Economic Studies*, *24*(1): 11–32.

Little, I.M.D. (1950) *A Critique of Welfare Economics*, Oxford: Clarendon Press.

Little, I.M.D. (1961) 'The real cost of labour and the choice between consumption and investment', *Quarterly Journal of Economics*, *75*: 1–15.

Little, I.M.D. and Mirrlees, J.A. (1974) *Project Appraisal and Planning for Developing Countries*, London: Heinemann Educational Books.

Little, I.M.D. and Mirrlees, J.A. (1990) 'Project appraisal and planning twenty years on', *Proceedings of the World Bank Annual Conference on Development Economics*, Washington, DC: The World Bank.

Little, I.M.D. and Mirrlees, J.A. (1994) 'The costs and benefits of analysis: project appraisal and planning twenty years on', in Layard, R.S. and Glaister, S. (eds) *Cost-Benefit Analysis*, Cambridge: Cambridge University Press.

Livermore, M. and Revesz, R. (2020) *Reviving Rationality: Saving Cost-Benefit Analysis for the Sake of the Environment and Our Health*. New York: Oxford University Press.

Londero, E.H. (2003) *Shadow Prices for Project Appraisal. Theory and Practice*, Cheltenham and Northampton, MA: Edward Elgar.

London Economics (1997) *Water Pricing: The Importance of Long Run Marginal Costs*, prepared for Ofwat – Office of Water Services.

López-Mosquera, N. and Sánchez, M. (2014) 'Cognitive and affective determinants of satisfaction, willingness to pay, and loyalty in suburban parks', *Urban Forestry & Urban Greening*, 13(2): 375-384,

Lyon, R. (1990) 'Federal discount rate policy, the shadow price of capital, and challenges for reforms', *Journal of Environmental Economics and Managements*, 18: S29–S50.

McFadden, D. (1975) 'The revealed preferences of a government bureaucracy: theory', *Bell Journal of Economics*, 6(2): 401–416.

McFadden, D. (1976) 'The revealed preferences of a government bureaucracy: empirical evidence', *Bell Journal of Economics*, 7(1): 55–72.

McKenzie, L.W. (1987) 'General equilibrium', 2: 498–512, in Eatwell, J., Peter Newman, P. and Milgate, M. (eds) *The New Palgrave: A Dictionary of Economics*, Four volumes, London: Macmillan.

Mackie, P. and Preston, J. (1998) 'Twenty-one sources of error and bias in transport project appraisal', *Transport Policy*, 5: 1–7.

Madden, D. (2009) '*Distributional characteristics for Ireland: a note*', Working Paper Series 2009, UCD Centre for Economic Research, University College Dublin.

McManus, M. (1959) 'Comments on the general theory of second best', *The Review of Economic Studies*, 26(3): 209–224.

Mahieu, P.-A., Andersson, H., Beaumais, O., Crastes, R. and Wolf, F.-C. (2014) '*Is choice experiment becoming more popular than contingent valuation? A systematic review in agriculture, environment and health*', FAERE Working Paper 2014.12.

Malinvaud, E. (1972) *Lectures on Microeconomic Theory*, Amsterdam: North-Holland.

Malinvaud, E. (1977) *The Theory of Unemployment Reconsidered*, Oxford: Basil Blackwell.

Malinvaud, E. and Nabli, M.K. (1997) 'The future of planning in market economies', Chapter 4 in Malinvaud, E., Milleron, J.-C., Nabli, M.K., Sen, A.K., Sengupta, A., Stern, N., Stiglitz, J.E. and Suzumura, K. (eds) *Development Strategy and Management of the Market Economy*, Vol. 1, Oxford: Oxford University Press.

Mangalam, S. and Vranic, G. (2020) *Use of New Technologies in Regulatory Delivery*, Cambridge: Donor Committee for Enterprise Development.

Marchand, M., Mintz, J. and Pestieau, P. (1984) 'Shadow pricing of labour and capital in an economy with unemployed labour', *European Economic Review*, 25: 239–252.

Marsden Jacob Associates (2004) '*Estimation of Long Run Marginal Cost (LRMC)*', report prepared for the Queensland Competition Authority. Online. http://www.qca.org.au/files/QCAL-RMCFinal.pdf.

Mason, A. (2013) '*Cost benefit analysis framework for broadband connectivity projects*', JASPERS Knowledge Economy and Energy Division, Staff Working Papers.

Mazumdar, D. (1976) 'The rural-urban wage gap, migration, and the shadow wage', *Oxford Economic Papers*, New Series, 28(3): 406–425.

Mendes, I. and Proença, I. (2005) '*Estimating the recreation value of ecosystems by using a travel cost method approach*', Working Paper 2005/08, Department of Economics at the School of Economics and Management (ISEG), Technical University of Lisbon.

Menon, M., Preali, F. and Rosati, F.C. (2005) '*The shadow wage of child labour: an application to Nepal*', UCW Working Paper.

Merret, J.A. and Sykes, A. (1963) *The Finance and Analysis of Capital Projects*, London: Longmans, Green & Co.

Merrifield, J. (1997) 'Sensitivity analysis in cost-benefit analysis: a key to increased use and acceptance', *Contemporary Economic Policy*, *15(3)*, 82–92.

Metropolis, N. (1987) 'The beginning of Monte Carlo method', *Los Alamos Science*, Special Issue dedicated to Stanislaw Ulam, (15): 125–130.

Milgate, M. (1979) 'On the origin of the notion of "intertemporal equilibrium"', *Economica*, *46(181)*: 1–10.

Milgate, M. (1987) 'Equilibrium: development of the concept', *1*: 179–182 in Eatwell, J., Peter Newman, P. and Milgate, M. (eds) *The New Palgrave: A Dictionary of Economics*, Four volumes, London: Macmillan.

Miniaci, R., Scarpa, C. and Valbonesi, P. (2014) 'Energy affordability and the benefits system in Italy', *Energy Policy*, 75: 289–300.

Mirrlees, J.A. (1976) 'Optimal tax theory: a synthesis', *Journal of Public Economics*, *6(4)*: 327–358.

Mishan, E.J. (1969) *Welfare Economics: An Assessment*, Amsterdam: North-Holland.

Mishan, E.J. (1976) *Cost-Benefit Analysis*, New York: Praeger.

Moore, M.A., Boardman, A.E. and Vining, A.R. (2013) 'The choice of the social discount rate and the opportunity cost of public funds', *Journal of Benefit-Cost Analysis*, *4(3)*: 401–409.

Moore, M.A., Boardman, A.E. and Vining, A.R. (2020) 'Social discount rates for seventeen latin american countries: theory and parameter estimation', *Public Finance Review*, *48(1)*: 43–71.

Mouter, N. (2018) 'A critical assessment of discounting policies for transport cost-benefit analysis in five European practices', *European Journal of Transport and Infrastructure Research*, *18(4)*: 389–412.

Mueller, D.C. (2003) *Public Choice III*, Cambridge and New York: Cambridge University Press.

Mukhopadhyay, N. (2000) *Probability and Statistical Inference*, New York: Dekker-CRC Press.

Murakami, H. (2016) 'A non-Walrasian microeconomic foundation of the "profit principle" of investment', in Matsumoto, A., Szidarovszky, F. and Asada, T. (eds) *Essays in Economic Dynamics*, Singapore: Springer.

Murty, M.N. and Gulati, S.C. (2004) '*A generalized method of hedonic prices: measuring benefits from reduced urban air pollution*', paper prepared as part of the research on 'Natural Research Accounting' financed by the Central Statistical Organization, Government of India.

Musgrave, R.A. (1969) 'Provision for social goods', in Margolis, J. and Guitton, H. (eds) *Public Economics*, London: Macmillan.

Myles, G. (1988) 'Some implications of quality differentials for optimal taxation', *Economic Journal* (Supplement), *98*: 148–160.

Myles, G. (1990) 'Vertical product differentiation can imply the Friedman-Savage utility function', *Economics Letters*, *33*: 5–9.

Myles, G.D. (1995) *Public Economics*, Cambridge: Cambridge University Press.

Myrdal, G. (1969) *Objectivity in Social Research*, New York: Pantheon.

National Audit Office (2007) Evaluation of Regulatory Impact Assessments 2006–2007.

Navajas, F. (2004) 'Structural reforms and the distributional effects of price changes in Argentina', in Bour, E., Heymann, D. and Navajas, F. (eds) *Latin American Macroeconomic Crisis, Trade and Labour*, London: Macmillan.

Neary, J.P. (1987) 'Rationing', 4: 92-96 in Eatwell, J., Peter Newman, P. and Milgate, M. (eds) *The new Palgrave: A Dictionary of Economics*, Four volumes, London: Macmillan.

Neary, J.P. and Roberts, K.W.S. (1980) 'The theory of household behaviour under rationing', *European Economic Review*, *1(13)*: 25–42.

Nepal, A. and Nelson, C. (2015) 'Estimation of shadow wage in agricultural household model in Nepal', 2015 Conference, Milan, Italy, International Association of Agricultural Economists.

Netherlands Discount Rate Working Group (2015) Rapport Werkgroep Discontovoet 2015, https://pure.uva.nl/ws/files/2661329/167999_rapport_werkgroep_discontovoet_2015_bijlage_2_.pdf (accessed on March 29th 2021).

Nevitt, P.K. (1989) *Project Financing*, London: Euromoney Publications.

Newbery, D. (1992) '*Long-term, discount rates for the forest enterprise*', paper commissioned by the Department of Forestry, Forestry Commission, Edinburgh.

Newbery, D. (1995) 'The distributional impact of price changes in Hungary and the United Kingdom', *Economic Journal, 105(431)*: 847–863.

Newbery, D. and Stern, N. (1987) (eds) *The Theory of Taxation for Developing Countries*, Oxford: Oxford University Press.

Newell, R.G. and Pizer, W.A. (2004) 'Uncertain discount rates in climate policy analysis', *Energy Policy, 32(4)*: 519–529.

New Zealand Government (2015) *Guide to Social Cost Benefit Analysis*, prepared by the Treasury. https://www.treasury.govt.nz/publications/guide/guide-social-cost-benefit-analysis (accessed on March 29th 2021).

New Zealand Government (2020) *Technical Note on Social Discount Rate*, prepared by the Treasury. https://www.treasury.govt.nz/information-and-services/state-sector-leadership/guidance/financial-reporting-policies-and-guidance/discount-rates (accessed on March 29th 2021).

Ni, J. (2017) *Discount Rate in Project Analysis*, Département Développement Durable et Numérique, France Stratégie. https://www.strategie.gouv.fr/sites/strategie.gouv.fr/files/atoms/files/10_fs_discount_rate_in_project_analysis.pdf (accessed on March 29th 2021).

Nicolaisen, M.S. and Driscoll, P.A. (2016) 'An international review of ex-post project evaluation schemes in the transport sector', *Journal of Environmental Assessment Policy and Management, 18(01)*: 1–33.

Nordhaus, W. (1993) 'Rolling the DICE: an optimal transition path for controlling greenhouse gases', *Resource and Energy Economics, 15*: 27–50.

Nordhaus, W. (2007) 'A review of the Stern review on the economics of climate change', *Journal of Economic Literature, 45(3)*: 686–702.

NOU (2012) *Cost-Benefit Analysis*, Official Norwegian Reports, NOU 2012: 16.

NSW Treasury (2017) *Guide to Cost-Benefit Analysis*, TPP 17–03. Sydney: NSW Treasury.

Nussbaum, M.C. (2000) *Women and Human Development: The Capabilities Approach*, Cambridge: Cambridge University Press.

O'Callaghan, d.a.n.i.e.l., Prior, s. and Unit, i. (2018) '*Central technical appraisal parameters: discount rate, time horizon, shadow price of public funds and shadow price of labour*', Staff Paper 2018. at https://igees.gov.ie/wp-content/uploads/2019/07/Parameters-Paper-Final-Version.pdf (accessed on March 29th 2021).

Odeck, J. (2013) 'How accurate are national road traffic growth-rate forecasts?—The case of Norway', *Transport Policy, 27*: 102–111.

Odeck, J. (2014) 'Do reforms reduce the magnitudes of cost overruns in road projects? Statistical evidence from Norway', *Transportation Research Part A: Policy and Practice, 65*: 68–79.

Odeck, J. and Welde, M. (2017) 'The accuracy of toll road traffic forecasts: An econometric evaluation Transport', *Res. Part A: Policy Pract., 101*: 73-85.

Odeck, J. and Kjerkreit, A. (2019) 'The accuracy of benefit-cost analyses (BCAs) in transportation: an ex-post evaluation of road projects', *Transportation Research Part A: Policy and Practice, 120*: 277–294.

OECD (1999) *Handbook of Incentive Measures for Biodiversity*, Paris: OECD.

OECD (2004) *The International Standard Cost Model Manual*, Paris: OECD.

OECD (2007) '*Use of discount rates in the estimation of the costs of inaction with respect to selected environmental concerns*', Working Party on National Environmental Policies, prepared by Hepburn, C., OECD.

OECD (2008) *Introductory Handbook for Undertaking Regulatory Impact Analysis* (RIA), Paris: OECD.

OECD (2010) *Producer and Consumer Support Estimates*, OECD Database 1986–2008. Online. http://www.oecd.org/agriculture/pse.

OECD (2012) *Mortality Risk Valuation in Environment, Health & Transport Policies*. Paris: OECD Publishing.

OECD (2014) *Regulatory Policy in Mexico*, Paris: OECD.

OECD (2015) *Regulatory Policy in Perspective*, Paris: OECD.

OECD (2018) *Cost-Benefit Analysis and the Environment: Further Developments and Policy Use*. Paris: OECD Publishing.

OECD (2019) *Tools and Ethics for Applied Behavioural Insights: The BASIC Toolkit*, Paris: OECD Publishing.

OECD (2020a) *A Closer Look at Proportionality and Threshold Tests for RIA*, Paris: OECD.

OECD (2020b) *Regulatory Impact Assessment*, Paris: OECD.

OECD (2021a) *How Do Laws and Regulations Affect Competitiveness: The Role for Regulatory Impact Assessment*, Paris: OECD.

OECD (2021b) *Regulatory Policy Outlook 2021*, Paris: OECD.

Office of Management and Budget – OMB (1992) *Circular a-94: Guidelines and Discount Rates for Benefit-Cost Analysis of Federal Programs*.

Office of Management and Budget – OMB (2003) *Circular No. A-4, "Regulatory Analysis"*.

Office of Management and Budget – OMB (2010) *Agency Checklist: Regulatory Impact Analysis*.

Office of Management and Budget – OMB (2011a) *Circular A-4, Regulatory Impact Analysis: Frequently Asked Questions (FAQs)*.

Office of Management and Budget – OMB (2011b) *Circular A-4, Regulatory Impact Analysis: A Primer*.

OPD/OED (1995) *A Review of the Quality of Economic Analysis in Staff Appraisal Reports for Projects Approved in 1993*, Washington, DC: Operations Policy Department/Operations Evaluation Department, The World Bank.

Ouchi, F. (2004) *A Literature Review on the Use of Expert Opinion in Probabilistic Risk Analysis*, Technical Report 3201, Washington, DC: The World Bank.

Overseas Development Administration (1988) *Appraisal of Projects in Developing Countries*, London: HMSO.

Papps, I. (1993) 'Shadow pricing with price controls', *Scottish Journal of Political Economy, 40(2)*: 199–209.

Pareto, V. (1909) *Manuel d'économie politique*, Paris: Giard.

Pareto, V. (1916) *Trattato di sociologia generale*, Florence: G. Barbèra.

Parfit, D. (1971) 'Personal identity', *The Philosopher Review, 80(1)*: 3–27.

Parliamentary Secretariat for the EU Presidency 2017 and EU Funds of Malta (2013) *Guidance Manual for Cost Benefit Analysis (CBAs) Appraisal in Malta*.

Payer, C. (1982) *The World Bank: A Critical Analysis*, New York: Monthly Review Press.

Pearce, D.W. (1993) *Economic Values and the Natural World*, London: Earthscan.

Pearce, D.W., Groom, B., Hepburn, C. and Koundouri, P. (2003) 'Valuing the future: recent advances in social discounting', *World Economics, 4(2)*: 121–141.

Pearce, D.W. and Ulph, D. (1995) *'A social discount rate for the United Kingdom'*, CSERGE Working Paper GEC 95–101.

Pearson, S., Chudleigh, P., Simpson, S. and Schofield, N. (2012) 'Learning to invest better: using *ex-post* investment analysis on agri-environmental research and development', *Research Evaluation, 21(2)*: 136–151.

Peon, G.-S.B. and Harberger, A.C. (2012) 'Measuring the social opportunity cost of labor in Mexico', *Journal of Benefit-Cost Analysis, 3(2)*: 1–41.

Percoco, M. (2008) 'A social discount rate for Italy', *Applied Economics Letters, 15(1)*: 73–77.

Percoco, M. (2012) 'Are project appraisers chiromancers?', *Applied Economics Letters, 19(3)*: 237–241.

Perkins, F. (1994) *Practical Cost Benefit Analysis*, South Melbourne: Macmillan.

Picard, P. (1993) *Wages and Unemployment: A Study in Non-walrasian Macroeconomics*, Cambridge: Cambridge University Press.

Picazo-Tadeo, A. and Reig-Martínez, E. (2005) 'Calculating shadow wages for family labour in agriculture: an analysis for Spanish citrus fruit farms', *Cahiers d'Economie et Sociologie Rurales*, 75: 5–21.

Picciotto, R. (2007) 'Is development evaluation relevant to the European project?', in Florio, M. (ed.) *Cost-Benefit Analysis and Incentives and Evaluation: The Structural Funds of the European Union*, Cheltenham: Edward Elgar.

Pigou, A.C. (1912) *Wealth and Welfare*, London: Macmillan.

Pinson, L. (2007) *Keeping the Books: Basic Recordkeeping and Accounting for the Successful Small Business*, Chicago, IL: Kaplan Pub.

Planning and Priorities Co-ordination Division (2013) *Guidance Manual for Cost Benefit Analysis (CBAs) Appraisal in Malta*.

Pohl, G. and Mihaljek, D. (1992) 'Project evaluation and uncertainty in practice: a statistical analysis of rate-of-return divergences of 1015 World Bank Projects', *The World Bank Economic Review*, 6: 255–277.

Potts, D. (2002) *Project Planning and Analysis for Development*, London: Lynne Rienner.

Potts, D. (2012a) 'Semi-input-output methods of shadow price estimation: are they still useful?', in Weiss, J. and Potts, D. (eds) *Current Issues in Project Analysis for Development*, Cheltenham and Northampton: Edward Elgar.

Potts, D. (2012b) 'Shadow wage rates in a changing world', in Weiss, J. and Potts, D. (eds) *Current Issues in Project Analysis for Development*, Cheltenham and Northampton: Edward Elgar.

Pouliquen, L.Y. (1970) '*Risk analysis in project appraisal*', World Bank Staff Occasional Papers Number 11, Baltimore, MD: Johns Hopkins University Press.

Powers, T. (ed.) (1981) *Estimating Accounting Price for Project Appraisal*, Washington, DC: Inter-American Development Bank.

Price, C. (1993) *Time, Discounting and Value*, Oxford: Blackwell.

Prud'homme, R. (2008) '*Policy evaluation in France: a tentative evaluation*', paper prepared for the World Bank. Online. http://www.rprudhomme.com/resources/2008+Policy+Evaluation+-France.pdf (accessed on March 18th 2013).

Qizilbash, M. (2005) 'Incommensurability and the first fundamental welfare theorem', *Oxford Economic Papers*, 57(4): 664–673.

Querbach, T. and Arndt, C. (2017) '*Regulatory policy in Latin America: an analysis of the state of play*', OECD Regulatory Policy Working Papers, No. 7, Paris: OECD Publishing.

Quinet, E. (2007) 'Cost benefit analysis of transport projects in France', in Florio, M. (ed.) *Cost Benefit Analysis and Incentives in Evaluation*, Cheltenham: Edward Elgar.

Quinet Commission (2013) L'évaluation socioéconomique des investissements publics Tome 1 Rapport final. Commissariat Generale a la strategie et a la Prospective.

Quinet, A. and Bueb, J. (2019) *La valeur de l'action pour le climat*. France stratégie, 3624–3648, https://www.strategie.gouv.fr/publications/de-laction-climat.

Rajaram, A., Le, Minh T., Biletska, N. and Brumby, J. (2010) '*A diagnostic framework for assessing public investment management*', Policy Research Working Paper 5397, Washington DC: The World Bank.

Ramsey, F.P. (1928) 'A mathematical theory of saving', *The Economic Journal*, 38(152): 543–559.

Ray, A. (1984) *Cost-Benefit Analysis: Issues and Methodologies*, Baltimore, MD: Johns Hopkins University Press.

Rawls, A. (1971) *Theory of Justice*, Cambridge, MA: Harvard University Press, Cambridge Press.

Regulatory Policy Committee (2020) *Impact Assessments: Room for Improvement?*.

Regulatory Scrutiny Board (2021) Annual Report 2020.

Renda, A. (2006) *Impact Assessment in the EU. The State of the Art and the Art of the State*. Brussels: Centre for European Policy Studies.

Renda, A. (2018) 'Cost-benefit analysis and EU policy: limits and opportunities'.

Republic of Serbia – Ministry of Infrastructure and Public Enterprise Roads of Serbia (2010) '*Manual cost benefit analysis Republic of Serbia*'. Online. http://www.putevi-srbije.rs/strategi-japdf/Manual_Cost_Benefit_Analysis.pdf.

Reutlinger, S. (1970) '*Techniques for project appraisal under uncertainty*', World Bank Staff Occasional Paper number 10, Baltimore, MD: Johns Hopkins University Press.

Riess, A. (2008) 'The economic cost of public funds in infrastructure investment', in H. Strauss (ed.) *EIB Papers: Infrastructure Investment, Growth and Cohesion*, Vol. 13, no. 1, Luxembourg: European Investment Bank.

Robbins, L. (1938) 'Interpersonal comparison of utility: a comment', *Economic Journal, 48*: 635–641.

Robert, C.P. and Casella, G. (2004) *Monte Carlo Statistical Methods*, New York, Springer.

Robert, C.P. and Casella, G. (2010) *Introducing Monte Carlo Methods with R*, New York, Springer.

Roberts, J. (1987) 'Perfectly and imperfectly competitive markets', 4: 198–200, in Eatwell, J., Peter Newman, P. and Milgate, M. (eds) *The New Palgrave: A Dictionary of Economics*, Four volumes, London: Macmillan.

Roberts, K. (1982) 'Desirable fiscal policies under Keynesian unemployment', *Oxford Economic Papers, 34(1)*: 1–22.

Roberts, K.W.S. (1980) 'Price independent welfare prescriptions', *Journal of Public Economics, 13(3)*: 277–297.

Roberts, T. and Marks, S. (1995) 'The cost-of-illness method and the social cost of Escherichia coli O157:H7 foodborne disease', Chapter 9 in Caswell, J.A. (ed.) *Valuing Food Safety Nutrition*, Boulder, CO: Westview Press.

Robinson, L.A., Hammitt, J.K. and Zeckhauser, R.J. (2016) 'Attention to distribution in U.S. regulatory analyses', *Review of Environmental Economics and Policy, 10*: 308–328.

Ross, S.A. (1995) 'Uses, abuses, and alternatives to the net-present-value rule', *Financial Management, 24(3)*: 96–102.

Ruschendorf, L. (2009) 'On the distributional transform, Sklar's theorem, and the empirical copula process', *Journal of Statistical Planning and Inference, 139(11)*: 3921–3927.

Saerbeck, R. (1990) '*Economic appraisal of projects. Guidelines for a simplified cost-benefit analysis*', EIB Paper no. 15, Luxembourg: European Investment Bank.

Sah, R.H. and Stiglitz, J. (1985) 'The social cost of labour and project evaluation: a general approach', *Journal of Public Economics, 28*: 135–163.

Saleh, I. (2004) 'Estimating shadow wages for economic project appraisal', *The Pakistan Development Review, 43(3)*: 253–266.

Salling, K.B. and Leleur, S. (2011) 'Transport appraisal and Monte Carlo simulation by use of the CBA-DK model', *Transport Policy, 18(1)*: 236–245.

Samuelson, P.A. (1937) 'A note on measurement of utility', *The Review of Economic Studies, 4(2)*: 155–161.

Samuelson, P.A. (1947) *Foundations of Economic Analysis*, Cambridge, MA: Harvard University Press.

Saunders, R.J., Warford, J.J. and Mann, P.C. (1977) '*Alternative concepts of marginal cost for public utility pricing: problems of application in the water supply sector*', World Bank Staff Working Paper No. 259.

Scarborough, H. and Bennett, J. (2012) *Cost-Benefit Analysis and Distributional Preferences: A Choice Modelling Approach*, Cheltenham: Edward Elgar.

Schempp, C. (2011) '*Application of the polluter pays principle (ppp) in waste management projects*', JAS-PERS Knowledge Economy, Energy and Waste Division. Staff Working Papers.

Schroyen, F. (2010) 'Operational expressions for the marginal cost of indirect taxation when merit arguments matter', *International Tax and Public Finance, 17(1)*: 43–51.

Schmitz, A. and Zerbe, R. (eds) (2009) *Applied Benefit-Cost Analysis*, Cheltenham: Edward Elgar.

Sell, A. (1991) *Project Evaluation: An Integrated Financial and Economic Analysis*, Aldershot: Brookfield.

Sen, A. (1972) 'Feasibility constraints: foreign exchange and shadow wages', *Economic Journal, 82*: 486–501.

Sen, A. (1986) 'Social choice theory', in Arrow, K.S. and Intriligator, M.D. (eds) *Handbook of Mathematical Economics*, Vol. 3, Amsterdam: North-Holland.

Sen, A. (1987) *On Ethics and Economics*, Oxford: Basil Blackwell.

Sen, A. (1992) *Inequality Reexamined*, Cambridge, MA: Harvard University Press.

Sen, A.K. (1966) 'Peasants and dualism with and without surplus labour', *Journal of Political Economy*, 74(5): 425–450.

Sezer, H. (2007) 'Derivation of regional welfare weights: an application to Turkey', in Florio, M. (ed.) *Cost-Benefit Analysis and Incentives in Evaluation: The Structural Funds of the European Union*, Cheltenham: Edward Elgar.

Shapiro, C. and Stiglitz, J.E. (1984) 'Equilibrium unemployment as a worker discipline device', *The American Economic Review*, 75(3): 433–444.

Shapley, L.S. (1969) 'Utility comparisons and the theory of games', in *La Décision*, Colloques internationaux du CNRS, Paris: CNRS.

Sidgwick, M.H. (1874) *Method of Ethics*, London: Macmillan.

Sidgwick, M.H. (1883) *Principles of Political Economy*, London: Macmillan.

Sidgwick, M.H. (1891) *Elements of Politics*, London: Macmillan.

Simon, C.P. and Blume, L.E. (1994) *Mathematics for Economists*, W.W. Norton & Company; trans. Zaffaroni, A. (ed.) (2002) *Matematica per l'Economia e le Scienze Sociali vol. 2*, Milan: Università Bocconi Editore.

Sivarethinamohan, R. (1964) *Operations Research*, New Delhi: Tata McGraw-Hill.

Sklar, M. (1959) 'Fonctions de répartition à *n* dimensions et leurs marges', *Publications de l'Institut de Statistique de L'Université de Paris*, 8: 229–231.

Skoufias, E. (1994) 'Using shadow wages to estimate labour supply of agricultural households', *American Journal of Agricultural Economics*, 76: 215–227.

Smets, H. (2009) 'Access to drinking water at an affordable price in developing countries', in El Moujabber, M., Mandi, L., Trisorio Liuzzi, G., Martin, I., Rabi, A. and Rodriguez, R. (eds) *Technological Perspectives for Rational Use of Water Resources in the Mediterranean Region*, Bari: Options Méditerranéennes, 57–68.

Smirnov, N. (1948) 'Tables for estimating the goodness of fit of empirical distributions', *Annals of Mathematical Statistics*, 19(2): 279–281.

Smith, A. (1776) *An Inquiry into the Nature and Causes of the Wealth of Nations*, McMaster University Archive for the History of Economic Thought.

Somanathan, E. (2006) 'Valuing lives equally: distributional weights for welfare analysis', *Economics Letters*, 90: 122–125.

Spackman, M. (2004) 'Time discounting and of the cost of capital in government', *Fiscal Studies*, 25(4): 467–518.

Spackman, M. (2007) 'Social discount rates for the European Union: an overview', in Florio, M. (ed.) *Cost-Benefit Analysis and Incentives in Evaluation: The Structural Funds of the European Union*, Cheltenham: Edward Elgar.

Squire, L. (1998) 'Professor Mirrlees' contribution to economic policy', *International Tax and Public Finance*, 5(1): 83–91.

Squire, L. and Tak, v.d.H.G. (1975) *Economic Analysis of Projects*, Baltimore, MD: Johns Hopkins University Press.

Starr, R. (1997) *General Equilibrium Theory: An introduction*, Cambridge: Cambridge University Press.

Starret, D. (1989) *Foundations of Public Economics*, Cambridge: Cambridge University Press.

Stern, N. (1977) 'Welfare weights and the elasticity of marginal utility of income', in Artis, M. and Nobay, R. (eds) *Proceedings of the Annual Conference of the Association of University Teachers of Economics*, Oxford: Blackwell.

Stern, N. (1987) 'The general theory of tax reform', in Newbery, D. and Stern, N. (eds) *The Theory of Taxation for Developing Countries*, Oxford: Oxford University Press.

Stern, N. (1990) 'Uniformity versus selectivity in indirect taxation', *Economics and Politics*, 2(1): 83–108.

Stern, N. (dir.) (2006) *The Stern Review Report: the Economics of Climate Change*, London: HM Treasury.

Stern, N. (2011) 'Presidential address: imperfections in the economics of public policy, imperfections in markets, and climate change', *Journal of European Economic Association*, 8(2–3): 253–288.

Stiglitz, J. (1994) *Whither Socialism?*, Cambridge: MIT Press.

Stiglitz, J., Fitoussi, J. and Durand, M. (2018) *Beyond GDP: Measuring What Counts for Economic and Social Performance*, Paris: OECD Publishing.

Stiglitz, J.E. and Dasgupta, P. (1971) 'Differential taxation, public goods and economic efficiency', *Review of Economic Studies*, 38(114): 151–174.

Stone, R. (1947) 'Definition and measurement of national income and related totals', *Appendix to the Report of the Sub-Committee on the National Income Statistics of the League of Nations Committee of Statistical Experts, Entitled: Measurement of National Income and the Construction of Social Accounts. Studies and Reports on Statistical Methods No 7*, United Nations Publication, Geneva.

Streissler, E. and Neudeck, W. (1986) 'Are there intellectual precursors to the idea of second best optimization?', *Journal of Economics*, 5: 227–242.

Sunstein, C. (2018) *The Cost-Benefit Revolution*, Cambridge: MIT Press.

Swales, J.K. (2009) 'A cost-benefit approach to the assessment of regional policy', in Farschi, M.A., Janne, O.E.M. and McCann, P. (eds) *Technological Change and Mature Industrial Regions*, Cheltenham: Edward Elgar.

Teichmann, D. and Schempp, C. (2013) '*Calculation of GHG emissions of waste management projects*', JASPERS Knowledge Economy and Energy Division. Staff Working Papers.

The DABLAS Task Force (2011) *Guide to Rapid Pre-appraisal of Urban Wastewater Projects*. Online. http://ec.europa.eu/environment/enlarg/dablas/downloads/pre_appraisal3.pdf.

The Treasury Board Secretariat of Canada (1998, 2nd edn 2002) *Benefit-Cost Analysis Guide*, Ottawa.

The White House (1992) *Circular A-94: Guidelines and Discount Rates for Benefit-Cost Analysis of Federal Programs*. Online. http://www.whitehouse.gov/omb/circulars_a094 (accessed on March 18th 2013).

The World Bank (1994a) 'Mexico – On-Farm and Minor Irrigation Networks Improvement Project', *Staff Appraisal Report 12280-ME*, Country Department II, Latin American and the Caribbean Region, Washington, DC.

The World Bank (1994b) *Pakistan – Balochistan Natural Resource Management Project*, Washington, DC. Online. http://documents.worldbank.org/curated/en/2000/11/5183999/pakistan-balochistan-natural-resource-management-project (accessed on July 12th 2013).

The World Bank (1998) *Handbook on Economic Analysis of Investment Operations*, Washington, DC: Operational Policy Department.

The World Bank (2010a) *Cost-Benefit Analysis in World Bank Projects*, Washington, DC: Independent Evaluation Group.

The World Bank (2010b) 'Report to the Board from the Committee on Development Effectiveness: Cost-Benefit Analysis in World Bank Projects and Draft Management Comments', *Report to the Board of Executive Directors from the Committee on Development Effectiveness*. Online. http://www-wds.worldbank.org/external/default/WDSContentServer/WDSP/IB/2010/10/19/000112742_20101019171732/Rendered/PDF/571950BR0CODE2010100591101PUBLIC1.pdf (accessed on March 20th 2013).

The World Bank (2015) *Operations Manual*. https://web.worldbank.org/archive/website01541/WEB/IMAGES/ENTIREOM.PDF.

The World Bank Independent Evaluation Group (2009) *Annual Review of Development Effectiveness – Achieving Sustainable Development*, Washington, DC.

Thureson, D. (2012) '*Avoiding path dependence of distributional weights. Lesson from climate change economic assessment*', Working Paper ISSN 1403–0586, Örebro University.

Treasury Board Secretary (2007) *Canadian Cost-Benefit Analysis Guide Regulatory Proposals*, https://www.tbs-sct.gc.ca/rtrap-parfa/analys/analys-eng.pdf (accessed on March 29th 2021).

Treasury Board Secretary (2020) *New policy on Cost-Benefit Analysis*. https://www.canada.ca/en/government/system/laws/developing-improving-federal-regulations/

requirements-developing-managing-reviewing-regulations/guidelines-tools/poli-cy-cost-benefit-analysis.html (accessed on March 29th 2021).

Tsuneki, A. (2002) 'Shadow-pricing interpretation of the pigovian rule for the optimal provision of public goods: a note', *International Tax and Public Finance, 9*(1): 93–104.

Turner, R.K. (1999) 'The place of economic values in environmental valuation', in Bateman, I.J. and Willis, K.G. (eds) *Valuing Environmental Preferences*, New York: Oxford University Press.

UNCTAD (2010) *Information Economy Report 2010. ICT, Enterprises and Poverty Alleviation*, Geneva: UNCTAD.

UNDP (1990) *Human Development Report 1990*, New York: Oxford University Press.

UNDP (2019) *'Human Development Report 2019 – Beyond Income, Beyond Averages, Beyond Today: Inequalities in Human Development in the 21st Century'*. Thecnical Notes available at http://hdr.undp.org/sites/default/files/hdr2019_technical_notes.pdf.

U.S. Department of Commerce, National Institute of Standards and Technology (2013) Energy Price Indices and Discount Factors for Life-Cycle Cost Analysis, https://nvlpubs.nist.gov/nistpubs/ir/2013/NIST.IR.85-3273-28.pdf.

US Environmental Protection Agency (2000a) *A Benefit Assessment of Water Pollution Control Programme since 1972*. Online. http://water.epa.gov/lawsregs/lawsguidance/cwa/316b/upload/2000_04_17_economics_assessment.pdf.

US Environmental Protection Agency (2000b) *Improving the Practice of Benefit Transfer: A Preference Calibration Approach*. Online. http://water.epa.gov/lawsregs/lawsguidance/cwa/316b/upload/2000_04_17_economics_benefits.pdf.

US Environmental Protection Agency (2000c) *A Retrospective Assessment of Cost of the Clean Water Act: 1972–1997*, http://water.epa.gov/lawsregs/lawsguidance/cwa/economics/upload/2000_10_23_economics_costs.pdf.

US Environmental Protection Agency (2010). *Guidelines for Preparing Economic Analysis*.

US Environmental Protection Agency (2013) *Technical Support Document: Technical Update of the Social Cost of Carbon for Regulatory Impact Analysis-under Executive Order 12866*, https://www.epa.gov/sites/production/files/2016-12/documents/scc_tsd_2010.pdf (accessed on March 29th 2021).

US Environmental Protection Agency (2018) Regulatory Impact Analysis for the Proposed Reconsideration of the Oil and Natural Gas Sector Emission Standards for New, Reconstructed, and Modified Sources, EPA-452/R-18-001, Washington, DC, September 2018.

USDOT, U.S. Department of Transportation (2021) *Benefit-Cost Analysis Guidance for Discretionary Grant Programs*, https://www.transportation.gov/sites/dot.gov/files/2021-02/Benefit%20Cost%20Analysis%20Guidance%202021.pdf.

U.S. Army (2018) *Cost Benefit Analysis Guide*, https://www.asafm.army.mil/Portals/72/Documents/Offices/CE/US%20Army%20Cost%20Benefit%20Analysis.pdf.

Vailhen, C.A. (1998) 'L'analyse financière entre méfiance et confiance', *Economies et sociétés, 32*(8–9): 235–250.

Varian, H.R. (1992) *Microeconomic Analysis*, 3rd edn, New York: W.W. Norton & Company.

Varian, H.R. (2014) *Intermediate Microeconomics with Calculus: A Modern Approach*. New York: WW Norton & Company.

Vining, A.R. and Boardman, A.E. (2006) 'Metachoice in policy analysis', *Journal of Comparative Policy Analysis: Research and Practice, 8*(1): 77–87.

Vining, A.R. and Weimer, D.L. (2015) 'Policy analysis', in *International Encyclopedia of the Social & Behavioral Sciences*, 2nd edn, New York: Routledge.

Viscusi, W. and Masterman, C. (2017) 'Income elasticities and global values of a statistical life', *Journal of Benefit-Cost Analysis, 8*(2): 226–250.

Viscusi, W.K. and Aldy, J. (2003) 'The value of statistical life: a critical review of market estimates throughout the world', *Journal of Risk and Uncertainty, 27*(1): 5–76.

Vohra, R. (1987) 'Planning', in Eatwell, J., Peter Newman, P. and Milgate, M. (eds) *The New Palgrave: A Dictionary of Economics*, Four volumes, London: Macmillan, 2: 885–891.

Vose, D. (2008) *Risk Analysis: A Quantitative Guide*, John Wiley and Sons, West Sussex: Chichester.

Walton, H., Longo, A. and Dawson, P. (2008) 'A contingent valuation of the 2012 London olympic games: a regional perspective', *Journal of Sports Economics*, 9: 304–317.

Walras, L. (1874) *Elements d'économie politique pure*, Lausanne: Corbaz.

Ward, W.A. (2019) 'Cost-benefit analysis theory versus practice at the World Bank 1960 to 2015', *Journal of Benefit-Cost Analysis*, 10(1): 124–144.

Ward, W.A., Deren, B.J. and D'Silva, E.H. (1991) *The Economics of Project Analysis: A Practitioner's Guide*, Washington, DC: World Bank Publication.

Warr, P. (1973) 'Saving propensities and the shadow wage', *Economica*, 40(160): 410–415.

Weintraub, E.R. (1974) *General Equilibrium Theory*, Macmillan Studies in Economics, London, Macmillan.

Weintraub, E.R. (1985) *General Equilibrium Analysis: Studies in Appraisal*, Historical Perspectives on Modern Economics, Cambridge: Cambridge University Press.

Weisbach, D.A. (2014) '*Distributionally-weighted cost benefit analysis: welfare economics meets organizational design*', Coase-Sandor Institute for Law & Economics Working Paper No. 689.

Weisbrod, B.A. (1972) 'Deriving an implicit set of government weights for income classes', in Layard, R. (ed.) *Cost-Benefit Analysis*, London: Penguin.

Weisbrod, B.A. (1986) 'Income redistribution effects & benefit-cost analysis', in Chase, S.B. Jr (ed.) *Problems of Public Expenditure Analysis*, Washington, DC: Brookings Institution.

Weiss, J. (1988) 'An introduction to shadow pricing in a semi-input-output approach', *Project Appraisal*, 3(4): 182–187.

Weiss, J. (1996) 'Project failure: the implications of a 25 per cent rule', in Kirkpatrick, C. and Weiss, J. (eds) *Cost-Benefit Analysis and Project Appraisal in Developing Countries*, Cheltenham: Edward Elgar.

Weiss, J. and Potts, D. (eds) (2012) *Current Issues in Project Analysis for Development*, Cheltenham: Edward Elgar.

Weitzman, M.L. (1994) 'On the environmental discount rate', *Journal of Environmental Economics and Management*, 26: 200–209.

Weitzman, M.L. (2001) 'Gamma discounting', *The American Economic Review*, 91(1): 260–271.

Weitzman, M.L. (2007) 'A review of the Stern review on the economics of climate change', *Journal of Economic Literature*, 45(3): 703–724.

Welde, M. and Odeck, J. (2011) 'Do planners get it right? The accuracy of travel demand forecasting in Norway', *European Journal of Transport and Infrastructure Research*, 11(1): 80–95.

Wendy, M., Dorothy, R., Hai-Yen, S. and Martha, M. (2004) *Valuing Human Life: Estimating the Present Value of Lifetime Earnings, 2000*, Center for Tobacco Control Research and Education, University of California.

Weymark, J. (2005) 'Shadow prices for a nonconvex public technology in the presence of private constant returns', *Advances in Public Economics: Utility, Choice and Welfare Theory and Decision Library*, 38: 61–71.

White, D. and VanLandingham, G. (2015) 'Benefit-cost analysis in the states: status, impact, and challenges', *Journal of Benefit-Cost Analysis*, 6(2): 369–399.

Whitehead, J.C. and Cherry, T.L. (2007) 'Willingness to pay for a Green Energy program: a comparison of ex-ante and ex-post hypothetical bias mitigation approaches', *Resource and Energy Economics*, 29(4): 247–261.

Wicksell, K. (1901) *Lectures on Political Economy*, Volumes I and II, London: Routledge.

Wicksell, K. (1958a) *Selected Papers in Economic Theory*, London: Allen and Unwin.

Wicksell, K. (1958b) 'Finanz theoretische Untersuchungen' (Jena: G. Fisher, 1896). Translated as 'A new principle of just taxation', in R.A. Musgrave and A.T. Peacock (eds) *Classics in the Theory of Public Finance*, London: Macmillan.

Williams, R. and Broughel, J. (2015) *Principles for Analyzing Distribution in Regulatory Impact Analysis*, Mercatus Center – George Mason University.

Willig, R.D. (1976) 'Consumer's surplus without apology', *The American Economic Review, 66*(4): 589–597.

Wilson, L.S. (1993) 'Regional employment subsidies and migration', *Canadian Journal of Economics, 22*(2): 245–262.

Wu, F. and Tsang, Y. (2004) 'Second-order Monte Carlo uncertainty/variability analysis using correlated model parameters: application to salmonid embryo survival risk assessment', *Ecological Modelling, 177*: 393–414.

Zerbe, R.O. and Dively, D.D. (1994) *Benefit Cost Analysis in Theory and Practice*, New York: Harper Collins.

Zhuang, L., Liang, Z., Lin, T. and Guzman, D.F. (2007) '*Theory and practice in the choice of social discount rate for cost benefit analysis: a survey*', ERD Working Paper No. 94, Asian Development Bank.

Index

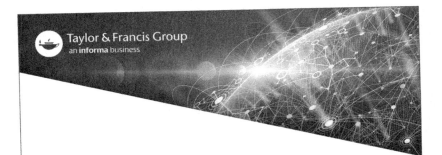

Printed in the United States
by Baker & Taylor Publisher Services